THE TORTURE REPORT

WHAT THE DOCUMENTS SAY ABOUT AMERICA'S POST-9/11 TORTURE PROGRAM

THE TORTURE REPORT

WHAT THE DOCUMENTS SAY ABOUT AMERICA'S POST-9/11 TORTURE PROGRAM

LARRY SIEMS

OR Books
New York · London

© 2011 Larry Siems

Published by OR Books, New York and London
Visit our website at www.orbooks.com

First printing 2011

Cataloging-in-Publication data is available from the Library of Congress
A catalog record for this book is available from the British Library

ISBN 978-1-935928-55-3 paperback
ISBN 978-1-935928-56-0 e-book

Typeset by Wordstop Technologies, Chennai, India

Printed by BookMobile in the United States and CPI Books Ltd in the United Kingdom
The U.S. printed edition of this book comes on Forest Stewardship Council-certified, 30% recycled paper. The printer, BookMobile, is 100% wind-powered.

CONTENTS

INTRODUCTION

This past Valentine's Day, I stood with the student body of the Charleston Law School at the intersection known locally as "The Four Corners of the Law," waiting to learn where a federal judge would hear one of the last surviving lawsuits against those who orchestrated the torture of prisoners during our country's "War on Terror."

It was a pristine, spring-promising low-country morning. An improbable power failure was keeping Judge Richard Gergel from welcoming the students—present, it turned out, at his invitation—to the courtroom where Thurgood Marshall argued the first of five cases leading to the *Brown v. Board of Education* Supreme Court decision, but nobody minded the delay. The students texted and smoked and cemented plans for the evening, soaking up the sun. The plaintiff, who had spent the better part of a decade pressing for this day, might have had something to say about the wait, but he was sealed inside a federal supermax prison in Colorado, two thousand miles away.

I had flown to South Carolina for the hearing that morning because over the course of eighteen months spent researching TheTortureReport. org, I'd come to understand that what that man, Jose Padilla, had endured for three and a half years at the U.S. naval base a few miles from where we were standing had been part of a kind of Ponzi scheme of torture. Padilla,

Abu Zubaydah, and British resident Binyam Mohamed had supposedly hatched a plot to detonate a "dirty bomb" in a major American city. But those three men had been serially tortured, Zubaydah in a secret CIA prison in Thailand, Mohamed by proxy torturers in Morocco and by U.S. agents in Pakistan and Afghanistan, and Padilla in the Charleston Navy Brig; their plans grew more fantastical the more they were abused. Theirs was a story not of an attack averted, but of how torture begets torture—first because bad information invented during torture led to more torture and invented information, and finally because interrogations were conducted not to thwart plots but to concoct cases to justify the detention and treatment of those who had been tortured.

Not that it matters why men are tortured. "No exceptional circumstances whatsoever, whether a state or war or a threat of war, internal political instability or any other public emergency, may be invoked as a justification of torture," the Convention against Torture and Other Cruel, Inhuman or Degrading Treatment or Punishment states. Under the Convention, which the U.S. ratified in 1994 and incorporated into a variety of domestic laws, those who order, carry out, or are complicit in torture are subject to criminal prosecution, no matter what they thought they were doing. And anyone who is tortured, no matter who he is, has "an enforceable right to fair and adequate compensation."

Padilla, an American citizen, was at last exercising this right: he was suing former Defense Secretary Donald Rumsfeld, former Defense Department General Counsel William J. "Jim" Haynes, and five other military officials for one dollar in damages for the abuse he suffered in the nearby brig. It was hard not to feel hopeful, that unseasonable morning, that an American court might at last shoulder our national responsibilities under the laws banning torture. Even U.S. District Judge Marcia Cooke, who presided over Padilla's criminal prosecution on charges having nothing to do with plots to attack the U.S. and who was privy to the record of his treatment at the brig, had suggested just such a lawsuit, writing in a footnote to one of her decisions, "Mr. Padilla is free to institute a *Bivens* action, an action for monetary damages, or any other form of redress he is legally entitled to pursue."

That optimism faded fast. Power never was restored in Charleston's old federal courtroom, the kind of genteel chamber where Tracy or Stewart or Peck would have stood up for vilified clients against the bigoted headwinds of the times. We settled instead into the modern, blond-paneled courtroom in the Hollings Judicial Center Annex around the corner, the law school students jamming the three rows of the gallery. So many attorneys for defendants Rumsfeld et al. filed in behind us that when Judge Gergel took the bench, he invited the ones who couldn't find chairs at the defense table to take seats in the jury box. Their presence there did little to further the impression that Padilla's claims would be getting a fair hearing.

"Everybody understands that when we intersect liberty and security, it creates challenges for all of us to sort out, and that's what we're here today to do our best to do," Judge Gergel began, narrating, as he would several times that morning, for the students' benefit. But when Haynes's attorney Greg Bowman rose to argue the defendants' motion to dismiss, Gergel lobbed a series of questions intimating that a great deal had already been sorted.

The motion hinged on whether, as Judge Cooke confidently suggested, Padilla could sue his tormentors under *Bivens v. Six Unknown Federal Narcotics Agents*, a 1971 Supreme Court precedent establishing that a person can hold individual federal officials liable for violating a constitutional right—and whether, even if he could bring a *Bivens* suit, the officials might still claim immunity for their deeds. "Are there special factors here that counsel against a court recognizing a *Bivens* action here?" Gergel prompted Bowman. "Some of the folks you're arguing on behalf of were actually people in the armed services obeying what they believed to be the order of the President, correct?" he nudged again. And again, "He was given the right to challenge his detention by way of habeas, correct?" Before long, Padilla's local counsel was leaning to Ben Wizner, the lead ACLU attorney arguing Padilla's case, muttering "I don't know what's happening, but it can't be *this*."

"It looks like I have my work cut out for me," Wizner addressed the court when he took the floor.

"Yes," Gergel admitted.

"It could not be more clearly established that the brutal abuse and incommunicado detention of an American citizen in an American prison is both unconstitutional and cognizable under *Bivens*," Wizner opened. In fact, he argued, this was precisely why the U.S. government had transferred him into total isolation in an empty wing of the Charleston Brig. "They did this to prevent lawyers and courts from interfering with their vicious years of interrogation," he suggested. "But I submit they also did it to prepare for this day, which they truly knew was coming, when the victim would be here to call them to account in a court of law. And to deny Jose Padilla a remedy, or to grant these defendants immunity, would be to reward them for their deliberate efforts."

For the next forty minutes, Wizner parried claims that courts had no business reviewing Padilla's case, and that Rumsfeld, Haynes, and their co-defendants could not be sued for actions Bush administration lawyers had said were legal. Gergel pressed Wizner to point to a case where a court had ruled that government officials could not treat presidentially-designated enemy combatants as they had Padilla. Wizner acknowledged the lack of precedents. But, he added,

> *There is also not a case from the Supreme Court, or any other court, that says that defendants or their agents could not go into Mr. Padilla's cell and literally beat him to death. There's no case that says that. But I hope we would all agree that even if a suspected enemy combatant were beaten to death in his cell, there would not be a qualified immunity argument simply because the designation of American citizen here as an enemy combatant was novel.*

"In this case," he went on,

> *Depriving someone of heat, light, manipulating temperatures, threatening him with death, injecting him with drugs and saying that it's truth serum, pumping noxious fumes into his cell, keeping him in isolation for almost two years without family contact, this is conduct you will not find if you read the cases the Supreme Court*

identified that shock the conscience. This conduct goes so far beyond that that we don't think any reasonable official could have thought it was acceptable to do these things to a U.S. citizen in a U.S. prison.

Toward the end of Wizner's argument, Gergel posited that trying Padilla's suit would unduly burden the military and risk exposing national secrets—but that perhaps just filing this lawsuit had discouraged Rumsfeld's and Haynes's successors from similarly abusing prisoners. "I certainly hope that what you've said is correct, Your Honor," Wizner countered. "But I don't have enough faith in that not to pursue a legal remedy for an American citizen who was subjected to unprecedented torture and abuse, not very far from this courtroom. And I believe that he is entitled to the remedy that he seeks in this case."

I had the impression that if Gergel, at that moment, had placed his decision in the hands of the overflow defense lawyers occupying the jury box, Padilla might have carried the day; a few even made a point of crossing the courtroom to congratulate Wizner after the hearing. But just three days later, Gergel dismissed the suit. Padilla's designation as an enemy combatant and his incommunicado detention involved "the most profound and sensitive issues of national security, foreign affairs, and military affairs," Gergel wrote in his opinion. "It is not for this Court, sitting comfortably in a federal courthouse nearly nine years after these events, to assess whether the policy was wise or the intelligence was accurate."

"Special factors counsel hesitation" in allowing a *Bivens* suit, he continued, insisting that trying the case "entangles the Court in issues normally reserved for the Executive Branch, such as those related to national security and intelligence." Furthermore, "a trial on the merits would be an international spectacle with Padilla, a convicted terrorist, summoning America's present and former leaders to a federal courthouse to answer his charges." Not that this would ever happen, Gergel concluded: if the case proceeded, Rumsfeld, Haynes, and their co-defendants were entitled to immunity for their actions because at the time of Padilla's detention by the Department of Defense, "there were few 'bright lines'" establishing that Padilla, as a so-called enemy combatant, had a right not to be tortured.

"To say the scope and nature of Padilla's legal rights at that time were unsettled would be an understatement," Judge Gergel wrote. "The Court finds that it was not clearly established at the time of his designation and detention that Padilla's treatment as an enemy combatant, including his interrogations, was a violation of law."

* * *

Here's what I learned from writing TheTortureReport.org.

The most senior members of the Bush administration, up to and including the President, broke international and domestic laws banning torture and cruel, inhuman, and degrading treatment. Worse, they had subordinates in the military and in civilian intelligence services break these laws for them.

When the men and women they enlisted to violate these prohibitions balked, knowing they'd be vulnerable to prosecution for the torture in the future—as they did from the outset, in the CIA, the FBI, and the military— these senior administration officials pretended to rewrite the law. They commissioned legal opinions they promised would shield those carrying out the abuses from being hauled into court, as the torture ban requires. "The law has been changed," detainees around the world were told. "No rules apply."

Then they tortured. They tortured men at military bases and detention facilities in Afghanistan and Iraq, in Guantánamo, and in U.S. Navy bases on American soil; they tortured men in secret CIA prisons set up across the globe specifically to terrorize and torture prisoners; they sent many more to countries with notoriously abusive regimes and asked them to do the torturing. When those carrying out the torture concluded there was no point to further torture, Washington at least twice ordered that prisoners be tortured more.

They tortured innocent people. They tortured people very likely guilty of terrorism-related crimes, but ruined all chance of prosecuting these people thanks to the torture. They tortured the innocent and the likely-guilty alike when the torture had nothing to do with imminent threats: they tortured people based on bad information extracted from people they had already tortured, as with Jose Padilla, Binyam Mohamed, and Abu Zubaydah; they tortured to get specific information they wanted, as when detainees were pressed about links between Saddam Hussein and Al Qaeda; they tortured to hide their mistakes, as when they used coerced statements by Guantánamo detainees to build cases against fellow detainees they had no business holding in the first place. They tortured people to break them, pure and simple.

And they conspired to cover up their crimes. They did this from the start, by creating secret facilities and secrecy regimes to keep what they were doing from the American people and the world. They did it by suppressing, and when necessary destroying, documentary evidence, including photographs and videotapes of the torture. They did it by subverting or denying legal process because, as the CIA's Inspector General noted ominously in a classified 2004 report, when you torture someone you create an "Endgame" problem, where "the Agency, like the military, has an interest in the disposition of detainees and particular interest in those who, if not kept in isolation, would likely divulge information about the circumstances of their detention."

I am hardly the first to learn these things or reach these conclusions. Dozens of outstanding journalists, lawyers, human rights investigators, bloggers, and members of Congress have discovered and reported similar conclusions for years. But I have reached them for myself, doing what I believe every citizen of conscience ought to do at moments like these, reading the documents themselves.

I learned one more thing as well, something that anyone who reads the record will also discover.

Over and over again, men and women in Afghanistan and Iraq, in Guantánamo, in secret CIA black sites, in Langley, in the Pentagon, in Congress, and in the administration itself recognized the torture for what it was and objected, protested, and fought to prevent, and then to end, these illegal and ill-advised interrogations. While those who devised and oversaw the torture program insist their decisions were colored by the consciousness of impending danger, these men and women, who spent their days in far closer proximity to deadly threats, decried the cruel treatment as ineffective, shortsighted, and wrong.

"As for 'the gloves need to come off,'" a military interrogator emailed from Iraq in 2003, just as the insurgency was gaining momentum and guerrilla attacks on U.S. forces were starting to soar, "we need to take a deep breath and remember who we are."

He was reacting to a message, forwarded to him under the comment "Sounds crazy, but we're just passing this on," asking ALCON, All Concerned, to "Provide an interrogation 'wish list' by 17 Aug 03." "The gloves are coming off gentlemen regarding these detainees," the interrogator's superiors announced. "[Redacted] has made it clear we want these individuals broken. Casualties are mounting and we need to start gathering info to help protect our soldiers from further attacks."

"Those gloves are most definitely NOT based on Cold War or WWII enemies," the soldier, whose name remains redacted in the FOIA documents, answered.

> They are based on clearly established standards of international law to which we are signatories and in part originators. Those in turn derive from practices commonly accepted as morally correct, the so-called "usages of war." It comes down to standards of right and wrong—something we cannot put aside when we find it inconvenient, any more than we can declare that we will "take no prisoners" and therefore shoot those who surrender to us just because we find a process inconvenient.

This sense of betrayal permeates the documents—not just of abstract values and principles, but of the women and men we commissioned to represent these values and principles to the world. In the earliest days of *The Torture Report* project, when I was still diving randomly into the tens of thousands of digital files, I came across the heartbreaking, handwritten sworn statement of a military translator working on an interrogation team in Kandahar in the early days of the Afghan War. She describes how, returning from a break, she found a mysterious Special Forces team crouched around a detainee her team had been interrogating, blowing cigarette smoke in his face. The prisoner was "visibly shaking and crying," she reported; "he said that they had hit him, told him he was going to die, blew smoke in his face, and shocked him with some kind of device."

She reports proudly that her team told the commandos "to get out and not to come back anywhere near anyone that we were talking to"; when she notified her superiors, "the chain of command took steps to ensure that nothing of the sort could happen again," even barring the Special Forces team from the facility. "I was very upset that such a thing could happen," she concluded for the record. "I take my responsibilities as an interrogator and as a human being very seriously. I understand the importance of the Geneva Convention and what it represents. If I don't honor it, what right do I have to expect any other military to do so?"

Her statement is dated February 13, 2002. Six days earlier and seven thousand miles away, President Bush had signed a memorandum to Dick Cheney, Colin Powell, Donald Rumsfeld, George Tenet, Alberto Gonzalez, Condoleezza Rice, and General Richard Myers declaring that Al Qaeda and Afghan Taliban prisoners did not merit Geneva Convention protections. As she was writing her statement, the Pentagon was contracting James Mitchell and Bruce Jessen, two military psychologists with no real-world interrogation experience whatsoever, to give a "crash course" for interrogators heading to Guantánamo on the very kinds of techniques she believed she had successfully confronted.

* * *

A few months after Judge Gergel dismissed Jose Padilla's lawsuit against Donald Rumsfeld and Jim Haynes for treatment those same two military psychologists helped devise, I was back in Charleston going through the files of Andy Savage, a local criminal defense attorney who had represented Ali al-Marri, one of the two other Bush-designated Enemy Combatants held for a time at the Charleston Brig.

I'd met Savage a few hours after the Padilla hearing, and he tried soothing the sting by recounting the role the brig Commandant and security chief played in reining in the abuses the three resident "ECs" endured. A Jesuit-educated New York Irishman who keeps his framed Manhattan hack license on a side table in his obviously prosperous practice, Savage relishes a good legal brawl; an Army veteran and former prosecutor, he also speaks the language of the brig's hybrid military and correctional culture. When his client, an accused Al Qaeda sleeper agent who had been confined, like Padilla, in a blacked-out isolation cell in his own wing of the building, exhibited signs of an impending mental breakdown, Savage found the brig's career servicemen as committed as he was to mitigating the damage of the Pentagon's abusive interrogations. As he pressed al-Marri's case, brig insiders shared DVDs full of logs and files documenting his ordeal.

In Savage's office, I clicked a video file on one of those DVDs and sat stunned as surveillance camera footage of al-Marri, Padilla, and Yasar Hamdi, each in his bare cell in his own isolation wing, filled the screen. The date stamp is June 2, 2004, just a few weeks before the Supreme Court upheld Hamdi's right to file a habeas corpus petition. For Hamdi and Padilla, the worst is over: in the upper left, Hamdi lounges on the blanket-covered mattress throughout the 10-minute clip, apparently reading; in the upper right, Padilla spends the whole time on the floor, back to the wall, occupied with papers spread between his legs. In the bottom right an agitated al-Marri, the only one of the three still undergoing interrogation, fidgets on a blanket atop a bare metal bedframe, waves sarcastically at the camera, then pinballs around the narrow cell.

In September 2002, Jack Goldsmith experienced a moment like this. Goldsmith, who a year later would replace Jay Bybee as head of the White House Office of Legal Counsel (OLC) and withdraw two of the "deeply flawed" foundational torture memos during his tenure, had traveled with David Addington, Jim Haynes, CIA chief counsel John Rizzo, and other lawyers from the Bush administration's self-titled "War Counsel" on a kind of field trip to observe interrogation operations; they flew to Guantánamo and then onto the Navy Brig in Norfolk, Virginia, where Hamdi was then being held. In his book *The Terror Presidency*, Goldsmith recalls how, on a day that happened to be his birthday, he found himself huddling with the other lawyers around a small black and white monitor in the Norfolk brig watching Hamdi—whose birthday it was that day as well—curled in a fetal position in his isolation cell.

"Before I saw him on the closed-circuit television, I had no sympathy for Hamdi, whom I knew had volunteered to fight for the tyrannical Taliban," Goldsmith wrote.

> *Witnessing an unmoving Hamdi on that fuzzy black-and-white screen, however, moved me. Something seemed wrong. It seemed unnecessarily extreme to hold a twenty-two-year-old foot soldier in a remote wing of a run-down prison in a tiny cell, isolated from almost all human contact and with no access to a lawyer. "This is what habeas corpus is for," I thought to myself, somewhat embarrassed at the squishy sentiment.*

Twice in the next several months, the Fourth Circuit Court of Appeals thwarted Hamdi's habeas application, first overturning a district court order that Hamdi be given access to an attorney, and then holding, essentially, that courts had no authority to challenge the President's determination that Hamdi was an Enemy Combatant subject to indefinite, incommunicado detention.

Not long after that second ruling, someone on the Norfolk brig staff emailed his superiors:

> *Sir are there any new developments with regard to the detainee's fate that can be passed along. I know I can not give him any false hope, but I fear the rubber band is nearing its breaking point here and not totally confident I can keep his head in the game much longer. I will continue to monitor his behavior and get [redacted] and [redacted] aboard, but fear that once this individual decides to go south, there will be little if anything, I can do to bring him back around. I have directed my staff to pay close attention to his behavior, to pick up their discussions with him and that I will conduct evening rounds in an effort to assure him we are concerned about his state of mind and health and welfare.*

When Andy Savage began visiting the Charleston Brig, these were the kind of servicemen he encountered, he told me. One of them, Air Force

Major Chris Ferry, sat outside his client's isolation cell every night for two weeks, talking al-Marri down from the ledge during a similar crisis.

Ferry took over security operations in 2005, not long after the Supreme Court ruled that Hamdi could in fact pursue a habeas corpus petition. Before he arrived, there had been an "open door policy" at the brig, as Ferry put it when I caught up with him where he is now stationed in Florida; agents from the Mitchell and Jessen school of interrogation entered the facility when they pleased and dictated conditions of the ECs' confinement. When Ferry, who had been through the military survival training regime those two psychologists had twisted into the Bush administration's Rendition, Detention, and Interrogation (RDI) program, learned what had been happening in the brig, he recognized the routine. "It was just like in Panama, with the music, lights on, lights off, banging on the bars," he told me, letting me know that kind of treatment was not without impact. "Locked in a box, you go crazy. You know if you give them something, anything, they'll stop."

But SERE training lasts just a week; Savage's client al-Marri had been in isolation for two years. "Why the fuck is his window still painted out?" Ferry remembers thinking. "Do you want him *really* to go crazy?" Not only that, Ferry thought: "You're just going to look like fools when these cases make their way through the courts."

So Ferry pressed for changes. "Open door" had been replaced by a strict-access regime, where visiting intelligence agents required approval from the Navy chain of command, and Ferry worked to rebuild the brig's traditional corrections protocols and professionalism. He pulled surveillance video to weed out aggressive guards, wanting, as he put it, to "nip in the bud corrections personnel thinking they're Billy Badass." And he went to al-Marri, whose response to isolation and harsh interrogation had been increasing incorrigibility, and introduced himself, breaking a Pentagon-imposed rule under which guards were forbidden from using their names. Ferry told him, "I'm not here to punish you. I'm here to treat you with respect. My job is to make sure you're safe. I'm not going to walk around like a drill sergeant, yelling at you."

Ferry specializes in a kind of amused self-deprecation: "I'm a dumbass,

I barely graduated from college," he told me; "I'm not the sharpest tack in the drawer." But he allowed that one of his strengths is communication, and that he was proud of his role in bringing the brig "to another level." "I feel good about that," he said simply. Still, he insisted, it was just a question of basic psychology. When holdovers ridiculed him for befriending an Enemy Combatant, he would answer, "You don't freakin' get it, do you? I'm trying to keep him *calm*." He reminded them—and me—that even with the improvements, al-Marri was still being punished. "So what if he can see out the window? You've got the guy's freedom already. People don't realize what that is, what that means."

And he could point to the results: through a milestone privileges program, al-Marri gradually mellowed. The ECs were allowed to address chits to the brig command about their conditions, and al-Marri became a spirited correspondent. In one remarkable document in Savage's files, al-Marri enumerates the abuses he endured during his eighteen-month incommunicado interrogation on the back of a photocopy of Clarence Thomas's dissent in the *Hamdi* habeas case—the opinion in which Thomas declared that detaining American citizens as Enemy Combatants under such conditions falls "squarely within the Federal Government's war powers, and we lack the expertise and capacity to second-guess that decision."

Eventually, al-Marri even did what he hadn't done during his incommunicado interrogation: he talked. Following his transfer to civilian custody to stand trial on material support charges, on the eve of his sentencing hearing, al-Marri met with David Risley from the U.S. District Attorney's office in Illinois and FBI Special Agent Tim Kirkham and for eight hours in a public visitation room at Pekin Federal Prison near Peoria voluntarily shared everything he knew about Al Qaeda acquaintances and operations.

But Ferry's improvements came too late for Padilla. Described by another brig staffer as docile "as a piece of furniture," Padilla "barely talked at all" in the two years Ferry headed security at the brig. "It was weird," he told me. "He was so reserved, even with his facial expression, and sometimes talked in the third person. 'Don't need anything, thanks,' was about all he would say."

When Padilla gained the privilege of watching television in a common area outside of his cell, he would automatically switch to ESPN. So Ferry studied up on Padilla's hometown Chicago Cubs and managed, finally, to hold trivial conversations. From these sparse chats, Ferry surmised the detainee "wasn't the smartest guy in the world"; he guessed that Padilla, a former Chicago gangbanger who converted to Islam in prison, had been set up for a fall. But he was a model prisoner, and Ferry kept urging him to submit chits suggesting improvements in his conditions. "I'm good," Padilla insisted. Finally, pressed one too many times, Padilla said he absolutely wouldn't put anything in writing. "If I ask for a book, the CIA will read it and say, 'What does he mean he wants a book?'" he snapped. "If I ask for a cup of water, they'll say, 'Why water?'"

"He was so afraid to say anything," Ferry told me. And he understood why. "I got to see a lot of the tapes," Ferry said, adding that "heavy stuff" is a good way to describe what went on during those Pentagon-directed interrogation sessions. Heavy, he wanted me to understand, did not mean waterboarding. It also didn't mean skillful or smart. "It was like Barney Fife stuff," Ferry said. "You've got to be friggin' *shitting* me," he recalls thinking as he was watching tapes of Padilla's interrogations. "Some of the techniques...are you *serious*?"

✳ ✳ ✳

Five and a half months after the Padilla hearing in South Carolina, on the ninth anniversary of the White House Office of Legal Counsel's secret August 1, 2002 torture memos, I was back in a Federal courtroom, this one on the nineteenth floor of the Daniel Patrick Moynihan U.S. Courthouse in lower Manhattan, similar in vintage to the one where Gergel shut down Padilla's suit, but with a better view. But if that hearing, with its legion of defense lawyers and gallery full of law students, was about whether we might someday see some fireworks, this one was about tracking down the last few embers from one of the few torture-related lawsuits to make it off the ground.

The first of those August 2002 memos, written by John Yoo and signed by Jay Bybee and titled "Standards of Conduct for Interrogation Under

18 U.S.C. §§ 2340-2340A," laid out the blueprint for evading prohibitions on torture, asserting that abuse becomes torture only if it results in organ failure, death, or years of mental torment, and then only if the torturer specifically intends to inflict such extreme damage; even then, Yoo, suggested, prosecuting White House-commissioned torturers could be an unconstitutional infringement on the President's war powers. The second Yoo-Bybee memo greenlighted the use of the so-called Enhanced Interrogation Techniques on Abu Zubaydah, who at that moment was in the hands of Dr. James Mitchell in the secret CIA dungeon in Thailand.

In June, 2004, *The Washington Post* published the "Standards of Conduct" memo, the first the public knew of the Bush administration's efforts to distort the definition of torture. The same month, the ACLU filed suit to force the CIA, the Justice Department, and the Department of Defense to comply with its Freedom of Information Act request, filed a year before, for all records relating to the treatment of detainees in U.S. custody. That suit, which *The New York Times* has called "among the most successful in the history of public disclosure," would produce some 130,000 pages of documents, the incredible trove I dug through over the eighteen months I worked on TheTortureReport.org.

But not all of the documents covered by that request were produced. Among the records the CIA failed to inventory for Judge Alvin Hellerstein were ninety-two videotapes of Mitchell's OLC-approved and White House-monitored interrogation of Abu Zubaydah. A little over a year after the FOIA suit was filed, the CIA destroyed what would have been the most blunt, visceral refutation of the OLC's claim that Enhanced Interrogation Techniques are not torture.

For ninety somber minutes, I watched the ACLU's lawyers press Hellerstein to find the CIA in Contempt of Court for destroying the tapes, arguing it is only right to cite a government agency for so blatantly disregarding judicial orders. The CIA's attorneys, looking too predictably like fraternity officers appearing before the dean, countered that their client has "stood up, heard the court, and taken responsibility here"; it should be enough, they argued, that the agency produced the lists the court requested after the tapes' destruction and offered to pay the ACLU's attorneys' fees.

"I'm not going to hold the CIA in contempt," Hellerstein finally announced. "In the final analysis, I think these things can happen in every organization. There are misguided officials, misguided in their belief that everything they do is correct, or that they are motivated to do the correct thing when, in fact, it is not the correct thing, I decline to hold an entire agency in contempt for the mistakes of some of its officials."

The feeling in the courtroom was less defeated than depleted. A kind of exhaustion has crept into judicial processes connected to the quest for accountability for the abuse of detainees in U.S. custody—the very processes mandated by U.S. law and international covenants banning torture. Leaving the courtroom, I keep thinking of an observation Judge Gergel made as he prepared to excuse himself from carrying out the Torture Convention's obligations at the Padilla hearing. "Mr. Padilla has had a good bit of process in our American court system," Gergel said. "I'm not sure how many citizens could claim to have been before three courts of appeals in a career." Those three trips to federal court had been required because the Bush administration played the courts like marks in a game of Three-card Monte—now you see him, now you don't—but Gergel was right in a sense, there had been plenty of judicial activity around Padilla's case. But what good is an abundance of process if there's no justice?

For if there's one thing that legal proceedings and investigations in the past five years have done, it is confirm the conclusions we are led to by the documents. Decisions of federal judges in Guantánamo habeas cases are now peppered with sentences like "The Court will not rely on the statements of Guantánamo detainees Hajj and Kazimi because there is unrebutted evidence that, at the time of the interrogation at which they made the statements, both men had been tortured," and "The government's problem is that its proof that Salahi gave material support to terrorists is so attenuated, or so tainted by coercion and mistreatment, or so classified, that it cannot support a criminal prosecution." In one opinion, Judge Gladys Kessler ordered Guantánamo detainee Farhi Saeed Bin Mohammed released because the evidence that he trained as an Al Qaeda fighter came largely from statements by Jose Padilla's alleged dirty bomb co-conspirator Binyam Mohamed—who, she found, had been subjected to "a constant barrage of physical and psychological abuse" throughout his detention in Pakistan, Morocco, and the CIA's secret "Dark Prison" in Afghanistan, all of it designed "to manipulate him into telling investigators what they wanted to hear."

There are judgments from our closest international partners as well. Both Binyam Mohamed, who is a resident of the United Kingdom, and Maher Arar, the Canadian citizen who was mistakenly detained at JFK airport and shipped off to Syria for torture, were denied their day in court in the U.S. when the Bush and Obama administrations claimed that adjudicating lawsuits for the restitution they are entitled to would endanger state secrets. But Britain and Canada found their countries' secondary roles in these human rights violations so troubling they conducted their own investigations—and, having verified their ordeals, awarded the men substantial compensation.

The list goes on. The European Parliament exhaustively documented the spiderweb of complicity woven by the CIA's rendition operations. An Italian court convicted twenty-two CIA agents and one U.S. Air Force officer in absentia for kidnapping a terrorism suspect off the street in broad daylight in Milan and sending him to Egypt to be tortured. The International Committee of the Red Cross (ICRC), the body authorized under international law to police detentions around the world, determined that Abu Zubaydah—whose account to ICRC investigators of his treatment in Thailand exactly matches the plan approved in the OLC memos—and thirteen others interrogated in secret CIA prisons endured both cruel, inhuman, and degrading treatment and torture.

And we have the judgments of our own servicemen and women who struggled through the legal mess created by circumventing long-established civil and military law. Susan Crawford, the former convening authority for the Guantánamo military commissions, confirmed publicly on the eve of Obama's inauguration that she could not prosecute detainee Mohammed al-Qahtani, whose "special interrogation" was orchestrated at the highest levels of the Pentagon, because he was tortured. When Mohammed Jawad, a minor when he was detained and sent to Guantánamo, came before the military commission, military judge Colonel Stephen Henley found that the "frequent flyer" program to which Jawad had been subjected, in which he was transferred from cell to cell 112 times in two weeks to deprive him of sleep, constituted cruel, abusive, and inhuman treatment.

Lieutenant Colonel Darrel Vandeveld, the Judge Advocate General lawyer assigned to prosecute Jawad, became instead the most forceful advocate for the young man's release, writing in an affidavit in support of Jawad's habeas corpus petition, "I lack the words to express the heartsickness I experienced when I came to understand the pointless, purely gratuitous treatment of Mr. Jawad by my fellow soldiers." Lieutenant Colonel Stuart Couch, the former marine pilot whose close friend captained one of the two planes terrorists hijacked and flew in the World Trade Center, happily accepted the assignment to prosecute alleged hijacker recruiter Mohammed Slahi, only to resign when he pieced together evidence that Slahi, another one of the Pentagon's "special projects," had been tortured in ways that violated both the law and fundamental religious precepts of the dignity of all human beings.

In short, we know what happened, and we know, from these better angels of our nature, how we should feel about it. But they have been left to carry the burden of conscience as well, as our institutions continue to let our leaders, and us, off the hook.

Last year, the Justice Department's Office of Professional Responsibility (OPR) published its much-delayed report on its investigation into whether the authors of the OLC's torture memos violated standards of professional ethics by so zealously working to blur the bright lines and "unsettle" the law. In a section of the report criticizing the August 1, 2002 "Standards of Conduct" memo's claim that agents who tortured detainees in U.S. custody could mount a necessity defense, the OPR specifically attacked the "ticking time bomb" scenario that Bybee and Yoo put forth as an example of when torture might be necessary.

> Reliance upon the scenario has been criticized because it assumes, among other things: (1) that a specific plot to attack exists; (2) that it will happen within hours or minutes; (3) that it will kill many people; (4) that the person in custody is known with absolute certainly to

be a perpetrator of the attack; (5) that he has information that will
prevent the attack; (6) that torture will produce immediate, truthful
information that will prevent the attack; (7) that no other means will
produce the information in time; and (8) that no other action could
be taken to avoid the harm.

The ticking bomb scenario is not only intellectually suspect, the OPR
found; it is entirely inapt to the circumstances Bybee and Yoo were justifying.
The interrogations of Abu Zubaydah, Khalid Sheikh Mohammed, Abd
al-Rahim al-Nashiri and other detainees subjected to the OLC-approved
Enhanced Interrogation Techniques never approached "the level of
imminence and certainty associated with the 'ticking time bomb' scenario,"
the OPR concluded. In fact, the investigators pointed out, the designers of
the abusive interrogation regime themselves never claimed their aim was
to deter imminent threats, but rather to "condition the detainee gradually
to break down his resistance to interrogation."

In the end, Jay Bybee and John Yoo escaped professional censure for
their legal distortions. Incredibly, rather than accept this gift quietly, when
the OPR invited now-Federal Judge Bybee to respond to a draft of its report,
he answered the OPR's criticism of the "ticking time bomb" scenario by
trotting out Jose Padilla's alleged "dirty bomb" plot. "The OLC attorneys
working on the 2002 Memo had been briefed on the apprehension of
Jose Padilla on May 8, 2002," Bybee wrote. "Padilla was believed to have
built and planted a dirty bomb—a radiological weapon which combines
radioactive material with conventional explosives—in New York City. It is
easy for OPR, seven years removed from the horror of 9/11, to scoff at the
notion of a ticking time bomb scenario, but the context in which these
memos were written simply cannot be forgotten."

Has anyone forgotten the 9/11 terrorist attacks and the fear they
engendered? Easily forgotten, though, as Bybee well knows, or at least
driven into the very margins of consciousness by the force of those
emotions, are facts. Jose Padilla could no more have planted a dirty bomb
in New York that you or I: he was apprehended at O'Hare airport as he
disembarked a flight from Zurich and had not been in the United States

for four years. Every Bush administration official knew this, and not one asserted at the time that a radiological bomb was ticking. In fact, within twenty-four hours of John Ashcroft's fevered pronouncement that Padilla had arrived in the United States with plans for such an attack, Deputy Defense Secretary Paul Wolfowitz was telling the press he didn't think there was even a plot "beyond some fairly loose talk."

This is what happens when no one is called to account, before the law, for torture: we submit to being lied to more, degrading ourselves and our democracy further.

Last November, three months before the Padilla hearing in Charleston, I flew to Geneva to watch the United States answer questions about its human rights record before the UN Human Rights Council. During the three-hour session, I sat amazed as Obama State Department Legal Advisor Harold Koh assured the world that the U.S. was committed to abiding by the Convention against Torture. "Notwithstanding recent public accusations, to our knowledge, all credible allegations of detainee abuse by United States forces have been thoroughly investigated and appropriate corrective action has been taken," he insisted.

That same week, former President Bush appeared before a packed auditorium at the opening event of the Miami Book Fair, promoting the memoir in which he wrote "Damn right!" he'd approved the waterboarding Khalid Sheikh Mohammed. In Miami, Bush again crowed that he'd approved the waterboarding of KSM, Zubaydah, and al-Nashiri, telling the crowd, to sustained applause, "Just so you know, in the book I walk you through getting this capability, this tool, passed by the United States Congress so it is now available to any president to use should he or she choose to do so."

Congress never passed legislation approving waterboarding or Enhanced Interrogation Techniques. Nor, in fact, did the Bush administration feel it needed Congressional approval for its abusive interrogations, asserting instead broad Presidential powers to define the treatment and determine the fate of prisoners in U.S. custody. Whether or not the president in fact possesses such powers is a question that continues to paralyze the courts and mesmerize the legal academy; meanwhile, what are we, the people, to do with the documentary record? Neither presidents nor dictators can order torture. Of course any of us, presidents included, can go beyond the law. The question, for those who would torture as much as for those who would plan and carry out terrorist attacks, the question for any of us, is how we answer to one another when we do wrong.

Larry Siems
September 2011, New York City

NOTES ON THE TEXT AND ACKNOWLEDGEMENTS

In September 2009, the American Civil Liberties Union launched the website TheTortureReport.org to open a window on some 130,000 pages of formerly secret documents relating to the abuse of prisoners in U.S. custody after the September 11, 2001. This book is a product of that innovative, interactive project.

The account that follows unfolded on TheTortureReport.org between September 2009 and March 2011. As the report's principal author, I would periodically post sections; as I did, a group of expert contributors made annotations on the text, offering comments, clarifications, and additional crucial information, and the public reacted to the posts in an open comments section. Between posts, I would update developments relating to the emerging narrative and explore related issues and key documents in a report diary. The narrative that developed, the comments, and the diary discussion were all meant to point the way to the website's most valuable feature, a publicly searchable database of the FOIA documents.

Much of that incredible trove remains untapped. I barely touched the substantial record of abuses of prisoners in military custody in Afghanistan and Iraq, for example. Instead, I concentrated on the three stories that for me most illuminated the workings—the origins, the structure and purposes, but also the central drama—of the torture program. In a sense, the three sections of this report form a kind of triptych of America's post-9/11 foray into torture: on the left, the CIA's White House-orchestrated interrogation of Abu Zubaydah and others in its illegal, secret prisons; on the right, the interrogations of Mohammed al-Qahtani and Mohamedou Ould Slahi, two of the Pentagon's "Special Projects," in Guantánamo Bay, Cuba; and in the middle panel, in a story that connects the CIA's black sites, Guantánamo, and the torture chambers of third countries, the rise and fall of an alleged "dirty bomb" plot involving Abu Zubaydah, Binyam Mohamed, and Jose Padilla.

These stories have three things in common: they are among the most well-documented in the record; they depict a clear chain of command emanating from the White House; and they portray treatment that was both recognized as torture at the time and unambiguously judged to be so afterwards. Much of the ground these narratives cover is not new—and yet so little of it, still, is widely known. I knew no more than the broad outlines when I began to reconstruct the record.

Few things appear more cold and impersonal than stacks of formerly classified documents about a torture program, but few things are more intimately and harrowingly human. My job, as I understood it, was to tell these stories entirely through the documentary evidence. As I did so, I tried to bring forth the voices of two groups in particular: the voices of those who endured the mistreatment, to whom we are obligated to listen if we are ever to fulfill our responsibilities under U.S. and international laws banning torture; and the voices of the men and women in the military and in the intelligence agencies who served as our collective moral compass as these events unfolded, often under great pressure and at considerable personal risk, who stood up to the abuses as they were happening and, in so doing, created crucial parts of this documentary record.

I am enormously grateful to the ACLU—first, for excavating these documents through Freedom of Information Act litigation and making them available for everyone to explore and draw their own conclusions, and then for giving me the opportunity, and the time and space, to do just that. I owe particular thanks, for their encouragement and patience, to the attorneys and staff of the ACLU's National Security Project, among them Jameel Jaffer, Alexander Abdo, Ben Wizner, Melissa Goodman, Jonathan Manes, Denny LeBoeuf, Hina Shamsi, Nusrat Choudhury, Ateqah Khaki, Leila Tabbaa, Benjamin Smyser, Hallie Pope, and Anna Estevao, and Steven Watt of the ACLU's Human Rights Program; and to Eric Schoenborn, who designed TheTortureReport.org, and Alex Vitrak, who kept it running. Thanks, too, to Steven Isenberg and Sarah Hoffman, my colleagues at PEN American Center, for making it possible for me to divide my time between this project and my usual duties. And thanks to John Oakes and OR Books for transforming this from web report to book form, and to Lara Tobin and Leily Kleinbard for their help with the manuscript.

One of the most dynamic elements of the website was the involvement of the expert contributors, a group that included Glenn Greenwald, Joanne Mariner, Deborah Popowski, John Sifton, Lisa Magarrell, Marcy Wheeler, Matthew Alexander, and David Frakt. Collectively and individually, they know far more than I do even now about the torture program and how it harmed us all. Their illuminating annotations appeared on the website throughout the text. Some of their work is lost in translation; many of their corrections and suggestions have been incorporated into the text as it appears here. However, several of their invaluable observations, comments, and reflections do appear, not in the text itself, but at the end of every section. I cannot thank them enough for their support for this project and for their own indispensable work.

ONE:

THE CIA'S EXPERIMENTS

ORIGINS

On September 17, 2001, six days after the terrorist attacks in New York and Washington, DC, President Bush signed a directive authorizing the CIA to set up and run secret prisons outside the United States.

Secret prisons are illegal. Every nation on earth must acknowledge its prisons, account for its prisoners, and allow those it is holding to communicate that they've been imprisoned. All prisoners must have some access to legal process. The International Committee of the Red Cross must be permitted to visit them and monitor the conditions of their imprisonment.

Seizing someone and delivering him to a secret facility where he is held incommunicado and unacknowledged is "enforced disappearance," a gross human rights violation associated with infamous, brutal regimes.[1] The laws against it are as absolute as those banning torture and cruel, inhuman, and degrading treatment, and the two crimes are closely linked. Invisible prisoners are abused prisoners, as a rule. But it is more than that: the uncertainty and fear disappearance engenders, not just in those who are disappeared but also in their families and communities, is itself considered a form of cruelty.[2]

Tens of thousands of pages of government documents and public reports, books, and articles now testify to the torture and cruel, inhuman, and degrading treatment of detainees that began in the CIA's "black sites" and spread through acknowledged and unacknowledged prisons in Guantánamo Bay, Afghanistan, and Iraq. Much of the most direct evidence remains secret, however. Videotapes of interrogations have been destroyed. Material still being withheld or redacted includes photographs, descriptions of the destroyed videotapes, real time cable traffic between interrogators and senior officials in Washington, and direct testimonies by victims of torture and abuse.

Still secret, too, is the document that first opened the space for torture and mistreatment to happen. In Freedom of Information Act proceedings, the CIA originally argued that the activities President Bush's September 17, 2001 Memorandum of Notification authorized were so sensitive the agency couldn't even acknowledge that the document existed.[3] But President Bush himself eventually disclosed the CIA's Rendition, Detention, and Interrogation program. In a speech on September 6, 2006, he revealed that the agency had been holding "a small number of suspected terrorist leaders and operatives" in secret sites overseas, and had been interrogating them with "an alternative set of procedures." After being held for as long as four and a half years, the President announced, the last fourteen of these CIA detainees had been transferred into military custody in Guantánamo.[4]

"Item 61," as the presidential directive became known in ongoing Freedom of Information Act (FOIA) litigation seeking all records relating to the abuse and torture of prisoners in U.S. detention centers overseas, is one of some two thousand documents the CIA was still withholding when President Obama officially ended the Rendition, Detention, and Interrogation program in January 2009. It includes the twelve-page Memorandum of Notification from the President to the National Security Council (NSC) establishing the program, plus a two-page "transmittal memorandum" from the NSC to CIA Director George Tenet with instructions on implementing the program and the list of those who had seen the document. In explaining the agency's refusal to produce this document at a hearing before Federal Judge Alvin Hellerstein on May 12, 2008, CIA attorneys argued that the level of classification of the document is so exceptional that even the font is classified.[5]

In the months following President Obama's inauguration, several more of those two thousand documents were released, most notably the report summarizing the results of an investigation by the CIA's own Office of the Inspector General (OIG) into the abuse of CIA detainees under the Rendition, Detention, and Interrogation program. That May 2004 OIG report depicts an agency struggling to implement a presidential order that put it on the wrong side of the law from the start:

> *The conduct of detention and interrogation activities presented new challenges for the CIA. These included determining where detention and interrogation facilities could be securely located and operated, and identifying and preparing qualified personnel to manage and carry out detention and interrogation activities. With the knowledge that Al-Qa'ida personnel had been trained in the use of resistance techniques, another challenge was to identify interrogation techniques that Agency personnel could lawfully use to overcome the resistance. . . . All of these considerations took place against the backdrop of pre-September 11, 2001 CIA avoidance of interrogations and repeated U.S. policy statements condemning torture and advocating the humane treatment of political prisoners and detainees in the international community.[6]*

Released in heavily redacted form in August 2009, the report summarizes the results of the Inspector General's investigation into the deaths of two detainees in CIA custody, allegations of the use of "unauthorized interrogation techniques" on CIA detainees, and information the Inspector General's office had received "that some employees were concerned that certain covert Agency activities at an overseas detention and interrogation site might involve violations of human rights."[7]

As it reviews specific incidents of torture, the report reveals the extent to which CIA interrogators in the black sites communicated their intentions and actions to their superiors in Washington, and their anxiety over the legality of their actions.[8] "During the course of this Review, a number of Agency officers expressed unsolicited concern about the possibility of recrimination or legal action resulting from their participation," the Inspector General reported. "One officer expressed concern that one day, Agency officers will wind up on some 'wanted list' to appear before the World Court for war crimes stemming from activities [redacted]."[9]

A week after the Inspector General's report was made public, Attorney General Eric Holder announced that he was directing a special prosecutor to review the very incidents examined in the Inspector General's 2004 report—a move former Vice President Dick Cheney immediately denounced as "an outrageous political act" and "an intensely partisan, politicized look back at the prior administration."[10] But CIA agents foresaw such an investigation early on, regardless of the political climate:

> A number of Agency officers of various grade levels who are involved with detention and interrogation activities are concerned that they may at some future dates be vulnerable to legal action in the United States or abroad, and that the U.S. Government will not stand behind them. Although the current detention and interrogation Program has been subject to DoJ legal review and Administration political approval, it diverges sharply from previous Agency policy and practice, rules that govern interrogations by U.S. military and law enforcement officers, statements of U.S. policy by the Department of State, and public statements by very senior U.S. officials, including the President, as well as the policies expressed by Members of Congress, other Western governments, international organizations, and human rights groups. In addition, some Agency officers are aware of interrogation activities that were outside the scope of written DoJ opinion. Officers are concerned that future public revelation of the CTC Program is inevitable and will seriously damage Agency officers' personal reputations, as well as the reputation and effectiveness of the Agency itself.[11]

As they carried out the September 17, 2001 presidential directive, CIA agents were left to wrestle with one of the fundamental problems enforced disappearance poses: the question of what the agency itself called the "endgame." What happens to those who have been treated in a way that undermines any possibility of reintroducing them into the legal system for prosecution and who, "if not kept in isolation, would likely divulge information about the circumstances of their detention"?[12] By May 2004 it was clear to the Inspector General that the CIA was trapped in the directive. "The Agency faces potentially serious long-term political and legal challenges as a result of the CTC Detention and Interrogation Program, particularly its use of [Enhanced Interrogation Techniques] and the inability of the U.S. Government to decide what it will ultimately do with terrorists detained by the Agency," he concluded.[13]

The U.S. government now acknowledges it held "fewer than 100 people" for up to five years in CIA black sites.[14] As President Bush announced, fourteen of these men were transferred to Guantánamo in 2006. These were not, as President Bush declared, the last of the black site detainees, however; two more CIA prisoners were moved to Guantánamo the following year. "Where the rest of those who disappeared into the Rendition, Detention, and Interrogation program are today is not clear. The government can point to many who are now in prisons in other countries, but several, it says, are missing or lost."[15]

The day before President Bush signed the September 17, 2001 directive, then-Vice President Cheney told a national audience on *Meet the Press* that the United States, in responding to the September 11 terrorist attacks, would have to work "the dark side," insisting "it's going to be vital for us to use any means at our disposal, basically, to achieve our objectives." The day after issuing the secret order, the President signed the Authorization for Use of Military Force in Response to the 9/11 Attacks, a Congressional joint resolution that had passed on a 98-0 vote in the Senate and a 420-1 vote in the House of Representatives. The resolution authorized the President

> *to use all necessary and appropriate force against those nations, organizations, or persons he determines planned, authorized,*

*committed, or aided the terrorist attacks that occurred on September
11, 2001, or harbored such organizations or persons, in order to
prevent any future acts of international terrorism against the United
States by such nations, organizations, or persons.*[16]

As expansive as that language is—so expansive the administration
would claim it conferred the power to conduct the National Security
Agency's illegal Terrorist Surveillance Program—it was narrower than the
administration wanted. Its proposed language would have authorized the
President "to deter and pre-empt any future acts of terrorism or aggression"
regardless of whether the targets had any connection to the September 11
attacks.[17] Moments before the Senate vote, the White House tried to insert
an additional phrase that would have permitted military and covert actions
inside the United States.[18]

When Congress passed a version that specifically rejected these
proposals, the administration responded in a way that would become a
hallmark of its antiterrorism efforts: it asked its lawyers to argue around
the legal restrictions. A week after the Congressional resolution was signed
into law, John Yoo, Deputy Assistant Attorney General in the Justice
Department's Office of Legal Counsel, issued a secret memorandum
asserting that the President had the power to take pre-emptive action
against terrorists or States that harbor them, whether or not they were
linked to 9/11. Yoo followed this a month later with a secret memorandum
insisting that the President had the authority to use military force within
the United States.[19]

At the time, few outside the administration knew that it was plotting
an antiterrorism strategy that recognized almost no legal restrictions, and
no one outside a handful of "special access" senior administration officials
knew that its plans specifically included enforced disappearance and
abusive interrogations.

Nevertheless, the international community was sufficiently alarmed
by what the phrase "all necessary and appropriate force" might entail and
what administration rhetoric might be signaling that it felt compelled to
remind the United States of its international obligations. On September

27, 2001, a delegation from the International Committee of the Red Cross met with State Department officials.[20] Two weeks later, the United Nations Committee against Torture issued this statement:

> *Although mindful of the terrible threat to civilised society of international terrorism, the Committee against Torture reminds State parties of the non-derogable nature of most of the obligations undertaken by them in ratifying the Convention against Torture.*
>
> *The obligations contained in Articles 2[21] and 15[22] are two such provisions and must be observed in all circumstances.*
>
> *The Committee against Torture is confident that whatever responses to the threat of international terrorism are adopted by State parties, such responses will be in conformity with the obligations undertaken by them in ratifying the Convention against Torture.*[23]

Annotations on this section from TheTortureReport.org

On the September 17, 2001 Presidential Memorandum of Notification, blogger Marcy Wheeler ("emptywheel") wrote,

> *It's important to note that the September 17, 2001 order also authorized renditions, and that the treatment of people like Ibn al-Sheikh al-Libi, described near the end of the report, was an early approach to fulfilling this part of the mandate. Also, it would be useful to point readers to a detailed explanation of the National Security Act's about Congressional notification, which are available at http://www.fas.org/sgp/crs/intel/m011806.pdf, and to note that the CIA did not inform Congress they were waterboarding until after they had already done a month of it with Abu Zubaydah.*

On the CIA's use of "authorized" and "unauthorized" techniques, Alexander Abdo of the ACLU's National Security Project wrote,

> *The CIA OIG report's revelations that interrogators used unauthorized techniques—like mock executions and threats on the lives of detainees—is*

particularly surprising given the excruciating level of senior oversight of the CIA's "enhanced interrogation" program. There are clearly two narratives at play and few answers about their interplay. On the one hand, senior-level officials have tried to wash their hands of the clear excesses of the CIA's interrogation program by pointing to the OLC memos. On the other, CIA interrogators have pleaded "good faith" reliance on legal advice that they clearly ignored at times.

On the fear some CIA agents expressed that they would face prosecutions for War Crimes before the World Court, Air Force Lieutenant Colonel and former lead defense counsel of the Office of Military Commissions in Guantánamo David Frakt wrote,

This fear reveals the ignorance of CIA Agents about international law. First of all, the correct name for the so-called "World Court" is the International Court of Justice. This court, in the Hague, resolves only legal disputes between nations (and provides advisory opinions to organs of the UN) and has no jurisdiction over individuals for war crimes. If the officers were referring to the International Criminal Court, the U.S. is not a party to the Rome Statute (President Clinton signed the statute, but President Bush unsigned it) and does not accept that the ICC has jurisdiction over U.S. citizens. Even if the Obama Administration were to sign on to the Rome Statue again, a move it is reportedly considering, and get the statute ratified by the Senate, it would not be retroactive.

On the section in general, former Air Force investigator and interrogator Matthew Alexander wrote,

Although some have argued that the crimes of torture and abuse, ghosting of detainees, and extraordinary rendition must be viewed within the context of the dark days after 9/11, I submit that there is no such language in any public oath of office. All oaths of office for U.S. public service require adherence to American law and principles at all times.

As horrific as 9/11 is in everyone's memory, it is a fundamental aspect of

leadership to be able to separate one's emotions from one's professional duty. As General George C. Marshall said, "Once an Army is involved in war, there is a beast in every fighting man which begins tugging at its chains...a good officer must learn early on how to keep the beast under control both in his men and in himself."

Our leaders failed to keep that 'beast' under control and, in failing to do so, became the very enemy we were fighting against. I believe these policies rise to a level above incompetence because they violated U.S. and international law. In that context, they can only be classified as crimes.

THE EXPERIMENT

When the International Committee of the Red Cross finally got to see Abu Zubaydah late in 2006, four and a half years after he disappeared into a secret CIA prison, this is what he said:

I woke up, naked, strapped to a bed, in a very white room. The room measured approximately 4m x 4m. The room had three solid walls, with the fourth wall consisting of metal bars separating it from a larger room. I am not sure how long I remained in the bed. After some time, I think it was several days, but can't remember exactly, I was transferred to a chair where I was kept, shackled by hands and feet for what I think was the next 2 or 3 weeks. During this time I developed blisters on the underside of my legs due to the constant sitting. I was only allowed to get up from the chair to go the toilet, which consisted of a bucket. Water for cleaning myself was provided in a plastic bottle.

I was given no solid food during the first two or three weeks, while sitting on the chair. I was only given Ensure and water to drink. At first the Ensure made me vomit, but this became less with time.

The cell and room were air-conditioned and were very cold. Very loud, shouting type music was constantly playing. It kept repeating every fifteen minutes twenty-four hours a day. Sometimes the music stopped and was replaced by a loud hissing or crackling noise.

The guards were American, but wore masks to conceal their faces. My interrogators did not wear masks.

During this first two to three week period I was questioned for about one to two hours each day. American interrogators would come to the room and speak to me through the bars of the cell. During the questioning the music was switched off, but was then put back on again afterwards. I could not sleep at all for the first two to three weeks. If I started to fall asleep one of the guards would come and spray water in my face.

After two or three weeks, Zubaydah told the Red Cross, he was given rice to eat once a day. "I would eat with my hand," he said, "but I was not allowed to wash."

It was also around this time that I was allowed to lie on the floor. I remained naked and in shackles, but I could sleep a little. It went on like this for about another one and a half months.

During the first few days a doctor came and gave me an injection. I was told it was an antibiotic. After about one and a half to two months I was examined by a female doctor who asked why I was still naked. My measurements were taken and the next day, I was provided with orange clothes to wear. This was followed however, by more threats that worse was to follow.

Indeed, the next day guards came into my cell. They told me to stand up and raise my arms above my head. They then cut the clothes off of me so that I was again naked and put me back on the chair for several days. I tried to sleep on the chair, but was again kept awake by the guards spraying water in my face.

When my interrogators had the impression that I was cooperating and providing the information they required, the clothes were given back to me. When they felt I was being less cooperative the clothes were again removed and I was again put back on the chair. This was repeated several times.

Eventually (I don't remember after how long), I was allowed to have a mattress and was given a towel to use as a sheet to cover myself with while sleeping. I was allowed some tissue paper to use when going to toilet on the bucket.

There then followed a period of about one month with no questioning, he reported. During that time, he was fed rice and beans once or twice a day, along with Ensure. The cell remained frigid, though the music was replaced by the round-the-clock "hissing and crackling noise" that he tried to block with earplugs fashioned from the tissue.

Then, about two and a half or three months after I arrived in this place, the interrogation began again, but with more intensity than before. Then the real torturing started.

Two black wooden boxes were brought into the room outside my cell. One was tall, slightly higher than me and narrow, measuring perhaps 1m x 0.75m and 2m in height. The other was shorter, perhaps only 1 meter in height. I was taken out of my cell and one of the interrogators wrapped a towel around my neck, they then used it to swing me around and smash me repeatedly against the hard walls of the room. I was also repeatedly slapped in the face. As I was still shackled, the pushing and pulling around meant that the shackles pulled painfully on my ankles.

I was then put into the tall box for what I think was about one and a half to two hours. The box was totally black on the inside as well as the outside. It had a bucket inside to use as a toilet and had water to drink provided in a bottle. They put a cloth or cover over the outside of the box to cut out the light and restrict my air supply. It was difficult to breathe. When I was let out of the box I saw that one of the walls of the room had been covered with plywood sheeting. From now on it was against this wall that I was then smashed with the towel around my neck. I think that the plywood was there to provide some absorption of the impact of my body. The interrogators realized that smashing me against the hard wall would probably quickly result in physical injury.

There was, he noted, a clear division of labor: "During these torture sessions many guards were present, plus two interrogators who did the actual beating, still asking questions, while the main interrogator left to return when the beating was over."

After the beating I was then placed in the small box. They placed a cloth or cover over the box to cut out all light and restrict my air supply. As it was not high enough even to sit upright, I had to crouch down. It was very difficult because of my wounds. The stress on my legs held in this position meant my wounds both in the leg and stomach became very painful. I think this occurred about 3 months after my last operation. It was always cold in the room, but when the cover was placed over the box it made it hot and sweaty inside. The wound on my leg began to open and started to bleed. I don't know how long I remained in the small box, I think I may have slept or maybe fainted.

I was then dragged from the small box, unable to walk properly and put on what looked like a hospital bed, and strapped down very tightly with belts. A black cloth was then placed over my face and the interrogators used a mineral water bottle to pour water on the cloth so that I could not breathe. After a few minutes the cloth was removed and the bed was rotated into an upright position. The pressure of the straps on my wounds was very painful. I vomited. The bed was then again lowered to a horizontal position and the same torture carried out again with the black cloth over my face and water poured on from a bottle. On this occasion my head was in a more backward, downwards position and the water was poured on for a longer time. I struggled against the straps, trying to breathe, but it was hopeless. I thought I was going to die. I lost control of my urine. Since then I still lose control of my urine when under stress.

I was then placed again in the tall box. While I was inside the box loud music was played again and somebody kept banging repeatedly on the box from the outside. I tried to sit down on the floor, but because of the small space the bucket with urine tipped over and spilt over me. I remained in the box for several hours, maybe overnight. I was then taken out and again a towel was wrapped around my neck and I was smashed into the wall with the plywood covering and repeatedly slapped in the face by the same two interrogators as before. I was then made to sit on the floor with a black hood over my head until the next session of torture began. The room was always kept very cold.

Zubaydah told the ICRC that this regime "went on for approximately one week," during which "the whole procedure was repeated five times."

On each occasion, apart from one, I was suffocated once or twice and was put in the vertical position on the bed in between. On one occasion the suffocation was repeated three times. I vomited each time I was put in the vertical position between the suffocation.

During that week I was not given any solid food. I was only given Ensure to drink. My head and beard were shaved everyday.

I collapsed and lost consciousness on several occasions. Eventually the torture was stopped by the intervention of the doctor.

I was told during this period that I was one of the first to receive these interrogation techniques, so no rules applied. It felt like they were experimenting and trying out techniques to be used later on other people.

Even then, the ordeal wasn't quite over.

At the end of this period two women and a man came to interrogate me. I was still naked and, because of this, I refused to answer any questions. So they again repeatedly slapped me in the face and smashed me against the wall using the towel around my neck. The following day I was given a towel to wear around my waist, but I was still very cold.

Then, little by little, things started to get better. I was again given rice to eat. Then my mattress was returned. I was allowed to clean my cell. The tall box was removed, but the short one remained in the room outside my cell, I think as a deliberate reminder as to what my interrogators were capable of. One week after the end of torture I was given a pair of green shorts and a top to wear. The food also improved with the addition of beans and fruit.

I was provided with water and allowed to wash inside the cell. However, the loud noise continued throughout the nine months I spent in that place. I was never given any outdoor time.[24]

In his September 2006 speech announcing the transfer of the fourteen "high value detainees" from CIA black sites to Guantánamo, President Bush described the group as "dangerous men with unparalleled knowledge about terrorist networks and their plans for new attacks." He reported that one of these men, Abu Zubaydah, a "senior terrorist leader and trusted associate of Osama bin Laden," had run a terrorist training camp in Afghanistan where some of the 9/11 hijackers trained and had helped smuggle Al Qaeda leaders out of Afghanistan. Zubaydah was severely wounded during his capture and survived thanks to medical care arranged by the CIA, the president said, and though he initially disclosed some "nominal" information during questioning, he ultimately proved "defiant and evasive."

> We knew that Zubaydah had more information that could save innocent lives, but he stopped talking. As his questioning proceeded, it became clear that he had received training on how to resist interrogation. And so the CIA used an alternative set of procedures. These procedures were designed to be safe, to comply with our laws, our Constitution, and our treaty obligations. The Department of Justice reviewed the authorized methods extensively and determined them to be lawful. I cannot describe the specific methods used—I think you understand why—if I did, it would help the terrorists learn how to resist questioning, and to keep information from us that we need to prevent new attacks on our country. But I can say the procedures were tough, and they were safe, and lawful, and necessary.[25]

The ICRC had no trouble ascertaining what these specific methods were from its interviews with the fourteen. Although they had been held in complete isolation in black sites scattered around the globe and interviewed separately in Guantánamo after their transfer, their accounts were so consistent that the ICRC assembled a list of the abusive techniques. It included suffocation by water; prolonged stress standing positions, naked, with arms extended and chained above the head; beatings by use of a collar; beating and kicking; confinement in a box; prolonged nudity; sleep deprivation; exposure to cold temperature or cold water; prolonged shackling of the hands and feet; threats of ill-treatment to the detainee or his family; forced shaving; and deprivation or restricted provision of solid food.

The Red Cross also discovered from those interviews that doctors or psychologists had monitored their interrogations, at times instructing interrogators on whether to continue, adjust, or stop particular methods. Noting that the "accepted role of the physician, or any health professional, clearly does not extend to ruling on the permissibility, or not, of any form of physical or psychological ill-treatment," and that in any case the presence of doctors and psychologists belies any claim that these methods are safe, the ICRC definitively concluded that the treatment of Abu Zubaydah and the other "high value detainees" included both torture and cruel, inhuman, and degrading treatment, both prohibited under the Geneva Conventions and the 1984 UN Convention against Torture.[26]

It's hardly a surprising conclusion, considering the genesis of these "alternate procedures."

* * *

In the first days of 2002, a soldier working as a translator for a team interrogating incoming prisoners at Kandahar Detention Facility in Afghanistan filed a sworn statement dutifully reporting what she recognized as illegal abuse of a detainee. She had taken a break with her team to review their notes. When they left the interrogation booth, she saw several "special forces" members enter, she wrote; when she returned from her break, she found the special forces members crouched around the prisoner.

They were blowing cigarette smoke in his face. The prisoner was extremely upset. It took a long time to calm him down and find out what had happened. The prisoner was visibly shaken and crying. [redacted] immediately told them to get out and not to come back anywhere near anyone that we were talking to. I could tell something was wrong. The prisoner was extremely upset. He said that they hit him, told him that he was going to die, blew smoke in his face, and had shocked him with some kind of device. He used the term "electricity."

In her statement, she notes that she reported the abuse and that the "chain of command took action to ensure that nothing of that sort could happen again." Nevertheless, she wrote,

> I was very upset that such a thing could happen. I take my job and my responsibilities as an interrogator and as a human being very seriously. I understand the importance of the Geneva Convention and what it represents. If I don't honor it, what right do I have to expect any other military to do so?[27]

As she was writing these words, two military psychologists were finalizing a paper titled "Recognizing and Developing Countermeasures to al-Qaeda Resistance to Interrogation Techniques," the first in a series of proposals that would turn this country's relationship to the Geneva Conventions upside-down.

In December 2001, the CIA had asked Dr. James Mitchell to prepare a paper on overcoming training Al Qaeda members receive to resist divulging information during interrogations. Mitchell, a recently-retired psychologist from the Air Force's Survival Evasion Resistance Escape (SERE) program, enlisted Dr. John "Bruce" Jessen, the program's active-duty senior psychologist, to help prepare a plan. The Department of Defense, too, was interested in their work; that same month, the DoD's General Counsel's office had contacted the Joint Personnel Recovery Agency (JPRA), which oversees SERE programs for all the armed services, looking for ideas on detainee "exploitation."[28]

SERE training, as the United States Senate Armed Services Committee explained in its November 2008 report on detainee abuse, is designed to simulate conditions U.S. military personnel might endure "if captured by an enemy that did not abide by the Geneva Conventions." All three of the services run SERE programs that expose service members at high risk of capture to forms of "illegal exploitation" U.S. prisoners of war have endured over the last fifty years.

> The techniques used in SERE school, based, in part, on Chinese Communist techniques used during the Korean war to elicit false

confessions, include stripping students of their clothing, placing them in stress positions, putting hoods over their heads, disrupting their sleep, treating them like animals, subjecting them to loud music and flashing lights, and exposing them to extreme temperatures. It can also include face and body slaps and until recently, for some who attended the Navy's SERE school, it included waterboarding.[29]

Neither Mitchell nor Jessen had any experience as interrogators. As SERE psychologists, their role was to ensure that volunteers were not harmed or traumatized by their experiences. Jessen had at one point acted the part of an enemy interrogator, but SERE interrogators are role players who have no experience in intelligence gathering or eliciting information. The whole exercise is tightly controlled and designed to fortify students to endure torture. Commanders and psychologists monitor instructors and make sure they don't suffer from "moral disengagement" and start to view students as prisoners or detainees. Students volunteer for the training, are regularly debriefed, and are given safe words to use in case the mock interrogations become too stressful.[30]

But Mitchell and Jessen proposed reverse engineering the process— which meant, essentially, replacing simulated capture scenarios meant to prepare U.S. servicemen to endure torture with actual, abusive interrogations. As they began formulating a plan, the Bush administration was working around the obvious hypocrisy of adopting interrogation techniques developed by some of the twentieth century's most abusive regimes. On January 9, 2002, John Yoo of the Justice Department's Office of Legal Counsel and Robert Delahunty, Special Counsel to Defense Department General Counsel William J. Haynes II, sent a legal memorandum to Haynes advising him that the Geneva Conventions, and particularly the Third Geneva Convention governing the treatment of prisoners of war, do not apply to captured Taliban fighters and members of Al Qaeda.[31]

White House Counsel Alberto Gonzales briefed President Bush on the memo on January 18, and the president agreed with its conclusion. The following day, Secretary of Defense Donald Rumsfeld instructed General

Richard Myers, Chairman of the Joint Chiefs of Staff, to inform all field commanders that Al Qaeda and Taliban members are "not entitled to prisoner of war status" under the Geneva Conventions, though they should "treat [detainees] humanely and, to the extent appropriate and consistent with military necessity, in a manner consistent with the principles of the Geneva Conventions of 1949."[32]

Secretary of State Colin Powell pushed the president to reconsider the decision. He argued that the policy put U.S. soldiers at risk of torture if they are captured; encouraged other countries to skirt the Conventions; discouraged countries from handing over terrorism suspects to the U.S.; hurt the U.S.'s international image; and undermined the high standards of U.S. military culture. Powell said he could agree that Al Qaeda and Taliban fighters might not be afforded POW status, but only on a case-by-case basis after a status hearing before a military board.

Gonzales pushed back. In a January 25, 2002 memorandum to the President, in which he famously suggested that the war on terrorism is a new kind of war that "renders obsolete Geneva's strict limitations on questioning of enemy prisoners" and "renders quaint some of its provisions," Gonzales dismissed Powell's arguments as "unpersuasive." In their place, he offered two in favor of denying Geneva Convention protections: first, that doing so "preserves flexibility" precisely because it eliminates the need for case-by-case determinations; and second, that it "substantially reduces the threat of domestic criminal prosecution under the War Crimes Act (18 U.S.C. 2441)." As Gonzales noted,

> That statute, enacted in 1996, prohibits the commission of a "war crime" by or against a U.S. person, including U.S. officials. "War crime" for these purposes is defined to include any grave breach of [Geneva Convention III on the Treatment of Prisoners of War (GPW)] or any violation of common Article 3 thereof (such as "outrages against personal dignity"). Some of these provisions apply (if the GPW applies) regardless of whether the individual being detained qualifies as a POW. Punishments for violations of Section 2441 include the death penalty. A determination that the GPW is not

*applicable to the Taliban would mean that Section 2441 would not
apply to actions taken with respect to the Taliban.*[33]

"Your determination [that GPW does not apply] would create a
reasonable basis in law that Section 2441 does not apply, which would
provide a solid defense to any future prosecution," Gonzales concluded.

On February 7, 2002, President Bush signed a memorandum to Dick
Cheney, Colin Powell, Donald Rumsfeld, Alberto Gonzales, Andrew Card,
George Tenet, Condoleezza Rice, and General Richard Myers memorializing
the position on the inapplicability of the Geneva Conventions. Five days
later, Mitchell and Jessen began circulating their paper to the CIA and the
Defense Department, which was overseeing a growing number of prisoners
in Afghanistan and Guantánamo.[34]

Within days, Mitchell, who was now working as a contract employee
for the CIA, and Jessen began giving training courses to put their ideas
into action. The Senate Armed Services Committee has documented how,
responding to a February 2002 request from the DoD's Defense Intelligence
Agency, Jessen and JPRA instructor Joseph Witsch gave an "ad hoc 'crash'
course" for a group of military interrogators headed for Guantánamo
and held a video teleconference to "pitch" how JPRA could assist with
interrogations. By March 8, they were presenting slide shows on detainee
"exploitation."[35]

In April, Jessen circulated his "Exploitation Draft Plan" to
"[h]old, manage, and exploit detainees to elicit critical information" at an
"exploitation facility" that would be inaccessible to non-essential personnel,
press, ICRC, or foreign observers.[36] In June, he led a two-day training
session for military interrogators headed for rotations "in Afghanistan and
elsewhere," and he held another one in July where Joseph Witsch acted
as the "beater" in a demonstration of SERE school scenarios and which
included instruction on waterboarding.[37]

Shortly after that training, Jessen retired from the Air Force and joined
Mitchell as a contract employee of the CIA. By then, Mitchell was in a secret
CIA prison in Thailand overseeing the use of "enhanced interrogations
techniques" in the questioning of Abu Zubaydah, personally delivering the

news, as Zubaydah would tell the ICRC five years later, that he "was one of the first to receive these interrogation techniques, so no rules applied."

* * *

There are two photographs from the night of Abu Zubaydah's capture, March 28, 2002. One is of two parallel, curving trails of blood leading into or out of a doorway. The other is an ABC news photograph of Zubaydah in the bed of a pickup truck, head on the tailgate, clean-shaven and wild-haired, obviously gravely wounded.[38]

That night, U.S. and Pakistani forces had simultaneously raided fourteen safehouses in and around Faisalbad, Pakistan, where the U.S. believed Zubaydah might be staying. Zubaydah, a Saudi-born Palestinian who had grown up in the West Bank, went to Afghanistan in 1991 to fight the Soviets and stayed on after the war, eventually becoming a coordinator of the Khalden training camp, which had trained mujahadeen fighters during the war and continued to operate until late 2000 or early 2001. The U.S. had been trying to track him since before 9/11, and by March 2002, based either on massive surveillance or on tips purchased from Pakistani authorities,[39] the search was narrowing.

During the raid, Zubaydah was shot in the stomach, testicle, and thigh. He was driven to a local hospital, and then quickly transferred to a better hospital in Lahore, where a team of doctors rushed from the United States performed surgery. Immediately afterwards—on March 31, 2002—he was strapped to a gurney and flown to a prison cell the CIA had set up in Thailand for his interrogation.

Abu Zubaydah, whose real name is Zayn al-Abidin Muhammad Husayn, was first questioned by two FBI agents who were flown to the black site right after Zubaydah's capture. One of the agents, then 30-year-old Ali Soufan, was one of the FBI's leading experts on Al Qaeda and a skilled interrogator who had been involved in many of the major terrorism investigations of the previous decade. Philip Zelikow, who served as Executive Director of the 9/11 Commission before joining the Bush administration in 2005, called him "one of the most impressive intelligence agents—from any agency" that the 9/11 Commission encountered.[40]

Soufan and his partner nursed Zubaydah as he recuperated, changing his dressings and holding ice to his lips for a fever, and Zubaydah was soon divulging important information. In testimony before the Senate Judiciary Committee in May 2009, Soufan explained his approach as "Informed Interrogation," the careful process of rapport-building that the intelligence agencies, law enforcement, and the military had been using, exclusively and successfully, to produce information. Under his questioning, Zubaydah identified Khalid Sheikh Mohammed by his alias "Mukhtar" and revealed Mohammed's role as the mastermind behind the 9/11 attacks. As Soufan told the Committee:

> *The information was so important that, as I later learned from open sources, it went to CIA Director George Tenet, who was so impressed that he initially ordered us to be congratulated. That was apparently quickly withdrawn as soon as Mr. Tenet was told that it was FBI agents who were responsible. He then immediately ordered a CIA [Counterterrorism Center] team to leave DC and head to the location to take over from us.*[41]

Over the next two months, Soufan clashed repeatedly with the CIA team, led by Dr. Mitchell, over Mitchell's proposed methods – methods Soufan insists were both abusive and ineffective:

> *A few days after we started questioning Abu Zubaydah, the CTC interrogation team finally arrived from DC with a contractor who was instructing them on how they should conduct the interrogations, and we were removed. Immediately, on the instructions of the contractor, harsh techniques were introduced, starting with nudity....*
>
> *The new techniques did not produce results as Abu Zubaydah shut down and stopped talking. At the time nudity and low-level sleep deprivation (between 24 and 48 hours) was being used. After a few days of getting no information, and after repeated inquiries from DC asking why all of a sudden no information was being transmitted*

(when before there had been a steady stream), we again were given control of the interrogation.

We then returned to using the Informed Interrogation Approach. Within a few hours, Abu Zubaydah again started talking and gave us important actionable intelligence.[42]

But Mitchell again interrupted the process:

After a few days, the contractor attempted to once again try his untested theory and he started re-implementing the harsh techniques. He moved this time further along the force continuum, introducing loud noise and then temperature manipulation.

Throughout this time, my fellow FBI agent and I, along with a top CIA interrogator who was working with us, protested, but we were overruled. I should also note that another colleague, an operational psychologist for the CIA, had left the location because he objected to what was being done.

Again, however, the technique wasn't working and Abu Zubaydah wasn't revealing any information, so we were once again brought back in to interrogate him. We found it harder to reengage him this time, because of how the techniques had affected him, but eventually, we succeeded, and he re-engaged again.

Once again, the contractor insisted on stepping up the notches of his experiment, and this time he requested the authorization to place Abu Zubaydah in a confinement box, as the next stage in the force continuum. While everything I saw to this point were nowhere near the severity later listed in the [Office of Legal Counsel] memos, the evolution of the contractor's theory, along with what I had seen till then, struck me as "borderline torture."

As the Department of Justice IG report released last year states, I protested to my superiors in the FBI and refused to be a part of what was happening. The Director of the FBI, a man I deeply respect, agreed, passing the message that "we don't do that," and I was pulled out....[43]

The departure of the FBI team did not give Mitchell a free hand, however. Every step of the interrogation process was coordinated with Washington, and every session was painstakingly documented. Cables began flowing from the Thai black site to CIA headquarters in Langley, Virginia, on April 13, 2002; at least five hundred and likely many more would be sent from the site to headquarters during the interrogation of Abu Zubaydah.[44] These cables were more than mere summary reports. John Kiriakou, one of the agents on Mitchell's team, told Brian Ross in a 2007 ABC news interview that the contents of the cable traffic was "extremely specific."

> It wasn't up to individual interrogators to decide, "Well, I'm gonna slap him. Or I'm going to shake him. Or I'm gonna make him stay up for 48 hours." Each one of these steps, even though they're minor steps, like the attention shake, or the open-handed belly slap, each one of these had to have the approval of the Deputy Director for Operations. So before you laid a hand on him, you had to send in the cable saying, "He's uncooperative. Request permission to do X." And that permission would come. "You're allowed to slap him one time in the belly with an open hand."[45]

✳ ✳ ✳

It wasn't just Kirakou's superiors at CIA headquarters at the other end of those cables. Though it was taking place in an underground cell in a secret CIA prison in Thailand, Mitchell and Jessen's experiment was unfolding in full view of the President and his closest circle of advisors. President Bush's September 17, 2001 order had authorized the CIA to capture terrorism suspects and hold and interrogate them in clandestine prisons, but CIA Director George Tenet wanted specific approval for the interrogation program for "high value detainees," so starting in the spring of 2002, then-National Security Advisor Condoleezza Rice chaired a series of meetings in the White House situation room where Tenet repeatedly briefed the "Principals Committee," which included Defense Secretary Rumsfeld, Secretary of State Powell, and Attorney General John Ashcroft, on the agency's plans for Abu Zubaydah.

The Principals had before them Mitchell and Jessen's list of eleven proposed "enhanced interrogation techniques" imported from SERE training. Rice told the Senate Armed Services Committee in 2008 that she asked the Attorney General "personally to review the legality of the proposed program," and that she understood that the legal advice "was being coordinated by Counsel to the President Alberto Gonzales."[46] Since December, Gonzales had been chairing meetings of a group of lawyers that included David Addington, Vice President Dick Cheney's legal counsel, Jim Haynes, General Counsel of the Department of Defense, and Timothy Flanigan and John Yoo of the Office of Legal Counsel. For the group, which took to calling itself the "War Council," "coordinating legal advice" meant more than analyzing the legality of proposals the various administration agencies submitted. Yoo, in his book *War By Other Means*, said the lawyers met repeatedly in late 2001 and 2002 "to develop policy in the war on terrorism."[47]

Two weeks before Abu Zubaydah was captured and disappeared into the CIA's black site, Yoo had issued a memo declaring the CIA's rendition program was legal;[48] now he turned his attention to advising on Zubaydah's interrogation, which by June 2002 was entirely in Mitchell's hands. At the NSC Principals meetings, Tenet would report on the CIA team's latest sessions and relay requests to move to more aggressive methods. Yoo and his colleagues would verbally declare the proposed treatment legal. So thorough was Tenet in sharing details of the interrogation and in seeking specific permission to proceed that Ashcroft would eventually object. "Why are we talking about this in the White House?" he is widely reported to have asked after one of the meetings. "History will not judge this kindly."[49]

As Mitchell progressed up the "force continuum," however, the CIA wanted more than oral approval. In his account to the ICRC, Abu Zubaydah described a month-long lull in his questioning "about two and a half or three months" after he had arrived at the black site. That would have been late June or early July, 2002. So far, he had been subjected to prolonged shackling, dietary manipulation, incessant loud noise, and had spent weeks naked in a bare, frigid cell, but at that point had only faced one of the eleven proposed EITs—sleep deprivation. Before Mitchell could move further into physical abuse and waterboarding, CIA attorneys ordered a pause to give Yoo and the Office of Legal Counsel time to prepare formal legal opinions declaring that methods that had been perfected by regimes that scorned the Geneva Conventions do not constitute torture. According to the CIA's Inspector General,

> *Eleven EITs were proposed for adoption in the CTC Interrogation Program. As proposed, use of EITs would be subject to a competent evaluation of the medical and psychological state of the detainee. The Agency eliminated one proposed technique – [REDACTED] – after learning from DoJ that this could delay the legal review.*[50]

That eleventh technique was evidently mock execution, a standard component of SERE training that is explicitly prohibited under the Convention against Torture and Other Cruel, Inhuman, and Degrading Treatment and under U.S. law codifying the Convention. The law specifically lists "the threat of imminent death" as an act that causes severe mental pain and suffering and is therefore criminal under the statute. But the phrase "mock execution" matches the redaction in the CIA Inspector General's report exactly, and there are clear indications that CIA interrogators initially included it in their repertoire. At the Thai black site, Ali Soufan erupted when he discovered Mitchell had constructed a coffin-shaped box for Zubaydah, calling Pasquale D'Amuro, the FBI assistant director for counterterrorism, and saying "I swear to God, I'm going to arrest these guys!" *Newsweek* reported that Mitchell told Soufan the box was for a "mock burial."[51]

The CIA ultimately requested formal legal opinions sanctioning ten Enhanced Interrogation Techniques: the attention grasp, walling, the facial hold, the facial or insult slap, cramped confinement, sleep deprivation, placing an insect in the confinement box, wall standing, stress positions, and waterboarding. As Yoo completed the memos, Rice personally informed Tenet that its interrogation plan could proceed as soon as the OLC issued its opinion. On July 24, the OLC told the CIA the techniques, including waterboarding, were legal and approved for use on Abu Zubaydah. That same day, the CIA delivered Mitchell's psychological assessment of Abu Zubaydah, which was to be attached to the memorandum, declaring Zubaydah physically and mentally fit for the interrogation.

Eight days later, on August 1, 2001, the OLC issued two memos written by John Yoo and signed by Jay Bybee, the Assistant Attorney General, giving Mitchell the green light to treat Abu Zubaydah in ways the ICRC would later have no difficulty identifying as torture.

The first, the now-infamous Memorandum to Alberto Gonzales on "Standards of Conduct for Interrogation under 18 U.S.C. 2340-2340A," narrows the Convention against Torture's proscriptions on acts inflicting severe physical and mental pain or suffering to the "most extreme" acts. According to the memo, severe physical pain must rise to the level "ordinarily associated with a sufficiently serious physical condition or injury such as death, organ failure, or serious impairment of body functions" in order to constitute torture.[52] Severe mental pain or suffering can only result from the four scenarios listed in the Convention—the intentional infliction of physical pain, the administration of mind-altering drugs, the threat of imminent death, or threats that another person will be tortured or killed in the prisoner's place—and then only if they result in prolonged, which is defined as lasting if not permanent, mental harm.[53]

To commit torture, the memo suggests, an interrogator's specific intention must be to inflict serious physical or mental pain or suffering, rather than, say, to extract information. Yoo ends by suggesting possible defenses in the event a prosecutor were to disagree with the memo's radical analysis: first, that the President's complete authority in the conduct of war includes the right to ignore the Convention against Torture; and second, that the torture was a necessary act of self defense.

The second August 1, 2002 memo, directed to John Rizzo, Acting General Counsel of the CIA, is titled "Interrogation of an al Qaeda Operative."[54] "You have asked for this Office's views on whether proposed conduct would violate the prohibition against torture found at Section 2340A of Title 18 of the United States Code," it begins. "You have asked for this advice in the course of conducting interrogations of Abu Zubaydah.... This letter memorializes our previous advice, given on July 24, 2002 and July

26, 2002, that the proposed conduct would not violate this prohibition." The memo summarizes the CIA's plan:

> As part of this increased pressure phase, Zubaydah will have contact only with a new interrogation specialist, whom he has not met previously, and the Survival, Evasion, Resistance, Escape ("SERE") training psychologist who has been involved with the interrogations since they began. This phase will likely last no more than several days but could last up to thirty days. In this phase, you would like to employ ten techniques that you believe will dislocate his expectations regarding the treatment he believes he will receive and encourage him to disclose the crucial information mentioned above. These ten techniques are: (1) attention grasp, (2) walling, (3) facial hold, (4) facial slap (insult slap), (5) cramped confinement, (6) wall standing, (7) stress positions, (8) sleep deprivation, (9) insects placed in a confinement box, and (10) the waterboard. You have informed us that the use of these techniques would be on an as-needed basis and that not all of these techniques will necessarily be used. The interrogation team would use these techniques in some combination to convince Zubaydah that the only way he can influence his surrounding environment is through cooperation. You have, however, informed us that you expect these techniques to be used in some sort of escalating fashion, culminating with the waterboard, though not necessarily ending with this technique.[55]

It then proceeds one-by-one down the list, affecting a naïve, disinterested tone: "You would like to place Zubaydah in a cramped confinement box with an insect. You have informed us that he appears to have a fear of insects," it says at one point, and later, "Finally, you would like to use a technique called the 'waterboard.'" Yoo's bland descriptions of the planned techniques stand in chilling contrast to Abu Zubaydah's account of the techniques in practice. For "Walling," for example, Yoo wrote

> [A] flexible false wall will be constructed. The individual is placed with his heels touching the wall. The interrogator pulls the individual

forward and then quickly and firmly pushes the individual into the wall. It is the individual's shoulder blades that hit the wall. During this motion, the head and neck are supported with a rolled hood or towel that provides a c-collar effect to prevent whiplash. To further reduce the probability of injury, the individual is allowed to rebound from the flexible wall. You have orally informed us that the false wall is in part constructed to create a loud sound when the individual hits it, which will further shock or surprise the individual.

The process Abu Zubaydah recounted to the Red Cross was far more violent:

I was taken out of my cell and one of the interrogators wrapped a towel around my neck, then they used it to swing me around and smash me repeatedly against the hard walls of the room...

When I was let out of the box I saw that one of the walls of the room had been covered with plywood sheeting. From now on it was against this wall that I was then smashed with the towel around my neck. I think that the plywood was there to provide some absorption of the impact of my body. The interrogators realized that smashing me against the hard wall would probably quickly result in physical injury.

Likewise, according to Yoo,

Cramped confinement involves the placement of the individual in a confined space, the dimensions of which restrict the individual's movement. The confined space is usually dark. The duration of confinement varies based upon the size of the container. For the larger confined space, the individual can stand up or sit down; the smaller space is large enough for the subject to sit down. Confinement in the larger space can last up to eighteen hours; for the smaller space, confinement lasts for no more than two hours.

But as Abu Zubaydah reported,

I was then put into the tall box for what I think was about one and a half to two hours. The box was totally black on the inside as well as the outside. It had a bucket inside to use as a toilet and had water to drink in a bottle. The put a cloth or cover over the outside of the box to cut out the light and restrict my air supply...

After the beating I was then placed in the small box. They placed a cloth or cover over the box to cut out all light and restrict my air supply. As it was not high enough even to sit upright, I had to crouch down. It was very difficult because of my wounds. The stress on my legs held in this position meant my wounds both in the leg and stomach became very painful.... The wound on my leg began to open and started to bleed. I don't know how long I remained in the small box. I think I may have slept or maybe fainted.

Yoo's cool description of the Enhanced Interrogation Techniques is followed by a fevered description of Abu Zubaydah himself, who, "though only 31, rose quickly from very low level mujahadeen to third or fourth man in al Qaeda" and who "has served as Usama Bin Laden's senior lieutenant." "Zubaydah has been involved in every major terrorist operation carried out by al Qaeda," the memo asserts, identifying him as a planner of a Millennium plot in Jordan, a plot to bomb the U.S. embassy in Paris, and the September 11 attacks. It cites the CIA psychological assessment's judgment that he is a "highly self-directed individual who prizes his independence" with "'narcissistic features' which are evidenced in the attention he pays to his personal appearance" and his "obvious 'efforts' to demonstrate that he is really a rather 'humble and regular guy.'" "According to your reports," Yoo records, "Zubaydah does not have any pre-existing mental conditions or problems that would make him likely to suffer prolonged mental harm from your proposed interrogation methods."[56]

The memo concludes by restating the creative reading of the torture statute outlined in the "Standards of Conduct" memo and breezily declaring that nine of the techniques fall well short of the line that memo established for torture:

The facial hold and attention grasp involve no physical pain. In the absence of such pain it is obvious that they cannot be said to inflict severe pain and suffering.[57]

As for sleep deprivation, it is clear that depriving someone of sleep does not involve severe physical pain within the meaning of the statute.[58]

Walling plainly is not a procedure calculated to disrupt profoundly the senses or personality. While walling involves what might be characterized as rough handling, it does not involve the threat of imminent death or, as discussed above, the infliction of severe physical pain.[59]

Nor does the use of the boxes threaten Zubaydah with severe physical pain or suffering. While additional time spent in the boxes may be threatened, their use is not accompanied by any express threats of severe physical pain or suffering.[60]

Only waterboarding poses a challenge. "We find that the use of the waterboard constitutes a threat of imminent death," the memo concedes.

As you have explained the waterboard procedure to us, it creates in the subject the uncontrollable physiological sensation that the subject is drowning. Although the procedure will be monitored by personnel with medical training and extensive SERE school experience with this procedure who will ensure the subject's mental and physical safety, the subject is not aware of any of these precautions. From the vantage point of any reasonable person undergoing this procedure in such circumstances, he would feel as if he is drowning at very [sic] moment of the procedure due to the uncontrollable physiological sensation he is experiencing. Thus, this procedure cannot be viewed as too uncertain to satisfy the imminence requirement. Accordingly, it constitutes a treat of imminent death and fulfills the predicate act requirement under the statute.[61]

But even though waterboarding simply and literally violates the prohibition on threatening death, Yoo's memo argues that it is permissible because it does not result in prolonged mental harm. "Indeed, you have advised us that the relief is almost immediate when the cloth is removed from the mouth and nose," it observes. "In the absence of prolonged mental harm, no severe mental pain or suffering would have been inflicted and the use of these procedures would not constitute torture within the meaning of the statute."[62] While acknowledging that it has just evaluated the EITs individually and that their use in combination could conceivably affect their impact and produce pain or suffering, the memo concludes that the regime would only constitute torture if the interrogators actually caused severe injury or prolonged mental harm—and then only if the interrogator specifically intended to inflict severe pain or suffering.

With these legal assurances secured, "the real torturing started," as Zubaydah told the ICRC. He was walled, confined in the tall box, walled again, confined in the small box, and waterboarded twice. He was confined again in a box, walled, and waterboarded some more. Zubaydah estimated that the process was repeated five times over the course of the week. In fact, he was waterboarded eighty-two times in August, 2002 before Mitchell and his team judged he was not concealing information. Washington, incredibly, was unconvinced. As the CIA's Inspector General recorded in his 2004 report,

> *According to a senior CTC officer, the interrogator team [REDACTED] considered Abu Zubaydah to be compliant and wanted to terminate EITs. [REDACTED] believed Abu Zubaydah continued to withhold information, [THREE LINES REDACTED] at the time it generated substantial pressure from Headquarters to continue use of the EITs. According to this senior officer, the decision to resume use of the waterboard on Abu Zubaydah was made by senior officers of the DO [ONE LINE REDACTED] to assess Abu Zubaydah's compliance and witnessed the final waterboard session, after which, they reported back to Headquarters that the EITs were no longer needed on Abu Zubaydah.*[63]

The incident makes its way into a footnote of a May 30, 2005 Office of Legal Counsel memo rearguing the legality of EITs:

> *This is not to say that the interrogation program has worked perfectly. According to the IG Report, the CIA, at least initially, could not always distinguish detainees who had information but were successfully resisting interrogation from those who did not actually have the information.... On at least one occasion, this may have resulted in what might be deemed in retrospect to have been the unnecessary use of enhanced techniques. On that occasion, although the on-scene interrogation team judged Zubaydah to be compliant, elements within CIA headquarters still believed he was withholding information. [REDACTED]...At the direction of CIA Headquarters interrogators therefore used the waterboard one more time on Zubaydah.*[64]

Abu Zubaydah's entire five-month interrogation, including this final session of waterboarding, was videotaped. Interrogators started recording their sessions as soon as he arrived at the black site "to ensure a record of Abu Zubaydah's medical condition and treatment should he succumb to his wounds and questions arise about the medical care provided him by CIA," the Inspector General reported. But as Mitchell's team took over, the "intense interest" at CIA Headquarters in "keeping abreast of all aspects of Abu Zubaydah's interrogation" now meant the videotapes served to document "compliance with the guidance provided to the site relative to the use of EITs."

What the tapes showed was that the sessions proceeded exactly according to plan. "There are ninety-two videotapes, twelve of which include EIT applications," the IG Report noted. "[A CIA Office of General Counsel] attorney reviewed the videotapes in November and December 2002 to ascertain compliance with the August 2002 DoJ opinion and compare what actually happened with what was reported to Headquarters. He reported that there was no deviation from the DoJ guidance or the written record."[65]

The Inspector General himself reviewed the videotapes several months later, during the investigation that culminated in his May 2004 report. He found eleven interrogation videotapes were blank; two were blank except for one or two minutes of recording; and two others were broken and could not be reviewed. When he compared the videotapes to the interrogation logs and cables, he calculated that twenty one hours of interrogation, including two waterboarding sessions, were missing from the tapes.[66]

In November 2005, all of the tapes were destroyed.

Annotations on this section from TheTortureReport.org

On adapting SERE techniques for real interrogations, Air Force Lieutenant Colonel and former lead defense counsel of the Office of Military Commissions in Guantánamo David Frakt wrote,

The techniques designed by the Chinese Communists, and further perfected by the Russians and North Vietnamese, were not necessarily intended to gather accurate (or, in the modern parlance, "actionable" intelligence). Rather, the techniques utilized at SERE were designed to elicit confessions, regardless of the truth of the contents of the confession, which could be exploited for propaganda purposes or used to frame individuals for crimes they did not commit. Psychologists who have studied these techniques have learned that those subjected to the techniques are likely to tell their captors whatever they think they want to hear in order to stop the abuse.

While this may include some accurate information, the subjects will also fabricate voluminous information in their desperation to provide something to stem the torture, and they will readily agree to whatever is suggested to them by their interrogators. This is why such techniques, in addition to being immoral and illegal, are largely worthless as intelligence-gathering tools.

and former Air Force criminal investigator and interrogator Matthew Alexander observed,

One has to question, if their intent was effective interrogations, why

would they not include our nation's foremost experts on interrogations in the discussion? Instead they relied on the advice of two psychologists, neither of whom had ever conducted an interrogation.

On the Yoo-Bybee memos, David Frakt wrote,

In my opinion, John Yoo and other Administration lawyers clearly overstepped their role. The function of the Office of Legal Counsel, according to its own website (www.usdoj.gov/olc) is to provide "authoritative legal advice to the President and all the Executive Branch agencies." Their role is essentially a reactive one—to respond to inquiries from the Executive Branch and to review proposed legislation. To the extent that it is appropriate for lawyers like the White House Counsel and DoD General Counsel to be proactive, it should be to help steer their clients away from problematic legal areas, not guide them directly into legal minefields. What Mr. Yoo and his colleagues did was to step out of the role of legal advisor or counselor and become advocates, seeking creative ways to advance their personal agenda and pet legal theories (such as unitary executive theory) or the agenda of the White House. While advocacy is certainly an appropriate role for some government legal offices, such as DoJ trial lawyers and the Solicitor General, it was a singularly inappropriate role for this group of legal advisors to assume.

and Matthew Alexander commented,

The legal memos justifying enhanced interrogation techniques (aka Torture and Abuse), never included obvious legal precedents that would have been easily retrievable through Lexus/Nexus by any novice attorney straight out of law school. For a comprehensive analysis of legal precedents establishing waterboarding as torture, read: "Drop by Drop: Forgetting the History of Water Torture in U.S. Courts" (available at http://www.pegc.us/archive/Articles/wallach_drop_by_drop_draft_20061016.pdf) by Evan Wallach.

As an interrogator and criminal investigator, I was trained to know that what is not said is often more important than what is said. The fact that flagrantly obvious, relevant legal precedents were omitted from the DoJ analysis and recommendations is evidence that the whole process was a rubber stamp for methods of torture and abuse that were already in use and that were to be continued.

On interrogation standards in the CIA and Armed Services in general, Matthew Alexander wrote,

For military personnel there was never a question of the legal definitions of torture and abuse or the prohibition against them. "The Army Field Manual 34-52" (available at http://www.fas.org/irp/doddir/army/fm34-52. pdf, replaced in September 2006 by "Army Field Manual 2-22.3") which governed interrogations stated: "The GWS, GPS, GC, and U.S. Policy expressly prohibit acts of violence or intimidation, including physical or mental torture, threats, insults, or exposure to inhuman treatment as a means of or aid to interrogation."

Although the legality of CIA personnel using enhanced interrogation techniques may have been argued under the August 1, 2002 OLC memos, military personnel conducting interrogations were always subject to the Army Field Manual prohibitions. Therefore, within the military, any use of enhanced interrogation methods would have been a direct violation of the Army's own regulations, at a minimum.

It is interesting to note as well that the Army Field Manual also specifically listed several of the counterproductive effects of using torture and abuse. Would those who authorized and used these methods contradict our own military's conclusions regarding these negative consequences?

The American people should realize that torture and abuse was not only harmful to the prisoners who were its victims. It also cost us the lives of Americans. Al Qaida used our policy as their most effective recruiting tool and those recruits killed American soldiers in Iraq.

BLACK SITES, LIES, AND VIDEOTAPES

On November 20, 2002, a suspected Afghan military in his early thirties named Gul Rahman was doused with water, shackled naked to the floor, and left overnight in a frigid cell in a CIA black site known as "The Salt Pit" on the outskirts of Kabul, Afghanistan. He died of hypothermia. The supervisor of the facility, an agent with no experience as an interrogator or a jailer, ordered him buried in an unmarked grave.[67]

As this was happening, the CIA was dispatching one of its lawyers to the black site in Thailand to review the videotapes of the Abu Zubaydah interrogation. For weeks the agency had been discussing destroying the tapes; a cable sent from the secret prison to headquarters in August, the month Zubaydah was waterboarded eighty-three times, discussed "the security risks of videotape retention" and suggested "new procedures for videotape retention and disposal." A September 6, 2002 email between CIA attorneys has as its subject "Destruction proposal on disposition of videotapes at field," and an email two months later "from a CIA officer to CIA officers and attorneys" dated November 6 follows up with the "proper procedures for destruction of the interrogation videotapes."[68]

But Langley had decided it wanted a "random independent review" of the tapes first, and so in late November, an attorney from the CIA General Counsel's office was sent to verify that Abu Zubaydah's torment had followed the approved script. With his assurances that it had, the discussion resumed: on November 27, a cable was sent from the black site "requesting approval for destruction of the interrogation tapes," and on December 3, 2002, headquarters responded with a cable with the subject line "Closing of facility and destruction of classified information" and an email "outlining the destruction plan for the videotapes."[69]

In the midst of this exchange, back in Afghanistan, CIA agents delivered a young mullah named Habibulah into the hands of army interrogators at Bagram Collection Point, a converted hangar at the former Soviet airbase about fifty kilometers north of Kabul. Within a week, an Armed Services Medical Examiner reported, "the remains" were "presented for autopsy clothed in a disposable diaper. No additional clothing or personal effects accompan[ied] the body."[70]

Habibulah had been "found unresponsive, restrained in his cell"— handcuffed to the wire mesh ceiling of the plywood-walled isolation cell, that is—at 12:15 a.m. on December 4, 2002. The military first claimed he had died of natural causes. The Medical Examiner, however, concluded the cause of death was "pulmonary embolism due to blunt force injuries"; the Manner of Death, "homicide."[71]

The day Habibulah was killed, the CIA switched off the video cameras and closed down its black site in Thailand.

In addition to the torture of Abu Zubaydah, they had for the previous two weeks been recording the interrogation of a second "high value detainee," Abd al-Rahim al-Nashiri, whose arrest the administration trumpeted on November 21, 2002. The alleged chief of Al Qaeda operations in the Persian Gulf and the suspected organizer of the 2000 bombing of the USS *Cole*, al-Nashiri was captured in Dubai in October and held for a time at the Salt Pit in Afghanistan before being flown to Thailand on November 15—where, as the CIA's Inspector General observes blandly, "The interrogation proceeded after [redacted] the necessary authorization."[72]

"Psychologist/interrogators began Al-Nashiri's interrogations using EITs immediately upon his arrival," the Inspector General reported. A largely redacted documented headed "Summary," "CTC's interrogation efforts" [redacted] "with the interrogation of Al-Nashiri" dated November 20, 2002 records that "Al-Nashiri has undergone [redacted] interrogation with the HVT interrogators using [redacted]" and "Al-Nashiri is becoming more compliant and is providing actionable intelligence."[73] Even so, Mitchell's team kept climbing the force continuum. The Inspector General found that although al-Nashiri "provided lead information on other terrorists during his first day of interrogation," the use of EITs continued for eleven more days, and on the twelfth day, "psychologist/interrogators administered two applications of the waterboard to Al-Nashiri during two separate interrogation sessions."

They didn't stop there. The cameras were switched off on December 4th; that day, al-Nashiri and Zubaydah were bundled onto a CIA-leased jet and flown to Dubai and on to a new secret CIA detention facility located near the airport in Szymany, Poland. The plane, a leased twenty two-seat Gulfstream jet carrying the two detainees and the six-person CIA rendition team, landed in Poland on December 5th; al-Nashiri's "enhanced interrogation" resumed immediately and continued for two more weeks, at which time his interrogators "assessed him to be 'compliant.'"[74]

Again, as in the interrogation of Abu Zubaydah, Washington wasn't satisfied:

> *Subsequently, CTC officers at Headquarters [redacted] sent a [redacted] senior operations officer (the debriefer) [redacted] to debrief and assess Al-Nashiri. The debriefer assessed Al-Nashiri as withholding information, at which point [redacted] reinstated [redacted] hooding, and handcuffing.*[75]

In a footnote elsewhere in his report, the Inspector General explains the difference between an interrogator and a debriefer:

> *Before 11 September 2001, Agency personnel sometimes used the terms* interrogation/interrogator *and* debriefing/debriefer *interchangeably. The use of these terms has since evolved and, today, CTC more clearly distinguishes their meanings. A debriefer engages a detainee solely through question and answer. An interrogator is a person who completes a two-week interrogations training program, which is designed to train, qualify, and certify a person to administer EITs. An interrogator can administer EITs during an interrogation of a detainee only after the field, in coordination with Headquarters, assesses the detainee as withholding information. An interrogator transitions the detainee from a non-cooperative to a cooperative phase in order that a debriefer can elicit actionable intelligence through non-aggressive techniques during debriefing sessions. An interrogator may debrief a detainee during an interrogation; however, a debriefer may not interrogate a detainee.*[76]

The CIA had begun offering two-week trainings for interrogators in

November 2002; "[s]everal CTC officers, including a former SERE instructor, designed the curriculum, which included a week of classroom instruction followed by a week of 'hands-on' training in EITs," the Inspector General reported. "Once certified, an interrogator is deemed qualified to conduct an interrogation employing EITs."[77] "Conducting" interrogations had clear limits, however. As in the "Mother may I" process Dr. James Mitchell had modeled during the interrogation of Abu Zubaydah, these newly-trained interrogators were required to seek permission from headquarters for each and every use of an enhanced interrogation technique.

But in the black site in Poland, ordered to resume al-Nashiri's interrogation but freed from the scrutiny of the video cameras, interrogators quickly began to stray from the DoJ-approved list of ten enhanced interrogation techniques. They smoked cigars and blew smoke in al-Nashiri's face during sessions.[78] They scrubbed him with a stiff brush "that was intended to induce pain." They stood on his ankle shackles, "which resulted in cuts and bruises." They "employed potentially injurious stress positions" on the prisoner:

> Al-Nashiri was required to kneel on the floor and lean back. On at least one occasion, an Agency officer reportedly pushed Al-Nashiri backward while he was in the stress position. On another occasion, [redacted] said he had to intercede after [redacted] expressed concern that Al-Nashiri's arms might be dislocated from his shoulders. [Redacted] explained that, at the time, the interrogators were attempting to put Al-Nashiri in a standing stress position. Al-Nashiri was reportedly lifted off the floor by his arms while his arms were bound behind his back with a belt.[79]

For two weeks, the "debriefer" who had been flown in from CIA headquarters oversaw this unscripted interrogation. Finally, the debriefer himself, who the Inspector General notes "was not a trained interrogator and was not authorized to use EITs," took over:

> Sometime between 28 December 2002 and 1 January 2003, the

debriefer used a semi-automatic handgun as a prop to frighten Al-Nashiri into disclosing information. After discussing this plan with [redacted] the debriefer entered the cell where Al-Nashiri sat shackled and racked the handgun once or twice close to Al-Nashiri's head.[80] *On what was probably the same day, the debriefer used a power drill to frighten Al-Nashiri. With [redacted] consent, the debriefer entered the detainee's cell and revved the drill while the detainee stood naked and hooded. The debriefer did not touch Al-Nashiri with the power drill."*[81]

When Congress codified the Convention against Torture and Other Cruel, Inhumane and Degrading Treatment or Punishment" in U.S. law in 1994, it specifically cited four acts that would produce the kind of "severe mental pain and suffering" that would be characterized as torture:

A. *the intentional infliction or threatened infliction of severe physical pain or suffering;*
B. *the administration or application, or threatened administration or application, of mind-altering substances or other procedures calculated to disrupt profoundly the senses or the personality;*
C. *the threat of imminent death; or*
D. *the threat that another person will imminently be subjected to death, severe physical pain or suffering, or the administration or application of mind-altering substances or other procedures calculated to disrupt profoundly the senses or personality.*[82]

The CIA had dropped "mock executions" from its proposed list of Enhanced Interrogation Techniques precisely because even the authors of the August 1, 2002 legal opinions couldn't argue that feigning an intention to kill a prisoner is ever permissible.[83] Now the CIA was facing a situation where agents involved in its Rendition, Detention and Interrogation program had clearly committed a premeditated felony under U.S. law.

* * *

In an August 31, 2009 interview with *Der Spiegel* magazine, John Helgerson said that one of the difficulties he encountered as the CIA's Inspector General while he was preparing the 2004 "Counterterrorism Detention and Interrogation Activities" Special Review was "the disorganization of the whole interrogation program. So much was being improvised in those early years in so many locations. There were no guidelines, no oversight, no training. How will you review a program handled differently in so many parts of the world?" "The agency went over bounds and outside the rules, that is for sure," he added.[84]

Helgerson was an Africa specialist who had served primarily on the research and analytical side of the agency before being appointed Inspector General, an office Congress had fortified in 1989 following its perceived shortcomings in investigating the Iran-Contra scandal. Like all but a handful of top CIA and administration officials, he knew nothing of the CIA's Rendition, Detention, and Interrogation program when he assumed the post in 2002; he learned of it in November, when Stephen Kappes, then the CIA's Deputy Director for Operations, informed him that the agency had sent a team to investigate the killing at the Salt Pit in Afghanistan. Kappes returned to Helgerson in January 2003 to report "that Agency personnel had used unauthorized techniques with a detainee, Abd Al-Rashin Al-Nashiri, at another foreign site," and to request that the IG's office investigate.[85]

In probing the gun and drill incident, Helgerson soon discovered that mock executions had been staged several times after they had been specifically excluded from the list of approved interrogation techniques.

The debriefer who employed the handgun and power drill on Al-Nashiri [redacted] advised that those actions were predicated on a technique he had participated in [redacted]. The debriefer stated that when he was [redacted] between September and October 2002, [redacted] offered to fire a handgun outside the interrogation room while the debriefer was interviewing a detainee who was thought to be withholding information. [Redacted] staged the incident, which included screaming and yelling outside the cell by other CIA officers and [redacted] guards. When the guards moved the detainee from the interrogation room, they passed a guard who was dressed as a hooded detainee, lying motionless on the ground, and made to appear as if he had been shot to death.

The debriefer claimed he did not think he needed to report this incident because the [redacted] had openly discussed this plan [redacted] several days prior to and after the incident. When the debriefer was later [redacted] and believed he needed a non-traditional technique to induce the detainee to cooperate, he told [redacted] he wanted to wave a handgun in front of the detainee to scare him. The debriefer said he did not believe he was required to notify Headquarters of this technique, citing the earlier, unreported mock execution [redacted].

A senior operations officer [redacted] recounted that around September 2002 [redacted] heard that the debriefer had staged a mock execution. [Redacted] was not present but understood it went badly; it was transparently a ruse and no benefit was derived from it. [Redacted] observed that there is a need to be creative as long as it is not considered torture. [Redacted] stated that if such a proposal were made now, it would involve a great deal of consultation. It would begin with [redacted] management and would include CTC/Legal, [redacted] and the CTC [redacted].

The [redacted] admitted staging a "mock execution" in the first days that [redacted] was open. According to the [redacted] the technique was his idea but was not effective because it came across as being staged. It was based on the concept, from SERE school, of showing something that looks real, but is not. The [redacted] recalled that a particular CTC interrogator later told him about employing the mock execution technique. The [redacted] did not know when this incident occurred or if it was successful. He viewed this technique as ineffective because it was not believable.

Four [redacted] who were interviewed admitted to either

participating in one of the above-described incidents or hearing about them. [Redacted] described staging a mock execution of a detainee. Reportedly, a detainee who witnessed the "body" in the aftermath of the ruse "sang like a bird."

[Redacted] revealed that approximately four days before his interview with OIG, the [redacted] stated he had conducted a mock execution [redacted] in October or November 2002. Reportedly, the firearm was discharged outside of the building, and it was done because the detainee reportedly possessed critical threat information. [Redacted] stated that he has not heard of a similar incident occurring [redacted] since then.[86]

It is clear from these accounts that there was a viral quality to the spread of interrogation techniques in 2002—and that the germ of the idea of what was permissible was the general understanding that the simulated torture methods employed in SERE training were now in play for U.S. interrogators. Other techniques that "caused concern because DoJ had not specifically approved them" included many of those to which al-Nashiri had been subjected, including one incident in which the debriefer "threatened Al-Nashiri by saying that if he did not talk, 'We could get your mother in here,' and 'We can bring your family in here.'" As Helgerson explained:

The debriefer reportedly wanted Al-Nashiri to infer, for psychological reasons, that the debriefer might be [redacted] intelligence officer based on his Arabic dialect, and that Al-Nashiri was in [redacted] custody because it was widely believed in Middle East circles that [redacted] interrogation technique involves sexually abusing female relatives in front of the detainee.[87]

In all, Helgerson concluded, "Agency personnel reported a range of improvised actions that interrogators and debriefers reportedly used at the time to assist in obtaining information in detainees. The extent of these actions is illustrative of the consequences of the lack of clear guidance at the time and the Agency's insufficient attention to interrogations in [redacted]."[88]

If Helgerson had limited his criticism to this—to the poor training and oversight of CIA agents in the program's early days—his work would have caused less consternation within the agency; after all, the CIA had been conscious from the outset that its interrogators were walking a fine line, and wanted to make sure the administration explicitly authorized its abusive methods and that its agents knew the rules.

Indeed, on January 28, 2003, days after Helgerson began his investigation, CIA Director George Tenet signed a three-page order entitled "Guidelines on Confinement Conditions for CIA Detainees" that formalized the requirements for CIA interrogations. The Guidelines instruct interrogators that "Unless otherwise approved by Headquarters, CIA officers may use only Permissible Interrogation Techniques. Permissible Interrogation Techniques consist of both (a) Standard Techniques and (b) Enhanced Techniques," and that "in each interrogation session in which an Enhanced Technique is employed, a contemporaneous record shall be created setting forth the nature and duration of each such technique employed, the identities of those present [redacted]." Interrogators were required to sign the order, acknowledging that they had read it and would comply with its terms.

But in a note explaining the genesis of his Special Review, Helgerson cited not only the request from Headquarters to investigate specific uses of unauthorized techniques, but also the fact that he had "received information that some employees were concerned that certain covert Agency activities at an overseas detention facility might involve violations of human rights."[89] As he explained in the *Der Spiegel* interview after leaving the CIA in 2009,

We wanted to respond to expressions of concern by some agency employees involved with the program who were uneasy about it. Actually there were a number of individuals who expressed to me their concern about various aspects of the program. They had the feeling that what the agency was doing was fundamentally inconsistent with past U.S. government policy and American values. It was something new and unprecedented for the agency. A critical legal opinion was missing which I believed was needed to protect agency employees and

detainees. It was then my own initiative to undertake this review.
And in the process we found things that we did not expect to find.[90]

In other words, Helgerson was determined to probe not just the
aberrations, but also the officially sanctioned interrogation program. As a
quasi-independent watchdog within the agency, the CIA Inspector General
has access by law to all CIA employees and files—which meant Helgerson
would be reviewing all the records of the Abu Zubaydah and al-Nashiri
interrogations, including the videotapes. And because CIA Inspectors
General are required to report the results of investigations and reviews to
Congressional overseers, others, too, would soon know that these records
existed.

On February 5, 2003, with Helgerson's investigation in motion, CIA
General Counsel Scott Muller briefed Porter Goss, who was then the
Chairman of the House Intelligence Committee, and Jane Harman, the
ranking Democrat on the committee, on the CIA's Rendition, Detention,
and Interrogation program and the use of enhanced interrogation
techniques in particular. At that meeting, Muller revealed that the CIA
had hundreds of hours of videotapes of the Thai black site interrogations,
which the Agency planned to destroy as soon as Helgerson completed his
review. Five days later, Harman wrote Muller:

Dear Mr. Muller:

*Last week's briefing brought home to me the difficult challenges
faced by the Central Intelligence Agency in the current threat
environment. I realize we are at a time when the balance between
security and liberty must be constantly evaluated and recalibrated in
order to protect our nation and its people from catastrophic terrorist
attack and I thus appreciate the obvious effort that you and your
Office have made to address the tough questions. At the briefing you
assured us that the [redacted] approved by the Attorney General
have been subject to an extensive review by lawyers at the Central
Intelligence Agency, the Department of Justice and the National
Security Council and found to be within the law.*

It is also the case, however, that what was described raises profound policy questions and I am concerned about whether these have been as rigorously examined as the legal questions. I would like to know what kind of policy review took place and what questions were examined. In particular, I would like to know whether the most senior levels of the White House have determined that these practices are consistent with the principles and policies of the United States. Have enhanced techniques been authorized and approved by the President?

You discussed the fact that there is videotape of Abu Zubaydah following his capture that will be destroyed after the Inspector General finishes his inquiry. I would urge the Agency to reconsider that plan. Even if the videotape does not constitute an official record that must be preserved under the law, the videotape would be the best proof that the written record is accurate, if such record is called into question in the future. The fact of destruction would reflect badly on the Agency.

I look forward to your response.[91]

Alarmed, CIA attorneys drafted an answer and carried it to a meeting at the White House on or before February 22, 2003 that was called to address "the CIA's response to a congressional inquiry."[92] Following that meeting, General Counsel Scott Muller sent a reply to Harman that ignored her admonition about the videotapes and brushed off her question about how the interrogation techniques accord with American values:

Thank you for your letter of 10 February following up on the briefing we gave you and Congressman Goss on 5 February concerning the Central Intelligence Agency's limited use of the handful of specially approved interrogation techniques we described. As we informed both you and the leadership of the Intelligence Committees last September, a number of Executive Branch lawyers including lawyers from the Department of Justice participated in the determination that, in the appropriate circumstances, use of these techniques is fully consistent with U.S. law. While I do not think it appropriate for me to comment

on issues that are a matter of policy, much less the nature and extent
of Executive Branch deliberations, I think it would be fair to assume
that policy as well as legal matters have been addressed within the
Executive Branch.[93]

* * *

Before Helgerson could watch the tapes—a February request for copies
was denied and he, too, would be required to travel to Thailand—the U.S.
had captured Khaled Shaikh Mohammed and waterboarded him 183 times
during a twenty five-day interrogation at the CIA black site in Poland.

Mohammed was seized on March 1, 2003 in a raid by Pakistani
intelligence and CIA operatives in Rawalpindi, Pakistan and transferred
immediately to Afghanistan. He was held there for three or four days,
shackled naked to the ceiling and doused routinely with cold water between
interrogation sessions. On or around March 6, he was hooded and flown
to another country where, as he told the International Committee of the
Red Cross when he was eventually interviewed in Guantánamo, "there was
snow on the ground" and everybody "was wearing black, with masks and
army boots, like Planet-X people." "I think the country was Poland," he told
the ICRC. "I think this because on one occasion a water bottle was brought
to me without the label removed. It had an email address ending in '.pl'. The
central-heating system was an old style one that I would expect only to see
in countries of the former communist system."[94]

At the black site near the Szymany airport, the interrogators told
Mohammed they had been given "the green-light from Washington to
give him 'a hard time,'" promising that he would be "brought to the verge
of death and back again."[95] He was kept naked for nearly a month, wrists
shackled to the ceiling and ankles to the floor, in a wooden-walled room
equipped with closed-circuit cameras where he was monitored twenty-four
hours a day by a doctor, psychologist and interrogator. For interrogations,
he was taken to another room where, with a doctor present, he was walled
and hosed down with cold water before male and female interrogators.[96]
The doctor also presided over the waterboarding, "standing out of sight
behind the head of the bed," "But I saw him when he came to fix a clip

to my finger which was connected to a machine," Mohammed recalled. "I think it was to measure my pulse and oxygen content in my blood. So they could take me to the breaking point."[97]

The process was repeated day in and day out, the punishment growing in intensity:

> The harshest period of the interrogation was just prior to the end of the first month. The beatings became worse and I had cold water directed at me from a hose-pipe by guards while I was still in my cell. The worst day was when I was beaten for about half an hour by one of the interrogators. My head was banged against the wall so hard that it started to bleed. Cold water was poured over my head. This was then repeated with other interrogators. Finally I was taken for a session of waterboarding. The torture on that day was finally stopped by the intervention of the doctor. I was allowed to sleep for about one hour and then put back in my cell standing with my hands shackled above my head....
>
> During the harshest period of my interrogation I gave a lot of false information in order to satisfy what I believed the interrogators wished to hear in order to make the ill-treatment stop. I later told the interrogators that their methods were stupid and counterproductive. I'm sure that the false information I was forced to invent in order to make the ill-treatment stop wasted a lot of their time and led to several false red-alerts being placed in the U.S.[98]

This would be the last time the U.S. waterboarded a detainee. Helgerson flew to the black site in Thailand some six weeks later, in May, to review the videotapes of the Abu Zubaydah interrogation and the first two weeks of the al-Nashiri interrogation. Although he found that fifteen of the ninety-two tapes that the CIA lawyer had reviewed in November were now blank or broken and twenty-one hours of interrogations described in the logs and cables were missing from the video record, including two waterboarding sessions, what he saw was more than enough for him to reach some damning conclusions.

Helgerson immediately saw that the antiseptic descriptions of the enhanced interrogation techniques in the OLC memos bore little resemblance to the techniques in actual practice. There was a critical difference between waterboarding as described in the August 1, 2002 "Interrogation of an al Qaeda Operative" memo[99] and the way it was being applied by Mitchell's interrogators. "The difference was in the manner in which the detainee's breathing was obstructed," he noted. "At the SERE school and in the DoJ opinion, the subject's airflow is disrupted by the firm application of a damp cloth over the air passages; the interrogator applies a small amount of water to the cloth in a controlled manner. By contrast, the Agency interrogator [redacted] continuously applied large volumes of water to a cloth that covered the detainee's mouth and nose."[100]

"One of the psychologists acknowledged that the Agency's use of the technique differed from that used in SERE training and explained that the Agency's technique is different because it is 'for real' and is more poignant and convincing," Helgerson reported.[101] The CIA, in other words, was employing torture as opposed to simulated torture.

Helgerson was shocked to discover that the CIA's own Office of Medical Services "was neither consulted nor involved in the initial analysis of the risk and benefits of EITs," and of waterboarding in particular:

> In retrospect, OMS contends that the reported sophistication of the preliminary EIT review was exaggerated, at least as it related to the waterboard, and that the power of this EIT was appreciably exaggerated...Furthermore, OMS contends that the expertise of the SERE psychologist/interrogators on the waterboard was probably misrepresented at the time, as the SERE waterboard experience is so different from the subsequent Agency usage as to make it almost irrelevant. Consequently, according to OMS, there was no a priori reason to believe that applying the waterboard with the frequency and intensity with which it was used by the psychologist/interrogators was either efficacious or medically safe.[102]

In fact, the administration had not only accepted Mitchell and Jessen's fanciful assurances on the proposed methods without consulting the agency's medical experts, they had outright ignored warnings from Mitchell and Jessen's former employer, the military's Joint Personnel Recovery Agency, about their effectiveness. An attachment to a 2002 memo from JPRA had cautioned:

> *The requirement to obtain information from an uncooperative source as quickly as possible—in time to prevent, for example, an impending terrorist attack that could result in loss of life—has been forwarded as a compelling argument for the use of torture. Conceptually, proponents envision the application of torture as a means to expedite the exploitation process. In essence, physical and/or psychological duress are viewed as an alternative to the more time-consuming conventional interrogation process. The error inherent in this line of thinking is the assumption that, through torture, the interrogator can extract reliable and accurate intelligence. History and a consideration of human behavior would appear to refute this assumption. (NOTE: The application of physical and or psychological duress will likely result in physical compliance. Additionally, prisoners may answer and/or comply as a result of threats of torture. However, the reliability and accuracy information must be questioned.)...*
>
> *In numerous cases, interrogation has been used as a tool of mass intimidation by oppressive regimes. Often, the interrogators operate from the assumption (often incorrect) that a prisoner possesses information of interest. When the prisoner is not forthcoming, physical and psychological pressures are increased. Eventually, the prisoner will provide answers that they feel the interrogator is seeking. In this instance, the information is neither reliable nor accurate (note: A critical element of the interrogation process is to assess the prisoner's knowledgeability. A reasoned assessment of what the prisoner should know, based on experience, training, position, and access should drive the questioning process.)*[103]

This is exactly what Helgerson saw when he watched the Abu Zubaydah and al-Nashiri tapes. "The Agency lacked adequate linguists or subject matter experts and had very little hard knowledge of what particular al-Qaeda leaders—who later became detainees—knew," he concluded. "This lack of knowledge led analysts to speculate about what a detainee 'should know'....When a detainee did not respond to a question posed to him, the assumption at Headquarters was that the detainee was holding back and knew more; consequently, Headquarters recommended resumption of EITs."[104]

Furthermore, Helgerson saw that headquarters and the White House were willing to bend or ignore even their own self-imposed rules. The memos permitted the repetition of techniques, for example, but noted agency assurances "that repetition will not be substantial because the techniques generally lose their effectiveness after several repetitions"; yet Abu Zubaydah was waterboarded eighty three times, and Khaled Shaikh Mohammed was waterboarded 183 times and subjected to sleep deprivation to the known limit of human endurance. Nevertheless, Scott Muller, the CIA's General Counsel, assured Helgerson that the Attorney General considered even these flagrant excesses "well within the scope of the DoJ opinion and the authority given to the CIA by that opinion."[105]

Helgerson disagreed. Not only did the waterboarding in practice, its risks versus results and its excessive, zealous, and unnecessary use, "[bring] into question the continued applicability of the DoJ opinion"; "the fact that precautions have been taken to provide on-site medical oversight in the use of all EITs is evidence that their use poses risks," he observed.[106] As for Yoo's August 1, 2002 memos, the Inspector General noted that "though they purport to assess whether EITs constitute torture, they don't address the separate question of whether the application of standard or enhanced techniques by Agency officers is consistent with the Torture Convention's requirement that countries also prevent 'cruel, inhuman, or degrading treatment or punishment.'"[107] Congress, in ratifying the Convention against Torture, had interpreted cruel, inhuman, or degrading treatment or punishment to mean treatment that violates the Eighth Amendment prohibition on cruel and unusual punishment or Fifth and Fourteenth Amendment bars against conduct that "shocks the conscience."

Filling this dangerous gap in the legal shield was a document entitled "Legal Principles Applicable to CIA Detention and Interrogation of Captured al-Qa'ida Personnel." This series of bullet points, which Muller sent to John Yoo on April 28, 2003 under the note "I would like to discuss this with you as soon as you get a chance," included two clearly aimed at protecting black site interrogators:

- *CIA interrogations of foreign nationals are not within the "special maritime or territorial jurisdiction" of the United States where the interrogation takes place on foreign territory in buildings that are not owned or leased by or under the legal jurisdiction of the U.S. Government.*

- *The use by CIA of the following techniques (and of comparable, approved techniques) in the interrogation of al-Qa'ida detainees is lawful, and violates neither Federal criminal law nor the Fifth, Eighth, or Fourteenth Amendments, in circumstances where the interrogators do not have the specific intent to cause the detainee to undergo severe physical or mental pain or suffering: isolation, sleep deprivation, reduced caloric intake (so long as the amount is calculated to maintain the general health of the detainee), deprivation of reading material, loud music or white noise (at a decibel level calculated to avoid damage to the detainee's hearing), the attention grasp, walling, the facial hold, the facial slap (insult slap), the abdominal slap, cramped confinement, wall standing, stress positions, sleep deprivation, the use of diapers, the use of harmless insects, and the water board.*[108]

Helgerson knew the latter was not true. After seeing the tapes, he was convinced that CIA interrogators, even when they were adhering absolutely to approved techniques and procedures, had at the minimum violated the ban on cruel, inhuman and degrading treatment.

On June 28, 2003, a month after Helgerson traveled to the Thai black site, President Bush released a statement marking the annual United Nations International Day in Support of Victims of Torture. Helgerson included this excerpt in his report:

The United States declares its strong solidarity with torture victims across the world. Torture anywhere is an affront to human dignity everywhere. We are committed to building a world where human rights are respected and protected by the rule of law.

Freedom from torture is an inalienable human right.... Yet torture continues to be practiced around the world by rogue regimes whose cruel methods match their determination to crush the human spirit....

Notorious human rights abusers...have sought to shield their abuses from the eyes of the world by staging elaborate deceptions and denying access to international human rights monitors....

The United States is committed to the worldwide elimination of torture and we are leading this fight by example. I call on all governments to join with the United States and the community of law-abiding nations in prohibiting, investigating, and prosecuting all acts of torture and in undertaking to prevent other cruel and unusual punishment.[109]

Coming in the midst of Helgerson's review, the statement rattled the agency. CIA General Counsel Scott Muller reportedly called the White House, worried about the morale and potential liability of CIA interrogators who had been following the president's program, and George Tenet met with the Principles to request new written approval for EITs that would plug the legal holes Helgerson had spotted. Sometime in July, the White House issued a still-classified memo that supposedly gave the agency its reinforced shield.[110] Then, Helgerson reports,

On 29 July 2003, the DCI and the General Counsel provided a detailed briefing to selected NSC Principals on CIA's detention and interrogation efforts involving "high value detainees," to include the expanded use of EITs. According to a Memorandum for the Record prepared by the General Counsel following that meeting, the Attorney General confirmed that DoJ approved the expanded use of various EITs including multiple applications of the waterboard. The General

Counsel said he believes everyone in attendance was aware of exactly what CIA was doing with respect to detention and interrogation, and approved of the effort.[111]

At the time, dozens of High Value Detainees had disappeared into CIA black sites, and floating around the agency was a Mitchell and Jessen business plan that presented black site interrogations as a project with a bright, booming future. One of the few unredacted pages reads:

2.2 Anticipated Future Demand

Results from the first Al Qaeda HVT interrogated using the aforementioned enhanced techniques, Abu Zubayda, have been outstanding. Abu Zubayda reached a satisfactory level of compliance in August 2002. Since April, the interrogation team has produced [redacted] actionable intelligence disseminations from Abu Zubaydah. This has ultimately led to some instances of the U.S. Government being able to neutralize Al Qaeda capabilities worldwide before there was an opportunity for those capabilities to engage in operations harmful to the United States. Because of this, U.S. Government decision makers have a positive view of the program, and there is pressure to increase HVT Interrogation Program capabilities in the shortest time possible.

As the success of the program and of other counter Al Qaeda activities continues to lead to the capture of additional HVT candidates, it can be reasonably expected that intelligence disseminations will lead to even more HVT candidate captures and the likewise increase in demand for more HVT program services.

2.3 Operational Assumptions

Required resources will be approved and available for the HVT Interrogation Program as depicted in Section 4. Such resources are critical to the success of the Program's ability to meet identified customer requirements.

The program will provide for the increase in demand of fully qualified [redacted] psychological services by carefully increasing the number of interrogation psychologists from a limited pool of appropriate candidates, maintaining expertise through an aggressive training and mentoring program with well documented oversight of all activities to ensure quality control.[112]

* * *

For months, the question of what to do with the videotapes seemed settled. A thirteen-page cable discussing the disposition of the tapes was sent just after the July 28, 2003 Principles meeting, and they had remained since then locked quietly in the vault in the black site in Thailand.[113]

Then, on April 28, 2004, CBS 60 Minutes II broadcast the first photographs of prisoner abuse at Abu Ghraib prison in Iraq. Just over a week later, on May 7, 2004, Helgerson circulated his completed, classified review of the CIA's RDI program within the CIA and the White House.

Any sense of security the CIA had derived from the 2003 legal assurances vanished. The visceral power of the pictures and their instant, global transmission drove home the particular dangers visual images pose, and Helgerson's report was just a hint of how the public, confronted not with candid snapshots by soldiers on the night shift but with film of hundreds of hours of Washington-directed torture, would react. As more photos surfaced in subsequent days in *The New Yorker* and *The Washington Post*, the CIA took the question of the tapes back to the White House.

On May 24, 2004, Scott Muller met with a group of lawyers that included Alberto Gonzales, David Addington, and NSA legal advisor John Bellinger about the photo scandal and the IG's report. Muller told the group that the CIA wanted to destroy the tapes, and meeting notes reportedly record that Bellinger advised against it. There are conflicting reports on how the others reacted. One *New York Times* account held that "one person familiar with the discussion said that in light of concerns raised in the inspector general's report that agency officers would be legally liable for harsh interrogations, there was a view at the time among some administration lawyers that the tapes should be preserved."[114] Another reported that "the emerging picture of White House involvement is more complex," and that "one former senior intelligence official with direct knowledge of the matter said there had been 'vigorous sentiment' among some top White House officials to destroy the tapes."[115] Jane Mayer, who gave the first account of the meeting in *The Dark Side*, wrote that Addington, aware they were discussing the possible destruction of evidence, was angry that the group was even being consulted on the question. One participant told her his attitude "was along the lines of 'Don't bring this into the White House.'"[116]

Meanwhile, the White House's Office of Legal Counsel was scrambling to contain the potential damage of Helgerson's report. On the same day the attorneys discussed the tapes, Jack Goldsmith sent a letter to Helgerson:

> *I understand that your office has been working on a report that, in part, discusses advice provided to CIA by my Office concerning interrogations in the war on terrorism. Scott Muller, the General Counsel of the CIA, recently provided me with a copy of the report and I would appreciate it if I could have time to review the description of my Office's advice and provide comments before the report is sent to Congress.*[117]

Goldsmith had taken over as head of the Office of Legal Counsel in October 2003, replacing Jay Bybee, who had resigned earlier in the year to become a federal judge, and from the start he had misgivings about the Bybee-Yoo legal advice. He had already challenged standing positions on the applicability of the Geneva Conventions and expressed serious doubts about the August 1, 2002 torture memos, which he reportedly learned of two weeks after taking office; in December 2003, he had also formally withdrawn another Yoo-authored memo authorizing the use of SERE-based techniques on detainees in military custody. On May 27, 2004, Goldsmith wrote a letter to Scott Muller noting the CIA IG's report "has raised concerns about certain aspects of interrogations in practice." He concluded

> *In light of the assertions in the Inspector General's Report, and the factual assumptions underlying our advice, we strongly recommend that any use of [the waterboard] remain suspended until we have had*

a more thorough opportunity to review the Report and the factual assertions in it. We recommend that with respect to the use of the other nine techniques, you review the steps you have already taken to ensure that in actual practice any use of those techniques adheres closely to the assumptions and limitations stated in our opinion of August 2002. Finally, the Report also includes information concerning interrogations that are not part of the enhanced interrogation techniques program. As you know, we have not provided advice on practices described in those portions of the Report.[118]

On July 3, 2004, citing "personal reasons," George Tenet submitted his resignation as Director of the Central Intelligence Agency. The next day, he sent a memo to National Security Adviser Condoleezza Rice looking for formal assurance of continued White House support for the CIA's secret interrogations. "As we have already discussed, the next logical step is for the Attorney General to complete the relevant legal analysis already in preparation," Rice responded.[119]

Before that could happen, the *Washington Post* ran an article by Dana Priest and R. Jeffrey Smith titled "Memo Offered Justification for the Use of Torture," that began, "In August 2002, the Justice Department advised the White House that torturing al Qaeda terrorists in captivity abroad 'may be justified,' and that international laws against torture 'may be unconstitutional if applied to interrogations' conducted in President Bush's war on terrorism, according to a newly obtained memo." The June 8, 2004 story went on to describe the "Standards of Conduct for Interrogation" memo in detail.[120] A week later, the newspaper posted a copy of the full memo online. His battle now public, Goldsmith immediately informed Attorney General John Ashcroft that he intended to withdraw the Yoo memo and planned to resign.

Tenet returned to the White House to press for official cover, and Scott Muller met with Bellinger and Deputy Assistant Attorney General James Comey on July 2, a meeting he summarized afterwards in a memo to Bellinger:

Subsequent to today's meeting we have had further discussions that clarified the extent of today's approval of certain techniques. The authorized techniques are those previously approved for use with Abu Zubaydah (with the exception of the waterboard) and the 24 approved by the Secretary of Defense on 16 April 2003 for use by the Department of Defense. I have relayed this information to the CIA's Counterterrorism Center.[121]

Finally, after a meeting where the Principals echoed the need for a new memo and a July 20, 2004 written request from the Agency for legal advice, the CIA reportedly received yet another still-secret legal shield that month.[122]

By then, Helgerson had briefed Pat Roberts and Jay Rockefeller, the Chairman and ranking Democrat of the Senate Intelligence Committee, and Porter Goss and Jane Harman on the House side, on his investigation and report. Rockefeller began pushing the agency on Helgerson's findings, but it was an election year and President Bush was pressing a reelection strategy calculated to keep Democrats on the defensive on national security issues, so growing anxieties in Congress about detainee abuse remained in check through the fall. But in May 2005, Rockefeller wrote Helgerson formally requesting documents cited in the report, including those relating to the General Counsel's 2002 review of the videotapes.

He wasn't the only one now on the trail of the tapes. That same month a federal judge presiding over the trial of Zacarias Moussaoui, who stood accused of planning to act as the "20th hijacker" in the 9/11 attacks, ordered the Justice Department to disclose whether the interrogation of Abu Zubaydah and others had been recorded. With the circle of those to whom the videotapes might eventually be produced expanding, pressure to destroy them was again on the rise. In July, Porter Goss, who had known of the debate over the tapes since he was briefed with Jane Harman in 2003 and who had replaced George Tenet as Director of the CIA in September, brought the problem of the tapes to John Negroponte, the newly installed Director of National Intelligence. Negroponte emphatically advised against destroying the tapes. A CIA attorney rendered a legal opinion on Negroponte's advice in an email to his "client" on July 28, 2005.

Again the tapes survived, and they survived again in September, when Rockefeller wrote to protest the CIA's refusal to respond to his request and to renew his demand for documents about the tapes.

Then, on November 2, 2005, *The Washington Post* published a front page, 2,700-word Dana Priest story exposing the network of secret CIA prisons in Afghanistan, Thailand, Guantánamo, and Eastern Europe. "More than 100 suspected terrorists have been sent by the CIA into the covert system," the piece revealed. "The top 30 al Qaeda prisoners exist in complete isolation from the outside world. Kept in dark, sometimes underground cells, they have no recognized legal rights, and no one outside the CIA is allowed to talk with or even see them, or otherwise verify their well-being."[123]

Less than a week later, still reeling from this leak, the agency learned that *The New York Times* was preparing to print a story that publicly revealed the existence of Helgerson's report and summarized its damning conclusions. "A classified report issued last year by the Central Intelligence Agency's inspector general warned that interrogation procedures approved by the CIA after the September 11 attacks might violate some provisions of the international Convention against Torture, current and former intelligence officials say," Douglas Jehl's piece would begin.[124]

On November 8, 2005, the day before this story ran, two cables were sent from the field to headquarters requesting permission to destroy the ninety-two videotapes. On November 9, someone at the CIA sent a fourteen-page email with the subject "Request approval to destroy field videotapes" that included three cables relating to the decision on their destruction. That same day, as the world was first learning of the report by the last person to view the tapes, a cable was sent to CIA headquarters confirming they had been destroyed.[125]

* * *

In the midst of the November 2005 revelations of the black sites and the CIA Inspector General's investigation, Judge Leonie Brinkema, the presiding judge in the Zacarias Moussaoui trial, again ordered the CIA to disclose whether the CIA had videotaped any interrogations that might have a bearing on Moussaoui's case, including the interrogation of Abu Zubaydah. The agency had answered her previous order with a sworn declaration that no tapes existed; on November 14, 2005, five days after the tapes were destroyed, the CIA again swore it had no videotapes.

Two years later, with Moussaoui's conviction up on appeal, federal prosecutors finally told the court that there were videotapes—and not, mysteriously, in the past tense, but rather two interrogation tapes the CIA had somehow discovered in September and October. The U.S. attorneys told the court they had personally reviewed the tapes and found them identical to a written transcript and related cables they were submitting to the court; all showed that the tapes had no relevance to Moussaoui's case, they insisted.

A month and a half later, on December, 6, 2007, CIA employees received an email from Michael Hayden, who had succeeded Porter Goss in 2006, headed "Message from Director: Taping of Early Detainee Interrogations":

The press has learned that back in 2002, during the initial stage of our terrorist detention program, CIA videotaped interrogations, and destroyed the tapes in 2005. I understand that the Agency did so only after it was determined they were no longer of intelligence value and not relevant to any internal, legislative, or judicial inquiries— including the trial of Zacarias Moussaoui. The decision to destroy the tapes was made within the CIA itself. The leaders of our oversight committees were informed of the videos years ago and of the Agency's intention to dispose of the material. Our oversight committees also have been told that the videos were, in fact, destroyed.

If past public commentary on the Agency's detention program is any guide, we may see misinterpretations of the facts in the days ahead. With that in mind, I want you to have some background now.

CIA's terrorist detention and interrogation program began after the capture of Abu Zubaydah in March 2002. Zubaydah, who had extensive knowledge of al-Qa'ida personnel and operations, had been seriously wounded in a firefight. When President Bush officially acknowledged in September 2006 the existence of CIA's counterterror initiative, he talked about Zubaydah, noting that this terrorist survived solely because of medical treatment arranged by CIA. Under normal questioning, Zubaydah became defiant and evasive. It was clear, in the President's words, that "Zubaydah had more information that could save innocent lives, but he stopped talking."

That made imperative the use of other means to obtain the information—means that were lawful, safe, and effective. To meet that need, CIA designed specific, appropriate interrogation procedures. Before they were used, they were reviewed and approved by the Department of Justice and by other elements of the Executive Branch. Even with the great care taken and detailed preparations made, the fact remains that this effort was new, and the Agency was determined that it proceed in accord with established legal and policy guidelines. So, on its own, CIA began to videotape interrogations.

The tapes were meant chiefly as an additional, internal check on the program in its early stages. At one point, it was thought the tapes could serve as a backstop to guarantee that other methods of documenting the interrogations—and the crucial information they produced—were accurate and complete. The Agency soon determined that its documentary reporting was full and exacting, removing any need for tapes. Indeed, videotaping stopped in 2002.

As part of the rigorous review that has defined the detention program, the Office of General Counsel examined the tapes and determined that they showed lawful methods of questioning. The Office of Inspector General also examined the tapes in 2003 as part of its look at the Agency's detention and interrogation practices. Beyond their lack of intelligence value—as the interrogation sessions had already been exhaustively detailed in written channels—and the absence of any legal or internal reason to keep them, the tapes posed a serious security risk. Were they ever to leak, they would permit identification of your CIA colleagues who had served in the program, exposing them and their families to retaliation from al-Qa'ida and its sympathizers.

These decisions were made years ago. But it is my responsibility, as Director today, to explain to you what was done, and why. What matters here is that it was done in line with the law. Over the course of its life, the Agency's interrogation program has been of great value to our country. It has helped disrupt terrorist operations and save lives. It was built on a solid foundation of legal review. It has been conducted with careful supervision. If the story of these tapes is told fairly, it will underscore those facts.

—*Mike Hayden*

The next day, *The New York Times* ran a Mark Mazetti story titled "C.I.A. Destroyed Two Tapes Showing Interrogations." Mazetti reported that Jose Rodriguez, Jr., who at the time directed the CIA's clandestine services, had ordered the tapes' destruction. Follow-up reporting by Mazetti and Scott Shane over the next three weeks established that Rodriguez had received legal advice from CIA attorneys Steven Hermes and Robert Eatinger sanctioning the action and that conversations about the tapes' fate over the years had included the top lawyers in the White House.

Hayden's assertion that the videotapes were "not relevant to any internal, legislative, or judicial inquiries" provoked a storm of protest. When Jane Harman warned the agency not to destroy the tapes in 2003, the chief legal question was whether doing so would violate the Federal Records Act; by the time they were destroyed, the number of requests for information that would include the videotapes, and the CIA's failure to acknowledge their existence or respond to these requests, meant the potential crimes had multiplied.

Harman, who now pressed the CIA to declassify her correspondence counseling against the destruction, told the *Times*, "How in the world could the CIA claim that these tapes were not relevant to a legislative committee?"[126] Thomas Kean and Lee Hamilton, the Chairman and Vice Chairman of the 9/11 Commission, published an op-ed entitled

"Stonewalled by the CIA," asserting that the agency "failed to respond to our lawful requests for information about the 9/11 plot. Those who knew about the videotapes—and did not tell us about them—obstructed our investigation."[127] Judge Brinkema had been lied to and her orders defied twice. A September 2004 order by another federal judge overseeing the ACLU's Freedom of Information Act lawsuit, which instructed the CIA, Defense Department, and a number of other governmental agencies "to produce or identify all records related to the treatment of detainees apprehended after September 1, 2007 and held in U.S. custody abroad," had been similarly, and repeatedly, defied.

On January 2, 2008, Attorney General Michael Mukasey announced that, "Following a preliminary inquiry into the destruction by CIA personnel of videotapes of detainee interrogations, the Department's National Security Division has recommended, and I have concluded, that there is a basis for initiating a criminal investigation of this matter." Mukasey appointed John Durham, a U.S. Attorney based in Connecticut, to conduct the investigation with the FBI. In the course of his investigation, Durham subpoenaed several CIA officials and employees to testify before a federal grand jury in Virginia.

Meanwhile, under a Contempt of Court motion filed shortly after the destruction of the tapes was revealed, the ACLU was pursuing all written records that describe or refer to the interrogations depicted in the tapes, including the interrogation logs and the back-and-forth cable traffic between the Thai black site and CIA headquarters. The CIA tried to argue that the tapes and related materials did not fall under the ACLU's FOIA request, but on August 20, 2008, Judge Alvin Hellerstein ordered the agency to produce a list describing each of the destroyed records; a list of any summaries, transcripts, or memoranda regarding the records, and of any reconstruction of the records' contents; and identification of any eyewitnesses who may have viewed the videotapes or retained custody of the videotapes before their destruction."[128] Judge Hellerstein twice deferred his order in consideration of Durham's criminal probe. When the second stay expired, government attorneys wrote to Hellerstein:

With the termination of the stay, the CIA is now gathering information and records responsive to the Court's order....In the meantime, the CIA can now identify the number of videotapes that were destroyed, which is information implicated by Point 1 of the August 20, 2008 Order. Ninety-two videotapes were destroyed. This information is included in the CIA Office of the Inspector General's Special Review Report, a redacted version of which was previously produced to the Plaintiffs. The CIA will unredact this information from the report and produce it to the Plaintiffs."[129]

The government subsequently produced several lists of cables and other key documents, but continued to withhold the documents themselves on two grounds: first, that they fall under an exemption to the Freedom of Information Act requests for materials that protect "intelligence sources and methods"; and second, that releasing the descriptions of the interrogations contained in the documents could serve as enemy propaganda—an argument the government also advanced in a separate portion of the same FOIA action to block the release of more photographs of prisoner abuse in Iraq and Afghanistan. The ACLU countered that under the law, FOIA exemptions cannot be used to hide illegal acts or save government agencies from embarrassment; the CIA should no longer be allowed to hide the records because President Obama has banned the enhanced interrogation techniques, because the techniques are no longer secret, and because they violate the Convention against Torture and are therefore outside the mandate of the CIA. As for propaganda, the ACLU pointed out that no court has ever allowed the withholding of purely textual description of government misconduct on the argument that the words would inflame our enemies.

In a hearing on September 30, 2009 in federal district court in New York, after reading several of the cables in a secret briefing in his chambers, Judge Hellerstein ruled that he would not address the question of whether, by committing torture, the CIA had forfeited its right to exempt the documents from the FOIA request. "I am not able to comment, particularly in the context of FOIA, on the nature of legality or illegality in the development of intelligence" the Judge said. "That has been a subject of intense comment and discussion for some time in our nation. And I have very strong personal views on the subject as well. But these personal views have to be cabined in and put into the context of my thoughts and thinking and activities as a private citizen, not as a judge."[130]

The court, Hellerstein asserted, was constrained by precedent from interfering with intelligence gathering and required to defer to the decisions of the agency on what to classify—and CIA Director Leon Panetta had submitted a classified affidavit insisting that the information remain secret to protect intelligence sources and methods. "Personally, I think the courts ought to have a more active role, but that's not what the law is," he said. "The Director of the CIA has made a strong representation about the needs of the CIA in relationship to its job to gather information and sources, and unless I am convinced that it is wrong, I have to give deference."[131]

ACLU attorneys insisted that little would be revealed by releasing descriptions of the Abu Zubaydah and al-Nashiri videotapes that is not already known from now-public documents like the OLC memos. Furthermore, any deference that might normally be due the agency had been surrendered by its willful destruction of the tapes.

Referring to the sample of the cable traffic he had just read *in camera*, Hellerstein responded:

> It is not the subtraction or the addition of details. It is the use in actual cases that makes a dramatic difference with the type of information that is presented.... You get a certain quality of information from a composite or an abstract or an exemplar or a summary, but you get a different quality of information in seeing how different things are used in different ways with different people at different times, what sequences are used, what order is used, what evaluations are made and so on. That's the very essence of intelligence gathering. It is not as if a generalized format is imposed by computer....
>
> You said something to the effect that deference is not owed when the government has admitted that what it did was wrong and where there is a tendency sometimes to use classification as a way of

avoiding embarrassment. It is a strong argument. But the fact that something was wrong, that it was admitted as wrong, does not change the bar, in my opinion, of deference...

If the tapes had been produced, the rationale to defer for classification probably would have been operative with regard to those tapes as well.[132]

* * *

One of the documents ACLU attorneys pointed to as an example of the wealth of information about black site interrogations now publicly available is a "Background Paper on CIA's Combined Use of Interrogation Techniques" that the CIA sent Daniel Levin, who was preparing a replacement for the Yoo memo in the Office of Legal Counsel, on December 30, 2004. The paper, submitted under a cover sheet with the note "Dan, A generic description of the process," explains:

In support of information previously sent to the Department of Justice, this paper provides additional background on how interrogation techniques are used, in combination and separately, to achieve interrogation objectives. Effective interrogation is based on the concept of using both physical and psychological pressures in a comprehensive, systematic, and cumulative manner to influence HVD behavior, to overcome a detainee's resistance posture. The goal of interrogation is to create a state of learned helplessness and dependence conducive to the collection of intelligence in a predictable, reliable, and sustainable manner. For the purposes of this paper, the interrogation process can be broken into three separate phases: Initial Conditions; Transition to Interrogation; and Interrogation.[133]

The paper summarizes Rendition ("during the flight, the detainee is securely shackled and is deprived of sight and sound through the use of blindfolds, earmuffs, and hoods..."), Reception at Black Site ("the HVD finds himself in the complete control of Americans.... The procedures he is subject to are precise, quiet, and almost clinical, and no one is mistreating him..."), and Transitioning to Interrogation ("The standard on participation is set very high during the Initial Interview. The HVD would have to willingly provide information on actionable threats and location information on High-Value Targets at large—not lower level information—for interrogators to continue with the neutral approach..."). It describes Interrogation as a three-step process of Conditioning Techniques, Corrective Techniques, and Coercive Techniques, and lists the permissible Enhanced Interrogation Techniques, minus the now-proscribed waterboard. Then it includes a section headed "Interrogation—A day-to-day look," which it explains "provides a look at a prototypical interrogation with an emphasis on the application of interrogation techniques, in combination and separately."

   2) Session One
   a. *The HVD is brought into the interrogation room, and under the direction of the interrogators, stripped of his clothes, and placed into shackles [redacted]*
   b. *The HVD is place standing with his back to the walling wall. The HVD remains hooded.*
   c. *Interrogators approach the HVD, place the walling collar over his head and around his neck, and stand in front of the HVD. [redacted]*
   d. *The interrogators remove the HVD's hood and [redacted] explain the HVD's situation to him, tell him that the interrogators will do what it takes to get important information, and that he can improve his conditions by participating with the interrogators. The insult slap is normally used as soon as the HVD does or says anything inconsistent with the interrogators' instructions.*
   e. *[redacted] If appropriate, an insult slap or abdominal slap will follow.*
   f. *The interrogators will likely use walling once it becomes clear that the HVD is lying, withholding information, or using other resistance techniques.*
   g. *The sequence [redacted] may continue for several more iterations as the interrogators continue to measure the HVD's resistance posture and apply a negative consequence to the HVD's resistance efforts.*
   h. *The interrogators, assisted by security officers (for security purposes)*

will place the HVD in the center of the interrogation room in the vertical shackling position and diaper the HVD to begin sleep deprivation. The HVD will be provided with Ensure Plus (liquid dietary supplement) to begin dietary manipulation. The HVD remains nude. White noise (not to exceed 79db) is used in the interrogation room. The first interrogation session terminates at this point.[134]

And later:

4) Session Three

a. *[redacted]. In addition, the medical and psychological personnel observing the interrogations must find no contraindications to continued interrogation.*

b. *The HVD remains in Sleep deprivation, dietary manipulation and is nude. [redacted]*

c. *Like the earlier sessions, the HVD begins the session standing against the walling wall with the walling collar around his neck.*

d. *If the HVD is still maintaining a resistance posture, interrogators will continue to use walling and water dousing. All of the Corrective Techniques (insult slap, abdominal slap, facial hold, attention grasp) may be used several times during this session based on the responses and actions of the HVD. Stress positions and wall standing will be integrated into interrogations [redacted]. Intense questioning and walling would be repeated multiple times. Interrogators will often use one technique to support another. As an example, interrogators would tell an HVD in a stress position that he (HVD) is going back to the walling wall (for walling) if he fails to hold the stress position until told otherwise by the HVD. This places additional stress on the HVD who typically will try to hold the stress position for as long as possible to avoid the walling wall. [redacted] interrogators will remind the HVD that he is responsible for this treatment and can stop it at any time by cooperating with the interrogators.*

e. *The interrogators, assisted by security officers, will place the HVD back into the vertical shackling position to resume sleep deprivation.*

Dietary manipulation also continues, and the HVD remains nude. White noise (not to exceed 79db) is used in the interrogation room. The interrogation session terminates at this point. In this example of the third session, the following techniques were used: sleep deprivation, nudity, dietary manipulation, walling, water dousing, attention grasp, insult slap, abdominal slap, stress positions, and wall standing.[135]

Noting that "The entire interrogation process outlined above, including transition, may last for thirty days," the paper concludes:

[T]here is no template or script that states with certainty when and how these techniques will be used in combination during interrogation. However, the exemplar above is a fair representation of how these techniques are actually employed.[136]

The paper was circulated eight months after the CIA's Inspector General completed his review—a review that revealed that even when CIA interrogators adhered exactly to an OLC-approved script they were likely violating the Convention against Torture; that the OLC's memos only offered the illusion of legal protection; and that, in any event, interrogators often strayed from the script. It came, as well, eight months after the Abu Ghraib photos showed how the sense of control and almost technological efficiency the paper strives to convey was an elaborate fiction, and that in fact the CIA program was nothing but a sum of abusive methods, many of which had mutated and spread. It also came one month after George Bush was reelected to a second term, an election he would call his "accountability moment."

Not long after the *Washington Post* broke the story about the CIA black sites and the *New York Times* report revealed the Inspector General's probe, the CIA fired a career agent named Mary McCarthy for "discussing operational matters with journalists." McCarthy had most recently served in the Inspector General's office, where she assisted in John Helgerson's Special Review and headed the office's investigation of CIA abuses in Iraq and Afghanistan. After her firing, the *Post* reported that "McCarthy became convinced that 'CIA people had lied'" during a June 2005 Congressional briefing by promising repeatedly that CIA interrogations did not violate the Convention against Torture, "not only because the agency had conducted abusive interrogations but also because its policies authorized treatment that she considered cruel, inhuman, and degrading." Similarly, she reportedly told friends that "a senior agency official failed to provide a full account of the CIA's detainee treatment policy at a closed hearing of the House Intelligence committee in February 2005, under questioning by Rep. Jane Harman."[137]

McCarthy's fate stands in contrast to that of peers and superiors who pushed, backed, carried out, and concealed or destroyed evidence of the agency's brutal excesses. On November 9, 2010, with the statute of limitations about to expire for filing criminal charges for the destruction of the Abu Zubaydah and al-Nashiri interrogation tapes, the Justice Department Public Affairs Director Matthew Miller released this short statement:

In January, 2008, Attorney General Michael Mukasey appointed Assistant United States Attorney John Durham to investigate the destruction by CIA personnel of videotapes of detainee interrogations. Since that time, a team of prosecutors and FBI agents led by Mr. Durham has conducted an exhaustive investigation into the matter. As a result of that investigation, Mr. Durham has concluded that he will not pursue criminal charges for the destruction of the interrogation tapes.[138]

November 9, 2010 was also the official publication date of former President George Bush's memoir *Decision Points*, in which he boasts of telling the CIA "Damn right!" he would approve the torture of Khalid Sheikh Mohammed. Defending the waterboarding of Mohammed, Abu Zubaydah, and Abd al-Rahim al-Nashiri, Bush continued to claim in publicity events to promote the book that the Enhanced Interrogation Techniques were legal under U.S. and international law. "We gained valuable information to protect the country, and it was the right thing to do, as far as I'm concerned," he insisted.

The world clearly disagreed. A few days earlier, a delegation from the United States appeared before the UN Human Rights Council to answer questions about its human rights record as part of the UN's mandatory Universal Periodic Review process. For three hours the delegation faced questions like this one, from Russia,

> What administrative and legislative steps are taken by the United States to hold accountable persons (including medical personnel) who had tortured detainees in U.S. secret prisons as well as detention centers in Bagram (Afghanistan) and Guantánamo Bay? What is being done to provide effective remedies to civilian victims of the "war on terror," including the detainees of the secret prisons and centers in Guantánamo and Bagram?

The Obama administration's State Department legal advisor Harold Koh assured the assembled nations that the United States was committed to abiding by the ban on torture and inhumane treatment—which explicitly requires nations to carry out criminal investigations of torture allegations, prosecute perpetrators, and make reparations to victims—and stated flatly, "Notwithstanding recent public allegations, to our knowledge, all credible allegations of detainee abuse by United States forces have been thoroughly investigated and appropriate corrective action has been taken." At a press conference after the session, Koh told the international press corps, "the Obama administration defines waterboarding as torture as a matter of law under the Convention against Torture; it's part of our legal obligation." Assistant Secretary of State Esther Brimmer, who led the U.S. delegation to Geneva, followed by declaring emphatically, "The prohibition against torture and cruel treatment applies to every U.S. official, every agency, everywhere in the world. There is an absolute prohibition as a matter of law and policy."

At a "Town Hall" meeting with NGOs later in the day, Koh elaborated on his claim that the U.S. had in fact investigated and settled all cases of torture, explaining that he was speaking specifically about abuse allegations involving detainees in the custody of the U.S. military; meanwhile, he said, the Justice Department had appointed Special Prosecutor John Durham to conduct an investigation of allegations involving civilians and civilian agencies, and that Durham's investigation was ongoing. When reporters asked Koh whether that investigation might reach those who had ordered waterboarding, Koh answered "the Attorney General has referred this very issue" to the Special Prosecutor. "Those investigations are ongoing. The question is not whether they would consider it; those discussions are going on right now."

When the Justice Department announced a few days later that Durham was declining to prosecute CIA officials for destroying the interrogation tapes, it signaled that he was indeed still considering criminal prosecutions relating to torture—but only in connection with the cases Helgerson had highlighted in his 2004 report where interrogators had used unauthorized techniques. Under investigation, still, were the CIA "debriefer" who had threatened al-Nashiri with the gun and drill—now known to be an Egyptian-American former FBI translator named "Albert"—and the agent who had doused Gul Rahman with water and left him shackled overnight in freezing temperatures in the Salt Pit in Afghanistan.

As Helgerson had discovered, Langley dispatched Albert to the Polish black site after Mitchell's team had judged al-Nashiri to be "compliant"; Albert "assessed" al-Nashiri and disagreed, ordering him hooded and shackled again and eventually threatening him with the handgun and power drill. In his report, Helgerson recorded that his office investigated the incident "and referred it findings to the criminal division of DoJ. On 11 September 2003, DoJ declined to prosecute and turned these matters over to CIA for disposition."[139] In September, 2010 the Associated Press learned that Albert and a superior identified as Mike had been reprimanded by the agency, and that Mike had retired and Albert had left the agency as well. But, the AP reported, "Albert returned at some point as a contractor, training CIA officers in northern Virginia to handle different scenarios they might face in the field, according to former officials."[140]

On June 30, 2011, Attorney General Eric Holder announced that Durham had completed his investigation:

Mr. Durham and his team reviewed a tremendous volume of information pertaining to the detainees. That review included both information and matters that had never previously been examined by the Department. Mr. Durham has advised me of the results of his investigation, and I have accepted his recommendation to conduct a full criminal investigation regarding the death in custody of two individuals. Those investigations are ongoing. The Department has determined that an expanded criminal investigation of the remaining matters is not warranted.[141]

Among the matters the Justice Department determined did not deserve further investigation was the mock execution of Abd al-Rahim al-Nashiri; once again, Albert escaped prosecution. Instead, after reportedly reviewing 101 cases involving detainees in CIA custody, federal prosecutors are reportedly still considering charges in connection with the death of Manadel al-Jawadi, whose ice-packed corpse was the subject of several celebratory Abu Ghraib photos,[142] and Gul Rahman at the Salt Pit in Afghanistan.

The Salt Pit investigation centers on a young agent identified as "Matt," a former Naval intelligence officer who joined the CIA and was put in charge of an operation for which he had no experience or training. In the weeks before he ordered Rahman to be dragged around his concrete cell, doused with water, and left shackled overnight as the temperature plummeted, Matt had repeatedly pressed the CIA's Afghanistan station chief for both heaters and guidance on running a secret prison. He received neither.[143]

When Helgerson conducted his Special Review, he faulted the agency for "fail[ing] to provide adequate staffing, guidance, and support to those involved with the detention and interrogation of detainees," but also specifically recommended that Gul Rahman's death be referred to the Justice Department for prosecution. The department declined to act, however, citing the contorted logic of the OLC memos. In his 2009 Classified Response to the Justice Department's Official of Professional Responsibility report on the shortcomings of those memos, Jay Bybee continued to insist that the agency's declination memorandum on the case "provides a *correct* explanation" of the August 1, 2002 Standards of Conduct's "specific intent" argument, and that if Matt, "as manager of the Saltpit site, did not intend for Rahman to suffer severe pain from low temperature in his cell, he would lack the specific intent under the anti-torture statute."[144]

If not for redaction errors in the declassified version of Bybee's response that left intact the names of Gul Rahman and the CIA's Salt Pit manager, Gul Rahman's family would never have known what happened to him. From the time he was seized from a home in Islamabad on October 29, 2002 until the OPR report was released in February, 2010, the man who was tortured to death in Afghanistan three weeks after he disappeared into U.S. custody had no name, and the United States had done nothing to notify his wife and four daughters or the International Committee of the Red Cross of his whereabouts or fate. Now the family, which reportedly lives in a refugee camp outside Peshawar, Pakistan, is trying to recover his body—the body "Matt" had spirited away to an unmarked grave. Covering the family's efforts in January, 2011, the Associated Press reported that the CIA had refused a Freedom of Information Act request for the autopsy report of Gul Rahman's killing and "declined to comment on the return of Rahman's remains."[145]

Annotations on this section from TheTortureReport.org

On the CIA's internal review of the videotapes, blogger Marcy Wheeler ("emptywheel") pointed to the September 19, 2009 sworn statement by a CIA information review officer Wendy Hilton, available at http://www.aclu.org/pdfs/safefree/acluvdod_decl_hilton_09222009.pdf:

The CIA has more recently said they also did the review to set up an affirmative defense for interrogators. Wendy Hilton's description of Doc 60 (which appears to be the January 9 document described as "reflect[ing] the CIA attorneys view on what facts were relevant to determine whether the interrogation of Abu Zubaydah was compliant with law and policy") noted:

"Throughout the CIA's terrorist interrogation program the CIA was

concerned that its officers could face civil and criminal liability for their actions. The CIA directed its attorneys to review the record of the first interrogations to ensure that they were conducted consistent with the Department of Justice's guidance, which could arguably provide a defense to possible domestic and international criminal and civil liability. Therefore, while the CIA attorneys may have performed their analysis to determine legal and policy compliance, that analysis was in the context of evaluating possible defenses for anticipated civil and criminal litigation."

On Mitchell and Jessen's methods, former Air Force criminal investigator and interrogator Matthew Alexander wrote,

Why would the CIA be permitted to use techniques that the U.S. military has clearly found to be both morally wrong and counterproductive? If our men and women in uniform were able to accomplish their missions without the use of enhanced interrogation techniques through the World Wars, Korea, Vietnam, and up to 9/11, what changed?

Some might argue that the enemy we face today is more capable in resisting interrogations and harsh (read: torture and abuse) interrogation techniques were required. If Major Sherwood Moran, a Marine during World War II and our country's most famous interrogator, were alive today, he would choke. Consider Imperial Japanese soldiers during World War II— suicide bombers, blind loyalty to their leader, brutal tactics, brainwashed, dedicated, formidable, aggressive, etc. Major Moran successfully interrogated captured Japanese soldiers because he used relationship-building approaches along with his knowledge of Japanese culture (he had been a missionary in Japan for forty years before the start of the war). The axioms that he put to paper in his "Suggestions for Japanese Interpreters Based on Work in the Field" lay out the methods he used to success in interrogating the Japanese— and not one mention of using an enhanced interrogation technique.

Perhaps the most disturbing part of this chapter is not the actual techniques or the cover-up of the unlawful use of torture and abuse, but the failure of leadership. Leaders failed to recognize that torture and abuse is

inconsistent with American principles and counterproductive to preventing future terrorist attacks. This wisdom is plainly laid out in every version of the Army Field Manual since 1949, but leaders shouldn't need a Field Manual to know that torture and abuse goes against every fiber of what it means to be American.

On the administration's interactions with Congress, Marcy Wheeler noted,

In their briefing on the IG report in July 2004, the CIA and Roberts/ Rockefeller specifically discussed the Convention against Torture; see http:// intelligence.senate.gov/pdfs/olcopinion.pdf. It appears clear from later issues that Rockefeller was pushing the Agency on whether the program complied with CAT.

TWO:

THE PONZI SCHEME

THE SCHEME

On November 19, 2009, U.S. Federal District Judge Gladys Kessler issued an opinion on the habeas corpus petition of a Guantánamo detainee named Farhi Saeed bin Mohammed, ordering the government to "take all necessary and appropriate diplomatic steps to facilitate Petitioner's release forthwith."[146]

Farhi Saeed bin Mohammed is a 50-year-old Algerian who had lived as an illegal immigrant in Europe since 1989, first in France, then Italy, and finally in the United Kingdom, which he entered on a false passport on January 7, 2001, hoping, he said, to find a better job. In June, he flew to Pakistan, and he went from Pakistan to Afghanistan in July, in pursuit, he has insisted, of a Swedish woman who had agreed to marry him and help regularize his immigration status. After the September 11, 2001 terrorist attacks and the U.S. invasion of Afghanistan in October, bin Mohammed crossed back into Pakistan, where he was picked up by Pakistani police. He was interviewed by Americans, turned over to American custody, and became one of the first captives to be flown to Guantánamo in February 2002.

Since the Supreme Court affirmed in 2008 that Guantánamo detainees have the constitutional right to file habeas corpus petitions in federal courts, the government had been required to show, by a "preponderance of evidence," that the prisoner's detention was justified; to be justified, the government had to show that the detainee was a member or "substantial supporter" of Al Qaeda or the Taliban. In Farhi Saeed bin Mohammed's case, as in many others, the government relied on a "mosaic" of evidence to establish bin Mohammed's status as an enemy combatant, in which the information supporting the allegation, taken as a whole, "comes together to support a conclusion that shows the Petitioner to be justifiably detained." That evidence can include hearsay and other information not admissible in criminal proceedings; in bin Mohammed's case, it ranged from "second-level hearsay to allegations…obtained by torture to the fact that no statement purports to be a verbatim account of what was said."[147]

The evidence that Farhi Saeed bin Mohammed belonged to Al Qaeda or the Taliban consisted of the fact that he had used aliases and false passports; that he attended mosques in London with extremist affiliations; that he had traveled to Pakistan, and from there to Afghanistan; that he stayed in a guesthouse in Afghanistan that facilitated the transfer of recruits to training camps in the region; and that he went from there to train at an Al Qaeda camp before fleeing to Pakistan after the September 11, 2001 terrorist attacks. Judge Kessler ruled that the government's evidence supported all of the allegations up through the alleged stay at the guesthouse. The court said,

> Mohammed's stated reason for going to Afghanistan is entirely implausible. Further, he provides inconsistent accounts of his stay at the Jalalabad guesthouse. These findings undermine his attempts to defeat credible evidence put forth by the Government that Mohammed lived among al-Qaida supporters while there. The Government has established that it is more likely than not that he traveled there as part of a recruiting pipeline. Therefore, the Court credits the Government's evidence regarding Petitioner's earlier conduct.[148]

But staying at a guesthouse with links to Al Qaeda did not prove that bin Mohammed had joined Al Qaeda or the Taliban. That assertion depended on the testimony of another detainee:

The Government argues that Petitioner left the Jalalabad guesthouse to train at an al-Qaida camp, and then returned to Jalalabad before fleeing the country for Pakistan after September 11.... Its chief support for this argument consists of the statement of Binyam Mohamed, who told interrogators at Guantánamo Bay in October and November of 2004 that Petitioner attended a training camp with him.[149]

There was, however, a problem with this allegation:

Petitioner contends that Binyam Mohamed's statements—the only other evidence placing Petitioner in a training camp—cannot be relied upon, because he suffered intense and sustained physical and psychological abuse while in American custody from 2002 to 2004. Petitioner argues that while Binyam Mohamed was detained at locations in Pakistan, Morocco, and Afghanistan, he was tortured and forced to admit a host of allegations, most of which he has since denied. When he arrived at Guantánamo Bay, Binyam Mohamed implicated Petitioner in training activities. However, after being released from Guantánamo Bay, he signed a sworn declaration claiming that he never met Petitioner until they were both detained at Guantánamo Bay, thereby disavowing the statements he made at Guantánamo Bay about training with Petitioner. In that sworn declaration Binyam Mohamed stated that he was forced to make untrue statements about many detainees, including Petitioner. Binyam Mohamed stated he made these statements because of "torture or coercion," that he was "fed a large amount of information" while in detention, and that he resorted to making up some stories.[150]

"The Government does not challenge Petitioner's evidence of Binyam Mohamed's abuse," Kessler noted. Rather, it argued that the statements made to an FBI interrogator once he got to Guantánamo were not coerced—that, in fact, he had been "cordial and cooperative." The report of his first interview in Cuba on October 29, 2004 "begins by describing various courtesies extended to the detainee, such as using a traditional Muslim greeting and offering him coffee...There was a brief exchange about Binyam Mohamed's health, and '[s]ubject detainee commented that he was doing well.' The meeting lasted for over two hours, was conducted in English, and was [redacted]"

> *After this prologue, the report indicates that Binyam Mohamed was shown a total of 27 photographs of various individuals, and identified 12 of them....He identified Petitioner by his kunya, "Abdullah," claiming that Petitioner "trained at the Algerian Camp with [him] and ... eventually traveled to Kandahar with to [sic] him....Special Agent [redacted] notes at the end of his report that the subject was "very cooperative and polite," and that he answered questions without betraying "signs of deception or resistance techniques." Further, Binyam Mohamed "at many times" spoke freely without being questioned or prompted, and the information that he provided was deemed to be consistent with earlier information that he provided, though it does not state where Binyam Mohamed provided the earlier information.[151]*

Binyam Mohamed repeated the assertions about Farhi Saeed bin Mohammed when he was interrogated again the next month—again, government attorneys insisted, without coercion. Whether or not he had been mistreated before he arrived at Guantánamo, the government argued, enough time had passed since he was abused and the circumstances of the Guantanámo interviews were sufficiently benign that these allegations were credible and admissible.

Judge Kessler disagreed. Courts have never held that after a certain amount of time the "taint of earlier mistreatment" dissipates, she ruled. "This Court concludes that the temporal break in this case was not long enough—given the length of the abuse, its severity, and the fact that it was targeted to overwhelm the Petitioner mentally as well as physically—to 'insulate the statement from the effect of all that went before.'"

First, Binyam Mohamed's lengthy and brutal experience in detention weighs heavily with the Court. For example, this is not a case where a person was repeatedly questioned by a police officer, in his own country, by his own fellow-citizens, at a police station, over several days without sleep and with only minimal amounts of food and water. See Ashcraft v. State of Tenn, 322 U.S. 143, 153-154 (1944); Reck v. Pate, 367 U.S. 433, 440-441 (1961) (murder suspect held incommunicado for eight days, questioned extensively for four, and interrogated while sick). While neither the Ashcroft nor Reck scenarios are to be approved, they can hardly compare with the facts alleged here.

The difference, of course, is that Binyam Mohamed's trauma lasted for two long years. During that time, he was physically and psychologically tortured. His genitals were mutilated. He was deprived of sleep and food. He was summarily transported from one foreign prison to another. Captors held him in stress positions for days at a time. He was forced to listen to piercingly loud music and the screams of other prisoners while locked in a pitch-black cell. All the while, he was forced to inculpate himself and others in various plots to imperil Americans. The Government does not dispute this evidence.[152]

She continues:

...[E]ven though the identity of individual interrogators changed (from nameless Pakistanis, to Moroccans, to Americans, and to Special Agent [redacted]), there is no question that throughout his ordeal Binyam Mohamed was being held at the behest of the United States. Captors changed the sites of his detention, and frequently changed his location within each detention facility. He was shuttled from country to country, and interrogated and beaten without having access to counsel until arriving at Guantánamo Bay, after being

interrogated by Special Agent [redacted]. See JE 72 (declaration of Binyam Mohamed's attorney, Clive Stafford Smith, stating that he did not meet with client until May of 2005).

From Binyam Mohamed's perspective, there was no legitimate reason to think that transfer to Guantánamo Bay foretold more humane treatment, it was, after all, the third time that he had been forced onto a plane and shuttled to a foreign country where he would be held under United States authority. Further, throughout his detention, a constant barrage of physical and psychological abuse was employed in order to manipulate him and program him into telling investigators what they wanted to hear. It is more than plausible that, in an effort to please Special Agent [redacted] (consistent with how captors taught him how to behave), he re-told such a story, adding details, such as Petitioner's presence at training, which he thought would be helpful and, above all, would bring an end to his nightmare.[153]

✻ ✻ ✻

When Abu Zubaydah was captured on March 28, 2002, seven others were also taken into custody in the raid on the safe house in Faisalbad, Pakistan. Six of these men were sent directly to Guantánamo. The seventh, a 19-year-old Syrian youth named Noor al-Deen, who was also shot during the raid, was not. As the *Washington Post* has reported, "Perhaps because of his youth and agitated state, he readily answered U.S. questions, officials said, and the questioning went on for months, first in Pakistan and later in a detention facility in Morocco." CIA agent John Kiriakou, who participated in the raid, told the reporter, "He was frightened—mostly over what we were going to do to him. He had come to the conclusion that his life was over."[154]

What al-Deen told his captors, and what he evidently repeated after being subjected to extraordinary rendition and imprisoned in Morocco, was that Abu Zubaydah, whom he reportedly idolized, was not a senior Al Qaeda figure, but rather someone who arranged travel and logistics for recruits looking for training in a variety of camps, some affiliated with Al Qaeda and some, like the Khalden camp with which Abu Zubaydah had been associated in the 1990s, frequently at odds with Al Qaeda and geared to training young men volunteering to fight in Bosnia and Chechnya. As such, though he interacted frequently with Al Qaeda's leaders, Abu Zubaydah was neither a planner nor a party to plans for the September 11, 2001 attacks or other major Al Qaeda operations.[155]

Despite al-Deen's warnings, on April 9, 2002, a little over a week after Abu Zubaydah had been strapped to a gurney and flown to the CIA black site in Thailand, George Bush told an audience at a Connecticut Republican Committee fundraising luncheon, "The other day, we hauled in a guy named Abu Zubaydah. He's one of the top operatives plotting death and destruction on the United States. He's not plotting and planning anymore. He's where he belongs."[156]

The next day, Binyam Mohamed was arrested with a false passport at Karachi airport as he tried to board a flight bound for London, where he had lived as a legal immigrant for the past seven years.

Mohamed, who was 23 at the time, was born in Ethiopia but left the country in 1992 when his father, an executive of the state-owned airline, looked for refuge overseas following the collapse of the regime of Mengistu Haile Mariam. They lived in the Washington DC area for two years, then tried the UK, and then, at 16, Binyam found himself on his own in London when his father decided to return to the U.S. for work. He attended high school and junior college, but by the time he was 20 he had an admitted drug problem. He got a job as a janitor in a West London mosque when he was 22, converted to Islam, and a few months later flew to Islamabad with the intention, he has insisted, of kicking his drug habit for good.

He has admitted spending time at a guest house in Jalalabad, where he met Chechen rebels, and then taking a forty-five-day "boot camp" course that included small arms training at a camp in Afghanistan, hoping, he says, to support the cause in Chechnya. He fled to Pakistan in the stream of refugees following the U.S. invasion of Afghanistan, determined to return to London. He booked a flight on April 3, 2002 but was turned away because his passport looked suspicious. He tried again a week later, and this time was apprehended. He spent ten days in a Pakistani prison without being interrogated.

Then, on April 20, 2002, he was moved to a Pakistani intelligence service interrogation center, where he was greeted by FBI agents. "He asked for an attorney and refused to speak with them, since he said the Americans had nothing to do with him," his attorney recorded in notes from his first interview with his client in Guantánamo in May of 2005. Mohamed told him, "I refused to talk in Karachi until they gave me a lawyer. I said it was my right to have a lawyer. The FBI said, The law has been changed. There are no lawyers. You can cooperate with us—the easy way, or the hard way."[157]

His attorney's notes continue:

There was 4 small cells, each 2m x 2.5m. While there, he was hung up for a week by a leather strap around the wrists. He could only just stand. He was only allowed down to go to the toilet twice a day. He was given food, normally rice and beans, once every second day. "It was the first thing that happened to me. I just thought it would end. There were threats of beating, though."

Mohamed described four FBI interrogators: "Chuck," a white male around 40; "Terry," a white male around 50; an unnamed light-skinned black male, 35, who spoke Swahili, and "Jenny," a fortyish white female.

The FBI seemed to think that because he had lived in the U.S. for a short while he had plans to do something there. "But I'm going to the UK," Binyam would say.

The FBI also seemed to think that he was some kind of top al-Qaida person.

"How? It's been less than six months since I converted to Islam! Before that, I was into using drugs," Binyam would say. Indeed, he had traveled in part to help try to kick the habit.

On the first day of interrogations, 'Chuck' said, "If you don't talk to me, you're going to Jordan. We can't do what we want here, the Pakistanis can't do exactly what we want them to. The Arabs will deal with you."

It was at this point that Binyam told them his name and address. Chuck checked with the British and this was true.

'Terry' asked the same questions. "I'm going to send you to Jordan or Israel," he said. Then he threatened to send him to the British. "The SAS know how to deal with people like you."

It was after Terry's visit that they started the torture.

The Pakistanis could not speak English, and Binyam could not understand them. They would just come in and beat him with a leather strap. It had a handle, and then leather with a joint making the rounded end part whip back on him.

One Pakistani pointed some kind of gun at Binyam's chest. It was a semi-automatic, and he loaded it in front of Binyam. "He pressed it against my chest. He just stood there. I knew I was going to die. He stood like that for five minutes. I looked into his eyes, and I saw my own fear reflected there. I had time to think about it. Maybe he will pull the trigger and I will not die, but be paralyzed. There was enough time to think the possibilities through."

'Chuck' came in after that. He said nothing. He stared at me and left.[158]

This interrogation lasted for a week. It played out at exactly the same time that the FBI and CIA interrogation teams were engaged in the tug-of-war over the interrogation of Abu Zubaydah in the CIA's black site in Thailand.[159] Mitchell's CIA interrogators had interrupted the apparently fruitful sessions with FBI agents Ali Soufan and his partner and instituted nudity and sleep deprivation, and Abu Zubaydah had stopped talking. As Soufan told the Senate Judiciary Committee in his May 13, 2009 testimony, "After a few days of getting no information, and after repeated inquiries from DC asking why all of a sudden no information was being transmitted (when before there had been a steady stream), we again were given control of the interrogation."[160]

"We then returned to using the Informed Interrogation Approach." Soufan told the Senate. "Within a few hours, Abu Zubaydah again started talking and gave us important actionable intelligence. This included the details of Jose Padilla, the so-called 'dirty bomber.'"[161] Despite the extraordinary secrecy surrounding the CIA's RDI program, on April 23, 2002, BBC news reported "The al-Qaeda terror network knows how to build a 'dirty bomb,' a senior Osama Bin Laden aide is reported to have told U.S. interrogators. Abu Zubaydah —Bin Laden's chief of operations until his capture in Pakistan last month—said the organization also knew how to smuggle it into the United States, unnamed U.S. officials have been quoted as saying." The report went on

> But the officials said there were highly skeptical of the credibility of Abu Zubaydah's claim, who also recently said al-Qaeda was targeting banks in the United States. That report was the basis of an FBI alert last week.
> "It could be he's not being truthful. It could be that he's boasting," a U.S. official told the Associated Press news agency.[162]

Nevertheless, the dirty bomb story immediately began to shape and dominate interrogations. "Every interrogator would ask questions about it," a former CIA officer said in a 2009 interview.[163] That week in Pakistan, Binyam Mohamed's FBI interrogators asked him if he had been trained in radiological weapons. Mohamed told 'Chuck' that when he was at the safe house in Afghanistan, he had visited a website with instructions on how to build an atomic bomb. The instructions, in fact, were from a 1979 satirical article by Barbara Ehrenreich, Peter Biskind, and Michio Kaku titled "How to Make Your Own H-Bomb"; the piece included directions such as

> First transform the gas into a liquid by subjecting it to pressure. You can use a bicycle pump for this. Then make a simple home centrifuge. Fill a standard-size bucket one-quarter full of liquid uranium hexafluoride. Attach a six-foot rope to the bucket handle. Now swing the rope (and attached bucket) around your head as fast as possible. Keep this up for about 45 minutes. Slow down gradually, and very

gently put the bucket on the floor. The U-235, which is lighter, will have risen to the top, where it can be skimmed off like cream.[164]

"It was obviously a joke: it never crossed my mind that anyone would take it seriously," Mohamed has said.

But that's when [Chuck] started getting all excited. Towards the end of April he began telling me about this A-bomb I was supposed to be building, and he started on about Osama Bin Laden and his top lieutenants, showing me pictures and making out I must have known them.[165]

Days later, on May 8, 2002, Jose Padilla was quietly arrested at Chicago O'Hare Airport. Five minutes before his flight from Zurich landed, then-U.S. District Court Judge Michael Mukasey signed a material witness warrant authorizing Padilla's arrest. That warrant was issued on the strength of a Material Witness Warrant Affidavit signed by FBI agent Joe Ennis. According to the government's description of that affidavit,

On or about April 23, 2002, Abu Zubaydah was shown two photographs, one that was taken from the U.S. passport of Jose Padilla, which had been recovered from Padilla's person. Abu Zubaydah identified the individual in that photograph as the person he knew as "Abdullah Al Muhajir." [The name Jose Padilla adopted when he converted to Islam] The other photograph was taken from a fake passport recovered from Binyam Muhammed, which Abu Zubaydah identified as the individual in the company of the "South American."

Abu Zubaydah further stated that Padilla and Binyam Muhammad had asked Abu Zubaydah for his opinion on their plan to build an explosive device that would combine uranium or other nuclear or radioactive material with an "ordinary" explosive device (hereinafter called a "dirty bomb") and then detonating the dirty bomb in the United States. Abu Zubaydah told Padilla and Binyam Muhammad that he (Abu Zubaydah) did not think the plan would work, but Binyam Muhammad thought it would work. Abu Zubaydah also indicated to the government that he did not think Padilla and Binyam Muhammad were members of Al Qaeda. Abu Zubaydah further stated that he believed the dirty bomb plan was still in the idea phase, as Padilla and Binyam Muhammad did not have any radioactive material yet, but they mentioned stealing radioactive material from an unnamed university. Abu Zubaydah believed that Padilla and Binyam Muhammad had consulted an unidentified Internet website to learn how to assemble a dirty bomb....

The affidavit then turned to information provided from an interview of Binyam Muhammad in early April, 2002. The affiant explained that Binyam Muhammad had been detained in Pakistan by the Pakistani authorities while trying to board a flight, on suspicions that his non-U.S. passport was fraudulent (which it was). The affiant explained that he had read reports prepared based on the interview of Binyam Muhammad, and had spoken with other law enforcement officers regarding this interview. Binyam Muhammad stated that he went to Pakistan at the behest of Abu Zubaydah to receive training in "wiring explosives." Binyam Muhammad further stated that, while in Pakistan, he and Padilla researched the construction of a uranium-enhanced device, which would be detonated in the United States. Binyam Muhammad and Padilla discussed this plan with Abu Zubaydah, who referred them to other members of Al Qaeda for further discussion of the operation.[166]

The affidavit makes no mention of the conditions under which this "interview" was conducted; nor, apparently, did an April 26, 2002 communication from the U.S. to the British Security Services, the "SyS," and the UK Secret Intelligence Service, the "SIS." The U.S. had alerted the British government on April 22 that it had detained someone using a fake British passport; four days later, the U.S. reported that the person had identified himself as Binyam Mohamed and that Mohamed had provided information that he was "planning to construct and detonate a 'dirty bomb.'"[167] Concluding from this that "BM was a person whose activities would be of importance to the SyS in protecting the vital interests of the national security of the United Kingdom," the British government insisted on sending its own agents to interview Mohamed.

Subsequent telegrams and communications from the U.S. were evidently more candid about the circumstances of his detention. Those reports, in the judgment of Britain's High Court of Justice, corroborated Mohamed's account of his interrogation in Pakistan sufficiently to "give rise to an arguable case of cruel, inhuman, or degrading treatment or torture."

By May, 2002, the U.S. and the Blair government had already had several skirmishes about the treatment of detainees in U.S. custody. British agents had deployed to Afghanistan in late September, 2001 to provide covert support for the impending U.S. military action, and in December the governments agreed that SyS agents could interview some detainees. The first agents arrived at Bagram Air Base on January 9, 2002, and the following day an SIS agent participated in an interrogation. Though he reported afterwards that the interview itself was conducted in accordance with the Geneva conventions, he expressed concern about the U.S. military's treatment of the detainee prior to the session. London wrote back, copying all SIS and SyS officers in Afghanistan:

> With regard to the status of the prisoners, under the various Geneva Conventions and protocols, all prisoners, however they are described, are entitled to the same levels of protections. You have commented on their treatment. It appears from your description that they may not be being treated in accordance with the appropriate standards....
>
> It is important that you do not engage in any activity yourself that involves inhumane or degrading treatment of prisoners. As a representative of a UK public authority, you are obliged to act in accordance with the Human Rights Act 2000 which prohibits torture, or inhumane or degrading treatment. Also as a Crown Servant, you are bound by Section 31 of the Criminal Justice Act 1948, which makes acts carried out overseas in the course of your official duties subject to UK criminal law. In other words, your actions incur criminal liability in the same way as if you were carrying out those acts in the UK."[168]

"The torture stopped when the British came," Mohamed told his lawyer when they met in Guantánamo in 2005. He described two British secret service agents, one named John and the other unnamed:

They gave me a cup of tea with a lot of sugar in it. I initially only took one.

"No, you need a lot more. Where you're going you need a lot of sugar." I didn't know exactly what he meant by this, but I figured he meant some poor country in Arabia. One of them did tell me that I was going to get tortured by the Arabs.

'John' questioned Binyam. Binyam said he wanted a lawyer.

"How can I help you?" he asked.

"I don't know," said Binyam.

"I'll see what we can do with the Americans," he said, promising to tell Binyam what would happen to him. He did not see him again.[169]

This meeting took place at the Pakistani secret services interrogation facility in Karachi on May 17, 2002. One of the two interrogators sent a cable to his superiors immediately afterwards describing the scene this way:

I told [BM] that he had an opportunity to help us and help himself. The U.S. authorities will be deciding what to do with him and this would depend to a very large degree on his degree of cooperation. I said that if he could persuade me he was telling the complete truth I would seek to use my influence to help him. He asked how, and said he didn't expect ever to get out of the situation he was in. I said it must be obvious to him that he would get more lenient treatment if he cooperated. I said that I could not and would not negotiate up front, but if he persuaded me he was cooperating fully then (and only then) I would explore what could be done for him with my U.S. colleagues. It was, however, clear that, while he appeared happy to answer any questions, he was holding back a great deal of information on who and what he knew in the UK and in Afghanistan.[170]

The agent specifically noted that during that interview, Mohamed dismissed the "dirty bomb" allegation as "the FBI perception." "The real story was that he had seen a file on a computer in Lahore and decided it was a joke—part of the instructions included adding bleach to uranium 238 in a bucket and rotating it around one's head for 45 minutes," the agent recorded.[171]

Nevertheless, despite the fact Mohamed had openly discussed his affiliations in London and his time at a training camp in Afghanistan, the agent concluded he was withholding information. And despite the fact that the agent had seen reports from U.S. intelligence agencies describing the treatment Mohamed had endured in Pakistan prior to this interview, treatment that included prolonged *strappado* suspension, sleep deprivation, and mock execution, the agent concluded, "I suspect that he will only begin to provide information of genuine value if he comes to believe that it is genuinely in his interests to do so. I don't think he has yet reached this point."[172]

* * *

On June 10, 2002, Attorney General John Ashcroft interrupted a series of meetings he was attending in Moscow to announce via satellite "a significant step forward in the war on terrorism." "We have captured a known terrorist who was exploring a plan to build and explode a radiological dispersion device, or 'dirty bomb,' in the United States," Ashcroft said gravely, citing "multiple independent and corroborating sources" for the intelligence behind the arrest. Insisting that the suspect's apprehension a month before at O'Hare Airport had "disrupted an unfolding terrorist plot to attack the United States," he broke the news that the administration was taking the historically unprecedented action of denying a U.S. citizen apprehended in the United States access to American courts.

Yesterday, after consultation with the acting secretary of defense and other senior officials, both the acting secretary of defense and I recommended that the president of the United States, in his capacity as commander in chief, determine that Abdullah al Muhajir, born Jose

Padilla, is an enemy combatant who poses a serious and continued threat to the American people and our national security. After the determination, Abdullah al Muhajir was transferred from the custody of the Justice Department to the custody of the Defense Department.[173]

At a Justice Department press conference in Washington later that day, Deputy Secretary of Defense Paul Wolfowitz announced that "as of today" Padilla was being held at the Naval Consolidated Brig in Charleston, South Carolina, and he reiterated that Padilla had "met with senior Al Qaeda members to discuss plans for exploding a radioactive device" and had "researched nuclear weapons." But the administration was already backpedaling on Ashcroft's assertion that Padilla's arrest had thwarted an attack in progress. Pressed by reporters on whether Padilla possessed the materials for a dirty bomb, FBI Director Robert Mueller said the plot had been "in the discussion stage," adding, "and it had not gone, as far as we know, much past the discussion stage, but there were substantial discussions undertaken."[174]

The next day, Wolfowitz went on national television again, this time to say "I don't think there was actually a plot beyond some fairly loose talk and his coming in here obviously to plan further deeds."[175] At the same time, the administration was leaking to Fox News that "the American accused of plotting with Al Qaeda terrorists to detonate a 'dirty bomb' to spread radioactive material, possibly targeting Washington," had an accomplice. "Law enforcement sources told Fox News another man named Benjamin Ahmed Mohammed was implicated in the plot and was taken into custody in Pakistan 'recently,' perhaps late last month," Fox reported. "One official said he would continue to be detained in Pakistan and there are currently no plans to bring him to the United States."[176] At a press briefing before a meeting with Congressional leaders at the White House, a reporter asked President Bush if "107 radiation sources" the Nuclear Regulatory Commission had reported missing might be in Al Qaeda's hands, and the President answered, "We will run down every lead, every hint. This guy Padilla's a bad guy, and he is where he needs to be, detained."[177]

Press descriptions of Padilla stressed his criminal past; he was a former

Chicago gang member who had spent several years in juvenile detention for his involvement in a robbery that ended in murder, and who had been jailed again as an adult in Florida for pulling a gun during a road rage incident. Ashcroft had suggested Padilla's path led straight from prison to Afghanistan; few follow-up reports mentioned that ten years had passed since he had been released from jail, during which he got married, worked alongside his wife at a Taco Bell, and converted with her to Islam, a process that had begun behind bars when he pledged to turn his life around and began reading the bible. Like Binyam Mohamed, Padilla looked to Islam for a sense of structure and stability. When his marriage faltered in 1998, Padilla went to Cairo to study Arabic and teach English, married again, and had two sons. He went to Saudi Arabia for the hajj in early 2000, and later to Afghanistan, hoping, he has said, that he could join the resistance in Chechnya.

Until his transfer to the brig in South Carolina, Padilla was held on a high security floor of the Metropolitan Correctional Facility in New York, where he had been delivered a week after he was taken into custody at O'Hare on the material witness warrant. It was by all accounts an undramatic arrest:

> Agents Fincher and Donnachie, along with Chicago FBI agents Robert Holley and Todd Schmitt, participated in an interview of Padilla in a conference room, which began at approximately 3:15 p.m. and ended sometime between 7:05 and 7:35 p.m. when Padilla declined to speak further to agents without an attorney....
>
> Near the end of the interview, but prior to actually placing Padilla under arrest, Agent Fincher told Padilla that he would like Padilla to work with him and help him more fully understand the issues they had discussed. If Padilla were to volunteer, Agent Fincher explained, the FBI would arrange for a hotel that evening and they would all travel to New York the next day so that Padilla could then testify in front of a grand jury in New York. Otherwise, Agent Fincher indicated that he would have to serve Padilla with a grand jury subpoena, which he showed to Padilla, to compel his testimony before the

grand jury. Padilla asked procedural questions about the grand jury
subpoena process, which Agent Fincher answered. After considering
the information, Padilla stated that he was not going to volunteer to
go to New York and that if Agent Fincher wanted him to go, he would
have to arrest Padilla. The same thing happened again: Agent Fincher
informed Padilla that he did have a Material Witness Warrant that
he could use to arrest Padilla, but that he would rather have Padilla
volunteer the information, and that he did not want to arrest Padilla.
Padilla responded that he was not going to volunteer and that Agent
Fincher would have to arrest him. Following this exchange, Padilla
was arrested by Agent Fincher and read his Miranda rights pursuant
to a Customs Advice of Rights Form.[178]

Padilla arrived at MCC on May 14, 2002. The following day he met
Donna Newman, his court-appointed attorney, when he was arraigned
before Judge Mukasey at the federal courthouse in New York. Over the
next several weeks the two met repeatedly; they were permitted to review
the Ennis affidavit on which the material witness warrant was based, and
Newman filed a motion arguing that material witnesses in grand jury
proceedings cannot legally be held in detention. Judge Mukasey was due
to rule on that motion on June 11. On Sunday, June 9, 2002, President
Bush signed a military order designating Padilla as an "enemy combatant"
and ordering the Justice Department to transfer him into the custody of
the Secretary of Defense, and Judge Mukasey granted the government's
application to vacate the material witness warrant. Newman was not
informed her client had been seized by the military until shortly before
Ashcroft's Moscow announcement the following day. She would not see
Padilla again for almost two years.

Meanwhile, in Pakistan the British government was growing uneasy
about its lack of access to Binyam Mohamed. SyS agents wanted to meet
with him again after the May 17 interview, but the U.S. had hinted he would
soon be transferred to Afghanistan. On June 11, the same day President
Bush was declaring Jose Padilla "a bad guy," SyS asked where he was and
requested to reinterview him, and the U.S. responded that his transfer was

imminent and asked that the British wait to interview Mohamed when he was in Afghanistan. A month later, an SyS telegram expressed frustration that it has received no further information on Mohamed's whereabouts and requested urgent information about his location. On July 15, the U.S. again told the SyS he would soon be sent to Afghanistan, where they would be able to see him. Another request by SyS for an update on July 31 went unanswered. Finally, "[o]n August 12, 2002, the SyS sought information from the SIS. They asked if on their routine visits to Bagram the SIS could check whether three individuals, including BM were at Bagram; the telegram stated "*** appear to have no information on his current whereabouts exclam."[179]

Around this time, Mohamed's brother and sister, both U.S. residents, received visits from FBI agents; when they asked where their brother was, the agents suggested he was in the custody of the Pakistani government. For the next several months, the siblings repeatedly sought further information from both the FBI and the Pakistani consulate in New York.[180]

By then, Binyam Mohamed was not in Pakistan or Afghanistan. On Friday July 19, 2002 Mohamed was flown on a commercial Pakistani International Airlines flight from Karachi to Islamabad, accompanied by two Pakistani officials but unrestrained. When the flight landed he was handcuffed and driven, first by bus then by pickup truck, to a detention facility where he was held until around 10 p.m. on Sunday night.[181] Then, as recorded in his attorney's notes,

> On July 21st, 2002, Binyam was taken to a military airport in Islamabad. There were two others with him. He was blindfolded, but it was very quiet. He was held there for about two hours.
>
> Once there, he was turned over to the Americans. The U.S. soldiers were dressed in black, with masks, wearing what looked like Timberland boots. They stripped him naked, took photos, put fingers up his anus, and dressed him in a tracksuit. He was shackled, with earphones, and blindfolded.
>
> He was put into a U.S. plane—he cannot say the size, but is sure it was some kind of official or military plane, rather than anything

*civilian, since it was so quiet on board before take off that there were
not many others on it.*

He was tied to the seat for the roughly 8 to 10 hour flight.[182]

Though the routine followed exactly the protocol described in the
CIA's December 30, 2004 "Background Paper on CIA's Combined Use
of Interrogation Techniques," Mohamed was not bound for a secret CIA
prison. And despite the fact that he had been identified publicly in the
U.S. as the accomplice of Jose Padilla, who was now being held as an
"enemy combatant," he was not headed either to Bagram or Guantánamo.
Instead,

*He was flown to an airport in Morocco where he arrived on July 22nd.
While he was blindfolded, he is sure there were two other prisoners
on the flight.*

He believes it may have been near Rabat.

Binyam believes that there was a U.S. military base near it.[183]

Flight records obtained in a 2006 investigation by Dick Marty, the
Swiss Rapporteur on Secret Detentions for the Parliamentary Assembly
of the Council of Europe, confirm that on July 21, 2002 a CIA-operated
Gulfstream V jet with the registration number N379P took off from
Islamabad and flew to Rabat, Morocco.[184]

When the flight landed, Mohamed was put in a van and driven for
forty-five minutes to a Moroccan interrogation facility, where he says the
purpose of his extraordinary rendition was immediately made clear:

*When I got to Morocco they said some big people in al-Qaida were
talking about me. They talked about Jose Padilla and they said I
was going to testify against him and big people. They named Khalid
Sheikh Mohammed, Abu Zubaydah, and Ibn Sheikh al-Libi. It was
hard to pin down the exact story because what they wanted changed
from Morocco to when later I was in the Dark Prison, to Bagram and
again in Guantánamo Bay.*

They told me that I must plead guilty. I'd have to say I was an al-Qaida operations man, an ideas man. I kept insisting that I had only been in Afghanistan a short while. "We don't care," was all they'd say.[185]

In his May 2005 conversation with his attorney in Guantánamo and in statements and interviews since, Mohamed has provided detailed and harrowing accounts of his treatment at this and another prison in Morocco over the next eighteen months. He described his "torture team" for his attorney, which included several Moroccans and one woman, "Sarah the Canadian," who was supposedly flown in to act as an intermediary.

The "Canadian" called "Sarah" came today. She said she was supposedly a "third party" only interested in talking to me, because I had refused to talk to the Moroccans and the Americans, so maybe I would talk to a Canadian.

"If you don't talk to me, then the Americans are getting ready to carry out the torture. They're going to electrocute you, beat you, and rape you." She seemed blasé about this, as if this was something normal. I listened to her, but I said I would not talk today.

A few days later:

Today "Sarah" came in with Mohammed, a Moroccan.

They had brought pictures, all of British people. "This is the British file," they said. "Sarah" picked up the pictures of two British people—Yusuf Jamaici and Amin Mohammed—and told their whole story, about how they were suspected of being al Qaida and other stuff.

They also brought pictures of about 25 of the "most wanted" al Qaida people. "I don't know these people."

"I'm giving you a last chance to think about cooperating with the U.S.," said 'Sarah.' They left me alone for a day to think about it, with no interrogation.[186]

At the end of this "softening up" phase, Mohamed was given to believe he would soon be released and returned to England. He was handcuffed as though he was about to be transported. Then, without warning, he was violently beaten. After that, Mohamed told his attorney, "the circle of torture began.

> They'd ask me a question. I'd say one thing. They'd say it was a lie. I'd say another. They'd say it was a lie. I could not work out what they wanted to hear.
> They say there's this guy who says you're the big man in al Qaida. I'd say it's a lie. They'd torture me. I'd say, okay it's true. They'd say, okay, tell us more. I'd say, I don't know more. They'd torture me again.[187]

After several such sessions, interspersed with beatings, one of his interrogators cut off his clothes with a scalpel and tied him against the wall.

> They took the scalpel to my right chest. It was only a small cut. Maybe an inch. At first I just screamed because the pain was just...I was just shocked, I wasn't expecting...
> Then they cut my left chest. This time I didn't want to scream because I knew it was coming.
> Marwan got agitated at this. "Just go ahead with the plan."
> One of them took my penis in his hand and began to make cuts. He did it once, and they stood still for maybe a minute, watching my reaction. I was in agony, crying, trying desperately to suppress myself, but I was screaming. I remember Marwan seemed to smoke a cigarette, throw it down, and start another.
> They must have done this 20 to 30 times, in maybe two hours. There was blood all over.[188]

Then, in September or October, 2002, shortly after Mitchell's CIA team had completed its month-long "enhanced interrogation" and repeated waterboarding of Abu Zubaydah in Thailand, Binyam Mohamed was

moved to another prison in Morocco. He would remain there for some
sixteen months. As Judge Kessler summarized Mohamed's accounts of his
experiences in this second location,

> *His new quarters are described in his diary in extreme detail,*
> *including a listing of the color of his sheets, the type of toothpaste he*
> *was given, and the brand of soap he was supplied. For days on end,*
> *he remained handcuffed with earphones on, and loud music blasted*
> *into his ears. This tactic, as well as others, interrupted his sleep for the*
> *whole time he was in Morocco. This treatment, in Binyam Mohamed's*
> *account, was the beginning of a campaign of mental torture designed*
> *to break him. He claims that his captors put mind-altering substances*
> *in his food, forced him to listen to sounds from adult films, drugged*
> *him, and paraded naked and semi-naked woman around his cell.*
>
> *He wrote that the mental torture led to "emotional breakdowns."*
> *Through this period, he was subject to two or three interrogations*
> *per month. These sessions are described as being "more like trainings,*
> *training [him on] what to say."*[189]

Around the time he was moved to this second location, on September
26, 2002, seven Bush administration lawyers, several of them members of
the self-proclaimed "War Council," boarded a Gulfstream jet in Washington
and flew to Guantánamo Bay, Cuba. The group, led by David Addington,
included White House Counsel Alberto Gonzales; William J. "Jim" Haynes
II, General Counsel of the Department of Defense; CIA attorney John
Rizzo; Alice Fisher, who worked for Michael Chertoff, then head of the
Criminal Division of the Justice Department; Patrick Philbin of the Office
of Legal Counsel; and Jack Goldsmith, who three weeks before had taken a
job in the General Counsel's office of the Pentagon.

The lawyers were on a field trip to check up on several of the
administration's more accessible interrogation experiments. At Guantánamo,
they toured a detention building at Camp Delta where two dozen detainees
were being held in wire cages, watched an interrogation, and grilled camp
commander General Michael Dunleavy about the unfolding interrogation

of Mohammed al-Qahtani. Three hours later, they reboarded the plane and flew to South Carolina.

Three and a half months before, on June 10, 2002, Padilla had signed two sheets of paper on his arrival at the modern naval prison in Charleston, agreeing to the brig rules.[190] Since then, he had been held alone in a wing of the brig in a cell whose windows were blackened so he couldn't tell whether it was night or day. He was being monitored constantly by video camera, fed through a slot in the door, refused a clock or calendar, and periodically denied light, a mattress, and the Koran. He had virtually no human contact other than with interrogators.[191]

There are no direct reports of what the White House attorneys saw during their hour tour and a briefing on Padilla's detention. After their visit, though, the lawyers flew on to Norfolk, Virginia to see the brig where the administration had been holding another U.S. citizen as an enemy combatant since April under a similar regime. Like Padilla, Yaser Hamdi was being detained in almost complete isolation in his own wing of a military prison and denied all contact with attorneys or the outside world. By the time Padilla was transferred to Charleston in June, Hamdi's Virginia jailers were already sending emails to their superiors expressing alarm about his mental state. "Unlike at Camp X-Ray this detainee has no other contact with his countrymen (as was and is still the case there), with nothing but time on his hands," one of the officers wrote. Writing again a week later to report that Hamdi was showing signs of depression, which he attributed to "the uncertainty of the detainees future and the unknown length of time he is to be incarcerated," the officer noted: "After eight months of incarceration in detention facilities (Kandahar, Camp X-Ray, Norfolk Brig) with no potential end in site and no encouraging news and isolated from his countrymen, I can understand how he feels."[192]

As the attorneys of the War Council toured the Norfolk Brig on September 26, 2002, at least one of them experienced a similar moment of empathy. Jack Goldsmith, who was celebrating his birthday that day, later wrote:

> *After being briefed on the conditions of Hamdi's confinement and learning about the very limited contact he had had with any human*

being during the previous six months, we shuffled through gloomy corridors to a guard station command center to have a look at Hamdi himself. Top administration lawyers crowded around the small black-and-white closed-circuit television bolted in the back corner of the room, and witnessed the barely twenty-two-year-old Hamdi—it was his birthday as well—in the corner of his small cell in an unused wing of the brig, crouched in a fetal position, apparently asleep.

Before I saw him on the closed-circuit television, I had no sympathy for Hamdi, whom I knew had volunteered to fight for the tyrannical Taliban. Witnessing the unmoving Hamdi on that fuzzy black-and-white screen, however, moved me. Something seemed wrong. It seemed unnecessarily extreme to hold a twenty-two-year-old foot soldier in a remote wing of a run-down prison in a tiny cell, isolated from almost all human contact and with no access to a lawyer. "This is what habeas corpus is for," I thought to myself, somewhat embarrassed at the squishy sentiment.[193]

In fact, both Hamdi and Padilla had pending habeas corpus petitions challenging their confinement in these conditions. In Padilla's case, Donna Newman had filed the writ the day after the White House announced he had been transferred to military custody. In it, she argued that the terms and conditions of Padilla's detention violated his rights under the Fourth, Fifth, and Sixth Amendments to the Constitution, and that holding him in military custody violated the Posse Comitatus Act's prohibitions on military involvement in domestic law enforcement activities.

At the end of August, as the CIA was completing its waterboarding of Abu Zubaydah and Binyam Mohamed was being tortured in Morocco, the government filed an affidavit in support of its position that the President was entitled to hold Padilla incommunicado. That affidavit, signed by Defense Department attorney Michael Mobbs, indicated that the information on which President Bush had relied in signing the June 9, 2002 order designating Padilla an enemy combatant and transferring him to military custody was largely the same as the information in the

Ennis affidavit used to secure the Material Witness warrant for his arrest the month before. But now, in addition to the alleged "dirty bomb" plot, Mobbs added that Padilla's discussions with Al Qaeda operatives also encompassed "other operations including the detonation of explosives in hotel rooms and gas stations." In a footnote, he explained, "These attacks were to involve multiple, simultaneous attacks on such targets, and also included train stations. The additional facts in this footnote were not included in the information provided to the President on June 9, 2002."[194]

Mobbs again cited "multiple intelligence sources, including reports of interviews with several confidential sources, two of whom were detained at locations outside of the United States," again without making any mention of the conditions of their detention or interrogation. In a footnote, though, he notes that one of the two "in a subsequent interview with a U.S. law enforcement officer recanted some of the information that he had provided, but most of this information has been independently corroborated by other sources."

On December 4, 2002 a U.S. District Court ruled that the President was entitled, as Commander-in-Chief, to arrest a U.S. citizen on American soil and transfer him to the military to hold as an enemy combatant. Moreover, in passing the 2001 Authorization for Use of Military Force, Congress had sanctioned the actions, and the courts, in deference to the president's war power, only had authority to conduct a minimal review to ensure there was "some evidence" to support his detention. However, the court ruled that Padilla should be allowed to consult with an attorney in preparing for such a review.

The administration refused, instead filing a motion for reconsideration of the ruling granting Padilla the right to see an attorney. Supporting this motion was a declaration by Vice Admiral Lowell Jacoby, Director of the Defense Intelligence Agency, insisting that any outside contact would interfere with Padilla's interrogation and making clear the administration intended to hold him until he broke. "One critical feature of the intelligence process is that it must be continuous," Lowell asserted. "Any interruption to the intelligence gathering process, especially from an external source, risks mission failure."[195]

Developing the kind of relationship of trust and dependency necessary for effective interrogations is a process that can take a significant amount of time. There are numerous examples of situations where interrogators have been unable to obtain valuable intelligence from a subject until months, or even years, after the interrogation process began.

Anything that threatens the perceived dependency and trust between the subject and interrogator directly threatens the value of interrogation as an intelligence gathering tool. Even seemingly minor interruptions can have profound psychological impacts on the delicate subject-interrogator relationship. Any insertion of counsel into the subject-interrogator relationship, for example—even if only for a limited duration or for a specific purpose—can undo months of work and may permanently shut down the interrogation process.[196]

"Padilla has been implicated in several plots to carry out attacks against the United States," Jacoby alleged, citing the "possible use of a 'dirty' radiological bomb in Washington DC or elsewhere," and also "the possible detonation of explosives in hotel rooms, gas stations, and train stations."[197]

In Pakistan, the British intelligence officer who interviewed Binyam Mohamed concluded he "would only provide information of genuine value if he comes to believe it is genuinely in his interests to do so," and the tool for this illumination was presumably more torture. For Padilla, Jacoby suggested, the tool was despair:

Permitting Padilla any access to counsel may substantially harm our national security interests. As with most detainees, Padilla is unlikely to cooperate if he believes that an attorney will intercede in his detention. DIA's assessment is that Padilla is even more inclined to resist interrogation that most detainees. DIA is aware that Padilla has had extensive experience in the United States criminal justice system and had access to counsel when he was being held as a material witness. These experiences have likely heightened his expectations that counsel will assist him in the interrogation process. Only after such time as Padilla has perceived that help is not on the way can

*the United States reasonably expect to obtain all possible intelligence
information from Padilla.*[198]

✷ ✷ ✷

For the next year, the three men remained in place, Abu Zubaydah in
the hands of the CIA in the black site in Poland, Jose Padilla under the
control of the Defense Intelligence Agency at the brig in Charleston, and
Binyam Mohamed in the custody of the Moroccans. Then, on January 21,
2004, the CIA dispatched another plane to Rabat, this one a Boeing 737
with the FAA registration N313P.[199]

"Farich—you're going home," Mohamed recounted being told, for the
second time.

*By now I would not believe it. I thought there was something special
coming along. The first time they said "farich" was the first time I
went to the torture chamber and they hung me up.*

*It was a cold night. I was cuffed, blindfolded, put in a van and
driven for about half an hour. Then they took me into a room, still
blindfolded. It was dark.*

*It was January 21st or 22nd, 2004, at about 10 pm. After waiting
about two hours, I heard a plane. I knew I was going to go. I heard
an American accent. I knew then I was being transferred back to the
Americans. It was me and two other prisoners.*

*There were five U.S. soldiers in black and grey, with face masks,
and again with Timberland type boots. The did not talk to me. They
cut off my clothes.*

*There was a white female with glasses. She took the pictures. One
of the soldiers held my penis and she took digital pictures. This took a
while, maybe half an hour.*

*She was one of the few Americans who ever showed me any
sympathy. She was about 5'6", short, blue eyes. When she saw the
injuries I had she gasped. She said, "Oh, my God, look at that." Then
all her mates looked at what she was pointing at and I could see the
shock and horror in her eyes.*

Later, when I was in Afghanistan they took more pictures. They were treating me, and one of them explained that the photos were "to show Washington it's healing."[200]

According to flight records, the Boeing 737 left Rabat at 2:05 a.m. on the morning of January 22, 2004, and landed in Kabul Afghanistan at 9:58 a.m. Mohamed was immediately transferred to a CIA black site known as the Dark Prison. Detainees who were held there have provided consistent accounts of a facility where prisoners were shackled in complete darkness virtually around the clock and bombarded with earsplitting, repetitive music and traumatizing noises. "A very very horrid horrid place," is how Bisher al-Rawi, who was detained there for two weeks in 2002, described it. "It's pitch dark. You can't see anything. You're on the floor. You need to use the toilet. You can't see how, you don't know what to do."[201]

As Binyam Mohamed reported to his attorney,

There was a hall with rooms apart from each other. I am guessing there were about 20 rooms. I was told special people were housed in it, and I was "special" which is why I was being taken there....

They knocked my head against a wall a few times until I could feel blood, then I was thrown into a cell. It was cell number 16 or 17, the second or third to last room from the shower room. The room was about 2 m by 2.5 m. The cell had a heavy metal door, all solid, then a second door with bars. There were speakers near the ceiling at both ends of the room. There was a watching hole low down on one wall. There was a hanging pole for people left there in the kneeling position. There was a bucket in the corner for a toilet.

I was put in shorts and a top, and chained to the floor with little or no room to manoeuver.

The mat was thin as a blanket, and the blanket was thin as a sheet. It was hard to use the toilet in the dark. All the shit and piss in the bucket got on my blanket, but when they let me lie down I had to use it, as it was all I had.

Showers were either weekly or monthly, as they wished.

It was pitch black, and no lights on in the rooms for most of the time. They used to turn the light on for a few hours, but that only made it worse when they turned it back off.

They hung me up. I was allowed a few hours of sleep on the second day, then hung up again, this time for two days. My legs had swollen. My wrists and hands had gone numb. I got food only once all this time. After a while I felt pretty much dead. I didn't feel I existed at all.

Then I was taken off the wall and left in the dark. There was loud music, Slim Shady and Dr. Dre for 20 days. I heard this non-stop over and over, I memorized the music, all of it, then they changed the sounds to horrible ghost laughter and Halloween sounds. It got really spooky in this black hole.[202]

The only light I saw came from the guards using flashlights to bring inedible food, mainly raw rice and beans for lunch, and bread and beans for dinner. Just the sauce, not the beans themselves. I lost 20 kg in the weeks of my stay. They used to come and weigh us every other day, it seemed like they were making sure we were losing weight.

Then there was a misunderstanding in interrogation that led to my being chained to the rails for a fortnight, all cause I said the truth about what I had and hadn't done, thinking the CIA interrogators looked understanding.[203]

In the Dark Prison, Mohamed's CIA interrogators were clear about their purpose:

I had interrogation most days. He started with pictures. I would say, "I don't know them." He would say, "You do know them." I'd said [sic], "Okay, I do know them." I would describe the people and what they did. I was just making stuff up, but it made the interrogator very happy. But then he went off and did his homework. He came back angry. "If you make up stories again, we're going to torture you." I asked him to tell me what he wanted, cos I didn't know what to say. "Just say what we want. Don't make things up." From then on they would give me the name and the story behind each picture. Most of them were Afghanis and Pakistanis. I was surprised at that, since I rarely had much of an interaction with an Afghani while I was there, because I did not speak the language.

In the Dark Prison, American solders, dressed all in black, came to me with a story. They said, "This is the story that Washington wants." It was about a dirty bomb. I was meant to steal the parts and build it with Padilla in New York. I did not even know what a dirty bomb was. At first, they talked about an atomic bomb, but then they talked about a dirty bomb. It was meant to be half A-bomb, half something else to make it explode. The story went round and round for the four months I spent in the Dark Prison. I could not understand what they were talking about, and got it wrong. They hung me up for ten days, almost non-stop. They had me in a sitting position on the floor, where I could not lie down. My hands were suspended above my head. There was a bucket next to me, but it was hard to maneuver to use it. I kept knocking over the bucket when I tried.[204]

That month, as Mohamed was being interrogated in the Dark Prison, Donna Newman and her co-counsel Andrew Patel and a delegation from the International Committee of the Red Cross were finally allowed to visit Jose Padilla in the brig in South Carolina.

On March 11, 2003, the district court granted the government's motion for reconsideration in part, but then had essentially affirmed its earlier decision, dismissing Vice Admiral Jacoby's statements as "speculative" and ruling that there was no way Padilla could pursue his habeas corpus claim without a lawyer. "Lest any confusion remain, this is not a suggestion or a request that Padilla be permitted to consult with counsel, and it is certainly not an invitation to conduct further 'dialogue' about whether he is permitted to do so," Judge Mukasey wrote in his opinion, insisting he "must have the opportunity to present evidence that undermines" the government's allegations.[205]

With Mukasey's ruling imminent, Newman and Patel met with Padilla on March 3, 2004. "The conditions of the meeting were extremely restrictive," Newman wrote later. "We were restricted in the topics we could discuss. The meeting was monitored and videotaped. Accordingly, we did not engage in any confidential discussions. The materials we sent to him were reviewed by the Department of Defense and redactions were made."[206]

Topics that were off limits included any discussion of Padilla's interrogation; on the table, though, were plans for a Supreme Court argument on his habeas petition the following month. In December 2003, the Second Circuit Court of Appeals had overturned Mukasey's ruling that the president had the power to detain a U.S. citizen detained in the U.S. as an enemy combatant in military custody. The Bush administration appealed, and on April 28, 2004, the same day *60 Minutes* broadcast the first Abu Ghraib photos, the Supreme Court heard *Rumsfeld v. Padilla* and *Hamdi v. Rumsfeld*, an appeal of the Fourth Circuit's rejection of Yaser Hamdi's habeas corpus petition.

With the Supreme Court now weighing two cases involving American citizens who were being held incommunicado and interrogated by the military, the administration was under increasing pressure to justify its actions. The week before the Supreme Court hearing, Senate Judiciary Committee Chairman Orrin Hatch had written Attorney General Alberto Gonzales asking the Justice and Defense departments to turn over whatever they could about Padilla's and Hamdi's cases. On May 28, 2004, the Justice Department released a declassified document entitled "Summary of Jose Padilla's Activities With Al Qaeda" that constructed an elaborate account of Padilla's terrorist plans based on Padilla's own admissions in custody and the interrogations of Abu Zubaydah, Binyam Mohamed (who is referred to as "the Accomplice"), Khalid Sheikh Mohammed, and two others identified as "Al Qaeda facilitators #1 and #2").

In this account, "Padilla admits he was first tasked with an operation to blow up apartment buildings in the United States with natural gas by [Mohammed] Atef...at a meeting in Qandahar in July or August 2001. Padilla accepted the tasking." Padilla and "another al Qaeda operative, Jafar Al-Tayar, received explosives training for this purpose"; however, "the mission was apparently abandoned after the training because Padilla and Jafar could not get along and Padilla told Atef he could not do the operation on his own." Padilla and Binyam Mohamed allegedly then proposed to

Abu Zubaydah an operation "in which they would travel to the United States to detonate a nuclear bomb they learned to make on the internet." Skeptical about their ability to carry out the plan, Abu Zubaydah is said to have arranged for them to meet Khalid Sheikh Mohammed instead. What follows is one of the document's most sensational passages:

> According to one statement by senior al Qaeda detainee #2, Padilla and the Accomplice did not commit to the apartment bombing mission, so KSM was unsure what operation they would finally pursue in the United States. According to that and other statements by this detainee, Padilla and his Accomplice were sent to KSM by Abu Zubaydah in March 2002, so that Padilla could propose the "dirty bomb" plan." KSM was very skeptical, and instead suggested that Padilla and his Accomplice undertake the apartment building operation originally conceived by Atef. They were to enter the United States via the Mexican border or Puerto Rico. Once in the U.S., Padilla and the Accomplice were to locate as many as three high-rise apartment buildings which had natural gas supplied to the floors. They would rent two apartments in each building, seal all the openings, turn on the gas, and set timers to detonate the building simultaneously at a later time. Selection of the target city in the United States was left up to Padilla. Padilla and his Accomplice discussed operational matters with KSM, were given communication training, and each received $20,000 for the operation. Although KSM had some doubts about the ability of Padilla and his Accomplice to successfully enter the United States, they had full authority from him to conduct an operation if they succeeded in entering the United States.
>
> According to the Accomplice, KSM first asked Padilla and his Accomplice to consider setting fire to a hotel or a gas station in the United States, but they told him it would be almost impossible to implement. KSM then asked Padilla to instead apply the explosives training he had received in Afghanistan to destroy an entire building in the central United States by fitting aluminum plates on the side of a room holding the pillars of the building, so that side would absorb all

the shock of the explosion, filling the room with natural gas, and then setting a detonator to go off in 24 hours. The Accomplice was tasked to build the detonator by connecting a programmable stopwatch to an electric detonator.

The Accomplice further states that KSM and Ammar al-Baluchi instructed Padilla and the Accomplice on the steps involved to execute this terrorist operation. Padilla would travel to Chicago after obtaining a new passport from the United States Embassy in Europe to expunge the record of Padilla's travel to Pakistan. Once in the United States, Padilla was to conduct an internet search on buildings that had natural gas heating. Padilla was to open a bank account and then obtain information about documents needed to rent an apartment; KSM advised they were to blow up approximately 20 buildings simultaneously, but Padilla pointed out that he could not possibly rent multiple apartments under one identity without drawing attention, and he might have to limit this operation to only two or three buildings. The Accomplice was to return to the United Kingdom, where he held refugee status, obtain a valid travel document, and then travel to the United States to meet Padilla in Chicago to assist him.[207]

The narrative is riddled with inconsistencies—first Padilla and Mohamed are supposed to enter the U.S. "via the Mexican border or Puerto Rico" and later Padilla is to secure a new passport in Europe and fly to Chicago and Mohamed is supposed to fly to the UK and then on to the U.S. with a valid travel document, for example—and the footnotes raise even more questions. In one, it becomes clear that KSM first identified Padilla's partner as Jafar, but in later statements "admits that the Accomplice was the second operative." Another, after alleging that the apartment plot was corroborated by Mohamed, Abu Zubaydah, and Al Qaeda facilitators #1 and #3, notes,

There are differences in detainee statements on the intended target of the apartment building mission, perhaps because it had not been finally determined, although the locations mentioned are all within

the United States. Padilla states that the primary target was New York City, although Florida and Washington, D.C. were discussed with KSM as well; selection of the apartment was left to Padilla's discretion. Padilla's Accomplice has stated that KSM instructed Padilla to conduct the operation in the central United States, or Chicago, and that he was assigned to meet Padilla in Chicago to assist him. Senior al Qaeda detainee #2 has said that KSM left selection of the target city up to Padilla, and has added in other statements that KSM intended the target to be along the Mexican-U.S. border, perhaps in Texas; that KSM advised Padilla to conduct the operation in California or somewhere in the U.S. Southwest; and that New York and Florida were never considered.[208]

Finally, a footnote observes, "There are a number of instances in his statements where Padilla attempts to downplay or deny his commitment to *al Qaeda* and the apartment building mission." It notes, for example, that "Padilla claims that he never pledged *bayat* (an oath of loyalty) to [Usama Bin Laden] and was not part of *al Qaeda*"; that "He says he and his Accomplice proposed the dirty bomb plot only as a way to get out of Pakistan and avoid combat in Afghanistan, yet save face with Abu Zubaydah"; and "that he returned to the U.S. with no intention of carrying out the apartment building operations."[209]

These inconsistencies and qualifications were absent three days later when Deputy Attorney General James Comey stood before the press and spun the "Summary of Jose Padilla's Activities With Al Qaeda" into a spellbinding narrative of Padilla's travels, training, and intentions. At the end, he drove home the point of the story:

Much of this information has been uncovered because Jose Padilla has been detained as an enemy combatant and questioned. We have learned many things from Padilla that I'm not going to discuss today and that we did not include in our answer to Sen. Hatch.

Had we tried to make a case against Jose Padilla through our criminal justice system, something that I, as the United States attorney in New York, could not do at that time without jeopardizing intelligence sources, he would very likely have followed his lawyer's advice and said nothing, which would have been his constitutional right.

He would likely have ended up a free man, with our only hope being to try to follow him 24 hours a day, seven days a week and hope—pray, really—that we didn't lose him.

But Jose Padilla was more than a criminal defendant with a broad menu of rights that we offer in our great criminal justice system. On May the 8th of 2002, a soldier of our enemy, a trained, funded and equipped terrorist, stepped off that plane at Chicago's O'Hare: a highly trained al Qaeda soldier who had accepted an assignment to kill hundreds of innocent men, women and children by destroying apartment buildings; an al Qaeda soldier who still hoped and planned to do even more by detonating a radiological device, a dirty bomb, in this country; an al Qaeda soldier who was trusted enough to spend hour after hour with the leaders of al Qaeda, Mohammed Atef, Abu Zubaida, Khalid Shaikh Mohammed; an al Qaeda soldier who had vital information about our enemy and its plans; and lastly an al Qaeda soldier who, as an American citizen, was free to move in, within, and out of this country.

Two years ago, the president of the United States faced a very difficult choice. After a careful process, he decided to declare Jose Padilla for what he was, an enemy combatant, a member of a terrorist army bent on waiting war against innocent civilians. And the president's decision was to hold him to protect the American people and to find out what he knows.

We now know much of what Jose Padilla knows. And what we have learned confirms that the president of the United States made the right call and that that call saved lives.[210]

The grandstanding bought the administration some time. Two months later, on June 28, 2004, the United States Supreme Court dismissed Jose Padilla's habeas corpus petition not on its merits but on technical grounds.

The 5-4 majority held that Padilla's attorneys had improperly filed the writ in federal court in New York instead of South Carolina, where Padilla was actually being detained, and that the petition had erred in naming Secretary of Defense Donald Rumsfeld as the respondent instead of the Naval Brig's commanding officer.

Meanwhile, in late May, as the administration was preparing this public relations offensive, Binyam Mohamed was moved again, this time with a group of detainees by helicopter from the Dark Prison to the detention facility at Bagram Airfield. Mohamed told his attorney

I was in Bagram from the end of May until I was taken to Guantánamo in September 2004.

They said there were ten of us meant to go to court. Some had to write statements. Some just had to sign statements that had been written by U.S. interrogators. They said we were meant to go to court right on arrival in Cuba.

They made me write something out for them in Bagram. It was long—about twenty pages—but the first fifteen pages were just an autobiography. The actual story was only a couple of pages. By then, the story was something like this. First, Jose Padilla and I were meant to have good connections, because we both spoke English. We were meant to have been hanging out together. The FBI showed me Jose Padilla's picture as early as April 2002 when I was in Pakistan. When I was in Morocco I was shown a news clip of him. The truth is that I do not know Jose Padilla, I did not recognize him in the photograph.

Second, I was meant to have come from Afghanistan with him. The truth is that I have no idea whether I did. I was in a group of people for two or three days coming out of Afghanistan. I have no idea whether he was in it, or even whether he had been in Afghanistan. I did not know him, and kept to myself, and I can say that I have certainly never spoken with him. But, of course, by the time I was in Bagram I was telling them whatever they wanted to hear.

Third, I was meant to say that Jose Padilla and I were going to go to the U.S. to explode a dirty bomb.

I don't really remember, because by then I just did what they told me. But I think that was about the total of it by then.[211]

Mohamed's lead interrogator at Bagram is identified as Special Agent 3 in Judge Kessler's opinion granting the habeas corpus petition of Farhi Saeed bin Mohammed. Special Agent 3 clearly leads one of the FBI's "clean teams," groups of interrogators whose job is to reinterview detainees who had previously been tortured to try to elicit the same information by non-coercive means. "Special Agent 3 began his questioning of Binyam Mohamed at Bagram in July of 2004, just over two months after he was transferred from the Dark Prison," Judge Kessler found. Special Agent 3 interviewed Mohamed first on July 21 and then several times at Bagram. In one of those sessions, Judge Kessler records, "Special Agent 3 made him write out his narrative."[212]

Finally, on September 19, 2004, more than two years after he had been detained at the Karachi airport, Binyam Mohamed was flown to Guantánamo. There, on October 29, 2004, Mohamed and Special Agent 3 met again. In that session, which began with the "various courtesies" including the traditional Muslim greeting and the offer of coffee, Mohamed was shown twenty-seven photos and identified twelve of them. Among those he identified was Farhi Saeed bin Mohammed, who, he said, had been a training camp companion.

Annotations on this section from TheTortureReport.org

On Binyam's interrogation by American interrogators in Pakistan, former Air Force criminal investigator and interrogator Matthew Alexander wrote,

It's clear that interrogators did little to build rapport and establish a relationship of trust, necessary to convince a detainee to cooperate. There was little analysis of what makes Mohamed tick. If he was planning to assist Al Qaida, why? Why did he start using drugs in the UK? Mohamed was

a perfect interrogation subject, a searching soul who the interrogators could have approached in a spirit of cooperation, not dominance.

On Defense Intelligence Agency Director Vice Admiral Lowell Jacoby's claims that "Anything that threatens the perceived dependency and trust between the subject and interrogator directly threatens the value of interrogation as an intelligence gathering tool," Matthew Alexander wrote,

These comments ignore the simple fact that numerous repeat offenders are routinely interrogated successfully in the U.S. every day by competent, professional detectives despite the Constitutional guarantees given to them. Interrogation is not about domination or creating dependencies or intimidation or establishing a sense of futility. It is about convincing a detainee to cooperate willingly by leveraging a relationship built on trust, not dominance. A professional, trained interrogator could have refuted these misconceptions about the art of interrogation and established a valid interrogation plan that would have been consistent with the law and American principles.

THE STORY UNRAVELS

Jose Padilla

In November 2005, President George Bush signed a memorandum to Secretary of Defense Donald Rumsfeld that read

> *Based on the information available to me [redacted] I hereby determine that it is in the interest of the United States that Jose Padilla be released from detention by the Secretary of Defense and transferred to the control of the Attorney General for the purpose of criminal proceedings against him.*
>
> *Accordingly, by the authority vested in me as President by the Constitution and the laws of the United States, I hereby direct you to transfer Mr. Padilla to the control of the Attorney General upon the Attorney General's request. This memorandum supersedes my directive to you of June 9, 2002, and, upon such transfer, your authority to detain Mr. Padilla provided in that order shall cease.*[213]

The order came a week before the administration's deadline for filing a Supreme Court brief in answer to Padilla's redirected habeas corpus petition, and this time it was clear that the justices intended to hear the case.

The year before, in June 2004, the Justices had decided Yaser Hamdi's habeas petition, ruling that though Congress had authorized the president to detain enemy combatants captured on the Afghan battlefield, Hamdi was entitled to a fair process to challenge his enemy combatant designation; Hamdi's incommunicado detention in a Naval Brig had not provided such a process. "An interrogation by one's captor, however effective an intelligence-gathering tool, hardly constitutes a constitutionally adequate fact-finding before a neutral decision-maker," Justice Sandra Day O'Connor wrote famously in the Court's plurality opinion. "We have long since made clear that a state of war is not a blank check for the President when it comes to the rights of the nation's citizens."[214] Faced with a requirement that it bring Yaser Hamdi's case before a "neutral decision-maker," the administration had instead quietly released Hamdi in October 2004, deporting him to

Saudi Arabia where he was freed on the condition he renounce his U.S. citizenship, accept a ban on travel to the U.S. and several other countries, and promise not to sue the United States over his detention.

Now it was to be Padilla's turn. His attorneys had refiled his habeas corpus petition in South Carolina against the commander of the Charleston Brig, and in March 2005 a federal judge had ruled that the case was "a law enforcement matter, not a military matter" and given the government forty-five days to charge him or set him free. The administration appealed directly to the Supreme Court, but the court again dodged a hearing, saying the Fourth Circuit Court of Appeals—generally considered the most conservative appellate court in the country—must review the district court's decision first. On, September 9, 2005, Judge J. Michael Luttig issued a unanimous opinion on behalf of a three-judge panel of the Fourth Circuit court that read,

> *The exceedingly important question before us is whether the President of the United States possesses the authority to detain militarily a citizen of this country who is closely associated with al Qaeda, an entity with which the United States is at war; who took up arms on behalf of that enemy and against our country in a foreign combat zone of that war; and who thereafter traveled to the United States for the avowed purpose of further prosecuting that war on American soil, against American citizens and targets.*
>
> *We conclude that the President does possess such authority pursuant to the Authorization for Use of Military Force Joint Resolution enacted by Congress in the wake of the attacks on the United States of September 11, 2001. Accordingly, the judgment of the district court is reversed.*[215]

Both Luttig and the administration knew the opinion would be reviewed by the Supreme Court, which was sure to reiterate its *Hamdi* position that Padilla was entitled to some means to challenge his enemy combatant status. So to avoid a ruling that would lead to a hearing on whether he was the would-be apartment building and "dirty" bomber the administration had been portraying, President Bush executed the transfer order on November 20. Two days later, Attorney General Alberto Gonzales held a press conference in New York to announce that a federal court in the Southern District of Florida had returned an indictment charging Padilla "with providing—and conspiring to provide—material support to terrorists, and conspiring to murder individuals who are overseas." Gonzales explained,

> *The indictment alleges that Padilla traveled overseas to train as a terrorist with the intention of fighting in "violent jihad"—a short hand term to describe a radical Islamic fundamentalist ideology that advocates using physical force and violence to oppose governments, institutions, and individuals who do not share their view of Islam. These groups routinely engage in acts of physical violence such as murder, maiming, kidnapping, and hostage-taking against innocent civilians.*
>
> *Mr. Padilla is now a new co-defendant—along with Canadian national Kassem Daher—in a criminal prosecution that previously charged defendants Adham Hassoun, Mohomed Youssef, and Kifah Jayyousi with terrorism-related crimes. All of these defendants are alleged members of a violent terrorist support cell that operated in the United States and Canada.*[216]

"As you know, under our criminal justice system all defendants are presumed innocent unless and until proven guilty," Gonzales added, without a hint of irony.

The indictment of the man the administration had publicly condemned as a "bad guy" who it said been apprehended on his way to carry out attacks calculated to cost scores, perhaps hundreds, of American lives, made no reference whatsoever to this murderous conspiracy. Instead, Padilla and his co-defendants were now charged with operating and participating "in a North American support cell that sent money, physical assets, and mujahideen recruits to overseas conflicts for the purpose of fighting violent jihad." The most serious charge, Count 1 of the indictment, alleged Conspiracy to Murder, Kidnap, and Maim Persons in a Foreign

Country; "Beginning at a time uncertain, but no later than in or about October 1993, and continuing until on or about November 1, 2001," the indictment read, the five defendants "did knowingly and willfully combine, conspire, confederate, and agree with others, known and unknown to the Grand Jury, to commit at any place outside the United States, acts that would constitute murder, that is, the unlawful killing of human beings with malice aforethought, kidnapping, and maiming...and did commit one or more acts within the jurisdiction of the United States, to affect the purpose and object of the conspiracy."[217]

Nearly all of the group's alleged activities had taken place in the eight years preceding 9/11, and their "purpose and object" had nothing to do with the United States or its citizens; rather, the group was accused of supporting and participating in "armed confrontations in specific locations outside the United States" "for the purpose of opposing existing governments and civilian factions and establishing Islamic states under Sharia." Over that eight-year period their countries of concern included Chechnya, Bosnia, Libya, and Somalia; in 1998, when Padilla left the U.S., the group's main interest was Kosovo, where war had broken out that year. The indictment alleged that Padilla had gone to Egypt to study with financial support from the group; two years later, on July 24, 2000, he filled out a "Mujahideen Data Form," in essence a training camp application; a few months later, the indictment asserted, phone calls intercepted in 2000 showed that Padilla had entered Afghanistan, presumably for training.

Judge Luttig—who had referred to Padilla in his opinion as someone who took up arms against the United States on behalf of Al Qaeda and traveled to the U.S. to wage war on American soil—was so incensed at the indictment and the apparent arbitrariness of Padilla's treatment that he rejected the government's request to authorize Padilla's transfer to civilian custody, insisting that he should remain in the brig in order to force the Supreme Court to review his own court's decision on the scope of presidential powers. But the administration went over his head, petitioning the Supreme Court directly to grant the transfer request, and on and January 3, 2006 Padilla was released from the Charleston Brig and flown to the Federal Detention Center in Miami.

In a pre-trial hearing in Miami in June, U.S. District Judge Marcia G. Cooke called the government's indictment "light on facts" and ordered prosecutors to turn over more specific information about its allegations.[218] Two months later, on August 21, 2006, she dismissed the conspiracy to murder charge, ruling it duplicated the two other material support-related charges, dropping Padilla's maximum sentence if convicted from life to fifteen years in prison.[219] Meanwhile, with the government again seeking to avoid scrutiny of Padilla's treatment by pledging it would introduce no evidence gathered in the brig, Padilla's attorneys were pursuing two strategies to bring his interrogation into Judge Cooke's courtroom—the first an assertion that his torture had left him unable to participate effectively in his own defense and therefore incompetent to stand trial, and the second a motion to dismiss the case for "outrageous government conduct."

Padilla's attorneys subpoenaed navy records and other information about his time in the brig to help build their case, and among the materials the government turned over to his attorneys were eighty-seven videotapes of Padilla in Charleston. *New York Times* reporter Deborah Sontag viewed a scene from one of them in early December. The recording documented a mundane event: "Today is May 21," a voice tells the camera. "Right now we're ready to do a root canal treatment on Jose Padilla, our enemy combatant."[220] Sontag's *Times* story included a still frame from the video, an indelible image of Padilla in blackout goggles and headphones surrounded by three corpsmen in camouflage riot gear.[221] In a subsequent NPR interview, she described what she had seen on the videotape this way:

> *Several guards approached the door of the cell in full riot gear. They unlock a rectangular panel at the bottom, and you see these feet—kind of pale feet—slide out through the hole. He's shackled. They then unlock a panel on the top. His hands come out and are cuffed.*
>
> *They unlock the door and they all push into the cell, turn him around, tie his cuffed hands to a metal belt at his waist so that he's completely chained, swivel him around and lead him out the door,*

at which point—very, very briefly—he gives the appearance of being somewhat catatonic. And he raises his head briefly. His eyes meet the camera completely blankly.

His head goes back down, and they put sort of a blackened ski mask over his eyes and very large noise-blocking headphones over his ears. And then the guards put their leather black-gloved hands on his shoulders and they all—they walk this masked, clanking prisoner down the hall to the dentist, and then he has a two-hour root canal procedure.[222]

This treatment was not disciplinary. Padilla was by all accounts a model prisoner; in an affidavit submitted in support of the motion for a mental competency hearing, attorney Andrew Patel reported that on one of his visits to the brig, the brig staff had told him that "Mr. Padilla's temperament was so docile and inactive that his behavior was like that of 'a piece of furniture.'" Patel added, "I was also told that the Brig staff was concerned about the damage that could occur from the extended isolation that Mr. Padilla experienced in the Brig."[223]

Patel, who first visited Padilla with co-counsel Donna Newman on March 3, 2004, met with his client "ten or eleven times" in the Charleston Brig. During one of those meetings, Patel recalled,

I asked him a question concerning a simple fact based on an event that had happened prior to his arrest. In observing Mr. Padilla's physical reaction to this question, I noted that his posture changed from relaxed to bolt upright in his chair. He began to blink his eyes and he appeared to have goose bumps on his arms and his neck. Mr. Padilla's reaction to my innocuous question was the same reaction that I would have expected if he had been stuck by a cattle prod.[224]

"Mr. Padilla retains the belief that he will be returned to the Brig if he discusses events that occurred there," Patel concluded. Despite repeated meetings and conversations about his defense, Patel said, "as of the date of this affirmation, Mr. Padilla remains unsure if I and the other attorneys working on his case are actually his attorneys or another component of the government's interrogation scheme."[225]

To Angela Hegarty, a forensic psychiatrist who examined Padilla and submitted an affidavit in his defense, Padilla exhibited some of the characteristics associated with "Stockholm Syndrome," the condition in which captives form intense bonds with their captors. "Mr. Padilla tends to identify with the interests of the government more than his own interests at times," she wrote.

> For example, after defense counsel cross-examined FBI agents regarding their interrogation of the defendant in Chicago establishing inconsistencies and aggressive behavior, Mr. Padilla's reaction was concern that the agents could get in trouble. Instead of being pleased with his attorney's efforts to get out the truth, he was more concerned about the effect it could have upon the agents, or the possibility that these efforts on his behalf might result in his return to the brig.[226]

He also appeared concerned that he might be considered mentally ill. Hegarty found that, far from "malingering" or exaggerating his symptoms, Padilla actually "strives to present himself as stress and symptom free on interview and on testing." "He is terrified of appearing or being seen as 'crazy,'" she reported. "He recalled being told by one of his interrogators that if he were to relate a particular experience to someone 'on the outside,' they would see him as 'crazy.' He was completely unable to describe those experiences for me."[227]

Though reluctant to describe his interrogation, Padilla had been willing to answer yes or no to a list of interrogation techniques Hegarty presented based on the leaked Bybee memo, and the psychiatrist told the court,

> Mr. Padilla was willing to affirm or deny whether he had been subject to interrogation techniques that had been commonly reported in the media. He denied being sexually assaulted or humiliated. He denied being water-boarded with uncharacteristic intensity and insistence. He acknowledged being kept in the dark or with the lights on for very

long periods of time, being shackled and left alone for long periods of time, of being kept in a cold environment for long periods of time, and above all, of being certain he would die in the brig.

In particular, he described periods of sleep deprivation caused by the discomfort of lying on a steel bunk without a mattress and with the lights on. Also, the slamming of adjacent cell doors at regular intervals prevented his sleep. Mr. Padilla recalled asking for medication for pain and being told by staff they were not authorized to give him anything for his pain. He also described an incident during which he felt intense pressure on his chest "like two hundred pounds" and was convinced he was going to die from that intense pressure.

During my interview, Mr. Padilla briefly conveyed obviously painful recollections of being taken out of his cell to a "recreation" cage. Mr. Padilla recalled how he begged his guards not to take him out and put him in the cage. He would not say what went on in the cage or why it upset him so. Mr. Padilla also made it clear to me that he had not told me everything that had been done to him in the brig and that he was unwilling to do so.

Mr. Padilla told me that he had no way of keeping track of time while in the brig. He was the sole occupant on the lower level of the brig. There were long periods of darkness and long periods of bright artificial light. There were no clocks or calendars. He had no access of any kind to the outside world. He was unable to put events in chronological order for me. He was clear that early on, for what seemed like months, there was a "terrible time," although he could not be more specific as to what constituted that "terrible time."228

As a result of his experiences, Hegarty told the court, Padilla presented a textbook case of Post Traumatic Stress Disorder. She concluded,

He has endured a traumatic event that involved actual or threatened death or serious injury, or a threat to the physical integrity of self or others and his response involved intense fear and helplessness. The use of prolonged isolation along with tactics designed to have

an individual reveal facts they otherwise might not wish to reveal, as well as the fostering of dependence on interrogators not only creates the conditions in which individuals might reveal important information, but also the conditions that induce intense fear, feelings of helplessness and loss of control characteristic of the traumatic experience. Sleep deprivation, physiological stress, and repeated questioning only exacerbate the traumatic nature of the experience. Mr. Padilla believed he was going to die on a number of occasions during his detention. He believed his family would be harmed if he did not comply. He learned that no matter whether he was cooperative, or whether he pleaded with his captors, he was utterly helpless and absolutely dependent on them for everything. He believed and still believes they have the ultimate power to decide what happens in his life, his case, and whether he is released or ultimately is returned to the brig.[229]

A 1985 Supreme Court decision had established that for a defendant to be considered competent to stand trial, the state only needs to show that he understands the charges against him, the penalty he faces, and the adversarial nature of the proceedings, and that he is able to assist his attorneys in his defense. Padilla's attorneys concentrated on this last factor, arguing that he was too traumatized and fearful to cooperate fully in preparing his case. During the mental competency hearings, both Hegarty and a second psychiatrist testifying on behalf of the defense, Dr. Patricia Zapf, supported this conclusion. Dr. Zapf testified that Padilla was "immobilized by anxiety" and unsure whether his attorneys might not in fact be government agents; convinced he would be returned to the brig, where he would remain until he died, he was, she reported, fatalistic about the proceedings. "He'd say, 'What does it matter? It doesn't matter. My fate has been decided. It's better to let things be.'"[230]

Incredibly, in the course of the competency hearing, Assistant U.S. Attorney Stephanie K. Pell revealed that the Defense Department had not turned over all of its videotapes of Padilla's interrogations to his attorneys—and that the tape it hadn't produced was the recording of

Padilla's last interrogation session on March 2, 2004, the day before he was finally allowed, after almost two years in isolation, to meet with his attorneys. "We have a good faith belief the tape existed," Pell told Judge Cooke at the hearing in February 2007, insisting the tape had been "lost" and that "an exhaustive search was conducted" but the video "could not be located."[231]

"Do you understand how it might be difficult to understand that a tape related to this particular individual just got mislaid?" Judge Cooke countered.[232] But there was little she could do. When Padilla's attorneys had filed notice that they planned to introduce scenes from the eighty-seven tapes in his defense, government attorneys argued that the tapes "contain isolated, historical sideshows, meant to divert this Court's attention away from the central issue before it, which is Padilla's present ability to understand the proceedings and communicate with his counsel." The tapes were "completely irrelevant to Padilla's present ability to communicate with his attorneys," the government insisted; moreover, while it was understood that the classified tapes would not be played in open court, "this Court should not even consider them in the privacy of chambers."[233]

In fact, the government argued, defense attorneys should be barred from making any reference to the conditions the tapes depicted in their cross examination of a court-appointed Bureau of Prisons psychologist who had deemed Padilla competent to stand trial.

Perhaps anticipating that the request to use the videotape excerpts will be denied, counsel for Padilla signaled at the last hearing that they intend to put "hypothetical" questions to the court-appointed expert, based on what occurred during the videotaped interrogations at issue. More specifically, counsel for Padilla plan to ask whether the court-appointed expert's opinion would change if he knew that so-and-so had occurred, with the so-and-so being something that appears on the classified videotapes.

Doing so, U.S. attorneys asserted, would violate a court order on the use of classified evidence.[234]

Judge Cooke had ruled for the government, rejecting Padilla's petition to play portions of the eighty-seven tapes. Now, confronted with the fact that the government had withheld the video of Padilla's final interrogation and its dubious claim that the tape had disappeared, his attorneys protested again. What happened during that last session with interrogators, on the day before he was allowed to meet his attorneys "directly impacts upon his relationship with his attorneys," his lawyers insisted.[235] But again, though clearly troubled by the government's claim that the tape had gone missing, Judge Cooke concluded that this tape, too, would have been inadmissible under her previous ruling.

She did, however, allow one window into the government's treatment of Padilla in the brig. Rudolfo Buigas, the court-appointed Bureau of Prisons psychologist, had not formally examined Padilla; because Padilla had refused to submit to another psychiatric evaluation, Buigas had interviewed him for about five hours instead, and then had spoken with Sanford Seymour, the technical director of the Charleston Brig, and brig psychologist Craig Noble about his state of mind in detention. Based on these interviews, Buigas had concluded that Padilla suffered from anxiety and an unnamed personality disorder, but that he was mentally fit to stand trial. Because Buigas's assessment had depended in part on their descriptions of their encounters with Padilla, Cooke ordered Seymour and Noble to testify at the hearing— though, again, they could not discuss his treatment or the conditions of his confinement, only their observations on his mental state.

During cross-examination, Seymour acknowledged that Padilla had been held in isolation with no clock or access to natural light; he said he had twice seen Padilla weeping. Noble testified that he had interviewed Padilla twice—once for a mental health intake assessment when he arrived at the brig on June 10, 2002, and the second time two years later when he had briefly spoken with Padilla, not face to face, but through the hatch in his cell door through which his meals were passed. He said Padilla's health was "unremarkable" both times. Padilla's attorneys asked whether those interviews had lasted less than two minutes, as brig records suggested, but the government objected, and he was not allowed to answer because Buigas had not questioned him about the length of their discussions.[236]

On February 28, 2007, Judge Cooke ruled that Padilla was competent to stand trial. She explained her decision relied in large part her own observations of Padilla. Though he had arrived in her courtroom shackled, she had ordered him unbound and he had remained unshackled throughout the pre-trial hearings without incident; moreover, she had found him "keenly aware" of the court proceedings and said he "clearly has the capacity to assist his attorneys"[237] She also noted that Padilla had signed an affidavit swearing to the descriptions of his treatment in the brig that his attorneys had presented, something they could not ethically have asked him to do were he incompetent. *Newsweek* reported that after her ruling, "Padilla, who has sat largely emotionless through the past few days of testimony about his mental competency, stood up and smiled, making a point of shaking the hands of each one of his defense attorneys."[238]

Judge Cooke made clear that her decision that Padilla could stand trial on the charges before her should not be considered as a rejection of his claims of abuse during his detention in the brig. "Those claims are for another day," she said, suggesting they would be reviewed in the course of his motion to dismiss based on "outrageous government conduct." But like the incompetence claim, the "outrageous government conduct" motion was a legal longshot; the doctrine has been applied almost exclusively in cases of entrapment, where the government participates in or facilitates the crime for which the defendant is eventually charged. In April, Judge Cooke issued an order denying Padilla's Motion to Dismiss, finding his argument had "numerous legal infirmities" because his treatment in the brig was not connected to the present charges that prior to 9/11 he had conspired to support terrorism overseas.

> *First, the fact that the governmental conduct occurred at a time and place removed from the crimes charged makes the remedy Padilla is seeking considerably more attenuated and arbitrary. Short of resorting to a 'two wrongs make a right' judicial process, it is difficult for this Court to ascertain how the remedy sought emanates from the infirmity defendant describes. This is considerably distinguishable from a government entrapment scenario, where the crime that the*

defendant is charged with is the crux of the outrageous government conduct claim.

Second, the outrageous conduct occurred while Padilla was under military control at the Naval Brig in Charleston, South Carolina. At this time, Padilla was being held under Presidential orders in connection with his enemy combatant status and had not been charged with the crimes he is currently facing. This further attenuates Padilla's outrageous government conduct claim. Even if Padilla's due process rights were violated while being held at the Naval Brig as an enemy combatant, he fails to explain how this violation should result in the dismissal of distinct crimes that he was not charged with at that point.

Third, Mr. Padilla fails to explain why suppressing governmental use of any evidence obtained from him at the Naval Brig is insufficient for purposes of this trial. In his motion, Padilla acknowledges that the government has already averred not to seek introduction of any of the Naval Brig evidence at trial. Despite summarily rejecting this remedy as "clearly inadequate," Padilla fails to support this contention or explain why his requested remedy is more appropriate.[239]

However, she concluded, "should the government decide to make use of any such evidence, an appropriate hearing will be scheduled to determine to what extent it is admissible."[240]

In a footnote, Judge Cooke emphasized that her order to deny Padilla's motion shouldn't be read as denying his assertions of abuse at the hands of the U.S. government. "This Court makes no finding with regard to Mr. Padilla's treatment at the Naval Brig. By stating that Mr. Padilla has failed to state a claim of 'outrageous government conduct,' the Court is merely rejecting the merits of Mr. Padilla's legal argument. Within the framework of this Order, the phrase 'outrageous government conduct' should be interpreted as a legal term of art and not defined in a conventional sense," she wrote.[241] In another footnote, she added, "This court's holding does not imply that this is Mr. Padilla's only remedy with regard to any alleged mistreatment at the Naval Brig, only that it is the most appropriate remedy within the framework of this prosecution. Mr. Padilla is free to institute a *Bivens* action, an action for monetary damages or any other form of redress that he is legally entitled to pursue."[242]

The trial of Jose Padilla, Adham Hassoun, and Kifah Jayyousi opened on May 14, 2007. The most serious charge against them was once again conspiracy to commit murder: in January, the 11th Circuit Court of Appeals had reversed Judge Cooke and reinstated Count 1 of the indictment. In late June, in a show of unity that observers believed augured ill for the defense, eleven of the twelve jurors came to court dressed entirely in black; on July 3, the entire jury sat through the proceedings dressed in coordinated rows of red, white, and blue. They heard almost nothing about Padilla's time in the brig during the three-month trial; indeed, days would go by with little mention of him at all. But in closing arguments, Assistant U.S. Attorney Brian Frazier directed the jury's attention to Padilla, Hassoun and Jayyousi's "star recruit." The main piece of evidence against him was the "mujahadeen data form" which a disguised CIA agent testified he had found in a raid in 2001 in Afghanistan and which allegedly bore seven of Padilla's fingerprints. "You don't mail away for it" Frazier told the jury. "You are already inside the Al Qaeda organization when you get this form." It was one of more than one hundred times he invoked Al Qaeda in a closing argument that seemed calculated to evoke the administration's early characterizations of the enemy combatant Padilla. Padilla "trained to kill," Frazier concluded.[243]

On August 16, 2007, after a day and a half of deliberations, the jury returned guilty verdicts on all three main counts, including conspiracy to murder, and it was generally assumed that Padilla would be condemned to life behind bars. But on January 23, 2008, Judge Cooke announced she was sentencing him to seventeen years in federal prison. She cited two factors in justifying her marked departure from federal sentencing guidelines. The first reflected her continuing discomfort with the conspiracy to murder charge. Prosecutors had presented nothing linking the defendants to specific acts of terrorism, she noted: "There is no evidence that these defendants personally maimed, kidnapped or killed anyone in the United States or elsewhere; there was never a plot to overthrow the United States government." The second, she made clear, had to do with what she had learned about his treatment in the Charleston Brig. Cooke was crediting Padilla for the three and a half years he had been held incommunicado and deprived of a mattress, clock, the Koran, or human contact, she explained. "I do find the conditions were so harsh for Mr. Padilla that they warrant consideration of the court's fashioning of a sentence in this case."[144]

On January 4, 2008, Padilla's attorneys filed a lawsuit against John Yoo, the author of the so-called Bybee memos, alleging that "During his time in the military brig, Mr. Padilla was intentionally subjected to a systematic program of illegal interrogation and conditions of confinement that Defendant Yoo justified through legal opinions purporting to permit illegal conduct."[245] The Complaint alleges:

> Plaintiff Jose Padilla is a United States citizen who was imprisoned as an "enemy combatant" in a military brig, without charge and without ability to defend himself or challenge his conditions of confinement for three years and eight months. Throughout those years, Mr. Padilla suffered gross physical and psychological abuse at the hands of federal officials as part of a systematic program of abusive interrogation intended to break down Mr. Padilla's humanity and his will to live. For nearly two years, Mr. Padilla was held in complete isolation and denied all access to the court system, legal counsel and his family. He was subjected to mistreatment including but not limited to extreme and prolonged sleep and sensory deprivation designed to inflict severe mental pain and suffering; exposure to extreme temperatures; interrogation under threat of torture, deportation and even death; denial of access to necessary medical and psychiatric care; and interference with his ability to practice his religion. In the year and a half that Mr. Padilla remained in the Brig after he was granted limited access to legal counsel, much of this severe abuse continued....
>
> The grave violations suffered by Padilla were not isolated occurrences by rogue lower-level officials; to the contrary, Defendant John Yoo, along with other senior officials, deliberately removed Mr. Padilla from due process protections traditionally available to

U.S. citizens detained by their government and barred all access to the outside world, including to counsel. On information and belief, Defendant Yoo and other senior officials then personally formulated and/or approved and/or failed to act upon actual or constructive knowledge of, a systematic program of illegal detention and interrogation, which was specifically designed to inflict, and did inflict, severe physical and mental pain and suffering on Mr. Padilla for the purpose of extracting information from him and/or punishing him without due process of law.... Defendant Yoo personally provided numerous legal memoranda that purported to provide to senior government officials a legal basis to implement an extreme and unprecedented interrogation and detention program—even though such tactics are unprecedented in U.S. history and clearly contrary to the U.S. Constitution and the law of war.[246]

Padilla's lawsuit, which seeks a judgment declaring that abuses described in the complaint "are unlawful and violate the Constitution of the United States" and one dollar in compensatory damages, is what Judge Cooke referred to as a *Bivens* action, named for a Supreme Court case in which Webster Bivens successfully sued six unnamed DEA agents who had searched his home and arrested him without a warrant. Yoo's attorneys moved to dismiss the case, arguing the president had the authority to authorize Padilla's detention as an enemy combatant and his interrogation, and that Yoo is entitled to immunity for his role in drafting the memos. But on June 12, 2009, U.S. District Judge Jeffrey S. White—a George W. Bush appointee—rejected those arguments and ruled that Padilla's suit can go forward.

This may well be Padilla's last opportunity to submit his treatment at the hands of the Bush administration to legal scrutiny.[247] By transferring him from the brig to civilian custody, the administration was hoping to avoid a Supreme Court showdown over Padilla's habeas corpus petition, a showdown it knew from the Hamdi decision it was likely to lose. Yet it remained afraid that the court would take the case anyway, as a way of reviewing Judge Luttig's 4th Circuit opinion "that the President possesses the authority under the Authorization of the Use of Military Force to detain enemy combatants who have taken up arms against the United States abroad and entered into this country for the purposes of attacking America and its citizens from within."

But on April 3, 2006, by a 6-3 vote, the Supreme Court denied Padilla's request for review of the Fourth Circuit decision, with Justices Roberts, Stevens, Kennedy, Scalia, Thomas, and Alito holding that Padilla's petition was moot now that he was in civilian custody. Justices Ginsburg, Souter, and Breyer disagreed, with Justice Ginsberg writing in dissent,

> This case, here for the second time, raises a question "of profound importance to the Nation," Does the President have authority to imprison indefinitely a United States citizen arrested on United States soil distant from a zone of combat, based on an Executive declaration that the citizen was, at the time of his arrest, an "enemy combatant"? It is a question the Court heard, and should have decided, two years ago. Nothing the Government has yet done purports to retract the assertion of Executive power Padilla protests.
>
> Although the Government has recently lodged charges against Padilla in a civilian court, nothing prevents the Executive from returning to the road it earlier constructed and defended. A party's voluntary cessation does not make a case less capable of repetition or less evasive of review.[248]

Even some members of the majority seemed uneasy with leaving Padilla's fate so completely in the president's hands. In an opinion co-signed by Roberts and Stevens, Justice Kennedy cautioned:

> In light of the previous changes in his custody status and the fact that nearly four years have passed since he first was detained, Padilla, it must be acknowledged, has a continuing concern that his status might be altered again. That concern, however, can be addressed if the necessity arises.... Were the Government to seek to change the status or conditions of Padilla's custody...the District Court, as well

as other courts of competent jurisdiction, should act promptly to ensure that the office and purposes of the writ of habeas corpus are not compromised. Padilla, moreover, retains the option of seeking a writ of habeas corpus.[249]

But the jurist who was most outraged by the Padilla saga was Judge Michael Luttig, whose opinion, in the end, escaped Supreme Court review. When the administration asked Luttig to authorize Padilla's transfer to civilian custody, it had also asked him to withdraw his opinion, fearing that Supreme Court would hear the case even though Padilla was now to be tried in a civilian court. It was a reasonable fear: Justice Stevens, who sided with the 6-3 majority declining to hear the appeal, had previously insisted that what was "at stake in this case is nothing less than a free society." But it was not, to Luttig, a reasonable request. In his opinion denying the request for authorization to transfer, Luttig wrote:

[T]he government's actions since this court's decision issued on September 9, culminating in and including its urging that our opinion be withdrawn, together with the timing of these actions in relation both to the period for which Padilla has already been held and to the government's scheduled response to Padilla's certiorari petition in the Supreme court, have given rise to at least an appearance that the purpose of these actions may be to avoid consideration of our decision by the Supreme Court...

[W]e would regard the intentional mooting by the government of a case of this import out of concern for the Supreme Court consideration not as legitimate justification but as admission of attempted avoidance of review. The government cannot be seen as conducting litigation with the enormous implications of this litigation – litigation imbued with significant public interest – in such a way as to select by which forum as between the supreme Court of the United States and an inferior appellate court it wishes to be bound.[250]

Luttig summarized the administration's actions in the Padilla case this way:

> *The government has held Padilla militarily for three and a half years, steadfastly maintaining that it was imperative in the interest of national security that he be so held. However, a short time after our decision issued on the government's representation that Padilla's military custody was indeed necessary in the interest of national security, the government determined that it was no longer necessary that Padilla be held militarily. Instead, it announced, Padilla would be transferred to the custody of federal civilian law enforcement authorities and criminally prosecuted in Florida for alleged offenses considerably different from, and less serious than, those acts for which the government had militarily detained Padilla. The indictment of Padilla in Florida, unsealed the same day as the announcement of that indictment, made no mention of the acts upon which the government purported to base its military detention of Padilla and upon which we had concluded only several weeks before that the President possessed the authority to detain Padilla, namely, that Padilla had taken up arms against United States forces in Afghanistan and had thereafter entered into this country for the purpose of blowing up buildings in American cities in continued prosecution of al Qaeda's war of terrorism against the United States.*
>
> *The announcement of indictment came only two business days before the government's brief in response to Padilla's petition for certiorari was due to be filed in the Supreme Court of the United States, and only days before the District Court in South Carolina, pursuant to our remand, was to accept briefing on the question whether Padilla had been properly designated an enemy combatant by the President.*
>
> *The same day as Padilla's indictment was unsealed in Florida, the government filed with us a motion pursuant to Supreme Court Rule 36 for authorization to transfer Padilla to Florida, a motion that included no reference to, or explanation of, the difference in*

the facts asserted to justify Padilla's military detention and those for which Padilla was indicted. In a plea that was notable given that the government had held Padilla militarily for three and a half years and that the Supreme Court was expected within only days either to deny certiorari or to assume jurisdiction over the case for eventual disposition on the merits, the government urged that we act as expeditiously as possible to authorize the transfer. The government styled its motion as an "emergency application," but it provided no explanation as to what comprised the asserted exigency.[251]

In a stinging conclusion, Luttig warned that such actions will inevitably have consequences "not only for the public perception of the war on terror but also for the government's credibility before the courts in litigation ancillary to that war"—and that "we cannot help but believe that those consequences have been underestimated":

For, as the government surely must understand, although the various facts it has asserted are not necessarily inconsistent or without basis, its actions have left not only the impression that Padilla may have been held for these years, even if justifiably, by mistake—an impression we would have thought the government could ill afford to leave extant. They have left the impression that the government may even have come to the belief that the principle in reliance upon which it has detained Padilla for this time, that the President possesses the authority to detain enemy combatants who enter into this country for the purpose of attacking America and its citizens from within, can, in the end, yield to expediency with little or no cost to its conduct of the war against terror—an impression we would have thought the government likewise could ill afford to leave extant. And these impressions have been left, we fear, at what may ultimately prove to be substantial cost to the government's credibility before the courts, to whom it will one day need to argue again in support of a principle of assertedly like importance and necessity to the one that it seems to abandon today. While there could be an objective that could command such a price as all of this, it is difficult to imagine what that objective would be.[252]

Annotations on this section from TheTortureReport.org

On the administration's legal machinations surrounding Jose Padilla, blogger Marcy Wheeler ("emptywheel") wrote,

These strategies of moving from civilian to military courts and attempting to craft charges from before the period of abuse were used in other cases as well. For the former, there's Ali al-Marri. And for the latter, the same thing was done with Abu Zubaydah and Ahmed Ghailani, at least.

On the treatment of Jose Padilla, and particularly masking and shackling him to escort him to the dental procedure, former Air Force criminal investigator and interrogator Matthew Alexander observed,

Compare this treatment to Japanese POWs who often weren't even handcuffed for transportation. The legendary WWII interrogator Major Sherwood Moran said, "Better to let the prisoner forget you are enemies than to remind him." In terms of his treatment in the brig in general, why were no Uniformed Code of Military Justice charges ever filed against the commander of the brig? Or other commanders who participated in his detention and/or ordered the policies? The UCMJ was completely ignored for more than seven years and is now plagued by the failure of military investigative commanders to open criminal cases in light of obvious evidence of criminal wrongdoing.

THE STORY UNRAVELS

Binyam Mohamed

On November 10, 2004, two months after Binyam Mohamed was delivered to Guantánamo and about two weeks after "Special Agent 3" had him identify the photographs of Farhi Saeed bin Mohammed and eleven others, the Combatant Status Review Board sent a memo to his appointed "Personal Representative" summarizing the evidence against him. It read:

1. Under the provisions of the Secretary of the Navy Memorandum, dated 29 July 2004, Implementation of Combatant Status Review Tribunal Procedures for Enemy Combatants Detained at Guantánamo Bay Naval Base Cuba, a Tribunal has been appointed to review the detainee's designation as an enemy combatant.

2. An enemy combatant has been defined as "an individual who was part of or supporting the Taliban or al Qaida forces, or associated forces that are engaged in hostilities against the United States or its coalition partners. This includes any person who committed a belligerent act or has directly supported hostilities in aid of enemy armed forces."

3. The United States Government has previously determined that the detainee is an enemy combatant. This determination is based on information possessed by the United States that indicates that the detainee is associated with al Qaida or the Taliban.

A. The detainee is associated with al Qaida or the Taliban.
1. The detainee is an Ethiopian who lived in the United States from 1992 to 1994, and in London, United Kingdom, until he departed for Pakistan in 2001.
2. The detainee arrived in Islamabad, Pakistan, in June 2001, and traveled to the al Faruq training camp in Afghanistan, to receive paramilitary training.
3. At the al Faruq camp, the detainee received 40 days of training in light arms handling, explosives, and principles of topography.

4. *The detainee was taught to falsify documents, and received instruction from a senior al Qaida operative on how to encode telephone numbers before passing them to another individual.*

5. *The detainee proposed, to senior al Qaida leaders, the idea of attacking subway trains in the United States.*

6. *The detainee was extracted from Afghanistan to Karachi, Pakistan, where he received explosives and remote-controlled-detonator training from an al Qaida operative.*

7. *The detainee met with an al Qaida operative and was directed to travel to the United States to assist in terrorist operations.*

8. *The detainee attempted to leave Pakistan for the United States but was detained and interrogated by Pakistani authorities, revealing his membership in al Qaida, the identities of Mujahidins he knew, and his plan to use a "dirty bomb" to carry out a terrorist attack in the United States.*

4. The detainee has the opportunity to contest his designation as an enemy combatant. The Tribunal will endeavor to arrange for the presence of any reasonably available witnesses or evidence that the detainee desires to call or introduce to prove that he is not an enemy combatant. The Tribunal President will determine the reasonable availability of evidence of witnesses.[253]

A week later, the U.S. Air Force major assigned to be his Personal Representative met with him for an hour and twenty minutes, and afterwards recorded these notes:

During the initial interview on 18 Nov 04, detainee elected to NOT participate in the Tribunal. He had no witnesses or documentary evidence but requested that his Personal Representative provide statements made during the interview. Those statements follow:

- *Detainee informed PR that the interrogators told him that the tribunals were a "pass by" to get to the courts. He stated that he had no evidence on him (plans, materials, weapons, etc.) when captured and was interrogated by the British Secret Service (M6) who said that he was not accused of anything. He told me he made statements while being (mentally and physically) tortured while in Pakistani jails. Detainee admitted items 3A1-4 on the UNCLASS summary of evidence, but stated he went for training to fight in Chechnya, which was not illegal. The detainee stated that the other items were rubbish or made under duress. He further stated that he traveled before 11 Sep 2001, which means he had different plans other than going to fight America. After 9/11, there was no way out of AF other than the groups who could get him out of AF, through PK, and back to Britain (namely al Qaida). Finally, detainee stated that his plane ticket at time of capture was a ticket from Karachi to Zurich to England, so how could he have plans to carry out attacks in the United States.*[254]

The Combatant Status Review Tribunals were a new feature at Guantánamo, created that summer following the Supreme Court's *Hamdi* decision and its 6-3 ruling in June in *Rasul v. Bush* that detainees at the U.S. naval prison in Cuba, too, had a right to pursue habeas corpus petitions in U.S. courts. The Pentagon described the CSRTs as a "formal review of all the information related to a detainee to determine whether each person meets the criteria to be designated as an enemy combatant"; they were meant to satisfy Justice O'Conner's admonition that those the administration was detaining were entitled to a "fact-finding before a neutral decision maker."[255]

But Mohamed was having none of it. Instead, he managed to get word to Clive Stafford Smith, a British lawyer already representing several other UK-based detainees, that he wanted Stafford Smith to take his case as well. Stafford Smith immediately filed a habeas corpus petition for Mohamed, and met him for the first time in person on May 2, 2005. Stafford Smith recalled that first meeting in his 2007 book *Eight O'clock Ferry to the Windward Side:*

Binyam was twenty-seven. He was tall and gangling, dark-skinned, originally from Ethiopia. He smiled and immediately told me how glad he was to see me. He spoke quietly, with a particular dignity. Some prisoners would take many hours of convincing that I was not from the CIA, but Binyam immediately opened up. I explained what we needed to do, and he started talking. He barely paused for breath during the three consecutive days we met. I have become so used to typing that the effort of handwriting notes was exhausting. Absorbing what he told me about being tortured would be far more difficult.[256]

At that time, Binyam Mohamed was one of around 540 alleged enemy combatants in Guantánamo. Not one of them had yet been brought before the problem-plagued military tribunals, the bodies President Bush had created by presidential order in October 2001 to prosecute detainees accused of acts of terrorism or war crimes, and a recent push toward prosecutions had prompted an embarrassing round of resignations of military prosecutors who were preparing cases for the tribunals. In their resignation letters to chief prosecutor Colonel Fred Borch, one of them, Air Force Captain John Carr, called the tribunal system "a half hearted and disorganized effort by a skeleton group of relatively inexperienced attorneys to prosecute fairly low-level accused in a process that appears to be rigged"; another, Air Force Major Robert Preston, observed simply, "writing a motion saying that the process will be full and fair when you don't really believe it is kind of hard—particularly when you want to call yourself an officer and a lawyer."[257]

Testifying in Congress after the Supreme Court struck down this first version of the military tribunal proceedings as unconstitutional in 2006, Lt. Commander Charles Swift raised the critical question of "whether military commissions can ever actually deliver the full and fair trails promised by the President's Order. Based on the past five years the inescapable conclusion is that the commission consistently failed to meet the President's mandate for full and fair trials." The system's "many shortcomings" ranged from the fact that all of the personnel involved, including the officers serving as jurors, were handpicked by the Appointing Authority, the same official who approved the charges, to the fact that the defense had limited power to call witnesses and that defense counsel, when they were granted access to secret government documents, could not share them with their clients. Most outrageously, Swift told the Senate, "the military commission system had no rule preventing the admissibility of statements obtained by coercion," and "had inadequate rules to ensure that the Defense would receive exculpatory evidence in the government's possession"—including evidence that the information relied upon by the prosecutors was the fruit of torture. This was especially true, Swift made clear, if the source of that information was the CIA.

> *Providing the defense with exculpatory evidence in the government's possession promotes not only a tribunal's fairness, but also the accuracy of its results. That is why the Supreme Court has held that an "individual prosecutor has a duty to learn of any favorable evidence known to the others acting on the government's behalf in the case, including the police." Yet in the military commission system, the Prosecution had no obligation to give the Defense exculpatory evidence in the possession of other government agencies. This was significant because, according to one former military commission prosecutor, government agencies intended to deliberately exploit this gap in discovery obligations to keep the defense from obtaining exculpatory evidence. Commission prosecutor Captain John Carr wrote to the commission system's Chief Prosecutor, "In our meeting with [a government agency], they told us that the exculpatory information, if it existed, would be in the 10% that we will not get with our agreed upon searches. I again brought up the problem that this presents to us in the car on the way back from the meeting, and you told me that the rules were written in such a way as to not require that we conduct such thorough searches, and that we weren't going to worry about it."[258]*

That was the situation Mohamed and Stafford Smith were facing on November 4, 2005, when the Appointing Authority for Military Commissions approved charges against Mohamed for conspiring with "Usama Bin Laden (a/k/a Abu Abdullah), Saif al Adel, Dr. Ayman al Zawahiri (a/k/a "the Doctor"), Mohammad Atef (a/k/a Abu Hafs al

Masri), Abd al Hadi al Iraq, Zayn al Abidin Muammad Husayn (a/k/a
Abu Zubayda hereinafter "Abu Zubayda"), Jose Padilla, and Khalid
Sheikh Mohammad" to commit acts of terrorism. The charge sheet is a
compendium of alleged plots connecting Mohamed to this who's who of
alleged terrorist leaders:

> 14. *In furtherance of this enterprise and conspiracy, Binyam*
> *Muhammad [sic] and other members or associates of al Qaida*
> *committed the following overt acts:*
>   a. *On or about May 2001, after a recent conversion to Islam, Binyam*
>   *Muhammad, a trained electrical engineer, traveled to Afghanistan*
>   *and attended al Qaida's al Farouq training camp, where he received*
>   *training in light weapons such as the Kalishnikov, Simonov, PKA,*
>   *rocket-propelled grenades (RPGs) and crew-served weapons.*
>   b. *In early summer 2001, which Binyam Muhammad was at al*
>   *Farouq, Usama Bin Laden visited the camp several times and*
>   *lectured Binyam Muhammad and other trainees about the*
>   *importance of conducting operations against the United States,*
>   *Europe, and Israel. During one of these lectures Usama bin Laden*
>   *told the group "something big is going to happen in the future" and*
>   *to "get ready" or words to that effect.*
>   c. *During August 2001, after completing his training at al Farouq,*
>   *Binyam Muhammad attended a city warfare course in Kabul where*
>   *he was to receive ten days of pistol training, ten days of training on*
>   *the AK-47, and ten days of "room to room" combat. Due to lack*
>   *of ammunition, Binyam Muhammed only received training on the*
>   *AK-47 assault rifle.*
>   d. *In September 2001, after completing his abbreviated city warfare*
>   *course, Binyam Muhammad moved to the front lines in Bagram to*
>   *experience fighting between the Taliban and the Northern Alliance.*
>   *While on the front lines, Binyam Muhammad took a course in*
>   *firing mortars, map reading, targeting and firing.*
>   e. *After a short time on the front lines in Bagram, Binyam Muhammad*
>   *attended an explosives training camp in Kabul where he received*

training on explosives and "homemade" bomb-making. Also in attendance at this camp was Richard Reid.

f. *After traveling from Kabul to Khandahar, Binyam Muhammed was directed to go to Zormat, Afghanistan where he met with Abd al Hadi al Iraqi. While in Zormat, Binyam Muhammad was told al Qaida had a "mission" for him.*

g. *Binyam Muhammad then traveled to Birmel, Afghanistan, and was introduced to Abu Zubayda. Abu Zubayda promised him training in Pakistan building remote-control-detonation devices for explosives that were to be used against American forces. After his training was complete, Binyam Muhammad was to return to Afghanistan to make detonation devices and teach others how to construct them.*

h. *Binyam Muhammad traveled with Abu Zubayda from Khost into Pakistan, stopping at several guesthouses and a madrassa (religious school) where he first met Jose Padilla, Ghassan al Sharbi and Jabran Said al Qahtani. Abd al Hadi al Iraqi and Abu Zubayda directed Binyam Muhammad (along with al Sharbi and al Qahtani) to receive training on building remote-controlled detonation devices for explosives.*

i. *From the madrassa in Khost Binyam Muhammad traveled to a guesthouse in Lahore, Pakistan, where he and Jose Padilla reviewed instructions on a computer in the guesthouse on how to make an improvised "dirty bomb." Ghassan al Sharbi translated these instructions into Arabic and read them aloud to a group in the guest house.*

j. *After arriving in Lahore, Binyam Muhammad and Jose Padilla met with Abu Zubayda in private and discussed plans for attacks against the United States. Abu Zubayda stated that he preferred Binyam Muhammad conduct an "overseas" operation instead of going back to Afghanistan as originally planned. Binyam Muhammad agreed to carry out an operation in the United States.*

k. *While in Lahore, Binyam Muhammad, Jose Padilla and Abu Zubayda discussed the feasibility of constructing the improvised "dirty" bomb from the instructions they had read on the computer. Abu Zubayda also discussed other plans against the United States with Binyam Muhammad and Jose Padilla, such as blowing up gas tankers and spraying people with cyanide in nightclubs. Abu Zubayda told Binyam Muhammad that one of the purposes for the attacks on the United States was to help "free the prisoners in Cuba."*

l. *After spending a few days in guest houses in Lahore and Faisalabad, Binyam Muhammad and Jose Padilla were sent to Karachi to meet Saif al Adel (the head of al Qaida's security committee) and Khalid Sheikh Mohammad (a top level al Qaida planner and leader). Saif al Adel and Khalid Sheikh Mohammad told Binyam Muhammad that their mission would involve targeting high-rise apartment buildings that utilized natural gas for its heat and also targeting gas stations. The apartment building plan called for renting an apartment and utilizing the natural gas in the buildings to detonate an explosion that would collapse all of the floors above. Binyam Muhammad and Jose Padilla agreed to conduct such an operation.*

m. *In early April 2002, Binyam Muhammad was given approximately $6,000 U.S. dollars and Jose Padilla was given approximately $10,000 U.S. dollars to get to the United States and met with Khalid Sheikh Mohammad for last minute briefings.*

n. *On of about April 4, 2002, Binyam Muhammad and Jose Padilla were both detained at passport control at the airport in Karachi (Binyam Muhammad for a forged passport and Jose Padilla due to visa violations), but were released the next morning. Khalid Skeikh Mohammad arranged to get Binyam Muhammad a different forged passport while Jose Padilla continued on to Chicago, Illinois.*

15. On or about April 10, 2002, Binyam Muhammad was arrested at an airport in Karachi, Pakistan, attempting to get back to London using a forged passport.[259]

Just over two weeks after this charge sheet was issued, Attorney

General Alberto Gonzales announced that Jose Padilla had been indicted in Florida and would be transferred from the military brig in Charleston, South Carolina to stand trial in Miami for conspiring to support violent jihad overseas. Speaking anonymously to reporters the next day, "current and former government officials" acknowledged that the decision to try Padilla on charges unrelated to the "dirty bomb" plot was connected to the fact that the "dirty bomb" case depended heavily on the testimony of Abu Zubaydah and Khalid Sheikh Mohammed—who were still being held in secret CIA black sites—and on Padilla's own self-incriminating statements in the brig. As Douglas Jehl and Eric Lightblau reported in *The New York Times*, "Mr. Mohammed and Mr. Zubaydah could almost certainly not be used as witnesses, because that could expose classified information and could open up charges from defense lawyers that their earlier statements were a result of torture, officials said." Without that testimony it would be "nearly impossible to prove the charges," the administration sources officials told the reporters.

But in Guantánamo, unencumbered by such basic due process requirements as the right to confront one's accuser or to challenge coerced testimony and confessions, the administration was pressing ahead against Binyam Mohamed. On December 12, 2005, Military Commissions Appointing Authority John Altenburg, Jr. signed an order referring the charges against Mohamed "as a non-capital case" to the Military Commission, ordering that "as soon as practicable, the Presiding Officer will conduct those sessions he deems appropriate to the expeditious conduct of the trial."[260] Nine other Guantánamo detainees had charges referred to the Military Commission for trial at about the same time; the charges against three of them, Ghassan Abdullah al-Sharbi, Sufyian Barhoumi, and Jabrad Said bin al-Qahtani also linked them with Abu Zubaydah. U.S. Marine Corps Colonel Ralph Kohlmann, the Presiding Officer named to try the cases, scheduled pre-trial hearings beginning in March, 2006. When attorneys for some of the detainees asked for more time to prepare their cases, Air Force Colonel Morris "Moe" Davis, the Chief Prosecutor for the Commissions, told reporters, "Remember if you dragged Dracula out into the sunlight he melted. Well that's kind of the way it is trying to drag a detainee into the courtroom. The facts are like the sunlight to Dracula. The last thing they want is to face the facts in the courtroom."[261]

For Binyam Mohamed, who had requested to see a lawyer the moment he was detained in Pakistan and who had been secretly detained literally thousands of miles away from any legal proceeding, the remark must have been especially galling. As Smith and Air Force Lieutenant Colonel Yvonne Bradley, his Commission-assigned defense attorney, prepared for his first hearing, Mohamed made some preparations of his own, telling his attorneys he planned to represent himself and requesting that they bring him a shirt dyed prisoner-orange and a notepad and marker on the day of the proceedings.[262]

At the hearing, Mohamed was irrepressible. After a scripted opening, which he interrupted to point out that they had spelled his name wrong and suggested they may therefore have the wrong person in court, Colonel Kohlmann read a long description of the defendant's rights and asked if he understood. "Am I allowed to answer this question now?" Assured that he was, Mohamed began,

You addressed me as Mr. Muhammad. I keep referring to this because this is a big issue. You have the wrong person on the seat. I mean, I don't understand what kind of system, after four years of torture and renditions, still gets the wrong person to be on the stand. I am not Mr. Muhammad, and if you are going by your books, I mean, how can you charge me with something and I am not the person. You got the wrong…the wrong man here.

Do you understand what I'm talking about? I think you're a reasonable person, that's why you're sitting over there. And to have in court a person who the cops put under interrogation for four years and then find out he's the wrong man, I mean, what kind of worthiness do these people have, man? Ask yourself, what kind of worthiness do they have bragging about Dracula and about this island that is getting them a lot of information, a gold mine? I'm innocent; I'm not—I'm not—I'm not supposed to be here. Mr. Muhammad, as you call him, is not here…is not present, so how can we go on?

I don't know if Congress gave you the right to change names, I don't know. Sure. I mean, they give you the right to change laws and play around with them, but I don't know about names. And this is an issue. I can't call you Ralph Kallmann rather than Kohlmann, can I, and arrest you and put you in jail? Because that's not you? Four years of—what do you call it, enhanced torture techniques, and we have the wrong person in court. I mean, that bothers me; I don't know how it doesn't bother you.[263]

Kohlmann tried to steer the hearing back to question of Mohamed's rights.

> BINYAM MOHAMED: *I'm…maybe I'm mistaken about…could you explain what the rights are? I mean, maybe I…I don't want to look stupid in court.*
>
> COL. KOHLMANN: *No, not at all.*
>
> BINYAM MOHAMED: *What is this rights you're talking about? Because I have been four years without rights and now all of the sudden I got rights. I am surprised.*
>
> COL. KOHLMANN: *If at any time during these proceedings you are confused, OK, you should ask for recess and then you can discuss things with your counsel. In this case I am going to explain them to you again because they are actually pretty concisely stated here in the trial guide. First, the one was— the right about a military—detailed military counsel, and I explained to you the right with regard to the Detailed Defense Counsel. And do you recall that explanation?*
>
> BINYAM MOHAMED: *Yeah.*
>
> COL. KOHLMANN: *OK. Do you want me to read it to you again?*
>
> BINYAM MOHAMED: *I don't want to…to go too deep into this because my interest is I've had—I haven't had rights for four years. If I had rights, I don't think I would have been touring the world. Could you explain what is…what is…what is rights? I mean, she can't explain it because I've asked her.*

When Kohlman turned to Lt. Col. Bradley, she elaborated. "The problem is I don't understand commission law," she told the Colonel Kohlmann. "I mean, I don't think anyone understands commission law and...I have to go by seventeen years of experience of law, of legal cases, of precedents. There is nothing out there, so when you send me back to advise him on something, I can only tell him what has existed, not what is being formulated—created—in these commissions." As Kohlmann lectured Bradley on tribunal decorum, Mohamed sat writing "CON-MISSION" on the notepad. "I don't consider this place as a commission," he began again, holding up the sign for reporters.

> So, I mean, I'll call it something else. I've been referring to this place as "the room." I'm happy she stood up there and said she's confused, and I can understand why she's confused about these commissions because this is not a commission, this is a con-mission, is a mission to con the world, and that's what it is, you understand.

Mohamed concluded:

> You said...there is a saying that says preach what you practice. You're preaching something and then practice something else. America preaches democracy and then creates a con-mission because it just wants certain non-citizens to be convicted. I didn't ask for a trial. You can kill me tomorrow; I don't really care. But then I have an obligation to the world that such crap cannot be accepted because of this, I have the right to say it.
>
> If you think your war, you are going to win the war by convicting ten people here, that is very stupid. I am not saying you. I am saying your government.
>
> I'll give you another example. Iran goes around saying, "I have to have a nuclear bomb." America says, "You know what, you can't, because we are stronger than you are." Iran says, "You have a bomb. Why can't I have a bomb?" So tomorrow you are going to have Australia saying, "You know what, you had a con-mission. Why can't

I have a con-mission?" When are you going to stop this? This is not the way to deal with this issue.

That is why I don't want to call this place a courtroom, because I don't think it is a courtroom.

I'm sure you wouldn't agree with it because if you was arrested somewhere in Arabia and bin Laden says, "You know what, you are my enemy but I am going to force you to have a lawyer and I give you some bearded turban person," I don't think you will agree with that. Forget the rules, regulations and crap...you wouldn't deal with that. That is where we are. This is a bad place. You are in charge of it. I don't know if you want to be a general. Because I can tell something, if you want to be a general you have to go along with this, but if you want to stay as colonel, like you are, you have to make real big decisions here.

I am done. You can stop looking at the watch.[264]

* * *

That hearing was as far as the government would get in its first attempt to try Mohamed before a military tribunal.

Three days after the conspiracy charge was entered against him at Guantánamo, the Supreme Court announced it would hear Salim Ahmed Hamdan's appeal challenging the legality of the military commissions. The following month, on December 30, 2005, Congress passed the Detainee Treatment Act of 2005, a schizophrenic piece of legislation that purportedly protected detainees from torture—which was already illegal—while also shielding U.S. personnel accused of abusive interrogations from liability and denying Guantánamo detainees the right to pursue habeas corpus petitions in U.S. courts. In February 2006, citing the DTA, the administration moved to have the Supreme Court dismiss the case, but the Justices heard oral arguments the following month, just as Colonel Kohlmann was presiding over preliminary hearings in Guantánamo.

The Court rejected the administration's argument that the DTA's habeas-stripping provision meant the Supreme Court could no longer consider Hamdan's case, with a 5-3 majority finding that Congress had in fact exempted pending petitions.[265] Asserting its power to review the way the administration proposed to try Hamdan, the Court went on to rule that the military commission created under President Bush's October 2001 order was not a "regularly constituted court affording all the judicial guarantees which are recognized as indispensable by civilized peoples."

To be legal, the Court ruled, the administration's military commissions either needed to comply with the Uniform Code of Military Justice, which codified the Geneva Conventions and international laws of war into U.S. law, or have specific Congressional authorization. The administration argued the 2001 Authorization for Use of Military Force granted the president power to create this new justice system, but Justice Stevens, writing for the majority, disagreed: "There is nothing in the text or legislative history of the AUMF even hinting that Congress intended to expand or alter the authorization set forth in Article 21 of the UCMJ." And the commissions the administration created clearly did not meet the due process requirements of the UCMJ or the "rules and precepts of the law of nations." For instance, though defendants are entitled to see a copy of the charges against them and to a presumption of innocence, "[t]hese rights are subject, however, to one glaring condition:"

> *The accused and his civilian counsel may be excluded from, and precluded from ever learning, what evidence was presented during, any part of the proceeding that either the Appointing Authority or the presiding officer chooses to "close." Grounds for such closure "include the protection of information classified or classifiable....intelligence and law enforcement sources, methods, or activities, and other national security interests."*[266]

Moreover, Stevens wrote, "the accused and his civilian counsel may be denied access to evidence in the form of "protected information" (which includes classified information as well as..."information concerning other national security interests") so long as the presiding officer concludes that the evidence is "probative" under §6(D)(1) and that its admission without the accused's knowledge would not "result in the denial of a full and fair trial."[267]

For the military commissions to comply with both the UCMJ and Geneva Conventions—Common Article 3 of which, at a minimum, applies to the detainees—the Supreme Court held that the same procedural rules must apply for the commissions as for military courts martial "unless such uniformity proves impracticable." The administration insisted that the danger posed by international terrorism made court-martial procedures impracticable, but Stevens disagreed, concluding, "Without for one moment underestimating that danger, it is not evident to us why it should require, in the case of Hamdan's trial, any variance from the rules that govern courts-martial."[268]

The administration returned to Congress following its *Hamdan* defeat, and in the waning hours of the final legislative sessions before recessing for the 2006 midterm elections, Congress answered the *Hamdan* decision by passing the Military Commissions Act, which President Bush signed into law on October 17, 2006. The bill's announced purpose was "to authorize trial by military commission for violations of the law of war and other purposes"; it largely replicated the procedures the administration had previously prescribed for the commission and this time made clear it was stripping all detainees of habeas corpus rights, including those, like Binyam Mohamed, who had habeas cases pending in federal courts in the U.S. The MCA also included provisions retroactively narrowing the definition of what kinds of detainee mistreatment might violate the War Crimes Act, so that now U.S. officials could face prosecution only for "grave breaches" of Common Article 3 of the Geneva Conventions, and extending immunity to interrogators who relied in good faith on the administration's legal advice.

The day after the Act was signed, the government served notice on 197 Guantánamo detainees that

The MCA, among other things, amends 28 U.S.C. § 2241 to provide that "no court, justice, or judge shall have jurisdiction" to consider either (1) habeas petitions "filed by or on behalf of an alien detained by the United States who has been determined by the United States to have been properly detained as an enemy combatant or is awaiting

such determination" or (2) "any other action against the United
States or its agents relating to any aspect of the detention, transfer,
treatment, trial, or conditions of confinement of an alien who is
or was detained by the United States" as an enemy combatant.....
Further, the new amendment to § 2241 takes effect on the date of
enactment and applies specifically "to all cases, without exception,
pending on or after the date of the enactment of this Act which relate
to any aspect of the detention, transfer, treatment, trial, or conditions
of detention of an alien detained by the United States since September
11, 2001.[269]

Three cases had been brought before these reconstituted military
commissions at Guantánamo by the time Mohamed was recharged.
Australian David Hicks was released under a plea bargain to serve a
nine-month sentence in his home country. Two others, Salim Ahmed
Hamdan and Omar Khadr, had the charges against them dismissed on
technicalities.[270] Also by the time Mohamed was recharged, Jose Padilla
had been convicted in Miami on the pre-9/11 conspiracy charges. The
International Red Cross had delivered its report on the treatment of
the fourteen high-value detainees from the CIA black sites to the U.S.
government; and though that report was not yet public, the general outlines
of Abu Zubaydah's treatment were well known.

In March, 2008, the London law firm of Leigh Day and Company sent
an "Extremely Urgent Letter Before Claim to British Foreign Secretary
David Miliband" announcing "We act on behalf of Binyam Mohamed, a
British resident currently held in U.S. custody in Guantánamo Bay, and who
is facing the imminent probability of military commission proceedings."
Noting that Mohamed was facing a deadline of April 6, 2008 and that his
attorney Clive Stafford Smith would file a lawsuit if necessary, the letter
explained that its purpose was

to make an urgent request for access to the documents and evidence
set out in the attached Appendix. Such documents and evidence

are likely to be exculpatory in the likely forthcoming U.S. military commission proceedings.

The context could scarcely be more important. The liberty (and possibly, the life) of Mr. Mohamed is at stake in U.S. military commission proceedings, and there is a strong reason to believe that the UK holds exculpatory evidence that would assist in Mr. Mohamed's defence. As such, it is under a clear obligation to provide such material and assistance to Mr. Mohamed, to help ensure that he can challenge the serious allegations that are likely to be made against him. The public interest in the disclosure of such material is overwhelming.[271]

The letter's appendix provided a list of "the categories of exculpatory evidence in the possession of the UK government that would assist Mr. Mohamed in defending against charges before a U.S. Military Commission in Cuba." Leading the list was "Any evidence of UK knowledge of Mr. Mohamed's upcoming rendition whilst he was held in Pakistan in April–July 2002, including any information known about the decision to render Mr. Mohamed to Morocco for torture."

Evidence is required to counter this. In particular, we seek the identity of the U.S. agents involved, so that they can be traced and interviewed or subpoenaed.

Indeed, the U.S. continues to deny that anyone was rendered to a foreign country by U.S. agents to be tortured. It is crucial that Mr Mohamed rebut this denial in order to establish that evidence obtained under or as a result of torture is inadmissible. Since the U.S. practice of extraordinary rendition for torture is a crime of universal jurisdiction under UK law pursuant to section 134 of the Criminal Justice Act 1988, there can be no conceivable basis on which this information should not be provided to assist in Mr Mohamed's defence. Indeed, it is our view that failure to provide this information would amount to complicity in torture, contrary to Article 4 of the UN Convention Against Torture which the UK has ratified and is committed to upholding.[272]

The letter also demanded "all information provided to the U.S. by the UK about Mr. Mohamed (including the fact that he was a 'nobody', only a cleaner from London)"; the opportunity "to interview and take statements from the UK agents who (it was conceded) spoke to Mr Mohamed whilst he was detained in Pakistan"; "full details and copies of the information [UK authorities] either passed direct to Morocco or via U.S. authorities"; and information concerning conditions in the "dark prison." Finally,

> *Mr. Mohamed was subsequently transferred to Bagram Air Force Base, before being moved to Guantánamo Bay. Due to prohibitions imposed by the U.S. government, Mr. Stafford Smith is unable to reveal the full nature of the case against Mr Mohamed to this firm. However, it is likely (based on the approach taken in other cases) that the U.S. will seek to use so-called "clean team" interrogation evidence against Mr Mohamed. They will only seek to rely on evidence obtained from Mr Mohamed after his overt torture in Morocco and the Dark Prison. However, evidence of prior torture arranged or carried out by U.S. agents is of course relevant to the admissibility and credibility of any such "clean team" interrogation evidence. In any event, we understand that British agents were often involved in the on-going interrogations at Bagram, and it is highly likely that the UK has plentiful evidence from multiple sources of allegations of coercion and abuse in Bagram (whether against Mr Mohamed or anyone else), or even of the homicides that were committed there by U.S. forces. Please provide such evidence.*[273]

Mohamed was formally recharged with conspiracy on May 28, 2008. The charge sheet is virtually identical to the one issued on November 4, 2005, except that Richard Reid's name has been removed from paragraph (e) and every reference to Abu Zubaydah has been purged from the document. Where before "Binyam Mohammad then traveled to Birmel, Afghanistan and was introduced to Abu Zubayda" and "Abu Zubayda promised him training in Pakistan building remote control devices for explosives," for example, now "Binyam Mohamed then traveled to Birmel Afghanistan, and trained on building remote control devices." "After arriving in Lahore, Binyam Mohammad and Jose Padilla met with Abu Zubayda in private and discussed plans for attacks against the United States" and "Abu Zubayda stated he preferred Binyam Mohamed conduct an 'overseas' operation instead of going back to Afghanistan" became "After arriving in Lahore, Binyam Mohamed and Jose Padilla plotted attacks against the United States. After these discussions, Mohamed and Padilla agreed to be sent to the United States to conduct these operations rather than returning to Afghanistan."[274]

Two days after the charges were filed, Clive Stafford Smith and Lt. Col. Yvonne Bradley wrote Susan Crawford, the Convening Authority for Military Commissions, asking the Convening Authority to investigate the evidence that the charges against Mohamed were based in part on evidence derived through torture, and that if her investigation confirmed that the charges were based at all on torture-derived evidence, the charges be dismissed. The Convening Authority answered first that "I will consider the information you provided before making a decision or the referral of charges in this case," and then, five days later, "the issues raised in your letters are best resolved through the formal military commission process."[275]

On June 12, 2008, the Supreme Court issued a decision in a case brought by Guantánamo detainee Lakhdar Boumediene challenging the MCA's habeas-stripping provision, ruling by a 5-4 majority that the Act "operated as an unconstitutional suspension of the writ" and that, because the United States exercises complete jurisdiction and control over the military base at Guantánamo, U.S. courts indeed have jurisdiction to hear habeas petitions of Guantánamo detainees. Stafford Smith and Bradley immediately wrote Crawford again, warning that "unless you inform us by 5:00 p.m. EST on Friday, June 20 that you agree to these reasonable requests, we will ask District Judge [Emmet] Sullivan, before whom Mr. Mohamed's habeas action is pending, to order the convening authority to take the requested actions."[276]

Meanwhile, Mohamed's UK attorneys had made good on their warning to the foreign secretary by filing suit to compel the British government to turn over to Mohamed any evidence it had that corroborated his account of extraordinary rendition and torture. The Foreign Secretary's office refused to say whether it possessed any exculpatory material, claiming "summary grounds of resistance" to the suit and moving for dismissal without a hearing. The court declined to dismiss, and on June 6, Miliband told the court that the Foreign office did have exculpatory evidence but would not disclose it to Mohamed's attorneys unless compelled; rather, Miliband said he would turn the materials over to U.S. military prosecutors in Guantánamo and let them decide whether or not to share the materials with Stafford Smith and Lt. Col. Bradley. At a hearing on June 20, 2008, a British judge criticized Miliband's actions as "very, very disturbing." Two days later, the U.S. reported to Miliband that it had reviewed the materials he sent, which included a description the CIA had sent to British intelligence describing Mohamed's interrogation in Afghanistan, and dismissed the allegations as "not credible."[277]

Under a principle of British law defined in a case called *Norwich Pharmacal*, a party may be required to turn over documents or information to a plaintiff in a lawsuit if the party is "involved or mixed up," even innocently, in the wrongdoing alleged in the suit; at issue before the UK court was whether the British government was involved or mixed up in Binyam Mohamed's incommunicado detention, abusive interrogation, or extraordinary rendition. In late August, after reviewing forty-two documents British intelligence services had received from the CIA concerning Mohamed's detention and treatment and hearing testimony from "Witness B," the secret service agent who interviewed Mohamed while he was being held in Pakistan, the court offered the following findings in support of its conclusion that British authorities were indeed mixed up in Mohamed's treatment at the hands of the Americans:

> (iii) It was clear from reports that BM was held incommunicado from 10 April 2002 whilst a series of interviews was conducted by the United States authorities in April 2002 during which he had asked for a lawyer and had been refused.
>
> (iv) In May 2002, the SyS and the SIS received reports containing information relating to BM's detention and treatment in Pakistan. The details of the reports are set out in the closed judgment....

(viii) During the interview Witness B saw himself as having a role to play in conjunction with the United States authorities in inducing BM to cooperate by making it clear that the United Kingdom would not help unless BM cooperated. We can well understand why, given the exigencies of the time, Witness B put matters in such stark terms as he did. It is clear that what he said to BM was, in effect, that the United Kingdom would not attempt to assist him unless BM persuaded him that he was cooperating fully with the United States authorities.

(ix) By 30 September 2002, it was clear to the SyS that BM was being held at a covert location (either by the authorities of the United States or under the direct control of the United States) which was not a United States military facility, such as Bagram. It is clear to us that they knew that he was not in a regular United States facility, that the facility in which he was being detained and questioned was that of a foreign government (other than Afghanistan) and that the United States authorities had direct access to information being obtained from him.

(x) The SyS were supplying information as well as questions which they knew were to be used in interviews of BM from the time of his arrest whilst he was held incommunicado and without access to a lawyer or review by a court or tribunal. They continued to supply information and questions after they knew of the circumstances of BM's detention and treatment as contained in the reports of the series of interviews in May 2002 and after September 2002 when they knew the circumstances related to his continued detention which we have described in subparagraph (ix)[278]

Subparagraph (iv)'s "information relating to Binyam's detention and treatment in Pakistan" was the forty-two CIA documents; the subparagraph itself was a placeholder marking the space where the court had redacted seven paragraphs summarizing their contents. It would be a year and a half before those paragraphs were restored to the public version of the court's judgment. As for the documents themselves, though, the court ruled that they were essential to Mohamed's defense, insisting "we can think of no good reason why the materials have not now been made available by the United States Government to Binyam Mohamed's lawyers."[279] Hinting that it was prepared to order the British government to turn the documents over to Mohamed, the court added,

> It is of particular significance that the United States Government has refused to provide any information as to BM's location during the period between May 2002 and May 2004.... It might have been thought self evident that the provision of information as to the whereabouts of a person in custody would cause no particular difficulty, given that it is a basic and long established value in any democracy that the location of those in custody is made known to the detainee's family and those representing him.
>
> In these circumstances to leave the issue of disclosure to the processes of the Military commission at some future time would be to deny to BM a real chance of providing some support to a limited part of his account and other essential assistance to his defence. To deny him this at this time would be to deny him the opportunity of timely justice in respect of the charges against him, a principle dating back to at least the time of Magna Carta and which is so basic a part of our common law and of democratic values.[280]

The next day, John Bellinger, who was now serving as Legal Advisor to Secretary of State Condoleezza Rice, wrote the British Foreign office pledging that the forty-two documents would be provided to the Convening Authority if the Convening Authority requested them, and that they would be produced to Lt. Col. Bradley if charges were referred to the military commission. A week later, the Foreign office told the court it had received a letter from the U.S. State Department confirming that the request had been received and the documents had been delivered to the Convening Authority. Satisfied for the moment that the materials would be available to Mohamed if his case went to trial, the court backed away from the threat to order their release.

But the British court's confidence in the Bush administration's assurances was short-lived, shaken by two events in the U.S. in September. First, Lt. Col. Darrel Vandeveld, the military prosecutor handling Mohamed's case, requested to resign from the Office of Military Prosecutors. Vandeveld was also prosecuting Mohammed Jawad, a Pakistani youth facing murder charges for allegedly throwing a grenade into a jeep in a passing military convoy in Afghanistan. In a sworn statement to the military commission dated September 22, 2008, Vandeveld declared,

I have divulged to [Jawad's military defender] Major Frakt those items of discovery that in my professional judgment the Rules for Professional Conduct, the Military Commissions Act, and the Manual for Military Commissions (MMC) have required me to relinquish, consistent with my ethical obligations as a prosecutor. In particular, I have forwarded to him immediately those items of evidence I considered to be exculpatory or in mitigation of the acts for which Mr. Jawad stands accused. Where I was unable to provide him with evidence that he requested, I attempted to give him an explanation for why I could not provide the evidence. In some cases, that has meant acknowledging that we have been unable to locate such evidence despite extensive searches. In other cases, that has meant identifying certain agencies, offices, individuals, or procedures which were preventing the disclosure, although I can swear under oath that I never revealed any classified information Major Frakt had not been entitled to receive; nor have I singled out any particular individual for condemnation....

My ethical qualms about continuing to serve as a prosecutor relate primarily to the procedures for affording defense counsel discovery. I am highly concerned, to the point that I believe I can no longer serve as a prosecutor at the Commissions, about the slipshod, uncertain "procedure" for affording defense counsel discovery. One would have thought that after six years since the Commissions had their fitful start that a functioning law office would have been set up and procedures and policies not only put into effect, but refined....

In my view, evidence we have an obligation as prosecutors and

officers of the court has not been made available to the defense.
Potentially exculpatory evidence has not been provided. My own
practice has been to relinquish immediately any piece of evidence I
have come across to the defense, even at the peril of the case against
Mohammed Jawad, and even though I sympathize and identify with
the victims in the case. To take one example, when I discovered
that Mr. Jawad had been placed in the "frequent flyer" program, I
notified the defense, sought an investigation, spoke to witnesses who
had not been identified by the law enforcement agencies assisting us,
and, in the end, conceded in a court filing that I had been wrong in
denouncing Mr. Jawad when he complained of the conduct toward
him in one of the first Commission proceedings. My personal practice
of disclosing exculpatory or mitigating evidence is not universally
practiced at OMC-P.[281]

Vandeveld would later elaborate on his experiences in a declaration
Jawad's attorneys submitted in his habeas corpus proceedings, a document
remarkable both for the misconduct it details and for Vandeveld's account
of his dawning awareness of the mistreatment Jawad had endured:

At some point during the hearing, Mr. Jawad erupted into a series
of harsh complaints about his mistreatment at Guantánamo, in
which he described having been moved repeatedly from cell to cell in
order to deprive him of sleep. Having at that point seen no evidence
substantiating this claim, and for which I could divine no legitimate
purpose, I dismissed his speech as an exaggeration....
    Over the next few weeks, I set about trying to gather the records
in response to Major Frakt's discovery request. I obtained a copy of the
Detainee Incident Management System (DIMS) records maintained
by JTF-GTMO. The DIMS are the official prison logs of all actions
and activities for each detainee. Every move, medical appointment,
chaplain visit, interrogation, and disciplinary action is recorded, and
much more. While reviewing the records, I noticed that they referred
to a suicide attempt by Mohammed Jawad on December 25, 2003,

which he sought to accomplish by banging his head repeatedly against one of his cell walls. I sent a copy of the records to Major Frakt. Shortly thereafter, Major Frakt contacted me with some follow-up questions about the records. The records reflected 112 unexplained moves from cell to cell over a two week period, an average of eight moves per day for 14 days. Upon further investigation, we were able to determine that Mr. Jawad had been subjected to a sleep deprivation program popularly referred to as the "frequent flyer" program. I realized that Mr. Jawad had been telling the truth at the last hearing. I lack the words to express the heartsickness I experienced when I came to understand the pointless, purely gratuitous mistreatment of Mr. Jawad by my fellow soldiers.

Over the course of the summer, my concerns and doubts about the strength of the case continued to mount. Despite a diligent search for the videotape of Mr. Jawad's original interrogation by U.S. personnel, a search that included a service-wide inquiry about the tape and where it might be located, I was never able to find the tape. I also failed to locate two alleged eyewitnesses to the attack who had allegedly told a U.S. investigator that they had personally witnessed Jawad throw the grenade. All I had were two paragraph summaries of interviews conducted through an interpreter of these witnesses several months after the attack. The information on these summaries identifying these two witnesses consisted solely of their names, both of which were common in Afghanistan.[282]

He concluded:

Ultimately, I decided that I could no longer ethically prosecute Mr. Jawad or, in good conscience, serve as a prosecutor at OMC-P. I have taken an oath to support and defend the Constitution of the United States, and I remain confident that I have done so, spending over four of the past seven years away from my family, my home, my civilian occupation—all without any expectation of or desire for any reward greater than the knowledge that I have remained true to my word and have done my level best to rise to our Nation's defense in its time of need. I did not "quit" the Commissions or resign; instead, I personally petitioned the Army's Judge Advocate General to allow me to serve the remaining six months of my two year voluntary obligation in Afghanistan or Iraq. In the exercise of his wisdom and discretion, he permitted me to be released from active duty. However, had I been returned to Afghanistan or Iraq, and had I encountered Mohammed Jawad in either of those hostile lands, where two of my friends have been killed in action and another one of my very best friends in the world had been terribly wounded, I have no doubt at all—none— that Mr. Jawad would pose no threat whatsoever to me, his former prosecutor and now-repentant persecutor. Six years is long enough for a boy of sixteen to serve in virtual solitary confinement, in a distant land, for reasons he may never fully understand. I respectfully ask this Court to find that Mr. Jawad's continued detention is unsupported by any credible evidence, any provision of the Detainee Treatment Act of 2005, the MCA, international law or our own Constitution. Mr. Jawad should be released to resume his life in a civil society, for his sake, and for our own sense of justice and perhaps to restore a measure of our basic humanity.[283]

Also on September 22, 2008, the same day Lt. Col. Vandeveld submitted his statement to the Military Commission, Judge Emmet Sullivan held a status conference on Binyam Mohamed's habeas corpus petition and ordered the U.S. government to turn over any exculpatory material held by any U.S. agencies by October 6, 2008.

On October 6, the government responded with a document that reiterated its assertions that Mohamed was a trained Al Qaeda operative who had planned to detonate a dirty bomb, explode a gas tanker, and release cyanide in nightclubs. When the UK court reviewed that document, it saw that the allegations were supported almost entirely by two pieces of evidence: Criminal Investigation Task Force reports of his interviews shortly after arriving in Guantánamo, and the twenty-one page confession he had produced in Bagram between July 28 and July 31, 2004, two months after he had been transferred from the Dark Prison, parts of which he had handwritten and parts of which he'd initialed. That confession ended with this exchange:

Q. *Have you made this statement of your own free will, without benefit, promise, or reward?*

A. *Yes.*

Q. *Has the interviewing agent promised you anything?*

A. *No.*

Q. *Has the interviewing agent treated you fairly, humanely, with respect and decency?*

A. *Yes.*

Q. *During your interviews with the interviewing agent have you been provided and/or offered food, beverage and toilet facilities?*

A. *Yes.*

Q. *Have you been treated well since you have been in U.S. military custody?*

A. *Yes.*

Q. *While in U.S. Military custody have you been treated in any way that you would consider abusive?*

A. *No.*

Q. *Has your ability to practice your religious beliefs been prevented since you have been in U.S. Military custody?*

A. *No.*

Q. *What would you say is your current state of health?*

A. *I feel healthy.*

Q. *While in U.S. Military custody, have you had access to medical care?*

A. *Yes.*

Q. *Are you willing to assist the U.S. Government by providing co-operative testimony and/or information during judicial proceedings and/or other legal processes?*

A. *I still haven't made up my mind.*

Q. *Has your co-operation thus far been of your own free will without benefit, reward, or promise?*

A. Yes.

Q. Is the information contained in this statement the truth?

A. Yes.[284]

But the administration also signaled it might be changing course. It notified Judge Sullivan that it had turned over seven of the forty-two documents, in the same heavily redacted form they had been released to the Convening Authority, to Mohamed's attorneys. It also announced that it was no longer relying on the allegations that Binyam Mohamed was plotting terrorist attacks in the United States to justify his detention as an enemy combatant.

Alarmed, Judge Sullivan ordered Mohamed's lawyers to make him aware of any documents they believed they needed for his defense, and scheduled another status conference for October 30, 2008. Equally troubled, the UK court notified the Foreign office and Mohamed's attorneys on October 21, 2008 that it would be handing down a judgment on releasing the 42 documents the following day.

That same day that the UK court issued this notice, the Pentagon announced it had dropped all charges against Binyam Mohamed and four other detainees whose original charge sheets had linked them to Abu Zubaydah. The day before, Convening Authority Susan Crawford had signed a directive declaring "The recommendation of the Legal Adviser in the Military Commission case of Binyam Mohamed is approved. All charges and specifications are dismissed without prejudice." Similar directives were issued for Ghassan Abdullah Sharbi, Sufyiam Barhoumi, Jabran Said bin al-Qahtani, and Noor Uthman Muhammed. Crawford offered no explanation for dropping the cases, but Michael Chapman, the Convening Authority's Legal Advisor, suggested that prosecutors needed more time to prepare their cases following Vandeveld's resignation. Vandeveld's replacements told Lt. Col. Bradley that they would file new charges against Mohamed within thirty days.[285]

At his October 30, 2008 status hearing, Judge Sullivan openly questioned the administration's motives for abandoning the "dirty bomb" charges and then dismissing the case against Binyam Mohamed just when two courts were on the verge of ordering it to release exculpatory documents. "That raises serious questions in this court's mind about whether the allegations were ever true," Sullivan declared.[286]

Judge Sullivan had before him a Notice of Service of Discovery that Mohamed's attorney had filed on October 27 asking the court for permission to depose Vandeveld and "Jane Payne," the member of Mohamed's rendition crew who he said had photographed the cuts on his penis; a seventeen-page Request for Admissions asking the government to stipulate to the truth of 199 specific details of Mohamed's account; and a Request for Production of Documents and Tangible Things relating to his treatment and interrogations in Pakistan, Morocco, the Dark Prison, Bagram, and Guantánamo.[287] At the hearing, Judge Sullivan ordered the government to turn over all exculpatory evidence relating to the withdrawn allegations of planned terrorist attacks in the U.S.

On December 1, he further ordered the government to release all exculpatory evidence "that would suggest that Petitioner should not be designated as an enemy combatant," and a week later he followed this with an order that within three days "the United States agent(s) who conducted the interviews with the Petitioner since he was brought into custody upon which Respondent relies in its Amended Factual Return shall submit a sworn declaration describing the circumstances surrounding the interviews and the resulting statements by Petitioner," and that the agent or agents must be made available for a deposition by Mohamed's attorneys before January 5, 2009. Meanwhile, he ordered Defense Secretary Robert Gates to provide a sworn affidavit under penalty of perjury that all exculpatory evidence had been turned over to Mohamed's lawyers.[288]

The UK court, meanwhile, had issued the ruling it promised in its October 22, 2008 opinion, a decision that essentially postponed ordering the release of the forty-two CIA documents to Mohamed's attorneys in deference to the habeas proceedings before Judge Sullivan in the U.S. The court emphasized that it found in the documents not only passages "relevant to the allegation made by BM that his confession had been the result of conduct that amounts to torture or cruel inhuman or degrading treatment," but also that it had publicly disclosed part of its finding on why the information in the documents was essential for Mohamed to receive a fair trial—not only relating to the dirty bomb plot charges, but to the allegations that he was an Al Qaeda associate and an enemy combatant as well.[289] But it would wait to see how Judge Sullivan ruled. "In light of his decision, this issue may become academic," the court wrote.

If not we will have the benefit of understanding the position of the United States Government and the benefit of Judge Sullivan's views when we proceed to determine the remaining issues in relation to the provision of the 42 documents. These issues include [Mohamed's attorneys'] submission that the Government of the United States is deliberately seeking to avoid disclosure of the 42 documents.

We must record that we have found the events set out in this judgment deeply disturbing. This matter must be brought to a just conclusion as soon as possible, given the delays and unexplained changes of course which have taken place on the part of the United States Government.[290]

That October 22 judgment contained a cryptic paragraph that read,

We refer in an annex (which it is not possible to make public now but which we will make public as soon as we can) to other matters before the Convening Authority.[291]

On March 23, 2009, the court released that annex, an astonishing document detailing the U.S. government's last-ditch effort to secure a plea bargain from Binyam Mohamed.

In August, before Lt. Col. Vandeveld's resignation, Vandeveld had asked Stafford Smith and Lt. Col. Bradley if Mohamed was open to a plea agreement. Unsure whether this time around the prosecution might seek the death penalty, and informed that even if Mohamed were acquitted he would continue to be detained as an enemy combatant until the ill-defined "end of hostilities," Stafford Smith and Bradley indicated that Mohamed was prepared to enter a *nolo contendere* plea to the May 28,

2008 charges in exchange for a sentence of no more than three years, with credit for time served since he was originally charged in 2005 and provided he was repatriated to the UK and not required to testify against others in Guantánamo. Vandeveld had countered with an offer of three years without credit for time served, during which Mohamed would agree to testify against other detainees. The negotiations ended there.

But on October 20, 2008, the day the Convening Authority dismissed the charges against Mohamed and the four others whose charge sheets mentioned Abu Zubaydah, Mohamed's attorneys received a draft plea agreement. In the annex, the UK court said, "It is important, we think, to set out some of the provisions of the agreement":

i)   *Clause 2 provided that BM agree to plead guilty to charge 1 and 2.*

ii) *Clause 5 provided that BM understood that the maximum statutory penalty, should his pleas of guilty be accepted for each charge, was confinement for life.*

iii) *Clause 7 provided as follows:*
   "The accused agrees not to participate in or support in any manner any litigation or challenge, in any forum, against the United States or any other nation or official of any nation, whether military or civilian, in their personal or official capacity with regard to the accused's capture, detention, prosecution, post conviction confinement and detainee combatant status. The accused further agrees to move to dismiss with prejudice any presently pending direct or collateral attack challenging the accused's capture, detention, prosecution and detainee combatant status. The accused assigns to the United States all legal rights to sign and submit any necessary documents, motions, or pleadings to implement this provision on behalf of the accused."

iv) *By Clause 10 BM agrees to submit to interviews and to appear before courts or Military commissions to testify if requested by the Government. By Clause 14, BM was to agree and accept as true an attachment setting out the facts supporting the charges. A copy of that was not provided to us.*

*v) By Clause 16, the maximum period of confinement that would
be adjudged and approved would be 10 years, but the Convening
Authority would order the suspension of the balance of the sentence
over one year. A condition was imposed that the Convening Authority
could decide that if BM failed to comply with the provisions of
Clause 10 (assisting the prosecution) the Convening Authority could
vacate the suspended portion of the sentence and order it be served
in full.*[292]

If Mohamed accepted the agreement, he would be forced to abandon
his claim before their court for disclosure of the documents, his attorneys
told the UK justices; likewise, if he pressed the Military Commission for
release of the materials, the deal would be rescinded. They pointed out that
he was being asked to agree to the arrangement at a time when there were
no pending charges against him but when he had been told new charges
were forthcoming, that he did not know what those charges would be and
he still had not seen the exculpatory documents, and that "the strategy of
the United States Government was to take advantage of the short period
of time in which [Binyam Mohamed's] defense lawyers could not see the
materials to conclude a plea bargain that was to the benefit of the United
States."[293]

The court concluded:

*We have provided these paragraphs in this annex to the parties on the
understanding that these are not to be made public at this time. We
do so on the basis that we have been told that these negotiations are
at this stage confidential.*

*However, in the light of the indications that the United States
Government would require in any plea bargain a confidentiality
statement by BM, we expressly enquired whether BM wished to
pursue this argument. We did so as we could not, consistently with our
principles of open justice and the rule of law, entertain this argument,
take it into account in our decision and then refuse to make it public
at an appropriate time. We were told that, notwithstanding this*

consequence, BM wished this issue to be addressed by us. He wanted it to be made clear to the world what had happened and how he had been treated by the United States Government since April 2002.

Accordingly, at an appropriate time after the plea bargain discussions are finally resolved, one way or the other, we shall make public this annex. We should add no plea agreement will be effective to prevent the making public of this annex, even if the proceedings are subsequently discontinued on terms that include a provision similar to clause 7 (set out at paragraph 5 iii) above). This is because this annex is an integral part of our judgment given on 22 October, 2008.[294]

Binyam Mohamed rejected the offer, and by the time the court published the annex, he was a free man in London.

* * *

Two days after his inauguration on January 20, 2009, President Obama signed three executive orders, the first ordering that the Guantánamo detention facility be closed within a year, the second banning torture and requiring that all interrogations comply with the army field manual, and the third establishing a task force to examine detention policies and review all individual cases. By February, pressure was mounting on the new administration to release Mohamed. Clive Stafford Smith wrote President Obama asking him to review the secret evidence of Mohamed's torture. On February 11, 2009 the British government announced that foreign office officials and a Metropolitan Police doctor were on their way to visit Mohamed in Guantánamo; Foreign Secretary Miliband announced the UK was working "as fast and hard as we can to secure his return."[295] That same day, Lt. Col. Bradley was in London appealing for action on Mohamed's behalf. In an op-ed published that morning in the *Guardian*, Lt. Col. Bradley wrote,

I am a lawyer and a soldier, and I act for Binyam Mohamed, who is currently on a hunger strike in Guantánamo Bay. I came to

England to ask everyone to work as hard as possible to get Binyam home. The new administration in the U.S. has said that it wants to close Guantánamo. The UK government says that it has been asking for Binyam's return since August 2007. Despite that, and despite England being the U.S.'s closest ally, Binyam is still in a cell in Guantánamo Bay. I believe that now is the time to press the new administration.

Guards told Binyam that he was going home in December, and so he is on a hunger strike (together with 50 or so other prisoners). This means that he is tube-fed while strapped to a chair, twice a day. Binyam has lost so much weight that he speaks of the pain he suffers from being strapped to the chair for hours each day—he speaks of feeling his bones against the chair. I am really worried that if Binyam does not come home soon, he will leave Guantánamo Bay in a coffin.

She concluded,

I profoundly hope that he is not being kept in Guantánamo to avoid information surrounding his rendition and torture [from] coming out. Clive Stafford Smith and I are testifying at the All Party Parliamentary Group on Extraordinary Rendition in Portcullis House, Westminster today, which is open to members of the public. I understand that a number of intelligence agents and politicians will also speak in an attempt to get Binyam home. I am meeting with David Miliband this Thursday, and I hope that he will assure me that Binyam is coming home.[296]

Twelve days later, Lt. Col. Bradley was among the group of family members and attorneys who welcomed Mohamed when a chartered Gulfstream jet landed at RAF Northolt airbase at 1:11 p.m. on February 23, 2010 following a ten-hour trip from Guantánamo. He was briefly detained under the Terrorism Act of 2000 and then set free. He said nothing to reporters, but shortly before the plane landed his attorneys released this statement on his behalf:

I hope you will understand that after everything I have been through I am neither physically nor mentally capable of facing the media on the moment of my arrival back to Britain. Please forgive me if I make a simple statement through my lawyer. I hope to be able to do better in days to come, when I am on the road to recovery.

I have been through an experience that I never thought to encounter in my darkest nightmares. Before this ordeal, "torture" was an abstract word to me. I could never have imagined that I would be its victim. It is still difficult for me to believe that I was abducted, hauled from one country to the next, and tortured in medieval ways—all orchestrated by the United States government....

And I have to say, more in sadness that in anger, that many have been complicit in my own horrors over the past seven years. For myself, the very worst moment came when I realised in Morocco that the people who were torturing me were receiving questions and materials from British intelligence. I had met with British intelligence in Pakistan. I had been open with them. Yet the very people who I hoped would come to my rescue, I later realised, had allied themselves with my abusers.

I am not asking for vengeance; only that the truth should be made known, so that nobody in the future should have to endure what I have endured.[297]

Even with the change of administrations, though, the United States has continued to thwart efforts to bring documents corroborating Mohamed's ordeal to light. In the UK court, first the Bush administration and then the Obama administration threatened that merely releasing the seven redacted paragraphs that summarize the forty-two secret documents could disrupt the intelligence sharing relationship between Britain and the United States. Foreign Secretary Miliband had successfully argued for the redaction from the court's August 2008 judgment by certifying to the court that

[D]isclosure of these documents by order of our courts or otherwise by United Kingdom authorities would seriously harm the existing intelligence sharing arrangements between the United Kingdom and

the United States and cause considerable damage to national security. I have also assessed that it may damage international relations of the United Kingdom more generally in liaison arrangements with third parties.

In reaching my assessment I have taken into account the fact that the U.S. administration on the basis of clear, consistent, and forceful communications, both written and oral, form senior officials, including at the highest national security levels from all of the departments and agencies concerned, have indicated that such damage is likely to occur.[298]

The court would later comment,

We characterized at several paragraphs in our fourth judgment that the reaction of the Bush Administration was a "threat." After the handing down of our judgment, the Foreign Secretary made a number of public statements disagreeing with our assessment that the statement made by the Bush Administration of the consequences which would follow could be characterized as a threat. In our judgment that is a matter of semantics. Whether this is characterised as "a threat" or "as a statement of consequences which will follow," what matters is substance.

On the evidence placed before us, it could not be disputed that the Bush Administration had made it clear that if the information in the redacted paragraphs was made public then reconsideration would be given to intelligence sharing arrangements. It was that specific matter, given the importance of intelligence sharing arrangements to the national security of the United Kingdom, that led us to conclude that the balance lay in favour of maintaining the redaction of the paragraphs from the first judgment.[299]

Persuaded by the Obama administration's strong public statements against torture and especially by the April 16, 2009 declassification and release of the four OLC memos—which, the court noted, publicly disclosed interrogations techniques which the fourty-two documents indicated had been applied to Mohamed in Pakistan—the court looked to the U.S. for signals that its position had changed on the release of the redacted paragraphs. But following an April 30, 2009 letter from CIA director Leon Panetta to the British secret service and face-to-face conversations with Secretary of State Hillary Clinton, Miliband again reported to the court,

> *She was fully aware of the issues and reiterated the U.S. position on public disclosure in this case had not changed with the change in Administration, the protection of intelligence going beyond party politics. She indicated that the U.S. remained opposed to the public disclosure of U.S. intelligence information in this case. The U.S. Secretary indicated further that public disclosure would affect intelligence sharing and would cause damage to the national security of both the U.S. and the UK. Comment by those representing the National Security Council at the same meeting made it clear, if further clarification was needed, that this was also the position of the White House.*[300]

This ban would likely have remained in place were it not for Judge Gladys Kessler's November 19, 2009 opinion in Farhi Saeed Bin Mohammed's habeas corpus case, where she ruled that the then 48-year-old Algerian must be released because the evidence against him was derived through the torture of Binyam Mohamed. Because her opinion graphically detailed Mohamed's interrogations in Pakistan and his rendition and torture in Morocco and again in the Dark Prison, the UK court concluded it could no longer reasonably be expected to keep seven paragraphs summarizing a small part of this same information secret, nor could the United States reasonably retaliate against Britain for revealing information that its own courts had proclaimed to be true. So on February 10, 2010, an appeals court composed of three of Britain's most senior judges ordered the release of these seven redacted paragraphs:

> *It was reported that a new series of interviews was conducted by*

*the United States authorities prior to 17 May 2002 as part of a new
strategy designed by an expert interviewer.*

*v) It was reported that at some stage during that further interview
process by the United States authorities, BM had been intentionally
subjected to continuous sleep deprivation. The effects of the sleep
deprivation were carefully observed.*

*vi) It was reported that combined with the sleep deprivation,
threats and inducements were made to him. His fears of being removed
from United States custody and "disappearing" were played upon.*

*vii) It was reported that the stress brought about by these deliberate
tactics was increased by him being shackled in his interviews*

*viii) It was clear not only from the reports of the content of the
interviews but also from the report that he was being kept under self-
harm observation, that the interviews were having a marked effect
upon him and causing him significant mental stress and suffering.*

*ix) We regret to have to conclude that the reports provided to the
SyS [security services] made clear to anyone reading them that BM
was being subjected to the treatment that we have described and the
effect upon him of that intentional treatment.*

*x) The treatment reported, if [it] had been administered on behalf
of the United Kingdom, would clearly have been in breach of the
undertakings given by the United Kingdom in 1972. Although it is not
necessary for us to categorise the treatment reported, it could readily
be contended to be at the very least cruel, inhuman and degrading
treatment by the United States authorities.*[301]

Because the UK court had already ruled that the fact that Mohamed
no longer faces trial in the U.S. meant the question of releasing the
documents themselves to his attorneys was essentially moot, the release
of these paragraphs effectively ended Mohamed's suit to have the British
government disclose what it knew about his treatment from 2002 through
2004. But Binyam Mohamed and four other UK-based former detainees
also had civil lawsuits pending in the U.S. and the UK against Jeppesen
Dataplan, Inc., a subsidiary of Boeing that handled the logistics of the CIA's

rendition flights, for "participation in the forced disappearance, torture and inhuman treatment of Plaintiffs…by agents of the United States and other governments." As the U.S. Complaint explained,

> *Flight records obtained by a European Parliamentary inquiry and a parallel investigation by the Council of Europe into CIA activities in Europe, together with other flight records obtained from national civil aviation authorities in Portugal, Spain, the Netherlands, and Italy in the course of criminal and journalistic investigations in those countries, reveal that over a four-year period, beginning on or around December 16, 2001, Jeppesen provided flight and logistical support to at least fifteen aircraft which made a total of seventy flights. The European Parliament and the Council of Europe concluded that all of these flights were made in the context of the extraordinary rendition program.*
>
> *Among the fifteen aircraft serviced by Jeppesen are a Gulfstream V aircraft formerly registered with the Federal Aviation Administration ("FAA") as N379P, and a Boeing-737 aircraft formerly registered with the FAA as N313P. On information and belief, Jeppesen provided flight and logistical services for all of the CIA flights for these two aircraft involving the rendition of terror suspects.*

Among the flights Jeppesen facilitated are these:

> *On July 21, 2002, the Gulfstream V aircraft was used to transport Plaintiff Binyam Mohamed from Islamabad to Rabat.*

and

> *On January 22, 2004, the Boeing-737 aircraft was used to transport Plaintiff Binyam Mohamed from Rabat, Morocco to a U.S. detention facility in Afghanistan.*[302]

The U.S. lawsuit was filed on May 30, 2007 under the Aliens Tort Claims Act. Jeppesen never responded to the Complaint; instead, the

Bush administration petitioned to intervene and moved to have the case dismissed on the grounds that the "very subject matter" of the lawsuit— that the U.S. had flown captives to be detained and interrogated in both foreign and secret CIA prisons—is a state secret. Then CIA director Michael Hayden asserted the state secret privilege in a declaration that said,

> *First, this lawsuit puts at issue whether or not Jeppesen assisted the CIA with any of the alleged detention and interrogation…. Disclosure of information that would tend to confirm or deny whether or not Jeppesen provided such assistance—even if such confirmations or denial come from a private party alleged to have cooperated with the United States and not the United States itself—would cause exponentially grave damage to the national security by disclosing whether or not the CIA utilizes particular sources and methods and, thus, revealing to foreign adversaries information about the CIA's intelligence capabilities or lack thereof.*
>
> *Second, this lawsuit puts at issues whether or not the CIA cooperated with particular foreign governments in the conduct of alleged clandestine intelligence activities. Adducing evidence that would tend to confirm or deny such allegations would result in extremely grave damage to the foreign relations and foreign activities of the United States.*[303]

On February 13, 2008, U.S. District Judge James Ware granted the government's motion to dismiss, ruling that the administration's invocation of the state secrets privilege meant the court lacked jurisdiction to hear the lawsuit. The ACLU appealed, and on April 28, 2009, a three judge panel of the Ninth Circuit Court of Appeals reversed Judge Ware's decision, holding that the case must be allowed to proceed and the government could invoke state secrets only with respect to specific pieces of evidence. This time it was the Obama administration arguing the state secrets privilege—the hearing came less than three weeks after inauguration day. But if there were questions as to whether the new administration was perhaps just seeing a legal process through as it reviewed Bush era policies and developed new positions, those questions were laid to rest when the Obama Justice Department appealed in June, 2009 for a rehearing en banc of the Ninth Circuit decision. An eleven-judge panel of the Ninth Circuit heard arguments on the government's appeal on December 15, 2009, and on September 8, 2010 issued a 6-5 decision affirming the District Court's ruling that trying the case would put state secrets at risk.

In a strongly-worded dissent he titled "A Flawed Procedure," Judge Michael Daly Hawkins protested,

> *Plaintiffs have alleged facts...that any reasonable person would agree to be gross violations of the norms of international law, remediable under the Alien Tort Statute. They have alleged in detail Jeppesen's complicity or recklessness in participating in these violations. The government intervened, and asserted that the suit would endanger state secrets. The majority opinion here accepts that threshold objection by the government, so Plaintiffs' attempt to prove their case in court is simply cut off. They are not even allowed to attempt to prove their case by the use of non-secret evidence in their own hands or in the hands of third parties.*[304]

Judge Hawkins attached to his opinion a vivid chart illustrating 112 pieces of publicly available information and evidence establishing that Jeppesen both operated the rendition flights and knew or should have known that the purpose of the flights was to render Mohamed and the four other plaintiffs to be tortured. The entries ranged from flight records and invoices to press clippings to official reports by the European Parliament and the government of Sweden.[305]

Writing for the majority, Judge Raymond Fisher conceded that the non-secret and public evidence was probably sufficient for Mohamed and his co-plaintiffs to press at least some of their claims without the need for classified materials. But, he held, "privileged information being inseparable from non-privileged information that will be necessary to the claims or defenses," "litigating the case to a judgment on the merits would present an unacceptable risk of disclosing state secrets."[306] Admitting that the majority's decision "deprives [the plaintiffs] of the opportunity to prove their alleged mistreatment and obtain damages," and eliminates an "important check on alleged abuse by government officials and putative contractors" Fisher insisted the court had reached its ruling "reluctantly," and that the decision "is not intended to foreclose—or to prejudge—possible non-judicial relief, should it be warranted for any of the plaintiffs."

> *First, that the judicial branch may have deferred to the executive branch's claim of privilege in the interest of national security does not preclude the government from honoring the fundamental principles of justice. The government, having access to the secret information, can determine whether plaintiffs' claims have merit and whether misjudgments or mistakes were made that violated plaintiffs' human rights. Should that be the case, the government may be able to find ways to remedy such alleged harms while still maintaining the secrecy national security demands. For instance, the government made reparations to Japanese Latin Americans abducted from Latin America for internment in the United States during World War II.*
>
> *Second, Congress has the authority to investigate alleged wrongdoing and restrain excesses by the executive branch....*
>
> *Third, Congress also has the power to enact private bills.... When national security interests deny alleged victims of wrongful governmental action meaningful access to a judicial forum, private bills may be an appropriate alternative remedy.*
>
> *Fourth, Congress has the authority to enact remedial legislation authorizing appropriate causes of action and procedures to address claims like those presented here. When the state secrets doctrine "compels the subordination of appellants' interest in the pursuit of their claims to the executive's duty to preserve our national security, this means that remedies for...violations that cannot be proven under existing legal standards, if there are to be such remedies, must be provided by Congress.*[307]

Judge Hawkins, in his dissenting opinion, scoffed at this suggestion that

the plaintiffs could expect justice from the White House and Congress—
the very branches of government that had run and tacitly supported the
Rendition, Detention, and Interrogation program:

> *The majority concludes its opinion with a recommendation of
> alternative remedies. Not only are these remedies insufficient, but
> their suggestion understates the severity of the consequences to
> Plaintiffs from the denial of judicial relief. Suggesting, for example,
> that the Executive could "honor[] the fundamental principles of
> justice" by determining "whether plaintiffs' claims have merit"
> disregards the concept of checks and balances. Permitting the
> executive to police its own errors and determine the remedy
> dispensed would not only deprive the judiciary of its role, but also
> deprive Plaintiffs of a fair assessment of their claims by a neutral
> arbiter. The majority's suggestion of a payment of reparations to the
> victims of extraordinary rendition, such as those paid to Japanese
> Latin Americans for the injustices suffered under Internment during
> World War II, over fifty years after those injustices were suffered,
> elevates the impractical to the point of absurdity. Similarly, a
> congressional investigation, private bill, or enactment of "remedial
> legislation" leaves to the legislative branch claims which the federal
> courts are better equipped to handle.*

Hawkins punctuated his point by citing Justice Scalia's dissenting
opinion in *Hamdi v. Rumsfeld*, in which the Supreme Court recognized the
right of Guantánamo detainees to challenge their detention in U.S. courts,
specifically referencing a passage in which Scalia, arguing the court's
decision did not go far enough to check potential presidential lawlessness,
quotes British jurist Sir William Blackstone:

> *Arbitrary imprisonment and torture under any circumstance is
> a "gross and notorious...act of despotism."' But "confinement
> [and abuse] of the person, by secretly hurrying him to [prison],
> where his sufferings are unknown or forgotten; is a less public, a*

*less striking, and therefore a more dangerous engine of arbitrary
government."*

Sir Blackstone wrote these words in 1765, before the creation of
the United States, and in Binyam Mohamed's case, they seem to hold
considerably more sway for politicians and courts to this day in their
country of origin. In July, 2009, at the invitation of Attorney General
Baroness Patricia Scotland, British police announced they had launched a
criminal investigation into whether individual secret service agents colluded
in the rendition and torture of Binyam Mohamed. In referring the case to
the Metropolitan Police, Baroness Scotland said she had reviewed the UK
court's open and closed judgments, transcripts of the deposition of "Witness
B," and the Foreign Secretary's secret evidence, adding, "I have concluded
that the appropriate course of action is to invite the commissioner of the
Metropolitan Police to commence an investigation into the allegations that
have been made in relation to Binyam Mohamed."[308]

At the same time, the British government has launched an official
investigation into its involvement in Binyam Mohamed's case. Following the
February 2010 release of a UN report on secret detention that concluded
the UK had been complicit in the forced disappearance of Mohamed and at
least four other UK-based detainees, and the publication that same week of
the seven secret paragraphs, former Attorney General Lord Peter Goldsmith
publicly demanded an official inquiry, saying "I believe [this issue] needs to
be clarified in the interest of the public and the intelligence agencies." "I'm
very troubled by what actually happened," he told reporters, "and that's
why I've said yes, these are matters which ought to be investigated. If there
was complicity, it's important that people are brought to book."[309]

The Blair government's support for the Iraq War and the Bush
administration's detention policies were an election issue when
parliamentary elections were held a few months later, and David
Cameron reiterated his own calls for an investigation when he became
Prime Minister in May 2010, promising to pursue settlements in lawsuits
Binyam Mohamed and other British-based Guantánamo detainees had
filed in England. On November 16, 2011, the British government agreed

to pay Binyam Mohamed and fifteen other former Guantánamo detainees substantial cash settlements in compensation for its complicity in their treatment while in U.S. custody; in Mohamed's case, the settlement reportedly exceeded one million pounds.

Meanwhile, with the dismissal of the Jeppesen suit in the United States, no avenues remain for Mohamed to pursue claims against those who were primarily responsible for his ordeal. There have been no parallel criminal or official investigations in the United States into the participation of American officials and intelligence agency personnel in the treatment of Binyam Mohamed, and there are none on the horizon.

Abu Zubaydah

When Attorney General Eric Holder announced on November 14, 2009 that the Obama administration intended to try five of the most notorious Guantánamo detainees in federal court for planning the September 11, 2001 attacks and five more before military commissions, conspicuously absent from either list was Abu Zubaydah. Khalid Sheikh Mohammed was there, slated for trial in New York, and Abd al-Rahim al-Nashiri, who was to appear before a military commission in connection with the USS *Cole* bombing. But Abu Zubaydah, the man the Bush administration identified as the "third or fourth man in al Qaeda" and the ringleader of the Padilla-Binyam Mohamed "dirty bomb" and apartment bombing plots, was once again not scheduled for prosecution of any kind.

In fact, Abu Zubaydah's only appearance in any courtroom since he was shot, captured, and spirited away to a secret prison in 2002 was at a Combatant Status Review Tribunal hearing on March 27, 2007, a month after Jose Padilla was declared competent to stand trial on the conspiracy charge in Miami. At the closing unclassified session of that hearing, Abu Zubaydah's Personal Representative read the following statement:

In the name of God the Merciful. Mr. President and Members of the Tribunal, I would have liked to have spoken to you today on my own, but I have been having seizures lately which have temporarily affected my ability to speak and write without difficulty. Therefore, I asked my Personal Representative to speak on my behalf. I hope from you justice, and I know that is what you seek.

Do not make the mistake [redacted] when they first arrested me on 28 March 2002. After months of suffering and torture, physically and mentally, they did not care about my injuries that they inflicted to my eye, to my stomach, to my bladder, and my left thigh and reproductive organs. They didn't care that I almost died from these injuries. Doctors told me that I nearly died four times. Then they transferred me in a way that a normal, ordinary person would be embarrassed to be treated, [four line redaction]. They did this to me because they thought I was the number three leader in al Qaida and a partner of Usama Bin Laden, as is mentioned in the unclassified Summary of Evidence against me.

After a few months went by, during which I almost lost my mind and my life, they made sure I didn't die. Therefore, year after year, I am losing my masculinity. Even my beard is falling out, not from injuries but from the lack of treatment. [Redacted] discovered after all of this that I am not Usama Bin Laden's partner, and that I am not number three in al Qaida, and that I'm not even in al Qaida.

After this, I started feeling the symptoms of my 1992 injury to my head, including the complete loss of my memory and an inability to speak, read, or write. But these abilities slowly came back to me although I still have shrapnel in my head. Also, another form of torture was when they wouldn't give me my diary, which caused me to have nearly 40 seizures. The mental anguish that came from broken promises in which they said that they would give me my diary back contributed to the seizures. Most importantly, my diary can refute the accusations against me and it can show that I am personally against the sort of acts that were committed.

"Dear Members of the Tribunal," Zubaydah's Personal Representative read on, "in saying all of this, I am not trying to gain your pity."

I am only trying for you to see the big picture, the true picture not the picture depicted by the media, which the CIA found out too late. Therefore, I would like you to know this truth before you make your decision. I know this is not a criminal trial, as you say, but all I hope from you is that you try me for something that I am proud of having done, not something I didn't do or am against, nor something that would shame me before the world.

I am not here to lie to you, or cheat you, or to lie to myself by saying that I am not an enemy of your injustice. I have been an enemy of yours since I was a child because of your unjust acts against my people, the Palestinians, through your help and partnership with Israel in occupying our land and by killing our men and raping our women and kicking out our people and turning them into refugees for more than 60 years. Until now, half of my people are refugees in refugee camps. I cannot deny that, since back when I was a child, I liked a lot of things in your country and your history and your culture. I am not lying by saying that, but it is the truth.

My moral position is not against the American people or America, but against the government which I see as a partner in oppression. A partner of a killer is also a killer. I also resent the military that is used by this government to inflict this oppression. In other words, dear members of the military, I am against you. My words are not hypocrisy, and I do respect you. I believe that even my enemy should be respected.

I don't deny that I am an enemy of your injustice, but I deny that I am an enemy combatant. I never conducted nor financially supported, nor helped in any operation against America. Yes, I write poetry against America and, yes, I feel good when operations by others are conducted against America but only against military targets such as the U.S.S. Cole. But, I get angry if they target civilians, such as those in the World Trade Center. This I am completely against, [one line redaction] My diary will prove that some of our accusations were not in my plans. How can I plan for operations that I don't believe in? What you call plans about what Bin Laden did on 9/11, I wrote in my diary in response to Bin Laden's action, noting that he had many choices on how to conduct war which are wrong in Islam, such as race war, killing civilians, burning cities, and targeting civilians in markets. This is what people of war do, and I am sorry you are one of them. This is the truth. If someone reads my diary with a biased mind, he will misinterpret my meaning.

Dear Members, this is what I have for you. As you have noticed, it wasn't a defense that contained much evidence [one line redaction] I also do not have a lawyer to defend me in front of this Tribunal. Take notice that if a lawyer was present, he would not have allowed me to say what I said because I said the truth without reservation. And I am willing to be hung for it for something I have done. I am not a lawyer to defend myself. I can't even speak clearly, temporarily, God willing. It is only to demonstrate to you.

The Commission President asked Abu Zubaydah directly whether he had anything to add to the statement. "No," Zubaydah answered. The President went on, "In your statement, you mentioned months of torture. Has anything that you provided us today regarding your written statements related to those that times that you have been tortured?"

ABU ZUBAYDAH: No. [conversation between Detainee and Language Analyst discussing the President's question] Actually, most of what they say I did in first months they take against me even for some things or like this they take I was—I was nearly half die plus what they do torture me—it—There I was not afraid from die because I do believe I will be shahid [Language Analyst translates] martyr, but as God make me as a human and I weak, so they say yes, I say okay, I do I do, but leave me. They say no, we don't want to. You to admit you do this, we want you to give us more information. This part I can't because I don't know. I say, "yes, I was partner of Bin Laden. I'm his number three in al Qaida and I'm his partner of [Ahmed] Ressam." I say okay but leave me. So they write but they want what's after, more information about more operations, so I can't. They keep torturing me, tell me why them self they discover you are not torturing. So some, not all, some what you have here even me say of me here in the paper, it is from FBI. But I don't know of the dealing; I was in the hands of FBI or CIA. But FBI people when I met them in the last month, I [one line redaction] And they have my part—four part of my diary and the origin is with them. So who's torture me taking over information. Maybe they are FBI, maybe are CIA, I don't know, till now. So here they say FBI—FBI, they not talk about the CIA, so I don't know.

PRESIDENT: *So did you make statements during that treatment?*

ABU ZUBAYDAH: *A lot.*

PRESIDENT: *And what you said, was it correct, was it incomplete or was it not correct or untrue in any way?*

ABU ZUBAYDAH: *They say "this in your diary." They say "see you want to make operation against America." I say no, the idea is different. They say no, torturing, torturing. I say, "okay, I do. I was decide to make operation." This first part the second part, okay. What is the operation? I not have the specifics; I talk about open idea. So most of this here the CIA, they admitted that I admitted too. [two line redaction] They start asking again and again about this thing. I tell them no. [one line redaction] I was like this, I was like this, I want to finish this. And something they not believe all what I do, say in that time. Some they believe, some they not believe. I don't know what they need or not need. They only ask and I answer.*

PRESIDENT: *In your previous statement, you were saying specific treatments. Can you describe a little bit more about what those treatments were?*

ABU ZUBAYDAH: *[Seventeen line redaction]*

PRESIDENT: *I understand.*

ABU ZUBAYDAH: *And they not give me chance all this. [68 line redaction] they start tell me the time for the pray and slowly, slowly circumstance became good. They told me sorry we discover that you are not number three, not a partner even not a fighter.*

PRESIDENT: *So I understand that during this treatment, you said things to make them stop and then those statements were actually untrue, is that correct?*

ABY ZUBAYDAH: *Yes.*[310]

In April, 2010, the U.S. government released a declassified version of a secret court filing it had submitted in Abu Zubaydah's habeas corpus case, where for the first time it officially acknowledged what Abu Zubaydah told the tribunal his interrogators had admitted to him years earlier.

"Evidence that Petitioner is not a member of al-Qaida" is "not inconsistent" with its new position on Abu Zubaydah, the government allowed; its understanding of the man John Yoo described in his "Interrogation of al-Qaeda Operative" memo as "involved in every major terrorist operation" carried out by the organization has, it explained, "evolved since his capture." In that document, the Justice Department fights a discovery request by arguing that since the United States government no longer claims that he had "any direct role in or advance knowledge of the terrorist attacks of September 11, 2001," or indeed "had knowledge of any specific terrorist operations" targeting the U.S., it cannot be compelled to turn over material relating to its earlier allegations. Now, it said, it is justifying his detention as an enemy combatant on the basis that he "supported enemy forces and participated in hostilities" and aided "the retreat and escape of enemy forces" following the United States' 2001 invasion of Afghanistan.[311]

Annotations on this section from TheTortureReport.org

On the admissibility testimony elicited through torture and other coerced testimony in Guantánamo legal proceedings, Air Force Lieutenant Colonel and former lead defense counsel of the Office of Military Commissions in Guantánamo David Frakt wrote,

Statements extracted through torture are explicitly excluded from admissibility in military commissions, consistent with the United States' obligation under the Convention against Torture. Under the CAT, statements which are the product of torture are not admissible in any legal proceeding of any kind. State Department Legal Adviser John B. Bellinger III acknowledged this obligation in response to questions from the UN and asserted that the U.S. recognized that this ban also applied in Combatant Status Review Tribunals.

Although there was, in theory, a ban on the use of statements produced by torture, the problem was in applying this rule. At the time of the initiation of the CSRTs and the first efforts at trying detainees in military commissions, the official position of the Bush Administration was that we never had tortured anyone. Since we hadn't tortured anyone, there weren't any statements produced by torture to exclude. In fairness to the officers who served on the CSRTs, it must be noted that the documents provided to them, typically summaries of statements produced in interrogation sessions, tended not to indicate the nature of the interrogation techniques used to extract the statements, so there was no reason for them to suspect that the statements were the product of torture. Furthermore, the evidence offered by the government in CSRTs, by regulation, was afforded a presumption of validity; this presumption was nearly impossible to overcome without the right to a defense lawyer (by regulation, the detainees' "personal representatives" weren't allowed to be lawyers), or any meaningful opportunity to call witnesses.

Once defense lawyers were allowed to be involved, they were sometimes able to prove that a statement that had been considered by a CSRT actually was the product of torture. For example, in Mohammed Jawad's case, his CSRT considered numerous summary interrogation reports as evidence that he was an enemy combatant. In Mr. Jawad's habeas corpus litigation, counsel for Mr. Jawad (including myself) filed a motion to suppress these reports on the basis that the statements contained therein were the product of torture. After initially indicating to the court that the government intended to rely on these statements, the government changed course and conceded that the statements were the product of torture and the motion to suppress *was granted. The government then informed the court that they no longer considered Mr. Jawad to be detainable, leading to Mr. Jawad's release shortly thereafter.*

Although statements obtained by torture were theoretically inadmissible, a major flaw of the military commissions was that statements which were merely the product of coercion were admissible. The admissibility of involuntary coerced statements is a fundamental due process violation.

On the Detainee Treatment Act of 2005 and the October 2006 Military Commissions Act, which established that only "grave breaches" of Common Article 3 of the Geneva Conventions could be prosecuted and extended immunity to interrogators who relied in good faith on the administration's legal advice, former Air Force criminal investigator and interrogator Matthew Alexander wrote,

How ironic is it that we needed acts of Congress to enforce acts of Congress that created the Military Justice system and gave us the authority to prosecute torture under federal statutes?

There is no grave breaches threshold in UCMJ or in federal statutes. There is only the law and, in the case of UCMJ, the elements of proof that define a crime. Immunity for interrogators who relied on good faith is a reversal of the Nuremberg trials and contrary to the military's own training, which emphasizes a soldier's legal obligation not to follow unlawful orders.

On alleged Al Qaeda training camps, attendance at those camps, and the role of Abu Zubaydah, blogger Marcy Wheeler ("emptywheel") wrote,

It is important to note that the training camps in Afghanistan were not all Al Qaeda camps, and Khalden, which a number of the detainees have ties to—including, most importantly, Abu Zubaydah and Ibn al-Shaykh al-Libi— pointedly wasn't. Particularly given U.S. funding of mujahadeen before the Russians withdrew, we ought to be having a discussion of what extent simple training at a camp can be used as evidence of involvement in terrorism, particularly if the camp did not have ties to Al Qaeda and/or participants could avoid pledging bayat.

As for Abu Zubaydah, his case reinforces everything you've said about Binyam Mohamed, but to a greater degree: Even for some of the most notorious detainees, the government has dramatically backed off any claim that they were actually part of Al Qaeda.

On the absence of criminal and official investigations into Binyam Mohamed's treatment in the United States, Matthew Alexander observed,

And herein lies a tragedy as terrible as the actual torture and abuse -- the refusal to investigate clear violations of the law. It brings the entire validity of the U.S. justice systems, military and civilian, into question.

THREE:

THE PENTAGON'S BATTLE LAB

A SPECIAL PROJECT

A week before President Obama's inauguration, *The Washington Post* published a story that began,

> *The top Bush administration official in charge of deciding whether to bring Guantánamo Bay detainees to trial has concluded that the U.S. military tortured a Saudi national who allegedly planned to participate in the Sept. 11, 2001, attacks, interrogating him with techniques that included sustained isolation, sleep deprivation, nudity and prolonged exposure to cold, leaving him in a "life-threatening condition."*
>
> *"We tortured [Mohammed al-]Qahtani," said Susan J. Crawford, in her first interview since being named convening authority of military commissions by Defense Secretary Robert M. Gates in February 2007. "His treatment met the legal definition of torture. And that's why I did not refer the case [for prosecution]."*[312]

That Mohammed al-Qahtani had been abused was hardly news: in June 2005, *Time* magazine published excerpts from an eighty-three-page log of a fifty-day stretch of Qahtani's interrogation, not in a CIA black site or a third-country prison, but by U.S. military interrogators in Guantánamo Bay, Cuba. The news was who was calling his treatment torture.

A career political appointee, Crawford had held a series of senior civilian Pentagon posts since Ronald Reagan named her General Counsel to the Department of the Army in 1983. In the elder Bush administration, she served as Inspector General of the Department of Defense under Defense Secretary Dick Cheney before Bush nominated her to be a judge on the Court of Appeals for the Armed Forces, the nation's highest military court. She spent four years of her fifteen-year term on the court as its Chief Justice. Reliably conservative, she was often to the right of her military peers; in one notable case, in which she was the lone dissenter in a 4-1 decision defining the rights of soldiers in death penalty cases, she even criticized her colleagues' "recent overreliance on due process."[313]

Crawford replaced John Altenburg, a career military officer, as Convening Authority of the problem-plagued Guantánamo Military Commissions in February 2007. Eight months later, the Chief Prosecutor for the Military Commissions resigned and published an op-ed in the *Los Angeles Times* insisting that under Crawford the commissions system had become "deeply politicized" to the point that "full, fair, and open trial were not possible." In that piece, titled "AWOL Military Justice," Colonel Morris "Moe" Davis wrote,

Altenburg's staff had kept its distance from the prosecution to preserve its impartiality. Crawford, on the other hand, had her staff assessing evidence before the filing of charges, directing the prosecution's pretrial preparation of cases (which began while I was on medical leave), drafting charges against those who were accused and assigning prosecutors to cases, among other things.

How can you direct someone to do something—use specific evidence to bring specific charges against a specific person at a specific time, for instance—and later make an impartial assessment of whether they behaved properly? Intermingling convening authority

and prosecutor roles perpetuates the perception of a rigged process
stacked against the accused.[314]

Whether or not she had a hand in its preparation, the sworn Charge Sheet
Crawford received on April 15, 2008 was the most momentous she would
review. Conferring capital war crimes charges against six alleged agents
of the September 11, 2001 terrorist attacks—Khalid Sheihk Mohammed,
Walid Muhammad Salih Mubarek bin Attash, Ramzi Binalshibh, Ali
Abdul Azis Ali, Mustafa Ahmed Adam al-Hawsawi, and Mohammed al-
Qahtani—the Charge Sheet listed crimes including conspiracy, attacking
civilians, murder in violation of the law of war, terrorism, and hijacking; it
was followed by a sixty-six-page appendix simply listing the names of the
attacks' 2,973 victims.

Qahtani's alleged role was not mastermind or facilitator of the attacks
but rather failed participant: the so-called twentieth hijacker, he had been
turned away when he tried to enter the U.S. just a month before 9/11.
According to the Charge Sheet,

107. *On or about July 14, 2001, in Riyadh, Saudi Arabia, **Mohamed al***
      ***Kahtani** received a visa to travel to the United States....*

117. *On or about August 4, 2001, at approximately 4:18 p.m., a vehicle*
      rented by Mohamed Atta (AA #11) entered a parking garage at
      Orlando International Airport, Orlando, Florida.

118. *On or about August 4, 2001, **Mohamed al Kahtani** traveled from*
      Dubai, United Arab Emirates, via Emirates Flight #7 to London-
      Gatwick, England, and Virgin Atlantic Flight #15 from London to
      Orlando, Florida, which was scheduled to arrive at 4:40 p.m.

119. *On or about August 4, 2001, **Mohamed al Kahtani** arrived at*
      Orlando International Airport, Orlando, Florida, with $2,800
      *in his possession, and attempted to enter the United States. **Al***
      ***Kahtani** also had an itinerary listing the telephone number 050*
      *52009905, a phone number associated with **Mustafa al Hawsawi**.*

120. *On or about August 4, 2001, **Mohamed al Kahtani** stated to an*
      officer of the United States Immigration and Naturalization Service

that there was someone "upstairs" in the airport to pick him up. When
asked the name of the person, so that the immigration inspector
could verify *al Kahtani's* intentions in the United States, *al Kahtani*
changed his story and stated that no one was waiting for him.

121.   On or about August 4, 2001, in between 4:30 p.m. and 8:30 p.m., a
total of five phone calls were placed using a calling card associated
with Mohamed Atta (AA #11) from a pay telephone in Orlando
International Airport to telephone number 91-50-520-9905, a
phone number associated with **Mustafa al Hawsawi**.

122.   On or about August 4, 2001, after being told his application for
entry into the United States was going to be denied, **Mohamed al
Kahtani** withdrew his application and was placed on board Virgin
Atlantic Fight 15, which was scheduled to depart Orlando, Florida,
at 8:25 p.m. and traveled back to Dubai, United Arab Emirates, via
London, England.[315]

On May 9, 2008, three weeks after receiving the sworn Charge Sheet,
Crawford drew a line through Qahtani's name, rejecting the charges against
him, and days later signed a new charge sheet against the five others with all
references to al-Qahtani removed. When the Pentagon publicly announced
the change, it offered no explanation, saying only that the charges against
Mohammed al-Qahtani had been dropped "without prejudice" and could
be reinstated in the future.[316]

But in the final hours of the Bush administration, Crawford publicly
declared that she had dismissed the charges against Qahtani because he
was tortured. "You think of torture, you think of some horrendous act
done to an individual," Crawford told the *Post's* Bob Woodward. "This was
not one particular act; this was just a combination of things that had a
medical impact on him, that hurt his health. It was abusive and uncalled
for. And coercive. Clearly coercive. It was that medical impact that pushed
me over the edge."[317]

Qahtani's treatment, Crawford was careful to emphasize, "met the legal
definition of torture." "The techniques they used were all authorized, but
the manner in which they applied them was overly aggressive and too

persistent," she explained. She named Defense Secretary Donald Rumsfeld as responsible for approving the abuse, adding "a lot of this happened on his watch." "It did shock me. I was upset by it. I was embarrassed by it," she told Woodward. "I sympathize with the intelligence gatherers in those days after 9/11, not knowing what was coming next and trying to gain information to keep us safe. But there still has to be a line that we should not cross. And unfortunately what this has done, I think, has tainted everything going forward."

* * *

The eighty-three-page document that was leaked to *Time* in 2005 begins

INTERROGATION LOG
DETAINEE 063

23 November 2002

> *0225: The detainee arrives at the interrogation booth at Camp X-Ray. His hood is removed and he is bolted to the floor. SGT A and SGT R are the interrogators. A DoD linguist and MAJ L (BSCT) are present.*[318]

It is the middle of the night. Qahtani is shackled to the floor by the wrists and ankles; we know this because several hours in, "one hand is uncuffed to allow him to eat." The interrogators are from military intelligence, Sergeant R, male, and Sergeant A, we soon learn, female. The Major is from the Joint Task Force Guantánamo's Behavioral Science Consultation Team. The "Biscuits," as they are known, are psychiatrists and psychologists whose job it is to assess and assist interrogators in exploiting detainees' fears and vulnerabilities. The three and their interpreter form one of three teams that will work on Qahtani around the clock for the next fifty days. In the room throughout, unnoted except when called upon to subdue Qahtani, are masked MPs. Not in the room but never far away is a medic, and often a guard dog and its handler as well. On call at all times is a doctor.

Though it's the beginning of the log, this is not the beginning of Qahtani's interrogation. He has been undergoing intense questioning in the Naval Brig in Guantánamo since July, when a fingerprint check revealed he had been denied entry to the U.S. a month before the attacks. The White House and Pentagon have been following the progress of his interrogation, and on their September 2002 field trip to Guantánamo the "War Council" sat in on one of his interrogation sessions. After their visit, Defense Department interrogators ratcheted up the pressure through the fall:

> In September or October of 2002, FBI agents observed that a canine was used in an aggressive manner to intimidate detainee #63 and, in November 2002, FBI agents observed Detainee #63 after he had been subjected to intense isolation for over three months. During that time period, #63 was totally isolated (with the exception of occasional interrogations) in a cell that was always flooded with light. By late November, the detainee was evidencing behavior consistent with extreme psychological trauma (talking to non-existent people, reporting hearing voices, crouching in a corner of the cell covered with a sheet for hours on end).[319]

The effects of weeks of isolation and sleep deprivation are obvious from log's first session. Barely an hour in, Qahtani "dozed off during a break." At 8:30 in the morning, he is allowed "two hours rest," and then at 10:35 he "is awakened and secured in chair," where he will remain, with the exception of bathroom breaks and an hour nap in the evening, until midnight. He announces he is on a hunger strike, and refuses both food and water, though the log records that at lunchtime, "at first he said he would eat, but then said that he was mentally not well and had only agreed because he was not thinking clearly." The logkeeper observes, "Detainee attempts to control the interrogation by complaining about his treatment, his mental illness, and his separation from his brothers in Cuba." Twice he breaks down and cries.

When the interrogation resumes at 4 a.m. the following morning, Qahtani alternately "engages in conversation" and "becomes unresponsive";

either way, he is accused of using resistance techniques outlined in the "Manchester Document," an Al Qaeda training manual discovered on a militant's computer in the UK in 2002. He asks Sergeant A if she really wants her questions answered, and Sergeant A tells him "she doesn't really need an answer." "The detainee seems disheartened by her response," the log observes.

At 8 a.m., just thirty hours into what will be a 1,200 hour interrogation, medical personnel appear:

0800: SGT A offers meal to detainee. The detainee refuses. SGT R explains that refusal to eat is unproductive. SGT A offers 30 minutes rest. The detainee refuses. Interrogators had Corpsman check the detainee's vital signs. The detainee has not taken fluids for over 24 hours. Corpsman states vital signs are good. The detainee still refuses to speak a word.

0820: SGT R removes food from table and tells the detainee he missed his chance. SGT R explains that the detainee's refusal to eat hurts only him. SGT R will not lose any sleep over it.

0830: SGT A uses "Level of Guilt" approach.

0840: SGT R has the detainee stand for 10 minutes to stretch and avoid sleeping

0900: SGT A asks the detainee if he wants to pray and sleep. The detainee says yes. SGT A says you have to drink water. The detainee says no. SGT R gives detainee 1 more chance. The detainee says no. SGT R empties water on floor and tells the detainee "you had your chance." The Corpsman then checks the detainee's vital signs, they are OK.

0925: SGT A discusses levels of guilt and sin.

0930: SGT A talks about the embarrassment of using a weak cover story and mixes in the "You can make this stop" approach. The detainee remains unresponsive.

0930: CAPT W advises SGT R that the Corpsman can administer IV fluids once Capt W and the Doctor on duty are notified and agree to it.

At 1:30 that afternoon, a "strap was hung from ceiling in anticipation of the doctor's arrival." At 6 p.m., "medical personnel checked vital signs and determined that detainee needed to be hydrated," and Qahtani is given two bags of fluids intravenously. Forty-five minutes later,

> 1845· *Medical doctor arrives to evaluate detainee to ensure he is physically able to continue. Detainee stated he wanted to sign a form or a release stating that he did not want any medications. The doctor explained that no such form exists. Detainee was informed that we would not let him die.*

The interrogation again continues until midnight; again Qahtani is awakened at 4 a.m. and his vitals are checked. He is now so dehydrated that the Corpsman is unable to find a vein; again "the Doctor was called to make a trip to perform an assessment." Incredibly, the interrogation continues:

> 0600: *To follow up on "Gods message," SGT R showed 9-11 DVD. SGT R stood behind detainee and whispered in his ear, "What is God telling you right now? Your 19 friends died in a fireball and you weren't with them. Was that God's choice? Is it God's will that you stay alive to tell us about his message?" At that point, detainee threw his head back and butted SGT R in the eye. The 2 MPs in the room wrestled detainee to the ground to regain control. SGT R crouched over the detainee and the detainee attempted to spit on him. SGT R stated "Go ahead and spit on me. It won't change anything. You're still here. I'm still talking to you, and you won't leave until you're given God's message. Detainee is put in chair.*
> 0630: *SGT A showed circumstantial evidence and told detainee repeatedly that she won't go away and neither will the evidence.*
> 0645: *Doctor attempted to put in IV and was unsuccessful. The doctor left to get more supplies.*
> 0700: *SGT A continued circumstantial evidence theme.*
> 0705: *Assessment – His reaction to SGT R was a combination of his*

guilt (possibly at not participating in the attack), his continuous interrogation, and his obvious hatred of SGT R. He was told after the episode that it proves he's not as weak and mentally ill as he wants us to believe.

0730: *Doctor arrived and ran an IV by putting in a temporary shunt to allow continuous IV*

0745: *SGT A ran the "already captured and talking" approach." When SGT R entered the booth the detainee reached for the IV. The guard stopped him and he reached again. The guards stopped him and cuffed his hands to the chair so he couldn't reach the IV. The detainee bent over and bit the IV tube completely in two. The guards strapped him to a stretcher and the corpsman attached a new IV. The detainee struggled through the entire process, but could no longer reach the IV.*

0900: *SGT A resumed the previous approach.*

0915: *Detainee requested to go to the bathroom but was given an opportunity to use a bottle instead. He was told he will not be unstrapped.*

0940: *Detainee was given three and one-half bags of IV. He started moaning and told the MPs he's willing to talk so he can urinate. SGT A entered the booth and asked the following questions: Who do you work for (Detainee answered: Al Qaida), Who was your leader (Detainee answered: Usama bin Laden), Why did you go to Orlando (Detainee answered: I wasn't told the mission), Who was meeting you? (Detainee answered: I don't know), Who was with you on the plane (Detainee answered: I was by myself). SGT R told detainee he was wasting SGT R's time. Detainee told SGT A he was willing to drink.*

1000: *Detainee again said he has to go to bathroom. SGT R said he can go in the bottle. Detainee said he wanted to go to the bathroom because it's more comfortable. SGT R said "You've ruined all trust, You can either go in the bottle or in your pants." Detainee goes in his pants. SGT A continued approach.*

1030: *Assessment – Detainee has a greater deal of animosity toward SGT*

R. He is beginning to understand the futility of his situation. He has to understand that his antics will not stop the interrogation at all. We feel he is slowly realizing that he will not outlast the battle of wills. He is much closer to compliance and cooperation now than at the beginning of the operation.

When the second team of interrogators finally releases Qahtani from the gurney and allows him to wash himself and change his clothes, he agrees to eat, but he immediately recants his earlier statements, insisting he didn't know bin Laden and "admitted to be al-Qaida because of the intense psychological pressure"; he "claimed to have been pressured into making a confession." The next day, as he is periodically made to elevate his feet and is handcuffed to the strap suspended from the ceiling to relieve dehydration-induced swelling in his extremities, the log records:

> 2300: *Detainee proclaims his innocence and requested that SGT M stop talking about Islam. (ie Usama bin Laden raped Islam. UBL hijacked Islam) Detainee stated, "If you interrogate me in the right way and the right position...you might find some answers*
> 2308: *Detainee claimed that the interrogations are based on malice, hate, and jealousy. He said, The treatment is wild and animalistic. Everybody has limits. Once those limits are crossed, what is somebody supposed to do?*
> 2310: *Detainee said, "If I told the truth, everybody would get mad. If you interrogated me correctly...maybe if you rested and I rested... One interrogator after another...God and his angels see what is happening."*
> 2315: *Detainee was on the verge of breaking.*

＊ ＊ ＊

Four days have passed. For four of the next seven, Qahtani is subjected to non-stop twenty-hour interrogations; the other three, he's allowed to nap an extra hour. He has dizzy spells; he's forced to receive an enema to relieve constipation. The interrogations become more aggressive: photographs of 9/11 victims are taped to the wall of the interrogation room, and then to his body. Videos of the 9/11 attacks are played over and over. "Liar," "Coward," "Failure" are written in Arabic on the plywood walls, and he is made to wear a sign saying "I am going to hell because I am full of hate." He is mocked relentlessly. On the morning on December 2, 2002, the tenth day of the interrogation,

> 1030: *Control began "birthday party" and placed party hat on detainee. Detainee offered birthday cake—refused. Interrogators and guards sing "God bless America." Detainee became very angry.*

The following morning,

> 0930: *Interrogators gave class to new MPs in view of detainee stating the resistance training, clouded thinking, series of mistakes, and attempts to gain control that the detainee has exhibited. Interrogators ran puppet show satirizing the detainee's involvement with Al Qaida.*

At 8:00 that evening, the log notes ominously, "Phase 1B begins."

> 2000: *Detainee awakened and told he is being taken back to Cuba, hooded, and loaded into ambulance. Ambulance drove a few feet and detainee was taken out and into a different interrogation booth. ENS S lead interrogator with a female DoD linguist. ENS S was in civilian clothes and ran an approach to plant seeds in the detainee's mind on how to end the interrogations. The approach centered around how Al Qaida had destroyed Islam and the detainee's life had been spared because it was now his jihad to tell the world about how 9-11 was wrong, and help rebuild Islam.*
> 2040: *Detainee hooded and taken to new primary interrogation booth that was decorated with photos of 9-11 victims, the U.S. flag, flags of coalition forces in the global war on terrorism, and red lighting. Detainee was subject to loud music for 20 minutes.*

> *2100: Hood was removed and U.S. National Anthem was played. CAPT W was lead interrogator with the same female DoD linguist.*
> *2105: Detainee's head and beard were shaved with electric clippers. Detainee started resistance when beard was shaved and MPs had to restrain. Shaving was halted until detainee was once more compliant. LTC P supervised shaving. No problems occurred. Photos were taken of detainee when the shaving was finished.*

The four-hour sleep period is shifted from midnight to 4 a.m. to 7:00 to 11:00 in the morning; on this first day of "Phase 1B" he is interrogated nonstop through the night. The assault on his senses increases: the lurid lighting, loud music during a showing of the popular Internet "devil in the smoke" 9/11 footage, and then, as if to announce the introduction of a new element in the interrogations, blared Christina Aguilera. Not long afterward SGT L, a female night shift interrogator, approaches and touches Qahtani, who struggles to get out of his restraints. All of this is closely monitored by a doctor, who checks his vital signs after the Aguilera plays and draws blood not long after to evaluate his kidney function.

"The rules have changed," he is told, and over the next three days, as medical personnel rehydrate him through an IV, the interrogators ratchet up the pressure. Then, on December 6, 2002, the fourteenth day of the interrogation, Qahtani is told another detainee has placed him at a safehouse in Kabul; he is accused of being a bin Laden bodyguard. "This will never end and things will get worse," his interrogators assure him. A few hours later, Qahtani offers another confession:

> *1400: Detainee taken to bathroom and walked 10 minutes. Corpsman replaced ankle bandages to prevent chafing from cuffs. Started "Al Qaida used Islam" and "bad muslim" themes. Detainee said "I will tell the truth" and told the interrogator to get out some paper. He also said "I am doing this to get out of here." Detainee began talking but would not give any information about people other than himself. Detainee talked about traveling to Afghanistan and meeting UBL who gave him money and sent him to America.*

Detainee also talked about his travel after he was turned away from Orlando.

1600: Detainee allowed to pray after promising to continue cooperating. Detainee asked for air conditioner to be turned off and asked for blanket—both were given.

1610: Detainee offered water and bathroom break— refused.

1715: Detainee allowed to pray.

But the lull is short-lived. Interrogators know this confession is fabricated, and shut down the interrogation session. When it resumes a few hours later, Qahtani is set upon twice, first by Sergeant L, a female interrogator, and then, evidently, by a guard dog:

1930: Third shift interrogation team enters the booth. The approaches were Pride and Ego down, Fear Up Harsh, and Invasion of Space by a Female. The detainee became very violent and irate. Detainee attempted to liberate himself from the chair in order to get away from the female. He struggled for approximately forty minutes attempting to move out of the presence of the female.

2030: Detainee was exercised for approximately fifteen minutes. The Medical Representative checked the detainee's blood pressure and weight. She cleared the detainee for further interrogation....

0001: First shift began. Detainee made to stand for the National Anthem. Interrogators began harsh Pride & Ego Down by poking holes in the new cover story and outlining the rules he must live by now.

0100: Detainee taken to the porch where he can see foraging banana rats and told that he chose this life with the rats. He is reminded of the good things in life that he chose to leave behind.

0120: Issues arise between MPs and dog handler. CAPT W talks with all parties and resolves issues.

0320: Detainee taken to bathroom and walked for 10 minutes. Corpsman checks vitals—O.K.

0345: Detainee offered food and water—refused. Detainee asked for

> *music to be turned off. Detainee was asked if he can find the verse*
> *in the Koran that prohibits music.*
>
> *0350: Corpsman checks vitals—detainee refuses Motrin and water.*
> *Corpsman asked detainee if he has dizziness or a headache—*
> *detainee says yes. Corpsman explains it is from lack of water. Vitals*
> *show dehydration is beginning. Corpsman calls doctor.*
>
> *0415: Detainee admits story he told interrogators was false. Stated he*
> *told the story because he was under pressure. Detainee was told he*
> *chose to be here, and was given the list of decisions he made that*
> *brought him here and was told he needs to take responsibility for*
> *his actions. Detainee was given an IV by corpsman. Detainee was*
> *told that we would not allow him to die.*

It is the second time he has heard this pledge.

When Qahtani is "put to bed" at 7 a.m. on December 7, the log states "24 HOUR RECUPERATION STAND-DOWN BEGINS"; his interrogation plan evidently called for a one-day hiatus after two solid weeks of questioning. But that break is not to include additional rest. He is roused as usual after four hours of sleep, and MPs are instructed "to offer water every hour, take detainee to bathroom and walk every one and a half hours, offer food once per shift, and keep music playing to prevent detainee from sleeping during stand-down. MPs are instructed not to converse with detainee except to issue commands." The "stand-down" is anything but recuperative, however, and the calm turns to panic that evening:

> *2000: Corpsman check vitals and finds the detainee's pulse is unusually*
> *slow. Doctor arrives and decides to perform an EKG—leaves to get*
> *EKG machine.*
>
> *2050: Doctor returns and performs EKG. Heartbeat is regular but slow—*
> *35 bpm. Doctor consults with another doctor.*
>
> *2130: Decision is made to take detainee to GTMO hospital to*
> *perform a CT scan of the detainee's brain to see if there are any*
> *irregularities.*
>
> *2215: Depart to hospital.*

2230: Arrive at hospital and begin CT scan.

2330: Doctors review scan and do not find any conclusive evidence of any conditions, but request the detainee be kept overnight until a radiologist can be flown in to ensure there are no anomalies. Detainee is placed in isolation ward and hooked up to monitor heart rhythm.

* * *

In December 1999, three years before this crisis played out in Guantánamo's Camp X-Ray, the American Medical Association amended its 152-year old Code of Medical Ethics to include this provision regarding torture:

Physicians must oppose and must not participate in torture for any reason. Participation in torture includes, but is not limited to, providing or withholding any services, substances, or knowledge to facilitate the practice of torture. Physicians must not be present when torture is used or threatened. Physicians may treat prisoners or detainees if doing so is in their best interest, but physicians should not treat individuals to verify their health so that torture can begin or continue. Physicians who treat torture victims should not be persecuted. Physicians should help provide support for victims of torture and, whenever possible, strive to change situations in which torture is practiced or the potential for torture is great.[320]

Nine times in the past two weeks—starting on Day 2 of the interrogation, when it is recorded that a "Medical doctor arrives to evaluate detainee to ensure he is physically able to continue"—military doctors have examined Qahtani. A doctor has installed a shunt in anticipation of the need for repeated IV rehydration and has drawn blood to check his kidney function. Now two doctors send Qahtani to the naval hospital and order a brain scan, and the military summons a radiologist from the Roosevelt Roads Naval Station in Puerto Rico. The log summarizes the events of the following day this way:

08 December 2002

> *Detainee's electrolytes are checked and corrected. Potassium*
> *was slightly below normal due to not eating. Detainee's left*
> *leg was swollen and an ultrasound was performed to check*
> *for blood clots. No blood clots were detected and the detainee's*
> *swelling went down naturally. A radiologist was flown in*
> *from Roosevelt Roads and checked the detainee's CT scan—*
> *no anomalies were found. No unusual heart rhythms were*
> *recorded by the monitor during the detainee's stay and his*
> *heart rate returned to normal naturally. The detainee slept*
> *most of the day between meals.*

Incredibly, by the following morning, plans are being made to resume
the interrogation, which is now well into its third week but barely a third
of the way through the logged sessions.

At six o'clock on the evening of December 09, Qahtani "is hooded,
shackled and restrained in a litter for transport to Camp X-Ray." One of
the evening-shift interrogators, Ensign C, rides with him, telling him he
can either "tell the whole truth" right there in the ambulance and rejoin
the other detainees in Camp Delta or remain silent and go back to Camp
X-Ray. A half hour later, "Detainee arrives at Camp X-Ray and is returned
to interrogation booth. ENS C enters booth with detainee and gives a last
chance to tell the whole truth. Detainee is uncooperative and ENS C leaves.
CAPT W enters booth and informs the detainee that he had been medically
cleared and only he could make it stop, otherwise it would get worse." This is
followed by a sardonic-sounding entry stating "Detainee was exercised for
good health." A medic checks his vital signs. "The interrogation continued."

Indeed, there is no change to his sleep schedule, no change in tactics.
That evening,

> 2340: *Detainee was repulsed by the female invasion of his personal*
> *space. He made several attempts to stand up in order to prevent*
> *her from entering his personal space. He attempted to appeal to*
> *SGT M but that was not effective. SGT M continued with fear*

up harsh until the detainee would give new information but the detainee continued to give old information so he was silenced by the interrogation team.

0000: *Interrogation team entered the booth and played the national anthem. Detainee was made to stand and put his hand over his heart. Lead explained rules to detainee. Ran pride and ego down approach. Played loud music to keep detainee awake.*

In a matter of hours, Qahtani is veering between anger and weeping; when he tries to speak, he is "silenced by interrogator yelling and loud music." He tells his tormentors he is "having emotional problems and need[s] to see a doctor for this." In response, he is again accused of using resistance techniques and mocked by interrogators who ask him to "perform the 'crazy Mohammed' facial expressions again." He is again "exercised for good circulation and overall good health, has his vital checked, and now is also weighed; 160 pounds when he arrived at Guantánamo,[321] he now weighs 119 pounds, "123 pounds with the three-piece suit," the vernacular for his wrist and ankle manacles. He urinates on himself when he is being led to the latrine.

Relentlessly, the humiliations escalate. He is taken to watch the foraging banana rats again and told they have "more love, freedom, and concern" than he does; "Detainee began to cry during this comparison." Interrogators stage an "exorcism to purge the evil Jinns that he claimed were controlling his emotions." They play childish games: "the lead held the coffee in front of the detainee and when the detainee reached for the coffee, the interrogator poured the coffee on the floor." He breaks down again, and asks that he be allowed to sleep in a separate room and only questioned in the interrogation room. When the interrogator asks him why he is making the request, the BSCT psychologist intervenes, announcing that he is "only trying to run an approach on the control and gain sympathy." With his vital signs again "not so good," three IV bags are administered, and the questioning continues through the night.

0150: *Interrogators gave detainee rules for the evening. 1) No talking. 2) Face forward. 3) Don't ask for anything. Detainee almost immediately began to speak. The interrogators screamed at detainee until he stopped. Detainee was reminded of his worthlessness as a human being. He was reminded of the fact that his standard of living is less than a Banana rat. While running the Pride and Ego (P/E) down approach, SGT M. showed the bottom of his boot to detainee. Detainee had one of the longest emotional outbursts seen yet. He went into a fit of rage yelling insults in English and Arabic to interrogators. He began to move his arms and legs in his chair as if to want to break away from the shackles and attack.*

Just after midnight the next night, an interrogator plays the call to prayer, but tells Qahtani "this is no longer the call to prayer. You're not allowed to pray. This is the call to interrogation. So pay attention." A sign reading "coward" is hung around his neck. He is "increasingly tired and incoherent," the log notes. He is again shown the banana rats. Then, after his four hour rest,

Interrogators began telling detainee how ungrateful and grumpy he was. In order to escalate the detainee's emotions, a mask was made from an MRE box with a smiley face on it and placed on the detainee's head for a few moments. A latex glove was inflated and labeled the "sissy slap" glove. This glove was touched to the detainee's face periodically after explaining the terminology to him. The mask was placed back on the detainee's head. While wearing the mask, the team began dance instruction with the detainee. The detainee became agitated and began shouting. The mask was removed and detainee was allowed to sit. Detainee shouted and addressed lead as "the oldest Christian here" and wanted to know why lead allowed the detainee to be treated this way.

That evening, three weeks into the interrogation and barely four days after the hospital emergency,

2200:   ...Medical representative took detainee's vital signs and removed the IV housing unit from the detainee's arm. The detainee's pulse rate was low (38) and his blood pressure was high (144/90). Detainee complained of having a boil on his left leg, just below his knee. The medical representative looked at his leg and phoned the doctor. The doctor instructed the corpsman to recheck the detainee's vitals in one hour.

2300:   Detainee refused water and food. He was taken to the latrine and exercised in order to assist in improving the detainee's vital signs.

2300:   The medical representative rechecked the detainee's vital signs. The detainee's blood pressure had improved but it was still high (138/80) and his pulse rate had improved but it remained low (42). The corpsman called the doctor to provide an update and the doctor said operations could continue since there had been no significant change. It was noted that historically the detainee's pulse sometimes drops in the 40's in the evenings.

* * *

14 December 2002

0001:   Interrogation team was briefed on condition of the detainee's mental and physical state. Detainee's hands were cuffed at his sides to prevent him from conducting his prayer ritual.

0025:   Lead begins berating detainee as a coward and liar. Lead taped picture of a 3 year old victim over detainee's heart. Detainee is told he will never leave Cuba. Lead states that if he does not tell the truth, the interrogator will keep talking to him everyday until he does. Control orders detainee to sit up and pay attention. Control dripped a few drops of water on detainees head to keep him awake. Detainee struggles when water is dropped on his head. Detainee attempts to talk, but both control and lead scream over the detainee until he stops.

0120:   Interrogators take a break and detainee listens to white noise.

> *Detainee goes to bathroom and is exercised while hooded.*
> *Detainee returns to booth and continues to listen to white noise.*
>
> 0140: *Interrogators enter the booth and play cards while conducting a*
> *[Pride & Ego] Down. Detainee is told that we get paid to mess with*
> *him so we might as well play cards, a leisure he cannot participate*
> *in. Detainee is told to shut up and stay awake. At times detainee*
> *began to fall asleep and water was dripped on his head as he was*
> *ridiculed. White noise was played in the background.*

Water is becoming a frequent tool to "assist him in maintaining his attention with interrogator." Sex is becoming the preferred torment. On December 17, "Control shows detainee photos from a fitness magazine of scantily clad women. Detainee called control an animal and stated that it was against his religion. Lead replied 'You can kill people and lie, but we can't show you pictures?' [Pride and Ego Down] continues." That night,

> *Detainee appeared to have been disturbed by the word*
> *homosexual. He did not appear to appreciate being called a*
> *homosexual. He denies being a homosexual. He appeared to be*
> *very annoyed by the use of his mother and sister as examples of*
> *prostitutes and whores. Detainee was taken to the latrine and*
> *exercised for approximately 10 minutes. He refuses to drink water*
> *again.*
>
> 2200: *Detainee was taken to the latrine and exercised. He did not desire*
> *water. He appeared disgusted by the photos of UBL and a variety*
> *of sexy females. Detainee would avoid looking at all of the photos*
> *shown to him.*

Interrogators have now taken to hanging pictures of swimsuit models around his neck; at 2 a.m. on December 19 "While walking out [to a bathroom break], detainee pulled a picture of a model off (it had been fashioned into a sign to hang around his neck) and began to struggle with MPs." The photos give rise to a new game: "[I]nterrogators added photos of fitness models to a binder. Once completed, the interrogators began showing the photos and asking the detainee detailed questions about the photos."

Toward dawn, Qahtani is led into a nearby interrogation booth, where interrogators have built a shrine to Osama bin Laden. He is "told he could now pray to his god—UBL." The log records, "Detainee was apprehensive and started to walk out of booth. Detainee was not allowed to leave and interrogator played the call to prayer. Detainee began to pray and openly cried." Then, after the four hours of sleep,

> *1100:*   *Detainee awakened, taken to bathroom and walked in the interrogation booth due to rain. Corpsman checked vitals—O.K.*
>
> *1115:*   *Detainee offered water—refused. Corpsman changed ankle bandages to prevent chafing. Interrogator began by reminding the detainee about the lessons in respect and how the detainee disrespected the interrogators. Told detainee that a dog is held in higher esteem because dogs know right from wrong and know to protect innocent people from bad people. Began teaching the detainee lessons such as stay, come, and bark to elevate his social status up to that of a dog. Detainee became very agitated.*
>
> *1230:*   *Detainee taken to bathroom and walked 30 minutes.*
>
> *1300:*   *Detainee offered food and water—refused. Dog tricks continued and detained stated he should be treated like a man. Detainee was told he would have to learn who to defend and who to attack. Interrogator showed photos of 9-11 victims and told detainee he should bark happy for these people. Interrogator also showed photos of Al Qaida terrorists and told detainee he should growl at these people. A towel was placed on the detainee's head like a burka with his face exposed and the interrogator proceeded to give the detainee dance lessons. The detainee became agitated and tried to kick an MP. No retaliation was used for the kick and the dance lesson continued.*

That evening, the log records, "The doctor spoke with the detainee. He was given an 800mg motrin for chest pains."[322] An hour later:

2145: *Detainee was taken to the latrine and exercised. His vitals were taken again. His blood pressure was normal but his pulse rate was high at 93. The medical representative will be monitoring the detainee's vitals closely until his pulse rate is lower.*

2200: *The detainee was stripped searched. Initially he was attempting to resist the guards. After approximately five minutes of nudity the detainee ceased to resist. He would only stare at the wall with GREAT focus. His eyes were squinted and stuck on one point on the wall directly in front of him. He later stated that he knew there was nothing he could do with so many guards around him, so why should he resist. He stated that he did not like the females viewing his naked body while being searched and if he felt he could have done something about it then he would have.*

2331: *Detainee's vital signs were taken again by the medical representative. All of his vital signs were normal. His blood pressure was 96/43 and his pulse rate was 61. He was taken to the latrine and exercised for approximately 10 minutes.*

21 December 2002

0001: *New interrogation shift enters the booth and begins "attention to detail" approach. Detainee looks at photos of fitness models and answers questions about the photos. Drops of water were sprinkled on detainee's head when he did not answer in previous sessions, but detainee is now viewing the photos and answering. Detainee rebuked interrogator under his breath several times.*

It is now the twenty-ninth day of the interrogation. "Phase II" has begun: Qahtani is allowed to sleep in a separate cell in a block where interrogators have placed an informant, but he still spends twenty hours a day in the interrogation booth. After four weeks of intense sleep deprivation, he is visibly subdued; on the morning of December 21, the logkeeper notes, "Detainee appeared very stoic at first and claimed he was just tired, which is unusual for this shift. It is possible the detainee did not sleep much due to the introduction of the confederate detainee." Interrogators take a softer approach, letting Qahtani pick the topic of conversation, and he asks rudimentary questions about Cuba: "Is there a mosque in Cuba, is Cuba part of the U.S., is Cuba in America, Europe, or Asia?" They ask Qahtani about "his dreams for getting out of this place." Qahtani tells them "he would like to get a job but not with the Saudi government. The detainee then announced in clear English 'I would like to be a supervisor or foreman.'"

That evening, however, Sergeant L presses the "invasion of personal space" to extremes. She records the events herself, in the first person:

2103: Detainee became very emotional during the discussion of taking the right and wrong paths in life. As we discussed taking the wrong path the discussion led into a discussion of consequences for taking the wrong path. This discussion of the consequences for taking the wrong path, led to the discussion of torture, beating and killing according to the Manchester document. At this point of the discussion I was forehead to forehead with the detainee and he stated that he would rather be beaten with an electrical wire than to have me constantly in his personal space. He stated that this is unbearable to him, my being in his personal space.

2223: Detainee was taken to the latrine and exercised. He refused to drink water. I sat the detainee on the floor and told him that he was considered to be beneath me and that he didn't deserve to be seated in a chair like civilized human beings. I told him constantly that he was a coward and weak minded individual who killed innocent women and children that God created. The discussion of the Saudi government followed the conversation of being beneath me. As I began to inform the detainee of the changes the Saudi government has been making in order to support the efforts of peace and terror free world I began to engage closeness with the detainee. This really evoked strong emotions within the detainee. He attempted to move away from me by all means. He was laid out on the floor so I straddled him without putting my weight on him. He would then attempt to move me off of him by bending *his legs in order to lift me off but this failed because the MPs were holding his legs down with their hands. The detainee began to pray loudly but this did not stop me from finishing informing the detainee about the Al Qaeda member, Qaed Salim Sinan al Harethi aka Abu Ali, that was killed by the CIA. When the linguist mentioned this killing she informed me that the detainee told her to get out of his face. She did not move and she continued to interpret as usual.*

* * *

Over the next week, Qahtani's exchanges with his interrogators grow more poignant as his desperation grows. Small talk and little indulgences alternate with the ritual humiliations. Allowed to speak, Qahtani tells interrogators "Muslims in America have it good because they can speak their minds, unlike in Saudi Arabia." He responds to interrogators' "Afghanistan theme" by offering his view that "the Afghans have their own problems that only they can solve," and he suggests that the reason "high ranking al Qaeda" captives are talking to interrogators is "because they have information and he does not." He speaks frankly about his treatment:

23 December 2002

0001: Upon entering booth, lead changed white noise music and hung pictures of swimsuit models around his neck. Detainee was left in booth listening to white noise.

0030: Lead entered booth and observed that detainee appeared troubled. Lead asked detainee how he was doing. Detainee related that he had problems. When lead first asked him what the problems were he stated that they were between him and god. Lead then told detainee to tell interrogator his problems because they could not be solved unless they were addressed. Detainee then addressed the following problems to lead:

i. Being subjected to pictures of swimsuit models and questions. – he began to cry quietly at this point.

j. Metal chair is too stiff and uncomfortable.

k. The overall treatment here. He cannot handle the treatment much longer – when he made this statement he began to cry and sob out loud.

Lead asked him if he had any other problems and he stated that the other problems he could deal with on his own. Ie: physical pain, sleeping arrangement etc. What he could not deal with much longer were his being subjected to the pictures and the treatment day after day.

A few hours later:

0230: *Detainee drank 1 cup of coffee. Upon completion he was told to go exercise and go to the bathroom. Detainee then asked lead if he could ask a question. Lead told detainee to ask his question. Detainee requested that lead add wearing the towel over his head to the list of detainee problems. Detainee related that he already knows where he is, so why does he continue to wear a towel over his head. Lead then told detainee that he will continue to wear a towel over his [head] and live this lifestyle until he has proven himself to be truthful, and provides answers to questions asked. He was reminded that he chooses when this treatment stops.*

0300: *Lead and translator played cards in front of detainee. Lead instructed detainee to drink 24 ounces of water. He was told that he needed to drink the 24 ounces by the time the next break approached. If he was not finished the remainder would be spilled over his head. Detainee completed the 24 ounces of water.*

0400: *Detainee was exercised and taken to the bathroom. MPs told lead that detainee cried quietly under the towel while exercising. When he returned to the booth lead asked, what is bothering you? Detainee immediately began to cry and sob loudly and when he regained his composure he stated "I'm tired of my life here" and continued to cry. Lead reinforced that he, detainee knew what he had to do to go back to his brothers in Cuba. Detainee then related, "I'm ready to tell my story." Lead told detainee that he has not proven himself to*

be able to answer questions in detail and truthfully, and therefore
lead did not want to hear his story at this time.

Again interrogators interpret Qahtani's behavior to suggest progress.
On Christmas eve, an interrogator notes "The detainee is thinking a lot
more on the themes when presented to him, seems to be on the verge of
breaking. " Then, on December 26th:

> 1945: *The doctor checked the detainee. The doctor looked at detainee's*
> *back to ensure there were no abrasions from sitting in the metal*
> *chair for long periods of time. The doctor said everything was good.*
>
> 2030: *Detainee stated the SGT L would be the cause of him committing*
> *suicide. He requested to write a will. His request was granted and*
> *he wrote a will with a crayon. Lead had will translated and it*
> *was a request that if he died here to have his body and passport*
> *sent back to his country quickly and to notify his mother. Lead*
> *entered booth with the detainee's will and told detainee that since*
> *he had allowed the detainee this opportunity, what would the*
> *detainee offer in return. The detainee said "thank you" and lead*
> *stated that was not enough. Lead told detainee that a single truth*
> *would be enough and asked the detainee "who recruited you into*
> *Al Qaida?" Detainee stated he was not Al Qaida and lead tore up*
> *the will in front of him.*

∗ ∗ ∗

Two days later—it is now the sixth week of the interrogation—
"Interrogators instructed MPs to unshackle the detainee except for his legs
to let him feel what it was like and give the detainee a chance to make
the decision to talk." Sergeant L is replaced by an interrogator Qahtani
recognizes from earlier interviews, before his "special interrogation" began;
he takes it as a "good sign." On New Year's Day, 2003, the log records
"DETAINEE WAS GIVEN 12 HOURS IN HIS SLEEP CELL," the first time
since he was hospitalized three weeks before that he has had an opportunity
to sleep more than four hours straight.

On the seventh of January, the Guantánamo Joint Task Force's Staff Judge Advocate, the base commandant's attorney, reviews the interrogation log, and again at 6:40 p.m. on January 10. What follows is the final night of Qahtani's logged interrogation:

2100: *Head break and 10 minutes exercise.*

2130: *Interrogation team entered the booth, IS1E and a DoD linguist. Interrogator covered previous night's topic of hopelessness unless the detainee cooperates fully so he can receive leniency. Detainee stated that the session this night was quieter and he liked that, and that he didn't like to talk about his case because the conversations would become harsh. Interrogator told detainee that conversations became harsh because the detainee lies. Detainee tried to deflect conversation when it turned to Al Qaida.*

2245: *Head break and 10 minute exercise. Interrogator allowed detainee to choose a topic to talk about. Detainee wanted to talk about dinosaurs. Interrogator gave history of dinosaurs and talked about the meteor that wiped them out, and equated this event with nuclear war. Detainee expresses great ignorance about dinosaurs and space, topics that are taught in U.S. grade schools. Detainee asked interrogator if the sun revolved around the earth.*

11 January 2003

0145: *Head break and 10 minutes exercise.*

0200: *Source ate 1 MRE and drank 1 bottle of water.*

0230: *Source received haircut. Detainee did not resist until the beard was cut. Detainee stated he would talk about anything if his beard was left alone. Interrogator asked detainee if he would be honest about himself. Detainee replied "if God wills." Beard was shaven. Detainee stated he was on strike from interrogation on all teams. A little water was poured over the detainee's head to reinforce control and wash hair off. Interrogator continued futility approach. Detainee began to cry when talking.*

0400: Head break and 10 minute walk.

0430: Nap

0545: Head break and 10 minute walk. Interrogator told detainee to choose a topic of discussion. Detainee asked to know about the rituals of Christianity. Interrogator told detainee to talk about the rituals of Islam first.

0650: Medical check, OK.

0700: Taken to X-ray for sleep period.

Five days later, at 8 p.m. on January 16, 2003, a doctor is called upon again, this time to certify Qahtani's condition. The entire one-page "MD Note" of that exam remains redacted. Unredacted is this final assessment: "Normal physical exam. No injuries or trauma. Plan: follow up with medical personnel."[323]

Annotations on this section from TheTortureReport.org

On the notion that the decision to torture was an emotional response or an overreaction to 9/11, former Air Force criminal investigator and interrogator Matthew Alexander wrote,

That could be argued perhaps for a soldier in the field, under fire, without adequate time to make decisions in the heat of the battle. We would not authorize such actions even in these extreme circumstances, but at least this "inability to separate emotions from professional duty" would hold more water. In the case of the U.S. torture story, this was certainly not the case. For months, years even, there were opportunities available from the President to the ranking officers in the field to say no to torture.

On the Qahtani interrogation logs, Matthew Alexander had several observations:

On the fact that he was shackled to the floor,

Not even WWII interrogators chained Japanese detainees to the floor. It reinforces that the detainee and interrogator are enemies. Rarely have detainees been constrained for interrogations in past wars.

On Qahtani telling his interrogators, "if you interrogate me in the right way and the right position, you might find some answers,"

Ironically, he was probably correct. A good interrogator would have asked what method was the correct one, according to the detainee, and let them lead the interrogator to the answer. The coercive nature of the entire interrogation process is working directly opposite against securing the prisoner's cooperation. The interrogator's attempt to use the "what God wants you to do" approach is run with such ignorance of Islam that it has zero chance of success.

On the puppet show,

This is just absolute buffoonery. Where are the officers? The senior interrogator? This is complete shenanigans, unprofessional, and absolute incompetence.

And on the aggressive use of female interrogators,

This is nowhere in the training or the Army Field Manual. These interrogations are so amateur, incompetent, and ludicrous that any experienced, professional interrogator overseeing them would have interceded long before, removed the interrogators, and issued appropriate disciplines. The interrogations violate Geneva Conventions, the Army Field Manual, the Uniformed Code of Military Justice, not to mention completely contradict the techniques taught in the interrogations training course and Field Manual.

MARCHING ORDERS

Discovered in a police raid in the UK a year before the September 11, 2001 attacks, "The Manchester Document" is a frank, fervent guide to Al Qaeda's tactics and methods, but its instructions on resisting interrogations are neither novel nor especially sophisticated. "From the first moment in captivity, the brother should proudly take a firm and opposing position against the enemy and not obey orders," the manual counsels. Stay "psychologically and mentally calm and maintain alertness and foresight." Don't trust benevolent-seeming interrogators. Don't talk to cellmates. Don't think that revealing something will improve your situation; "The one who gives one piece of information to avoid the lashes of the whip is deluding himself because the torture would intensify." Remember that "when I talk under torture, I do not mention unknown dates and places to the security personnel, but well known ones. When I mention dates or names, it is important to memorize them because they will ask about them again to know if I was truthful."[324]

Much less commonplace and far more detailed is the document's description of the two-tier interrogation process captives can expect to encounter:

> *Interrogation: Consists of a psychological warfare and intellectual combat between the intelligence agent and the suspect through questions and answers related to one or more topics. The interrogation uses all kinds of physical and psychological techniques to break the will of the suspect and lead him to a total collapse. The agency that conducts the interrogation is the government's questioning apparatus that belongs to the Ministry of Interior Affairs. The officers of that apparatus graduate from the police academy. In our country, that apparatus has no values or code of ethics. It does not hesitate to use all kinds of torture and bodily and emotional harm to obtain evidence that could incriminate the suspect.*
>
> *Questioning: Questioning is similar to interrogation in that they are both forms of psychological warfare and intellectual combat.*

The questioning, however, is conducted by the prosecution [office of district attorney], which is under the judicial branch. That authority is (apparently) independent from the government (executive branch) and from the people's parliament (legislative branch). The prosecution officials graduate from law school and use the technique of confrontation and repeated questioning, but without torture."[325]

The reader is warned that in the first interrogation session he will be blindfolded and handcuffed, but his interrogators will be friendly, urging him to confess or face painful torture. As he is questioned, his reaction is studied and "a plan is devised for dealing with the brother." Then,

[A]nother session is held using torture in order to control the brother through fright and orders (sit down, don't sit down, face the wall, don't talk, don't raise your voice, curses and insults). The brother should not weaken, but should try to disobey the interrogator's orders or take his time executing them. If the interrogators find that the torture technique is successful, they would intensify it. However, if they find that the brother is dodging them, they would resort to psychological torture techniques.

Some interrogators may try to confuse the brother, distort his reasoning, and tangle his thoughts by throwing many questions at him at the same time and not allowing him the chance to answer them. If the brother delays his answers, he would be struck. During that torture [session], the brother is given a chance to speak, even tell a lie, in return for halting the torture. He is given a sheet of paper and asked to write whatever he wants in return for his release, for not prosecuting him, etc.[326]

The document goes on to list the specific torture techniques captives may face:

Torture Methods: Secret agents use two methods of torture: A) Physical torture; B) Psychological torture

Methods of Physical Torture:

a. *Blindfolding and stripping of clothes*

b. *Hanging by the hands.*

c. *Hanging by the feet [upside down]*

d. *Beating with sticks and electrical wires*

e. *Whipping and beating with sticks and twisted rubber belts*

f. *Forcing the brother to stand naked for long periods of time*

g. *Pouring cold water on the brother's head*

h. *Putting out lighted cigarettes on the brother's skin*

i. *Shocking with an electrical current*

j. *Kicking and punching*

k. *Attacking the brother with vicious dogs*

l. *Making the brother sit on a stake*

m. *Throwing in a septic tank*

n. *Pulling out the nails and hair*

o. *Dragging*

p. *Tying the hands and feet from behind*

q. *Utilizing sharp objects, such as a pocketknife or piece of glass*

r. *Burning with fire*

s. *Sleeping on a bare marble floor without a cover and flooding the cell with salt water*

t. *Standing on toes and against a wall pressing with the fingers for long hours. The brother may be denied sleep, food, drink, and medicine*

u. *Beating on cuts and sore parts of the body*

v. *Giving the brother a lot of water or very watery fruits, such as watermelon, after denying him food and drink. After the brother drinks or eats the fruit, his hands and penis will be tied so the brother will not be able to urinate*

w. *Placing drugs and narcotics in the brother's food to weaken his will power*

x. *Placing the brother in a solitary confinement where the cells are made of a special kind of cement that gets extremely hot in the summer and cold in winter y. Hitting the brother's genitals with a stick or squeezing them by hand*

z. Dragging the brother over barb wires and fragments of glass and metal

Methods of Psychological Torture:

a. *Isolating the brother socially, cutting him off from public life, placing him in solitary confinement, and denying him news and information in order to make him feel lonely*

b. *Forbidding calling him by name, giving the brother a number, and calling him by that number in order to defeat his morale*

c. *Threatening to summon his sister, mother, wife, or daughter and rape her*

d. *Threatening to rape the brother himself*

e. *Threatening to confiscate his possessions and to have him fired from his employment*

f. *Threatening to cause a permanent physical disability or life imprisonment*

g. *Offer the brother certain enticements (apartment, car, passport, scholarship, etc.)*

h. *Using harsh treatment, insults, and curses to defeat his morale*

i. *Controlling everything the brother does, even in private, whether he is awake or asleep, to convince him that they are in charge. They would force him to bow his head and look down while talking with the guards.*

The list ends with this admonition:

Further, let no one think that the aforementioned techniques are fabrications of our imagination, or that we copied them from spy stories. On the contrary, these are factual incidents in the prisons of Egypt, Syria, Jordan, Saudi Arabia, and all other Arab countries.[327]

Where the Manchester Document instructs its reader to "ask that evidence of his torture be entered in subsequent legal proceedings," it is not directing him to fabricate abuse claims. Written in the expectation that its recruits would be detained by one of these enemy Arab regimes, the manual anticipates torture as an inevitable fact, and simply urges captives to report the treatment they receive. Through the years, senior Bush administration officials repeatedly distorted these instructions to cast doubt on abuse claims. "These detainees are trained to lie, they're trained to say they were tortured," Defense Secretary Donald Rumsfeld said in a June 21, 2005 interview on Fox News's "Tony Snow Show," "and the minute we release them or the minute they get a lawyer, very frequently they'll go out and they will announce that they've been tortured."[328]

* * *

It was the Manchester Document that former Air Force psychologist James Mitchell studied in December 2001 with future business partner John "Bruce" Jessen when they were preparing their paper proposing countermeasures to overcome Al Qaeda's resistance training.[329]

As they were completing their draft, John Yoo and Robert Delahunty, Special Counsel to Defense Department General Counsel William J. "Jim" Haynes II, were finalizing a legal opinion titled "Application of Treaties and Laws to al Qaeda and Taliban Detainees," a document concluding that neither Al Qaeda nor Taliban captives were entitled to Geneva Convention protections. On January 6, 2002, three days before they submitted their opinion to Haynes, the Pentagon ordered the Navy to refurbish an abandoned complex of chain link pens that had been built to house Haitian refugees at the naval base in Guantánamo Bay in the early 1990s, and to have the camp ready to receive up to one hundred detainees in four days.[330]

On January 11, 2002, a plane carrying the first twenty supposedly non-Geneva eligible enemy combatants arrived at Guantánamo. At a press briefing that afternoon in Washington, Defense Secretary Donald Rumsfeld and Joint Chiefs of Staff Chairman General Richard B. Myers described the group as "very very dangerous people." "I mean, these are people that would gnaw hydraulic lines in the back of a C-17 to bring it down," Myers famously added. Rumsfeld had hinted that one of the detainees had been sedated en route, and a reporter pressed for details, asking if he had in fact tried to chew through a hydraulic line. "'No, no' (laughter) 'Hyperbole,'" the transcript records Rumsfeld's answer, and Myers echoes, "'That was hyperbole' (More laughter)."[331]

Neither Myers nor Rumsfeld claimed the group contained Al Qaeda leaders; rather, Rumsfeld suggested that they were "people who probably reached a certain phase of interrogation" in Afghanistan and it was important to "free up openings there." Reporters grilled them on what standard of treatment the new arrivals would receive in Guantánamo:

Q: *Mr. Secretary, you said, that for the most part, the detainees will be treated in a manner consistent with the Geneva Convention. Exactly which parts, which rights, privileges of the Geneva Convention will they have, and who will decide, and when will it be decided on an ad hoc basis? And just as a follow-up, can you say if there's been any –*

Rumsfeld: *Well, let me work on that for a minute. That's a mouthful. What we've said from the beginning is that these are unlawful combatants in our view, and we're detaining them. We call them detainees, not prisoners of war. We call them detainees. We have said that, you know, being the kind of a country we are, it's our intention to recognize that there are certain standards that are generally appropriate for treating people who were—are prisoners of war, which these people are not, and—in our view— but there—and, you know, to the extent that it's reasonable, we will end up using roughly that standard. And that's what we're doing. I don't—I wouldn't want to say that I know in any instance where we would deviate from that or where we might exceed it. But I'm sure we'll probably be on both sides of it modestly....*

Q: *But why is it important that you not consider them—in other words, why not just treat them as prisoners of war? If prisoners of war get additional rights and protections, why not just treat them that way?*

Rumsfeld: *That's basically what we're doing. That's what I've said.*

> *We're generally conforming to the Geneva Convention as it*
> *applies to prisoners of war. That's what that—*
> Q: *Why not let it officially apply?*
> *Rumsfeld: Well, first of all, we don't have to. And second, I—we're*
> *still in the very early stages of this, and we're in the process of*
> *trying to figure out the answers to all of this and how— what's*
> *the best way to do it? What's the proper way to do it? How will*
> *we feel good about having done it a certain way? And what is*
> *appropriate? And those are the kinds of things that we're going*
> *through, because, as I say, there's hundreds of these people,*
> *and more coming from the ones that are being detained by*
> *our friends.*
>
> *And so we're trying to rapidly build detention areas that*
> *are appropriate, and we're trying to train people to—military*
> *people to handle hard-case detainees, and—when that isn't*
> *what they normally do when they get up in the morning. And*
> *we're just trying to get it right.*[332]

Over the next month, Rumsfeld's deliberately ambiguous comments were cemented as official policy. On January 18, 2002, White House Counsel Alberto Gonzales briefed President Bush on the Yoo-Delahunty memo, and Bush sanctioned its conclusions. The next day, Rumsfeld ordered the Joint Chiefs to instruct all field commanders that Taliban and Al Qaeda members are "not entitled to prisoner of war status," though they should "treat [detainees] humanely and, to the extent appropriate and consistent with military necessity, in a manner consistent with the principles of the Geneva Conventions of 1949"; the order was relayed down the line two days later.[333] On January 25, Gonzales delivered his memo dismissing Secretary of State Colin Powell's objections to suspending Geneva protections, and on February 7, 2002, President Bush issued the order accepting the Yoo-Delahunty legal conclusions and echoing Rumsfeld's instructions that detainees were not entitled to the protections but that

Of course, our values as a nation, values that we share with many

nations in the world, call for us to treat detainees humanely, including those who are not legally entitled to such treatment. Our nation has been and will continue to be a strong supporter of Geneva and its principles. As a matter of policy, the United States Armed Forces shall continue to treat detainees humanely and, to the extent appropriate and consistent with military necessity, in a manner consistent with the principles of Geneva.[334]

Mohammed al-Qahtani was delivered to Guantánamo six days later. Qahtani had been captured by the Pakistani military on December 15, 2001, one of a wave of alleged militants fleeing the battle of Tora Bora in Afghanistan. The Pakistanis turned him over to U.S. forces, and on February 13, 2002 he became Detainee 063 in Guantánamo's hastily-rigged Camp X-Ray. By then Navy Seabees had built more of the camp's open-air cells, eight-by-eight-by-ten foot metal-roofed cages guards would throw tarps over when it rained. Even at night, an FBI agent assigned to the base in those early days reported, "the entire camp was bathed with light"; she said she "could see light shining on the camp from her hootch." When she toured the camp, an agent from the Army's Criminal Investigation Division told her "they were keeping the lights on both as a security measure and a sleep deprivation technique."[335] Like all detainees, Qahtani was weighed during inprocessing. The 5' 6", 22 or 23 year-old Saudi weighed 132 pounds that day.[336]

Months later, another FBI agent arriving for a shift at the base was shown a film of detainee inprocessing in those early days; the agent later described the scene in an interview with the Justice Department's Inspector General:

[Redacted] recalled one portion of the video where the detainees were hooded and kneeling in what was referred to as the "pumpkin patch." Various military personnel were yelling and screaming at the detainees while they were kneeling in the pumpkin patch. [Redacted] advised that the "pumpkin patch" refers to the manner in which the detainees are placed on the tarmac when they arrive and are removed from the aircraft. [Redacted] recalled that while one soldier

*was yelling at a detainee in the pumpkin patch the detainee just
passed out. [Redacted] characterized the video as "hard core." Also,
[Redacted] thought at the time that it was bizarre the military was
showing them this video. [Redacted] recalled that there were some
military dogs in the video that were apparently used to control and
disorient the detainees when they first arrived.*[337]

The transfer to a prison camp on a tropical island thousands of miles from
Central Asia and the Middle East and the treatment on arrival and in Camp
X-Ray clearly had an effect. An FBI supervisor who "was in the tower
when the plane landed" with the first group of detainees and who regularly
returned to the base to debrief FBI interrogators reported that agents who
were assigned to question Guantánamo's early arrivals told him that "many
of the detainees came into the interviews shaking or visibly upset."

*The Agents often had to calm the detainees down b/c the detainees
thought that there were going to be killed after entering the interview
shacks. The detainees were used to a much different environment
in Afghanistan or their home country. Some detainees clearly felt
that they were going to be harshly treated or killed as part of being
questioned. The Agents had to reassure the detainees that all they
wanted to do [was] to talk to them.*[338]

In April 2002, a Chinese Uighur detainee who had been captured in
Afghanistan and transferred to Guantánamo in January was interrogated
in X-Ray's primitive, plywood interrogation rooms—not by the FBI or
military interrogators, but by what the Justice Department's Inspector
General identifies only as "Chinese officials." The detainee told an FBI
agent that before the session he had been "awakened at 15 minute intervals
the entire night and into the next day" and that he was "exposed to low
room temperatures for long periods of time and was deprived of at least
one meal." The treatment was evidently repeated with other Uighurs who
were transferred to Guantánamo later that year. According to the Inspector
General, "the agent stated that he understood that the treatment of the Uighur

detainees was either carried out by the Chinese interrogators or was carried out by U.S. military personnel at the behest of the Chinese interrogators."[339]

Forty-five years earlier, a 1956 CIA study entitled "Communist Control Techniques: An Analysis of the Methods Used by Communist State Police in the Arrest, Interrogation, and Indoctrination of Persons Regarded as 'Enemies of the State'" assessed the impact of post-capture anxiety and the manipulation of sleep, temperature, and diet this way:

> *Even in the absence of isolation, profound and uncontrolled anxiety is disorganizing...The newly arrested prisoner does not know how long he will be confined, how he will be punished, or with what he will be charged. He does know that his punishment may be anything up to death or permanent imprisonment. Many prisoners say that uncertainty is the most unbearable aspect of the whole experience....*
>
> *But, if these alone are not enough to produce the desired effect, the officer in charge has other simple and highly effective ways of applying pressure. Two of the most effective of these are fatigue and lack of sleep. The constant light in the cell and the necessity of maintaining a rigid position in bed compound the effects of anxiety and nightmares in producing sleep disturbances. If these are not enough, it is easy to have the guards awaken the prisoners at intervals. This is especially effective if the prisoner is always awakened as soon as he drops off to sleep. The guards can also shorten the hours available for sleep, or deny sleep altogether. Continued loss of sleep produces clouding of consciousness and a loss of alertness, both of which impair the victim's ability to sustain isolation. It also produces profound fatigue.*
>
> *Another simple and effective type of pressure is that of maintaining the temperature of the cell at a level which is either too hot or too cold for comfort. Continuous heat, at a level at which constant sweating is necessary in order to maintain body temperature, is enervating and fatigue producing. Sustained cold is uncomfortable and poorly tolerated. Yet another method of creating pressure is to reduce the food ration to the point at which the*

prisoner is constantly hungry. This usually involved loss of weight, which is often associated with weakness and asthenia. Furthermore, deprivation of food produces lassitude, loss of general interest and some breakdown of courage. Some people become profoundly depressed when deprived of food....

The Communists do not look upon these methods as "torture." Undoubtedly, they use the methods which they do in order to conform, in a typical legalistic manner to overt Communist principles which demand that "no force or torture be used in extracting information from prisoners." But these methods do, of course, constitute torture and physical coercion. All of them lead to serious disturbances of many bodily processes."[340]

The same year as that CIA study, U.S. Air Force sociologist Albert Biderman presented a paper at the New York Academy of Medicine that analyzed how communist Chinese interrogators had employed a range of such techniques to extract false confessions from U.S. airmen captured during the Korean War. In probing how these interrogators "gained compliance" from U.S. servicemen to the point that they were able to extort admissions that were in fact lies, Biderman was surprised to discover that the techniques they used were hardly novel and rarely involved physical abuse. Physical torture, Biderman found, interferes with the "teaching process" necessary to shape confessions by setting up a contest between the interrogator and the captive. "Can he endure pain beyond the point to which the interrogator will go in inflicting pain? The answer for the interrogator is all too frequently yes," Biderman wrote in a journal article on his research the following year.

"Generally," Biderman reported, "[physical violence] appears to have been limited to cuffs, slaps, and kicks, and sometimes merely to threats and insults." The exception, he noted, was forced standing, which pits the detainee against himself; "Returnees who underwent long periods of standing and sitting...report no other experience could be more excruciating." By avoiding violence—"by formal adherence," as Biderman put it, "to twisted norms of humaneness and legality"—interrogators were

CHART 1 – COMMUNIST COERCIVE METHODS
FOR ELICITING INDIVIDUAL COMPLIANCE

General Method	Effects (Purposes)	Variants
1. Isolation	Deprives Victim of all Social Support of his Ability to Resist. Develops an Intense Concern with Self. Makes Victim Dependent on Interrogator.	Complete Solitary Confinement Complete Isolation Semi-Isolation Group Isolation
2. Monopolization of Perception	Fixes Attention upon Immediate Predicament. Fosters Introspection. Eliminates Stimuli Competing with those Controlled by Captor. Frustrates all Actions not Consistent with Compliance	Physical Isolation Darkness or Bright Light Barren Environment Restricted Movement Monotonous Food
3. Induced Debilitation; Exhaustion	Weakens Mental and Physical Ability to Resist	Semi-Starvation Exposure Exploitation of Wounds Induced Illness Sleep Deprivation Prolonged Constraint Prolonged Interrogation or Forced Writing Over Exertion
4. Threats	Cultivates Anxiety and Despair	Threats of Death Threats of Non-repatriation Threats of Endless Isolation and Interrogation Vague threats Threats Against Family Mysterious Changes of Treatment
5. Occasional Indulgences	Provides Positive Motivation for Compliance. Hinders Adjustment to Deprivation.	Occasional Favors Fluctuations of Interrogators' Attitudes Promises Rewards for Partial Compliance Tantalizing
6. Demonstrating "Omnipotence" and "Omniscience"	Suggests Futility of Resistance	Confrontations Pretending Cooperation Taken for Granted Demonstrating Complete Control over Victim's Fate
7. Degradation	Makes Costs of Resistance Appear More Damaging to Self-Esteem than Capitulation. Reduces Prisoner to "Animal Level" Concerns	Personal Hygiene Prevented Filthy, Infested Surroundings Demeaning Punishments Insults and Taunts Denial of Privacy
8. Enforcing Trivial Demands	Develops Habit of Compliance	Forced Writing Enforcement of Minute Rules

able both to shape prisoner compliance in the desired direction and "gain a considerable propaganda advantage when victims who are released truthfully state that no one laid a hand on them."[341]

Biderman's paper concluded with a chart of methods Chinese interrogators used to move POWS from "complete resistance" to "defensive resistance" to "defensive compliance," and then to "active" and "complete" compliance.

It was out of these Cold War-era studies that the U.S. armed services developed their Survival, Evasion, Resistance, Escape (SERE) training programs, where American soldiers at risk of enemy capture have, for years, been trained to resist a range of pressures from insult slaps and sleep deprivation to a tightly controlled simulation of waterboarding. The SERE role-playing sessions are often constructed to test whether trainees can be coerced into signing a confession admitting to war crimes. Now, in April 2002, the U.S. military was facilitating the use of sleep deprivation and temperature manipulation by Chinese interrogators in Guantánamo's Camp X-Ray; SERE psychologist Bruce Jessen was circulating his "Exploitation Draft Plan" detailing how SERE techniques would be used on detainees held incommunicado at secret "exploitation facilities"; and James Mitchell was rushing to put the plan into practice, sending the first cables to CIA headquarters chronicling the interrogation of Abu Zubaydah at the CIA black site in Thailand.

In preparing the "Exploitation Draft Plan," Mitchell and Jessen knew they had two audiences: the CIA and the Pentagon. Their December 2001 paper on overcoming Al Qaeda resistance training had reached the Joint Chiefs in February, with a recommendation from Colonel John "Randy" Moulton, commander of the military's SERE-overseeing Joint Personnel Recovery Agency, that the JPRA send a team to Guantánamo to conduct a "short course" on "basic and advanced techniques and methods" that JPRA had used in its SERE training courses. The Defense Intelligence Agency responded with an official request for support, and in early March, Jessen and JPRA instructor Joseph Witsch held a two week "ad hoc 'crash course on interrogation' for the next crew (rotation) going to SOUTHCOM," the military command responsible for Guantánamo. They also held a teleconference with military interrogators in Guantánamo, which they followed with a pitch on how JPRA could assist.[342]

At the March training, Jessen and Witsch presented a PowerPoint presentation titled "Al Qaeda Resistance Contingency Training: Contingency Training for [redacted] Personnel Based on Recently Obtained al Qaeda Documents." In its 2008 "Inquiry into the Treatment of Detainees in U.S. Custody," the Senate Armed Services Committee reported,

> The presentation on detainee "exploitation" described phases of exploitation and included instruction on initial capture and handling, conducting interrogations, and long-term exploitation. The exploitation presentation also included slides on "isolation and degradation," "sensory deprivation," "physiological pressures," and "psychological pressures." At SERE school, each of these terms has special meaning.
>
> The [redacted] instructor guide describes "isolation" as "a main building block of the exploitation process" and says that it allows the captor total control over personal inputs to the captive." With respect to degradation, the guide contains examples of the methods used by SERE instructors to take away the "personal dignity" of students at SERE school. Examples of degradation techniques used at SERE school include [redacted]. Mr. Witsch, the JPRA instructor who led the March 8, 2002 training, told the Committee that stripping could also be considered a degradation tactic.[343]

In a footnote, the Committee added,

> Another slide describing captor motives states: establish absolute control, induce dependence to meet needs, elicit compliance, shape cooperation.... In other JPRA materials, techniques designed to achieve these goals include isolation or solitary confinement, induced physical weakness and exhaustion, degradation, conditioning, sensory deprivation, sensory overload, disruption of sleep and biorhythms, and manipulation of diet. Physical Pressures

Used in Resistance Training and Against American Prisoners and
Detainees.[344]

On March 18, 2002, just after the training, Jessen sent an email with a
vision for future trainings, where one day would "cover the basics of the
SERE techniques and another three days would be devoted to 'role play.'"[345]

As with the CIA, Mitchell and Jessen saw opportunity in the early
chaos of Guantánamo. SOUTHCOM, whose sphere is the Americas, had
little experience with the region from which Guantánamo was receiving its
detainees. Few of its interrogators had a background in terrorist networks
or investigations, and many were reservists who had never questioned an
actual prisoner. Its own linguists "were worthless," Major General Mike
Dunlavey would say later. "They came out of school and could order coffee,
but they were getting smoked by the detainees."[346]

Dunlavey was Commander of Joint Task Force 170, created on
February 16, 2002—nine days after President Bush issued the Geneva
Conventions directive—to run interrogation operations at Guantánamo.
While he nominally reported to SOUTHCOM Commander General James
Hill, Dunlavey had been installed from above, as he explained in a sworn
statement in 2005:

> *How I became the JTF-170 Commander? I was working at the*
> *National Security Agency. On 14 February 2002, I was contacted to*
> *meet with the SECDEF. I received a joint service billet description. I*
> *met with the SECDEF on the 20th or 21st of February 2002, along with*
> *the Deputy SECDEF, Wolfowitz and a number of other personnel.*
>
> *The SECDEF told me that DoD had accumulated a number of*
> *bad guys. He wanted to set up interrogation operations and to identify*
> *the senior Taliban and senior operatives and to obtain information on*
> *what they were going to do regarding their operations and structure.*
>
> *The SECDEF said he wanted a product and he wanted intelligence*
> *now. He told me what he wanted; not how to do it.*
>
> *Initially, I was told that I would answer to the SECDEF and*
> *USSOUTHCOM. I did not have to deal with USCENTCOM. Their*

mission had nothing to do with my mission. Everything had to go up to USSOUTHCOM then to JCS. The directions changed and I got my marching orders from the President of the United States. I was told by the SECDEF that he wanted me back in Washington DC every week to brief him.[347]

In the spring and summer of 2002, Dunlavey shared the command of the camp with Brigadier General Rick Baccus, whose Joint Task Force 160, composed largely of military police units, ran detention operations. When Baccus assumed the command of JTF 160 on March 27, X-Ray had reached its maximum capacity of three hundred detainees, and Baccus's troops had their hands full just policing the swelling prison population. "It was a very manpower-intensive situation," Baccus recalled in a 2005 *Frontline* Interview. "Camp X-Ray didn't have any internal facilities at all—no bathrooms, no source of water...[I]f [the detainees] wanted to do the smallest thing like go to the bathroom, the MPs were required to go in, shackle them, and then move them to a Port-A-John to have them go to the bathroom and take them back again."[348] But construction had begun on a more permanent facility, and on April 28 and 29, the population of Camp X-Ray was transferred to newly-constructed cellblocks in Camp Delta, where the open-air cells contained flush toilets, metal bed frames, and sinks with running water. Camp Delta added cellblocks through the spring and summer; by the end of June, Baccus's MPs were running a prison for 536 detainees.

Among the June arrivals was an 18-year-old Yemeni youth named Mohamed Hassan Odaini, who had been seized in a raid on a rooming house for Koranic studies students in Faisalabad, Pakistan in March. Far from a "very bad guy" or committed militant, Odaini was a serious student who was quite literally in the wrong place at the wrong time, having accepted an invitation to stay overnight at the house after joining the residents for dinner. That he was an innocent bystander was clear to his U.S. captors by the time he was shipped with fourteen of the guesthouse's residents to Guantánamo. The U.S. District Court that reviewed his habeas corpus petition eight years later found that an interrogator who interviewed Odaini just after his arrival concluded that he "appeared to be telling the truth" and recommended that he "be utilized to identify individuals at house in Faisalabad" and then he "should be considered for repatriation." "He was told shortly after being taken into custody and upon arrival at Guantánamo Bay that he would be released within two weeks," noted the court that finally ordered his release almost eight years later.[349]

In fact, by the summer of 2002 it was clear that Guantánamo's swelling population, which now ranged in age from early teens to mid-nineties, included many who didn't belong there. As the *New York Times* would report two months later, "[S]ome clues were obvious. Some of the detainees were elderly or infirm. One of those was Faiz Muhammad, a genial old man with a long wispy beard whom interrogators nicknamed "Al Qaeda Claus." Another, who was able to make the trip only after extensive medical care from Army doctors in Afghanistan, quickly became known as "Half-Dead Bob."[350] The notion that Camp Delta's cells were filled with hardened fighters steeped in the Manchester document was undercut by the fact that many of the detainees had never been to training camps and couldn't read or write; now, supposedly, they were receiving resistance training at the camp itself. "Although many of the detainees are illiterate and have not read the manual, a JTF source said there is a segment of the detained population who were trainers in the various terrorist camps and that these trainers have either, by example or through different modes of communication, disseminated the document's principles to the larger detainee population," an article on Joint Task Force Guantánamo's website later insisted.[351]

In his press conference announcing the delivery of the first group of detainees to Guantánamo in January, Rumsfeld had suggested what role he expected the island's population to play in intelligence gathering:

Q: *If these guys are so dangerous and they're so –*
Rumsfeld: *The implication being they're not?*
Q: *No, No, No.*
Rumsfeld: *Oh.*
Q: *I'm just saying, since they are, how is it that we're able to get specific information on, you know, al Qaeda leaders? In other words, they're obviously not willing to give us that kind of*

information. Are some of them just deciding that it's best for them to give us the information? Is there a large number of them that are willing to do the interviews?

Rumsfeld: There's several aspects to it, and one aspect is that there are Taliban who know things about al Qaeda. And they may not be as hard-core as the al Qaeda, but they may have worked in close proximity with them. They may have been functionaries for them. They may have been couriers for them. They may have been whatever. And so that's one location. Some other people just may decide that the better—you know, that—"that's enough of that, and maybe I'll just go ahead and cooperate and see if I can get myself in a better circumstance."[352]

FBI agents and military HUMINT ("human intelligence") agents had been questioning detainees separately since around the time Mohammed al-Qahtani arrived at Camp X-Ray in February. In May, "Tiger Teams" were created in an effort to coordinate military and FBI interrogations; each team included an FBI agent and a "BAU" analyst from the agency's Behavioral Analysis Unit, one military HUMINT interrogator, a contract linguist, and two investigators from the military's Criminal Investigation Task Force, which like the FBI questions suspects with an eye toward building cases for prosecution. Each team interviewed two detainees a day. The FBI agents and BAU analysts were generally the most experienced members of the team, and "tiger team" interrogations followed FBI protocol, under which detainees were not issued Miranda warnings but otherwise were questioned according to the agency's Legal Handbook requirement "that no attempt be made to obtain a statement by force, threats, or promises," and with the FBI's traditional emphasis on rapport-building.

The FBI considered these interrogations successful. But Washington was pressing Dunlavey for more "product," and Dunlavey in turn was demanding more from military interrogators. David Becker, who was Chief of the military's Interrogation Control Element (ICE) in Guantánamo at the time, told the Senate Armed Services Committee that during the summer of 2002 Dunlavey and Lieutenant Colonel Jerald Phifer, Dunlavey's Director for Intelligence, "urged him to be more aggressive in interrogations," and "repeatedly asked him during this period why he was not using stress positions in interrogations," even though a Standard Operating Procedure issued later in the summer explicitly stated "DETAINEES WILL NOT BE PLACED IN STRESS POSITIONS." Furthermore,

> *Mr. Becker also told the Committee that on several occasions, MG Dunlavey had advised him that the office of Deputy Secretary of Defense had called to express concern about the insufficient intelligence productions at GTMO. Mr. Becker recalled MG Dunlavey telling him after one of these calls, that the Deputy Secretary himself said that GTMO should use more aggressive techniques.*[353]

In its investigation, the Armed Services Committee found evidence suggesting that the pressure from Washington was driven not by concerns about the quantity of intelligence being gathered so much as a desire for a particular kind of information. Becker told the Committee that military interrogators were required to ask detainees about possible links between Al Qaeda and Iraq. Two years before Becker's Senate testimony, military psychiatrist Major Paul Burney described this pressure for the Army's Inspector General,

> *[T]his is my opinion, even though they were giving information and some of it was useful, while we were there a large part of the time we were focused on trying to establish a link between Al Qaeda and Iraq and we were not being successful in establishing a link between Al Qaeda and Iraq. The more frustrated people got in not being able to establish this link...there was more and more pressure to resort to measures that might produce more immediate results.*[354]

Major Burney arrived in Guantánamo in June as part of a three man team from the Army's 85th Medical Detachment Combat Stress Control Team; he and his teammates, a psychologist and a psychiatric technician, thought they had been deployed to the base to provide psychological services to U.S. servicemen working in the prison. Instead, as Burney told the Armed Services Committee,

> *Three of us; [redacted] [the enlisted psychiatric technician], and I, were hijacked and immediately inprocessed into Joint Task Force 170, the military intelligence command on the island. It turns out we were assigned to the interrogation element because Joint Task Force 170 had authorizations for a psychiatrist, a psychologist, and a psychiatric technician on its duty roster but nobody had been deployed to fill these positions. Nobody really knew what we were supposed to do for the unit, but at least the duty roster had its positions filled.*[355]

There was, in fact, a plan: the three were to become JTF 170's first Behavioral Science Consultation Team, or "BSCT." Like the FBI's BAU agents, the "biscuits," as they came to be known, were meant to analyze detainees and give interrogators advice on approaches and strategies. Complete novices in supporting interrogations, Burney and his team were pointed to the military's Joint Personnel Recovery Agency for instruction in how SERE techniques might be used in Guantánamo interrogations, and Burney began working with top JPRA psychologists to organize a training session aimed at drawing up a wish list of potentially useful SERE techniques.

That month, an FBI agent stumbled on a scene in which a detainee was "short-shackled" in "what appeared to be a stress position on his knees." A translator was yelling at the detainee, who was massaging his leg, while "two young soldiers" stood by, "laughing and snickering." The agent asked the soldiers if the treatment had been authorized. As the Justice Department's Inspector General later reported, "One soldier told the agent that the activity was authorized, but the agent was not convinced and he sought out a CITF legal advisor. The two of them brought this incident to the attention of Commanding General's JAG."

The agent and CITF legal advisor followed up with a meeting with Dunlavey's Deputy Commander. "[T]he Deputy Commander quickly lost his temper during this meeting," both the agent and the legal advisor told the Inspector General. "The FBI agent told us that the Deputy Commander misinterpreted the agent's concern as constituting a torture investigation." But in this first skirmish in what would become a running battle over the treatment of detainees, the agents thought they had prevailed; after the meeting, the two were told that the conduct in question was "unacceptable and required further training and supervision, but that an investigation was unnecessary." Henceforth, "detainees would have the opportunity to be seated during FBI and CITF interviews," they were assured, and the Defense Intelligence Agency's supervisor was also "instruct[ing] Defense HUMINT service interrogators to observe this rule."[356]

* * *

Days later, FBI investigators in Washington, sifting through fingerprints of Guantánamo detainees, matched the fingerprint of Mohammed al-Qahtani to that of a man who had been refused entry to the United States when he arrived at Orlando Airport from Dubai via London the month before the September 11 terrorist attacks. On July 15, word of the possible 9/11 connection was relayed to FBI agents in Guantánamo, who alerted the military. Attorney General John Ashcroft and President Bush were briefed as well, and word came back down from the White House that "there was no interest in prosecuting al Qahtani in a U.S. court"; David Nahmias, counsel to the Justice Department's Criminal Division, told the department's Inspector General that "someone had made a determination that 'not one single [detainee] will see the inside of a courtroom in the United States.'"[357]

In Guantánamo, Qahtani was suddenly "the ticket everybody wanted," as an FBI agent stationed there at the time put it.[358] The FBI moved quickly to assert its authority to lead Qahtani's interrogation, arguing that it had discovered the link and had overall control of the 9/11 investigation. Qahtani was moved to a new cell in Camp Delta and interviewed every day for a week by FBI and CITF agents, where he first claimed he had never been to the United States, and then admitted he had traveled to Florida but insisted it was in order to buy and sell used cars. On July 27, 2002, he was transferred again, to the maximum-security cellblock of Camp Delta "to minimize influence and social support from other detainees." The FBI then called on Ali Soufan, who four months earlier had questioned the wounded Abu Zubaydah in the CIA black site in Thailand and later faced down Mitchell's interrogation team over Zubaydah's treatment there.[359] Soufan "had already obtained confessions from [redacted] detainees" in Guantánamo and "was recognized by Michael E. Dunlavey as 'a national treasure,'" one of Soufan's FBI colleagues told the Inspector General, adding that, to his credit "when the Federal Bureau of Investigation had a .400 hitter in [redacted] down here, [Dunlavey] recognized it."[360]

In late July, as Mitchell's crew was gearing up for its month-long, White-House orchestrated torture of Abu Zubaydah in Thailand, Ali Soufan interviewed Mohammed al-Qahtani in Guantánamo. After that session, Soufan recommended that Qahtani "should go into some sort of isolation or segregation if the Federal Bureau of Investigation was going to have some shot of making progress with this guy," and came up with the idea of putting him in a "non-standard arrangement in the Navy Brig."[361] The recommendation raised concerns; as the Inspector General noted in a footnote to his 2008 report, "severe isolation of the type used on Qahtani for interrogation purposes rather than as a disciplinary or security measure would likely be considered to be coercive and contrary to FBI interviews in the United States."

Nevertheless, Soufan's request was approved up the FBI chain of command, and on August 8, 2002, Qahtani was forcibly removed from his cell and delivered by military ambulance to a specially prepared wing of the Guantánamo Naval Brig evidently modeled on the environments in which Yaser Hamdi and Jose Padilla were then being held at the Naval Brigs in Virginia and South Carolina. "There was a concerted effort to try to isolate him from any human contact with the guards," Soufan told the Inspector General. "A protocol was designed so that [Qahtani] would not be able to see the guards' faces"; "some guards covered their faces in some fashion and other times [he] was supposed to turn away so as not to look at the guards."[362] In a February 27, 2007 interview with the Inspector General, Qahtani himself called the brig "the worst place I was taken to." The IG recorded,

*He said he did not know when to pray because the window was
covered up and he could not tell what time of day it was. In addition,
he said that he did not know the direction of Mecca. Al-Qahtani told
the OIG that the entire time he was at the Brig the guards covered
their faces when they dealt with him. He also said he was not allowed
any recreation, and while he was allowed into the hallway outside his
cell, he never saw the sun. Al-Qahtani said the lights in his cell were
left on continuously for the entire time he was there, which he said
was half a year. Al-Qahtani also described the Brig as very, very cold.
He said he sometimes had a mattress, but if the interrogators did not
like his answers, they would take things like that away.*[363]

Immediately after the move, Soufan sat with Qahtani and told him
"this is your place until you change your story." Qahtani told the Inspector
General that Soufan had "some sense of humanity" and that he "did not use
aggression or physical violence." He did, however, make "actual or implied
threats" that the IG found troublesome:

*According to Al-Qahtani, [Soufan] said things such as "you will find
yourself in a difficult situation if you don't talk to me" and "if you're
not going to talk now, you will talk in the future." When asked if he
took this as a "warning or a threat," Al-Qahtani replied that it was "a
little bit of both."*

Soufan and other FBI agents questioned Qahtani for a month in the
Naval Brig. They offered to return him to Camp Delta if he would just
give them "a small piece of information"; he countered that if they moved
him, he would talk. They left him alone in his cell for long periods without
interrogating him. In one crisis moment, Soufan had to be "tracked down
at chow hall" and summoned to the brig by guards "concerned about his
behavior"; he had to walk Qahtani around outdoors to calm him down.
Soufan himself began to observe "strange behavior," noting that Qahtani's
"ritual washing before prayer started to turn into excessive compulsive

behavior, and that "he would use his blanket to make a cocoon-like structure in his cell."[364]

Soufan's FBI supervisor told the Inspector General that "within two weeks" of learning of the possible 9/11 connection, the military decided it "wanted a piece of Qahtani." Soufan himself reported that by mid-August, military interrogators were asking, "Is it soup yet?"[365] Over the previous month, senior Pentagon lawyers had written to JPRA Chief of Staff Daniel Baumgarten requesting a list of exploitation and interrogation techniques "that had been effective against Americans," and Baumgarten sent Jim Haynes a responsive memo noting that JPRA had already been "assist[ing] in the training of interrogators/exploiters from other governmental agencies" and assuring Haynes that "[s]everal of the techniques highlighted (Atch 1) as training tools in JPRA courses, used by other SERE schools, and used historically may be effective in inducing learned helplessness and 'breaking' the [Operation Enduring Freedom] detainees' will to resist." The attached list of techniques included facial and abdominal slaps, walling, stress positions, use of smoke, cramped confinement, water dousing, and waterboarding. The same July 26, 2002 memo and attachments were forwarded to the CIA in support of the OLC memos sanctioning the torture of Abu Zubaydah that were completed four days later, on August 1, 2002.[366]

On August 18, 2002, two and a half weeks into the Abu Zubaydah interrogation in Thailand and ten days into the FBI's sessions with Qahtani in the Guantánamo brig, the *Los Angeles Times* ran a story entitled "No Leaders of Al Qaeda Found at Guantánamo." "Despite intense interrogations and investigations, U.S. authorities have yet to identify any senior Al Qaeda leaders among the nearly 600 terrorism suspects from 42 countries in U.S. military custody at Guantánamo Bay, Cuba," the article announced. It quoted government sources who said there were "no big fish" in custody there and the island's detainees were not "high enough in the command and control structure to help counter-terrorism experts unravel al Qaeda's tightknit cell and security systems." "Some of these guys literally don't know the world is round," one of the sources added. Moreover, in recent weeks three detainees had "tried to hang themselves in their cells with camp-issued 'comfort items' such as towels and sheets, and another tried to slit his wrists with a plastic razor," the *Times* reported.[367]

That *Los Angeles Times* story appeared just after a CIA analyst had spent a week at Guantánamo conducting a survey of detainees. The analyst's top secret report, circulated in Washington a month later, mirrored the *Times* article's conclusion that a large number of the camp's detainees were either innocent or low-level militants who had rushed to the defense of the Taliban in Afghanistan after the October 2001 U.S. invasion.[368] The CIA's report only confirmed what many foreign governments had been telling the United States about their own citizens in U.S. custody, and in August the subject of how to deal with the many obviously wrongfully imprisoned detainees began to dominate Secretary of State Colin Powell's morning briefings. As Powell's Chief of Staff Col. Lawrence B. Wilkerson testified in March 2010 in the habeas corpus proceeding of detainee Abel Hassan Hamad,

> [I]t became apparent to me as early as August 2002, and probably earlier to other State Department personnel who were focused on these issues, that many of the prisoners detained at Guantánamo had been taken into custody without regard to whether they were truly enemy combatants, or in fact whether many of them were enemies at all. I soon realized from my conversations with military colleagues as well as foreign service officers in the field that many of the detainees were, in fact, the victims of incompetent battlefield vetting....
>
> In fact, by late August 2002, I found that of the initial 742 detainees that had arrived at Guantánamo, the majority of them had never seen a U.S. soldier in the process of their initial detention and their captivity had not been subject to any meaningful review.... Secretary Powell was...trying to bring pressure to bear regarding a number of specific detentions because children as young as 12 or 13 and elderly as old as 92 or 93 had been shipped to Guantánamo. By that time, I also understood that the deliberate choice to send detainees to Guantánamo was an attempt to place them outside the jurisdiction of the U.S. legal system.[369]

Even within Guantánamo, protests were mounting. JTF 160 Commander Rick Baccus told journalists touring the camp in August that his own uniformed officers were questioning the continuing designation of detainees as "enemy combatants" rather than "prisoners of war" entitled to Geneva protections.[370]

Against this backdrop, the Pentagon was conducting a Guantánamo review of its own—not grappling with the question of how detainees might receive some due process, but rather how to wring more intelligence out of the camp. The Joint Chiefs appointed Colonel John P. Custer, the assistant Commandant of the U.S. Army Intelligence Center and School at Ft. Huachuca, Arizona to carry out the study. Custer's report, which he delivered on September 10, 2002, reinforced a growing desire at the Pentagon to replace JTF 160 and JTF 170 with a single task force whose primary mission was interrogations. He specifically recommended melding the approaches of the FBI's Behavioral Analysis Unit and the BSCTs to create conditions "conducive to extracting information by exploiting detainee's vulnerabilities." In his report, Custer called Guantánamo "America's Battle Lab." The term, and concept, stuck. Colonel Britt Mallow, the Commander of the Criminal Investigative Task Force, told the Senate Armed Services Committee,

> MG Dunlavey and later MG Miller referred to GTMO as a "Battle Lab" meaning that interrogators and other procedures there were to some degree experimental, and their lessons would benefit DoD in other places. While this was logical in terms of learning lessons, I personally objected to the implied philosophy that interrogators should experiment with untested methods, particularly those in which they were not trained.[371]

* * *

The day after Custer delivered his report, on the first anniversary of the terrorist attacks, CITF Commander Brittain Mallow met with DoD General Counsel Jim Haynes to discuss his concerns over what everyone in Guantánamo could now see was coming. After that meeting, Mallow began to take steps to separate the men and women under his command from the military's plans to use SERE techniques in interrogations, drafting a Memorandum for the Record to "Provide additional guidance to Criminal Investigative Task Force (CITF) agents regarding the use of various techniques and methods" in Guantánamo detainee interviews. Under the heading "Guidance," Mallow wrote,

> The President's 7 Feb 2002 POTU.S. memo states, "As a matter of policy, the United States Armed Forces shall continue to treat detainees humanely and, to the extent appropriate and consistent with military necessity, in a manner consistent with the principle of Geneva." Therefore, CITF will employ interview methods or techniques that are consistent with the Geneva protections and the President's memo. These methods are designed to ensure that all information from [Detained Persons] is taken voluntarily.[372]

Mallow then listed techniques and methods consistent with the President's memo and permissible for CITF agents: prolonged interviews of up to twelve hours, interrupting sleep to interview detainees early in the morning or late at night ("to catch the [detainee] when he is less guarded, not to wear [him] down into confessing"), and a variety of conventional police interrogation techniques. "Unacceptable methods" that were "not necessarily in compliance with the President's memo" and off-limits to CITF agents included threats and "discomfort," specifically temperature manipulation, stress positions, and sensory deprivation. Mallow's draft concluded, "CITF agents will use methods and techniques that comply with the President's memo, and specifically designed to ensure all information from [detainee] is provided voluntarily."

On September 16, 2002, six days after Custer submitted his report, Major Burney's three-man BSCT team and four Defense Intelligence Agency interrogators flew from Guantánamo to Fort Bragg for a four day training session with Joseph Witsch and Gary Percival, Bruce Jessen's replacement as senior SERE psychologist. The training mirrored one Witsch and Percival had offered CIA interrogators in June and followed the principles outlined in Jessen's April 2002 Exploitation Draft Plan.[373]

In addition to guidance on such SERE techniques as walling, exposing students to cold until they shiver, and the use of phobias such as fear of spiders, the curriculum included slides suggesting the use of punishments that "might be offensive for Arab and Islamic detainees" and listing among possible resistance "countermeasures" "invasion of personal space by a female." The presentations came with caveats, however: Burney later told both Army and Senate investigators that the instructors didn't think that the SERE techniques should be brought back to Guantánamo and "stressed time and time again that psychological investigations have proven that harsh interrogations do not work. At best it will get you information that a prisoner thinks you want to hear to make the interrogation stop, but that information is strongly likely to be false."[374]

That hesitation is reflected in post-training communications from SERE instructor Joseph Witsch. In his after-action report, Witsch cautioned his superiors at JPRA,

> I highly recommend we continue to remain in an advisory role and not get directly involved in the actual operations—GTMO in particular. We have no actual experience in real world prisoner handling. The concepts we are most familiar with relate to our past enemies and we have developed our Code of Conduct based on these experiences. Without actual experience with [Designated Unlawful Combatants] we are making the assumption that procedures we use to exploit our personnel will be effective against the current detainees.

Witsch followed this a week later with a memo to the Chief of JPRA's Operational Support Office:

> What do we bring to the table? We are Code of Conduct instructors with a vast amount of experience training highly intelligent, disciplined, and motivated DoD personnel to resist captivity... We base our role-play laboratories on what we know our former enemies have done to our personnel in captivity. It is based on illegal exploitation (under the rules listed in the 1949 Geneva Convention

Relative to the Treatment of Prisoners of War) of prisoners over the last 50 years....

We are out of our sphere when we begin to profess the proper ways to exploit these detainees. We are now attempting to educate lower level personnel in DoD and OGAs with concepts and principles that are somewhat foreign to them and while it all sounds good they are not in a position nor do they have the depth of knowledge in these matters to effect change and do it in reasonable safety.

The handling of [Designated Unlawful Combatants] is a screwed up mess and everyone is scrambling to unscrew the mess."[375]

But back in Guantánamo, a newly-created JTF "special projects" team was already preparing to tell Ali Soufan and the FBI to "step aside" so it could assume control of Qahtani's interrogation.[376] On September 23, 2002, an alarmed CITF agent wrote to CITF's Deputy Commander,

DoD Intelligence personnel contacted FBI [Supervisory Special Agent] in order to conduct an interview of a detainee assigned to the FBI. The DoD personnel indicated that they intend to employ the following interrogation techniques: drive the hooded detainee around the island to disorient him, disrobe him to his underwear, have an interrogator with an Egyptian accent (it is known among the detainees that Egyptians are aggressive interrogators and commonly use coercion, to include maiming)....

As a law enforcement agency, CITF is clearly prohibited from participating in these techniques and we also do not want to turn a deaf ear when we learn of these issues.[377]

Two days later, flush with Mitchell and Jessen's inflated claims of the success of the CIA's torture of Abu Zubaydah the month before in Thailand, the lawyers of the "War Council" flew from Washington to tour Guantánamo and the brigs in Charleston, South Carolina and Norfolk, Virginia. Jack Goldsmith, invited by Jim Haynes the night before to join the trip when "a spot opened up on the plane," condensed the Guantánamo visit to a single paragraph in his book *The Terror Presidency*:

The purpose of the trip was to review the facilities for Taliban and al Qaeda detainees in U.S. military custody. On the plane I was introduced to many important legal players in the administration, including David Addington, Patrick Philbin, John Rizzo (then the number-two lawyer in the CIA, and now its acting General Counsel), Alice Fisher (now head of the Criminal Division at the Department of Justice), and several Pentagon lawyers. A little over three hours later, we landed in tropical Cuba, took a twenty-minute ferry across Guantánamo Bay, and boarded a bus for a brief ride to Camp Delta, the new detention facility. After a briefing on the operation of the camp from military officials, we walked through a detention building that held two-dozen orange jumpsuit-clad prisoners in mesh cells, each of which contained a bed, a sink, a toilet, and a copy of the Koran. Some of the detainees ignored us. Some stared at us with an empty gaze. Some looked at us with an anger that I had never before experienced. We next witnessed an ongoing interrogation, toured the camp's medical facilities, and saw the spot where construction was about to begin on a building to house military commissions. And then we took the bus and ferry trip back to the plane and, three hours after we arrived, left the island.[378]

A SOUTHCOM JAG's trip report of the lawyers' visit recorded that "[v]isitors asked very few questions and made very few comments"; however, it noted, MG [Dunlavey] "did take Mr. Haynes and a few others aside for private conversations."[379] The Senate Armed Services Committee reported,

MG Dunlavey held private conversations with Mr. Haynes and a few others and briefed the entire group on a number of issues including "policy constraints" affecting interrogations at the JTF. For example, MG Dunlavey told the group that JTF-170 would "like to take Koran away from some detainees—hold it as incentive" but that the issue

*was undergoing a policy determination by SOUTHCOM. The trip
report noted that Mr. Haynes "opined that JTF-170 should have the
authority in place to make those calls, per [the President's] order,
adding that he "[t]hought JTF-170 would have more freedom to
command." MG Dunlavey told the Committee that he may have told
the group during their visit that JTF-170 was working on a request for
authority to use additional interrogation techniques."*[380]

✶ ✶ ✶

Two days later, on the morning of September 27, 2002, an FBI Behavioral
Analysis Unit agent working in Camp Delta received a call asking him to
return to the FBI's Guantánamo command post immediately. "FBIHQ
[redacted] etc. had issues regarding #63, surprise, surprise," he later told the
Justice Department's Inspector General. The call followed an email from
the agent to headquarters referring to the "fun and games" the military
had planned for Qahtani.[381] On September 30, the agent emailed again to
report the military's plan involved moving Qahtani from the brig to Camp
Delta briefly to see if he would cooperate and then sending him to Camp
X-Ray for an open-ended phase of twenty-hour interrogation sessions. The
agent asked his supervisor for guidance because military intelligence agents
wanted him to be part of one of the interrogation teams; he was told that
"as long as there was no torture involved" he could participate and "provide
FBIHQ with updates of what was happening."[382]

On October 1, 2002, the agent wrote again:

Here's the latest regarding our friend.

*The most recent Interrogation Plan has been signed off on by
the appropriate (all the way up to the 2 star) DoD individuals. As
it presently stands, tomorrow night (10/2/2002–Wednesday @ 2300
hours) # 063 will be picked up at the Brig (totally manacled, hooded,
and gagged) for transport to Delta. After the transport, the detainee
will be unhooded, allowed to look around to ensure that he is in
fact at Delta. He will then be taken to one of the CTC trailers where
he will be asked four (4) 'core' questions. If he is uncooperative, as*

everyone believes he will be, he will then be immediately transported to a holding cell at Camp X-Ray.

Once at X-Ray, the DHS will begin the interrogation process with 2 interrogators and one of their 'Behavioral Scientists' observing. After a 6 hour session, the DHS has another team to continue with the scenario. The lead team will then take the third 6 hour sessions (myself and [redacted] been specifically asked to observe this team from a strictly behavioral perspective). After this 18 hour period, the detainee will be allowed to rest for 4 hours before the process will begin again for a yet-to-be determined time frame.

[Redacted] and I made it very clear that we would be available for observation only for the initial time at Delta and then for the initial lead DHS team 6 hour session. After that, we will be "on call" should something positive happen. We had an hour meeting this afternoon with all DHS team personnel to get everyone up to speed on what was happening. The DHS group, including Lt. Col. [redacted] feels confident that this will do what needs to be done to obtain #063's cooperation.

SSA [redacted] has been fully briefed of this session.

[Redacted] It is our recommendation [redacted] and myself) that should FBIHQ want to send anyone down to question # 063 concerning FBI issues, that they wait at least a week after the aforementioned DHS mission has been completed.[383]

The next day, General Dunlavey sent a memo to Brigadier General Rick Baccus, commander of JTF-160, requesting support for an operation involving an interrogation plan that, he assured his counterpart, "has been reviewed by my Staff Judge Advocate and determined to be legally sufficient."[384] That same day, BSCT Major Burney submitted a memo he had drafted in response to a request from Lieutenant Colonel Jerald Phifer, Dunlavey's Director for Intelligence, requesting SOUTHCOM approval for new interrogation authorities. Burney told the Senate Armed Services Committee that "by early October there was increasing pressure to get 'tougher' with detainee interrogations but nobody was quite willing to define what 'tougher' meant"; the task evidently fell to Burney, who was coached to the extent he was told that if his memo didn't contain coercive techniques it "wasn't going to go very far." He reported that he drafted the memo in one evening, and that he had learned some of its interrogation approaches during the Fort Bragg training and made up some of them himself.[385]

The memo suggested three categories of interrogation techniques be used in the interrogation booth "to develop rapport, promote cooperation, and counter resistance." Category I included incentives and "mildly adverse approaches" such as telling detainees they would be in Guantánamo forever unless they cooperated. Category II, for "high priority" detainees "suspected of having significant information relative to the security of the United States," included stress positions, isolation of up to thirty days, deprivation of food, and back-to-back twenty-hour interrogation sessions once a week. In Category III, "detainees that have evidenced resistance and are suspected of having significant information pertinent to national security" could be isolated without the right of visitation by treating medical professionals or the Red Cross and subjected to daily twenty-hour interrogations, death threats, forced nudity, and exposure to cold weather or water until they began to shiver. Not entirely comfortable with his work, Burney added this statement:

> Experts in the field of interrogation indicate the most effective interrogation strategy is a rapport-building approach. Interrogation techniques that rely on physical or adverse consequences are likely to garner inaccurate information and create an increased level of resistance.... There is no evidence that the level of fear or discomfort evoked by a given technique has any consistent correlation to the volume or quality of information obtained.... The interrogation tools outlined could affect the short term and/or long term physical and/ or mental health of the detainee. Physical and/or emotional harm from the above techniques may emerge months or years after their use. It is impossible to determine if a particular strategy will cause irreversible harm if employed.... Individuals employing Category II and Category III interrogation techniques must be thoroughly

trained...[and] carefully selected, to include a mental health screening (such screenings are SOP for SERE and other Special Operations personnel).[386]

Lieutenant Colonel Diane Beaver, Dunlavey's Staff Judge Advocate, convened a meeting that afternoon to discuss Burney's memo. In addition to JTF-170 personnel including Burney, BSCT teammate Leso, Phifer, and David Becker, JTF-170's chief of intelligence, the meeting had an unusual guest: Jonathan Fredman, chief counsel to the CIA's Counterterrorism Center, who had flown from Washington to participate. The meeting opened with Burney and Leso reporting on the Fort Bragg training and echoing the memo's warning that fear-based approaches are "unreliable, ineffective in almost all cases." The meeting minutes show that Phifer challenged Burney, asking, "Harsh techniques used on our service members have worked and will work on some, what about those?" Leso and Becker countered that force is risky and likely to be ineffective since the detainees "are used to seeing much more barbaric treatment."[387] At this point, the minutes record, "a discussion about ISN 63 ensued, recalling how he has responded to certain types of deprivation and psychological stressors." Then:

BSCT continued:	*Psychological stressors are extremely effective (ie, sleep deprivation, withholding food, isolation, loss of time)*
COL Cummings	*We can't do sleep deprivation*
LTC Beaver	*Yes, we can – with approval*
BSCT	*Disrupting the normal camp operations is vital. We need to create an environment of "controlled chaos"*
LTC Beaver	*We may need to curb the harsher operations while ICRC is around. It is better not to expose them to any controversial techniques. We must have the support of the DoD.*
Becker	*We have had many reports from Bagram about sleep deprivation being used.*

LTC Beaver   *True, but officially it is not happening. It is not being reported officially. The ICRC is a serious concern. They will be in and out, scrutinizing our operations, unless they are displeased and decide to protest and leave. This would draw a lot of negative attention.*

COL Cummings   *The new PSYOP plan has been passed up the chain*

LTC Beaver   *It's at J3 at SOUTHCOM*

At this point, Fredman takes the floor:

Fredman   *The DoJ has provided much guidance on this issue. The CIA is not held to the same rules as the military. In the past when the ICRC has made a big deal about certain detainees, the DoD has "moved" them away from the attention of the ICRC. Upon questioning from the ICRC about their whereabouts, the DoD's response has repeatedly been that the detainee merited no status under the Geneva Convention.*

The CIA has employed aggressive techniques on less than a handful of suspects since 9/11.

Under the Torture Convention, torture has been prohibited by international law, but the language of the statutes is written vaguely. Severe mental and physical pain is prohibited. The mental part is explained as poorly as the physical. Severe physical pain described as anything causing permanent damage to major organs or body parts. Mental torture described as anything leading to permanent profound damage to the senses or personality. It is basically subject to perception. If the detainee dies you're doing it wrong. So far, the techniques we have addressed have not proved to produce these types of results, which in a way challenges what the BSCT paper says about not being able to prove whether

> *these techniques will lead to permanent damage.*
> *Everything on the BSCT white paper is legal from a*
> *civilian standpoint [Any questions of severe weather or*
> *temperature conditions should be deferred to medical*
> *staff]. Any of the techniques that lie on the harshest end*
> *of the spectrum must be performed by a highly trained*
> *individual. Medical personnel should be present to*
> *treat any possible accidents. The CIA operates without*
> *military intervention. When the CIA has wanted to use*
> *more aggressive techniques in the past, the FBI has pulled*
> *their personnel from theatre. In those rare instances,*
> *aggressive techniques have proven very helpful.*
>
> LTC Beaver   *We will need documentation to protect us*
> Fredman   *Yes, if someone dies while aggressive techniques are*
> *being used, regardless of cause of death, the backlash*
> *of attention would be detrimental. Everything must be*
> *approved and documented.*

When Becker steps in to note that the FBI and CITF have indicated they will not participate in harsh techniques, Beaver insists that there is no legal reason why they can't, and that their decision is "more ethical and moral as opposed to legal." Yet when the question of videotaping interrogations arises, the group quickly agrees that "videotapes are subject to too much scrutiny in court," and that "videotapes of even totally legal techniques will look ugly." Fredman resumes,

> Fredman   *The Torture Convention prohibits torture and cruel,*
> *inhumane and degrading treatment. The U.S. did*
> *not sign up to the second part, because of the 8th*
> *amendment (cruel and unusual punishment), but we*
> *did sign the part about torture. This gives us more*
> *license to use more controversial techniques.*
>
> LTC Beaver   *Does SERE employ the "wet towel" technique?*
> Fredman   *If a well-trained individual is used to perform*

> *this technique it can feel like you're drowning. The*
> *lymphatic system will react as if you're suffocating, but*
> *your body will not cease to function. It is very effective*
> *to identify phobias with them (ie, insects, snakes,*
> *claustrophobia). The level of resistance is directly*
> *related to person's experience*

MAJ Burney   *Whether or not significant stress occurs lies in the eyes*
             of the beholder. The burden of proof is the big issue. It
             is very difficult to disprove someone else's PTSD

Fredman   *These techniques need involvement from interrogators,*
             psych, medical, legal, etc.

Becker   *Would we get blanket approval or would it be case by*
             case?

Fredman   *The CIA makes the call internally on most of the*
             types of techniques found in the BSCT paper, and this
             discussion. Significantly harsh techniques are approved
             through DoJ.

LTC Phifer   *Who approves ours? The CG? COUTHCOM CG?*

Fredman   *Does the Geneva Convention apply? The CIA rallied*
             for it not to.

LTC Phifer   *Can we get DoJ opinion about these topics on paper?*

LTC Beaver   *Will it go from DoJ to DoD?*

LTC Phifer   *Can we get to see a CIA request to use advanced*
             aggressive techniques?

Fredman   *Yes, but we can't provide you with a copy. You will*
             probably be able to look at it.

The meeting concludes with a brainstorming session on ways to manipulate the lives of all Guantánamo detainees to create an environment of "controlled chaos." The list includes "let[ting] detainee rest long enough to fall asleep and wake him about every thirty minutes and tell him it's time to pray again," and "Truth serum; even though it may not actually work, it does have a placebo effect."[388]

These meeting minutes would find their way to CITF agent Blaine

Thomas, who forwarded them to CITF legal advisor Sam McCahon with the note, "Sam, very interesting reading on how detainees are being treated for info." Mark Fallon, who was copied on that note, forwarded it again to McCahon with a note of his own:

> Sam:
>
> We need to ensure seniors at OGC are aware of the [JTF]170 strategies and how it might impact CITF and Commissions. This looks like the kinds of stuff Congressional hearings are made of. Quotes from LLTC Beaver regarding things that are not being reported give the appearance of impropriety. Other comments like "It is basically subject to perception. If the detainee dies you're doing it wrong" and "Any of the techniques that lie on the harshest end of the spectrum must be performed by a highly trained individual. Medical personnel should be present to treat any possible accidents" seem to stretch beyond the bounds of legal propriety. Talk of "wet towel treatment" which results in the lymphatic gland reacting as if you are suffocating, would in my opinion, shock the conscience of any legal body looking at using the results of the interrogations or possibly even the interrogators. Someone needs to be considering how history will look back at this.[389]

Two days after the meeting with Feldman, Major Burney wrote to Lieutenant Colonel Louie "Morgan" Banks, the chief psychologist for JPRA, relaying JTF 170's continuing interest in "pursuing the potential use of more aversive techniques." Burney asked Banks "where task force personnel could go to receive such training" and whether he knew "any consultants who could assist if any of these measures are eventually approved." Banks answered emphatically:

> I do not envy you. I suspect I know where this is coming from. The answer is no, I do not know of anyone who could provide that training.... The training that SERE instructors receive is designed to simulate that of a foreign power, and to do so in a manner that encourages resistance among the students. I do not believe that

training interrogators to use what SERE instructors use would be particularly productive.[390]

* * *

Within hours of the meeting with the CIA attorney, Qahtani was taken according to plan from the Naval Brig to Camp Delta There, two FBI agents joined in an unproductive two-hour, four-question interview, after which Qahtani was sent, hooded and shackled in the back of an ambulance, to one of the abandoned interview shacks in Camp X-Ray. The two agents are referred to pseudonymously in the Justice Department Inspector General's description of what happened next:

> *Al-Qahtani was interrogated by another military interrogation team from October 3 until the early morning hours of October 4. Lyle said Al-Qahtani was "aggressively" interrogated and that the plan was to "keep him up until he broke." Foy said he did not know if that ultimately is what happened, because he and Lyle stopped observing the process. Foy stated in an e-mail to the FBI Unit Chief and the OSC at GTMO the next morning that an FBI approach to Al-Qahtani the following week would not be worthwhile "due to the current mental/ physical status of the detainee."*
>
> *Foy and Lyle returned to Camp X-Ray in the late afternoon of October to continue their observations. Lyle told the OIG that one of the interrogators, a Marine Captain, had been interrogating Al-Qahtani by yelling at him and calling him names. Lyle stated that the Captain got up on the table in the room to yell at Al-Qahtani in a more intimidating fashion, at which point he squatted over a Koran that had been provided to Al-Qahtani. This action incensed Al-Qahtani, who lunged toward the Captain and the Koran. Al-Qahtani was quickly subdued by the military guards in the room. Foy gave a similar account of this incident....*
>
> *Lyle and Foy also described an incident the next day in which a guard received a signal to bring a working dog into the interrogation room where Al-Qahtani was being interrogated. Lyle said that the use*

of dogs as an interrogation tool was exclusively the military's idea,
based on their belief that Arabs feared dogs because they viewed dogs
as unclean. Lyle said that the guard handling the dog first agitated the
dog outside the interrogation room, and then brought the dog into the
room close to Al-Qahtani. Lyle said that the dog barked, growled, and
snarled at Al-Qahtani in very close proximity to him, but was never
allowed to have contact with him. Foy gave a similar account of the
incident, and told the OIG that he and Lyle were not comfortable
with the situation with the dog so they left the interrogation.[391]

Five days later, Qahtani was returned to the brig, and one of these
agents reported to FBI headquarters,

Hello from GTMO,

*As of 10/08/2002 (Tuesday) @ 1800 hours, DHS will **discontinue***
their current efforts regarding # 063. Besides the sleep deprivation,
they utilized loud music, bright lights, and "body placement
discomfort," all with negative results. They asked [redacted] and I to
participate in an 'after action' on this phase which we will probably
do. At present, the plan is for DHS to initiate their Phase II on # 063
sometime this weekend.

The detainee is down to around 100 pounds but is still as fervent
as ever. That's it for now, more to follow after the aforementioned
meeting.[392]

According to the Armed Services Committee, another FBI agent wrote
headquarters that same day "reflect[ing] upon the failed interrogation." "I
think we should consider leaving him alone, let him get healthy again, and
do something 'different'"[393]

Three days later, Major General Dunlavey sent a memorandum to
General Hill, Commander of SOUTHCOM, requesting formal approval
to use nineteen SERE-based techniques in Guantánamo interrogations.
The techniques, laid out in three categories in an accompanying memo
prepared by Lieutenant Colonel Phifer, were the same ones suggested in

the October 2, 2002 Burney memo, with two additions from that day's brainstorming session with the CIA attorney: the use of phobias and "the use of a wet towel and dripping water to induce the misperception of suffocation." Phifer would later tell the Senate Armed Services Committee that he was uncomfortable with the idea of using some of the techniques, but that he had been under pressure from Dunlavey to produce the memo; Dave Becker, JTF 170's intelligence chief, told the Senators simply that he thought the memo was "stupid." Dunlavey's request conveyed no such ambivalence, however. "I believe the methods and techniques delineated in the accompanying J-2 memorandum will enhance our efforts to extract additional information," he wrote, adding "I have concluded that these techniques do not violate U.S. or international laws."[394]

Dunlavey attached the document on which he said he was basing that conclusion, a legal brief prepared by his Staff Judge Advocate, Lieutenant Colonel Diane Beaver. Although there is no evidence that Beaver had seen the secret August 1, 2002 Yoo memos, Fredman had semaphored the essentials of Yoo's arguments at the October 2 meeting, including his conclusion that "severe physical pain" was on the order of organ failure or death; he had also signaled that the CIA had received official approval for techniques up to and including waterboarding. The gist of the White House's position was clear, and Beaver, thus instructed, wrote her seven-page memo the following weekend.

The memo begins by reviewing international, domestic, and military laws that constrain interrogations. Although Beaver finds that the European Court of Human Rights held that Britain's use of hooding, forced standing, white noise, and food and sleep deprivation on IRA prisoners in the 1970s violated the Convention against Torture's prohibition on cruel, inhuman, and degrading treatment, she waves off international law entirely in light of the determination that Guantánamo detainees are not protected by the Geneva Conventions. Under U.S. law, she acknowledges, interrogators are bound by the Torture Statute's incorporated Eighth Amendment prohibition on "cruel and unusual punishment," but that

so long as the force used could plausibly have been thought necessary in a particular situation to achieve a legitimate governmental objective, and it was applied in a good faith effort and not maliciously or sadistically for the very purpose of causing harm, the proposed techniques are likely to pass constitutional muster. The federal torture statute will not be violated so long as any of the proposed strategies are not specifically intended to cause severe physical pain or suffering or prolonged mental harm. Assuming that severe physical pain is not inflicted, absent any evidence that any of these strategies will in fact cause prolonged and long lasting mental harm, the proposed methods will not violate the statute.[395]

She then proceeds through the three categories of proposed techniques: "The use of mild and fear related approaches such as yelling at the detainee is not illegal because in order to communicate a threat, there must also exist an intent to injure." Category II techniques including stress positions, forced standing, prolonged isolation, and twenty-hour interrogations "are all legally permissible so long as no severe physical pain is inflicted and prolonged mental harm intended, and because there is a legitimate governmental objective in obtaining the information necessary that the high value detainees on which these methods would be utilized possess, for the protection of the national security of the United States, its citizens, and allies." Finally,

With respect to the Category III advanced counter-resistance strategies, the use of scenarios designed to convince the detainee that death or severely painful consequences are imminent is not illegal for the same aforementioned reasons that there is a compelling governmental interest and it is not done intentionally to cause harm. However, caution should be utilized with this technique because the torture statute specifically mentions making death threats as an example of inflicting mental pain and suffering. Exposure to cold weather or water is permissible with appropriate medical monitoring. The use of a wet towel to induce the misperception of suffocation would also be permissible if not done with the specific intent to cause prolonged mental harm, and absent medical evidence that it would. Caution should be exercised with this method, as foreign courts have already advised about the potential mental harm that this method may cause. The use of physical contact with the detainee, such as pushing and poking will technically constitute an assault under Article 128, UCMJ.[396]

Having reached the conclusion that some of the techniques are per se violations of the Uniform Code of Military Justice, Beaver suggests "It would be advisable to have permission or immunity in advance from the convening authority for military members to utilize these methods."[397]

If Phifer and Becker had misgivings about the list of techniques they were proposing, Beaver had grave doubts about her legal analysis. She had asked for help from lawyers at SOUTHCOM and the Pentagon in drafting the memo, and when that wasn't forthcoming, she assumed that her brief would be "carefully reviewed by legal and policy experts at the highest levels before a decision was reached." In a 2008 hearing before the Senate Armed Services Committee, Beaver said she was "shocked" to learn later that her memo "would become the final word on interrogation policies and practices within the Department of Defense," something that, for her, "was simply not foreseeable." As the Committee reported, "She stated she did not expect to be the only lawyer issuing an opinion on this monumentally important issue" and that "in hindsight, [she] could not 'help but conclude that the others chose not to write on this issued to avoid being linked to it.'"[398]

In fact, when SOUTHCOM Commander James Hill relayed Dunlavey's request for approval of the nineteen techniques to the Joint Chiefs two weeks later, he expressed uneasiness with Beaver's conclusion and specifically requested additional legal review.

I am uncertain whether all the techniques in the third category are legal under U.S. law, given the absence of judicial interpretation of the U.S. torture statute. I am particularly troubled by the use of implied or expressed threats of death of the detainee or his family. However, I desire to have as many options as possible at my disposal and therefore request the Department of Defense and Department of Justice lawyers review the third category of techniques.[399]

One of Hill's SOUTHCOM lawyers, Assistant Staff Advocate Mark Gingras, later told the Army's Inspector General that Hill's team had doubts about both the Category II and Category III techniques, but that it was clear that in conveying their reservations to Washington they were bucking a headwind:

> *As lawyers we're talking about adherence to the rule of law being important, and that's what we're trying to tell everybody as we travel around the world to these other countries. That's paramount to democracy. And so suddenly we look like we're brushing this aside or we're twisting the law. The feeling was that the decision makers within the Pentagon didn't much care about that. They cared about winning the War on Terrorism. And if that meant you had to pull out fingernails you'd pull out fingernails, figuratively speaking.*[400]

When Dunlavey's request reached the Pentagon, Captain Jane Dalton, the Joint Chief's legal counsel, also found Beaver's legal analysis "woefully inadequate." Dalton forwarded the request and attachments to each of the branches of the armed services for comment, and received a chorus of protests in return. The Air Force came back with a memo expressing "serious concerns regarding the legality of many of the proposed techniques" and suggesting that "some of these techniques could be construed as 'torture' as that crime is defined by 18 U.S.C. 2340." The Navy called for "a more detailed interagency legal and policy review." The Marine Corps concluded that "several of the Category II and III techniques arguably violate federal law, and would expose our service members to possible prosecution" under U.S. law and the UCMJ. The Army submitted two memoranda, one from its Office of the Judge Advocate General and one from its Criminal Investigative Task Force.

The Judge Advocate General's office warned that death threats and waterboarding "appear to be clear violations of the federal torture

statute" and that techniques such as stress positions, deprivation of light
and auditory stimuli, the use of individual phobias, removal of clothing,
and forced grooming "crosses the line of 'humane' treatment" and could
well violate the UCMJ and the Federal anti-torture statute. The CITF's
memo concurred that "[Category] III and [Category] II techniques may
subject service members to punitive articles of the UCMJ" and warned
that military personnel who witness or become aware of the use of such
techniques could be exposed to criminal liability for failing to intercede or
report the abuses. The CITF's legal advisor concluded, "I cannot advocate
any action, interrogation or otherwise, that is predicated on the principle
that all is well if the ends justify the means and others are not aware of how
we conduct our business."[401]

Captain Jane Dalton briefed Joint Chiefs Chairman General Richard
Myers on the services' reactions and set up a teleconference with the
Defense Intelligence Agency, the Army's Ft. Huachuca Intelligence School,
SOUTHCOM, and Guantánamo to learn more about the proposed
techniques and prepare for an independent legal review. She also drafted a
memo for Myers to send to SOUTHCOM stating, "We do not believe the
proposed plan is legally sufficient" and warning that "several of the Category
III techniques arguably violate federal law, and could expose interrogators
to possible prosecution."[402] The Myers memo was to recommend "in-depth
technical, policy, and legal assessment" of the techniques before they were
approved. But as the Senate Armed Services Committee reported,

*According to CAPT Dalton, after she and her staff initiated their
analysis, CJCS GEN Myers directed her to stop that review. CAPT
Dalton said that GEN Myers returned from a meeting and "advised
me that [DoD General Counsel] Mr. Haynes wanted me...to cancel
the video teleconference and to stop" conducting the review because
of concerns that "people were going to see" the GTMO request and
the military services' analysis of it. According to CAPT Dalton, Mr.
Haynes "wanted to keep it much more close hold." When CAPT Dalton
"learned that [the DoD General Counsel] did not want that broad
based legal and policy review to take place," she and her staff stopped*

the review. This was the only time that CAPT Dalton had ever been asked to stop analyzing a request that came to her for her review.[403]

* * *

It was now early November. Over the past month, following their one-week interrogation of Qahtani in Camp X-Ray, military interrogators had been expanding their use of aggressive techniques in other interrogations as well, regardless of the lack of official approval for anything beyond the Field Manual's proven methods. On October 15, 2002, two FBI agents were questioning a detainee in Camp Delta when a "giggling" military interrogator entered the interrogation room and told them "You guys have to come see this." They were shown to a nearby room where a detainee sat handcuffed to the I-bolt in the floor, his head wrapped in duct tape. Two guards and two military interrogators were in the room, one of whom was screaming at the detainee. "Was he spitting on someone?" one of the FBI agents asked. "No, he just wouldn't stop chanting the Koran," their guide answered.[404] FBI agents were reporting other incidents as well—of sleep deprivation, of a female interrogator exposing her breasts to a detainee, of an interrogator smearing a detainee with vegetable oil while telling him it was "pig's oil."[405] "Stupid, demeaning, and ineffective" is how David Nahmias, Assistant Attorney General for the Criminal Division, later characterized such improvisations.[406]

Nahmias and the head of the FBI's Military Liaison and Detainee Unit traveled to Guantánamo on October 15, 2002. During their three-day visit, the military boasted to Nahmias that it had "broken" Qahtani, and that deep into a marathon interrogation he had blurted Mohammed's Atta's name. Agents from the FBI's Behavioral Analysis Unit dismissed the claim, insisting that Qahtani "was just giving the interrogators what they wanted so they would let him eat or go to the bathroom." Nahmias and the MLDU Unit Chief challenged the military on its claim directly during a videoconference with Major General Geoffrey Miller, the incoming Commander of the combined JTF-GTMO, Lieutenant Colonel Phifer, the chief CITF psychologist, Pentagon officials, and a representative of the CIA. During that teleconference, Phifer presented the military's plan for an even more aggressive interrogation of Qahtani, trumpeting the information

military intelligence had extracted in its recent sessions. According to the
Justice Department's Inspector General,

> *At that point the FBI Unit Chief said he spoke up and said "look,
> everything you've gotten thus far is what the FBI gave you on Al-
> Qahtani from its paper investigation." The Unit Chief said the
> conversation became heated. According to the Unit Chief, the Chief
> CITF Psychologist and Nahmias agreed that the information the
> Lieutenant Colonel presented had been provided by the FBI and that
> the Lieutenant Colonel's suggested interrogation methods were not
> effective and were not providing positive intelligence. The Unit Chief
> said that the meeting ended because of the controversy.*[407]

Nahmias and the Unit Chief left Guantánao on October 18, convinced
that the military's interrogation plan wouldn't work and that the military
was "completely ineffective in getting any kind of intelligence" out of
Qahtani.[408] Back in Washington, Nahmias shared his concerns with Michael
Chertoff, then Assistant Attorney General for the Criminal Division, and
the two of them brought the issue to Attorney General John Ashcroft and
Deputy AG Larry Thompson. Ashcroft and Chertoff reportedly supported
the FBI's position, raising questions about the effectiveness of the military's
interrogation of Qahtani and suggesting that the DoD's descriptions of the
information Qahtani had provided was often inaccurate, either because
he was lying or because the military was misrepresenting what he said.[409]
By early November, the dispute over Qahtani's treatment was the subject
of "ongoing, long-standing trench warfare in the interagency discussions"
between the FBI and the military, including at the Principals Committee,"
Ashcroft's Chief of Staff later told the Justice Department's Inspector
General. According to Nahmias, Chertoff and Ashcroft "were continually
frustrated by their inability to get any changes or make progress with
regard to the Al-Qahtani matter."[410]

In early November, General Geoffrey Miller assumed command of
Joint Task Force GTMO, which replaced the divided JTF 160 and JTF 170
command structure at Guantánamo. Miller arrived with a clear sense of his

mission: Baccus had been relieved of the command of JTF 160 in October, four days after the *Washington Times* reported on the growing rift between Baccus and Dunlavey over the treatment of prisoners; the *Times* article pointed in particular to a decision by Baccus to allow the Red Cross to hang posters informing inmates they were required to provide only name, rank, and serial numbers to interrogators. Pentagon sources quoted in the article berated Baccus, who allegedly had begun greeting detainees with "Peace be with you," as "too nice," and insinuated he had been interfering with Dunlavey's intelligence gathering operations. As a combined unit whose primary emphasis was the production of intelligence, JTF-GTMO was meant to eliminate such tensions and reorganize camp life to better serve that purpose.[411]

On November 12, 2002, having received none of the extra legal guidance he requested and over the expressed reservations of all four services, the FBI, the CITF, and those two agency's most seasoned interrogators, SOUTHCOM Commander General Hill gave Miller verbal approval for the use of the Category I and Category II techniques on Qahtani—a list that included stress positions, isolation of up to thirty days, sensory deprivation, hooding, nudity, forced grooming, and the use of individuals phobias and twenty-hour interrogations. That same day, Lieutenant Colonel Phifer sent an email to General Miller with a four-page attachment stating, "[h]ere is the Interrogation Plan for ISN:063 as approved by you. Request you fwd to Gen. Hill, info J2/J3/COS. We will begin at 0001 15 Nov per your guidance."[412]

The attached "Special Interrogation Plan" described a four-phase operation whose purpose was to "break the detainee and establish his role in the attacks of September 11, 2001." "Prior to the Interrogation, we would like to have the detainee's head and beard shaved," the plan began. "This is to be done for both psychological and hygiene purposes." Qahtani would be interrogated in twenty-hour sessions and allowed four hours rest in an indefinitely repeating cycle. "During the interrogation the detainee will at all times be placed in stress positions and blindfolded. If necessary the detainee may have his mouth taped shut in order to keep him from talking. Written approval for the tape and for the presence of dogs will be submitted and obtained prior to implementation." The tape had a particular purpose: in Phase I of the plan, interrogators would harangue and berate Qahtani for days and not allow him to speak, with the idea that, when finally given the opportunity, he would "provide his whole story."

In Phase II, a military translator posing as a detainee would be placed in a Camp X-Ray cell near Qahtani's in a ruse to get him to reveal the secrets he was withholding between interrogation sessions. If this didn't work,

> *The third phase of the plan to exploit 063 requires OSD approval for the SERE interrogation technique training and approval of the level three counter interrogation resistance training submitted by JTF-GTMO. Once the approvals are in place, those interrogation techniques will be implemented to encourage 063 to cooperate.*

Finally, if this phase employing the Category II and III techniques failed, the military would move to Phase IV, titled "Coalition Exploitation":

> *The fourth phase of the plan to exploit 063 required that he be sent off-island either temporarily or permanently to either Jordan or Egypt, or another country to allow those countries to employ interrogation techniques that will enable them to obtain the requisite information.*[413]

On November 14, 2002, anticipating the furious objections that were to follow, Lieutenant Colonel Beaver sent an email to Major Sam McCahon, the CITF's legal advisor, saying, "[c]oncerning 63, my understanding is that NSC has weighed in and stated that intel on this guy is utmost matter of national security…We are driving forward with support from SOUTHCOM. Not sure anything else needs to be said."[414] But both CITF and the FBI were determined to derail the plan. That same day, CITF Commander Colonel Britt Mallow emailed General Miller directly:

> *I strongly disagree with the use of many of the proposed [Category] 3 and some [Category] 2 techniques. I feel they will be largely ineffective, and that will have serious negative material and legal*

effects on our investigations. I also am extremely concerned that the use of many of these techniques will open our military members up for potential criminal charges, and that my agents, as well as other [military personnel] will face both legal and ethical problems if they become aware of their use."[415]

The next day, unaware that Captain Dalton's legal review had been aborted, McCahan submitted a legal memo to Miller stating that CITF had raised "formal legal objections" to the interrogation and that SOUTHCOM was in no position to approve a plan that was "currently under legal review" at the Pentagon General Counsel's office. McCahon reiterated that "the reliability of any information gained from aggressive techniques will be highly questionable." He specifically objected to all of the SERE-based "physical stresses" in Phase III of the plan, and decried Phase IV's implication "that third country nationals with harsher interrogation standards could be used to convey threats to persons of family or inflict harm contrary to the Convention against Torture."[416]

FBI agents who saw the interrogation plan likewise judged it "deeply flawed." Two BAU agents who had recently arrived in Guantánamo reported to headquarters that at least one of the "techniques," preventing Qahtani from speaking in anticipation he would later tell all, had an especially dubious provenance: "It is our information," the agents wrote, "that this interrogation technique was recommended by…an Army linguist, who claims to have a number of years of 'Agency' experience. Other than the word of this agent, there has been no data proffered which justifies the use of this technique." Objecting in particular to the proposed Phase IV rendition to Egypt or Jordan, the two concluded, "[u]nless this plan is modified to exclude aspects that have not been approved for FBI personnel, we cannot be a signatory."[417] A few days later, these two agents carried these concerns into an "interrogation strategy session" with defense intelligence officers. Disturbed by the "utter lack of sophistication" and "circus-like atmosphere" of the meeting, the agents later described to the Justice Department's Inspector General the "'glee' with which the would-be participants discussed their respective roles in carrying out the techniques."[418]

As protests grew, Miller postponed the plan's start date by a week and told his interrogators and the FBI and CITF to find some "common ground." In preparation for a meeting on November 20, the FBI and CITF drew up an alternative interrogation plan that would rely on long-term rapport building. According to the Inspector General, their joint plan pointed out that Qahtani's negative interrogation "only reinforces Al-Qaeda stereotypes about evil Americans and validates their expectation of harsh treatment and potential torture." The FBI pressed its approach at a meeting with General Miller himself, stressing the effectiveness of rapport-building methods with even the most hardened criminals and pointing out that, in the case of suspected Al Qaeda militants, inflicting suffering on someone who believes his suffering will be rewarded by God is almost certainly counterproductive. Miller acknowledged "positive aspects of rapport building" at the meeting, but clearly backed the military plan, which he described as "relentless" and "a sustained attack."

When the agencies sat down together on the evening of November 20, it was immediately clear to the FBI "that the military could not agree to a plan that did not include the application of SERE techniques and a phase which involved sending Al-Qahtani to a third country where he could be tortured to get information."[419] But by the end of the meeting the FBI had floated, and believed it had won military support for, a third, "hybrid" interrogation plan that would give the FBI one more week with Qahtani in the hope it might gather enough information to scuttle the rest of the military's plan. The following morning, anticipating a videoconference with Washington later that day that would decide Qahtani's fate, the BAU agents wrote to FBI headquarters,

> As promised, attached is a "hybrid" plan for #63 that incorporates a phase where our desired techniques are employed. DoD here on the ground agreed to this plan and will discuss it during the 1600 meeting today. I believe that is the same meeting you are attending. We are also sending the plan to the BAU for their review. We remain ambivalent about this hybrid approach even though they bought off on a rapport building phase one. One of the downsides is that it is

not a plan that allows for a long term rapport building technique. Success or failure will be determined in 5-7 days before moving on to the next phase. Also attached is a narrative written by [redacted] which advocates a long term approach—also being sent to BAU. A concern with embracing the hybrid approach is that there will be many variables that we will have no control over. As I understand it, we are not to participate with DoD in the actual interrogation. I think this is wise. However, in order to further diplomacy we met with DoD at its request, to determine if there was any middle ground between their approach and our proposed approach. The hybrid approach was that middle ground. But we still have misgivings:

1. *The DHS plan seems better suited for the battlefield and not for long-term detainees*

2. *Although very enthusiastic, DHS interrogators appear to have limited experience in any kind of interview approach which emphasized patience or being friendly over a long period of time. They appear to be highly susceptible to pressure to get quick results, and this pressure will be reflected in they improvise plans as they go along.*

3. *The reliability of the interview techniques is questionable. Worse, there appears to be no one on the DHS side who seems to be concerned about this. They are quick to dismiss any approach that extends beyond their experience or imagination.*

4. *Their embracement of a fear-based approach is consistent with the military environment in which they operate, but may not be conducive to the long term goal of obtaining reliable intelligence.*

I know that you may have news for us following your 1600 meet. Please review the documents attached and advise as to whether we should participate further in any way or gracefully back out on this one. If you want us to back out, I request that HQ provide a written communication directing us not to get involved. Otherwise, our continued dealings with the other agencies are cramped.

[From [redacted]>> Although I agree with the above, I think DHS will likely revert back to their original plan, which basically

*begins with Phase II of this hybrid plan, if we don't give our blessing
to the hybrid plan. While the hybrid is not the best plan, I do
believe it is the lesser of two evils. I also believe that this hybrid plan
does simulate some of the important factors found in Stockholm
Syndrome cases. Specifically, extended hours awake under increased
stress continuing over a number of days, extended periods of time
where rapport may be developed and the interviewer can become
humanized in the detainee's eyes, opportunity for the detainee to be
convinced that they are going through this ordeal together, all work
together to possibly accelerate the bonding process. For these reasons
I think this hybrid has more opportunity for success than the DHS
original plan.*[420]

During the November 21, 2002 videoconference, which connected
Miller, Phifer, and CITF and FBI personnel in Guantánamo with
SOUTHCOM in Florida and Jim Haynes's office in Washington, the
military made no mention of either the new joint FBI/CITF plan or the
FBI's propose hybrid. Instead, Phifer—identified by the Inspector General
as "the same Lieutenant Colonel who had falsely claimed in the October
2002 teleconference that the DoD had obtained information from Al-
Qahtani using aggressive methods"—now claimed the FBI had helped
develop, and supported, the military's interrogation plan. As one of the
FBI's BAU agents later reported, during the "awkward teleconference,"
Phifer "blatantly misled the Pentagon into believing that the BAU endorsed
[military intelligence's] aggressive and controversial Interrogation Plan."[421]

The military's final version of the plan included a new Phase I that
mirrored the FBI's proposal to use non-aggressive methods, but under
the control of military interrogators, not FBI agents. Phase II, like the first
plan's Phase I, would commence with forced shaving and include the shut-
up-and-talk routine, for which, the plan specifically noted, General Miller
had now approved "the use of hospital gauze to restrain the detainee's
mouth to prevent him from becoming argumentative and verbally abusive."
Phase III was now the ruse of the linguist posing as a detainee, and Phase
IV the use of SERE techniques, minus stress positions and dogs, which

Miller later insisted were removed from the plan on his instructions. "The intent of raising the stakes to this level is to convince 063 that it is futile to resist," the plan said. "Success of [this phase] is when his sense of futility is raised to a high enough level that source gives in and provides the necessary information." The phase ends "with success or a standstill, after the exhaustion of all tools JTF-GTMO has to offer.⁴²²

Finally, though Phase V retained the original Phase IV title "Coalition Exploitation," it hedged the question of what might await Qahtani in the event Phase IV ended in a "standstill." While still hinting at the possibility of rendition to a third country, it stated, "The fifth phase of the plan to exploit 063 will be determined at the national interagency level where the future disposition of 063 will be determined.⁴²³

The FBI made no move during the videoconference to object to Phifer's claim that the agency backed the military's plan. But the FBI's on-site supervisor and two agents met with Miller afterwards to press their case. Miller reportedly "thanked them for their views, but told them JTF-GTMO staff knew what they were doing.⁴²⁴ Later that day, the supervisor wrote a memorandum to Miller summarizing for the record the events of the previous week:

From: FBI Guantánamo Bay
Subject: VTC 21 November 2002
To: Major General Miller

The purpose of this correspondence is to bring to the Commanding General's attention concerns that FBI has regarding representations that were made about the FBI's position on the proposed operational approach to [redacted] at the 21 November VTC.

At the direction of the Commanding General and in an effort to find some methodological common ground with respect to an Interrogation Plan for detainee [redacted] the FBI On-site Supervisor and Supervisors from the FBI Behavioral Analysis Unit met with JTF GTMO staff members on the evening of 20 November. During this meeting, DHS presented its draft Interrogation Plan. The FBI voiced misgivings about the overall coercive nature and possible illegality of elements of this plan. The FBI also voiced its strong objections regarding the efficacy of a fear-based approach.

The FBI offered in writing an alternative interrogation approach based on long term rapport-building. This approach was previously discussed extensively between FBI Behavioral experts and DHS and JTF staff members. At the 20 November meeting, DHS and JTF staff members recognized advantages of the FBI's approach, and decided to revise their plan by incorporating some of the FBI's rapport-building aspects. Despite the close working environment of this consultation, JIG and DHS staff never advised FBI personnel that the revised plan would be presented the following day to the Pentagon Office of General Counsel. In fact, the FBI representatives stated clearly to the JIG and DHS representative that the techniques proposed in the plan must be reviewed and formally approved by FBIHQ and BAU officials prior to any implementation.

Had the JIG advised the FBI of his intentions to present the revised DHS plan to DoD at the 21 November VTC as an FBI/ DHS plan, FBI representatives would have strenuously objected. Additionally, although all agencies were aware that the NCIS Chief Psychologist, Dr. [redacted] was scheduled to arrive on 21 November for the purpose of evaluating the DHS and FBI plans, the JIG did not solicit Dr. [redacted] professional opinion.[425]

That Naval Criminal Investigative Service Chief Psychologist was Michael Gelles, who submitted his review of the military's plan—a plan he concluded "lacks substantive and thoughtful consideration"—the following day. Gelles, too, cautioned that "the choice to use force with this adversary in an interrogation may only reinforce his resistance," and added, by way of a warning, that if the plan went forward, "I would have trouble not finding myself from a professional perspective, being forced into an adversary position through cross examination in a military tribunal as an expert on interrogation."[426]

Ignoring him as well, Miller approved the military's plan that same day,

November 22, 2002, and by 2:25 a.m. the following morning Qahtani was back bolted to the floor of an interrogation booth in Camp X-Ray.

* * *

Against the FBI's advice that he be allowed to "get well" after his one-week interrogation in Camp X-Ray at the beginning of October, Qahtani had spent the intervening weeks in complete isolation in the Navy Brig, subjected to bright lights, noise, and sleep deprivation. One hundred and fifty-seven pounds on July 2, 2002, he weighed 108 pounds on November 15, a week before the "Special Interrogation" began.[427] He arrived in the booth depleted and frail—and according to the BSCT psychiatrist who participated in the seven-week interrogation, deliberately disoriented. When he was transferred, Qahtani was "made [to] believe he was sent to a hostile country which advocated torture," and "led to believe he himself might be killed if he did not cooperate with questioning," the BSCT told the Senate Armed Services Committee.[428]

Two days after the "Special Interrogation" began, CITF legal advisor Sam McCahon emailed Diane Beaver, formally declaring that "CITF is not on board with aggressive techniques including twenty hour [plus] interrogations. Therefore, according to our policy, we will 'stand clear' and not offer participation, advisements, support, or recommendations as to its implementation."[429] The FBI was following a similar course, telling its agents to "stand well clear of it" and formally registering protests up the chain of command.

On December 2, 2002, an FBI agent and attorney submitted his legal review of the military's Category I through III techniques concluding "All the Category III techniques and many of those in Category II, including hooding, nudity, stress positions, 20 hour interrogations, and the use of individual phobias such as fear of dogs to reduce stress, were coercive interrogation techniques which are not permitted under the U.S. Constitution's Eighth Amendment prohibition on cruel and unusual punishment"; moreover, many of those techniques are also "examples of coercive interrogation techniques which may violate 18 U.S.C. §2340, the 'Torture Statute.'" Therefore, the analysis concluded, "It is possible that those who employ these techniques may be prosecuted, and possibly convicted if the trier of fact determines that the user had the requisite intent."[430]

That same day, Defense Secretary Donald Rumsfeld signed a memo approving the use of all of the Category I and Category II interrogation techniques proposed in Dunlavey's October 11 memo and one, the use of "mild, non-injurious physical contact," from Category III. Rumsfeld's General Counsel Jim Haynes had submitted the recommendation on November 27, 2002, under pressure from Rumsfeld, who had been expressing "exasperation that he didn't have a recommendation." Rumsfeld could have simply signed his name indicating his approval, but a handwritten note on the bottom of the memo seemed to underscore, as his deputies had for months in their weekly calls with Dunlavey and Miller, which side of the line he wanted military interrogators to lean. "However, I stand for 8-10 hours a day. Why is standing limited to 4 hours?" Rumsfeld asked rhetorically.[431]

In "the Battle Lab," the message came through loud and clear. Timothy James, the CITF's Special Agent in Charge in Guantánamo, told the Senate Armed Services Committee he was "in shock" when he saw Rumsfeld's authorization; it "told us we had lost the battle," he said. At 8:00 p.m. the following night, Qahtani's interrogation log notes, "Phase 1B" began. Qahtani was told he was being returned to Cuba, bundled hooded in the back of an ambulance and driven to another interrogation booth, where he was bombarded with music and forcibly shaved. Four days later he was in the hospital recovering from a dangerously slow heart beat and low core temperature and hypothermia. Two days after that, he was back in the booth, and the assault resumed.

By then, military interrogators were preparing a document titled "JTF-GTMO 'SERE' Interrogation Standard Operating Procedure," which began,

This SOP document promulgates procedures to be followed by JTF-GTMO personnel engaged in interrogation operations on detained persons. The premise behind this is that the interrogation tactics used at U.S. military SERE schools are appropriate for use in real-world interrogations. These tactics and techniques are used at SERE school

*to 'break' detainees. The same tactics and techniques can by used to
break real detainees during interrogation operations.*

"Note that all tactics are strictly intended to be non-lethal," the authors
felt compelled to add.[432]

The draft "Standard Operating Procedure" developed protocols for
using the Rumsfeld-approved SERE techniques camp-wide: it laid out
how the insult slap" and "stomach slap" are administered "to shock and
intimidate the detainee"; explained that "stripping" meant "forceful removal
of detainee's clothing"; and described kneeling, standing, and "Worship the
Gods" stress positions. A December 18 version of the SOP instructed that a
"corpsman or medic should be onsite, and a doctor on-call should medical
care be necessary," and that JTF-GTMO's military and civilian interrogators
"will undergo training by certified SERE instructors prior to being approved
for use of any of the techniques described in this document."

While the SOP was being drafted, Rumsfeld issued a letter directing the
JPRA to send two SERE trainers to Guantánamo to instruct JTF-GTMO's
Intelligence Control Element on the "theory and application of the physical
pressures" used in the Navy's SERE school. A similar SERE workshop the
month before for CIA agents posted to the black sites had been a "fiasco,"
according to the SERE psychologist who organized the sessions; there, CIA
interrogators had taken the lead in demonstrations, waterboarding one
another and showcasing a technique to "enhance" the "pain threshold"—a
technique the trainers themselves later said they believed would be "totally
inappropriate to do to anybody, whether it's an American or a foreign
detainee" for fear it might cause "permanent physical damage."[433]

SERE trainers John Rankin and Christopher Ross arrived in
Guantánamo on December 30, 2002. In their sessions with JTF-GTMO,
Rankin and Ross concentrated not on the more extreme physical abuses
featured in the CIA sessions, but on the "theory" of the Rumsfeld-approved
Category II and Category III-level pressures. "On the morning of 31 Dec
02, Mr. Ross and I initiated training with an in-depth class on Biderman's
Principles…to approximately 24 ICE personnel," Rankin recounted in his
after action report; he attached the hand-out he had given the ICE with

"Biderman's Chart of Coersion." Rankin and Ross followed this with a class "covering interrogation fundamentals and resistance to interrogation," a session Rankin said was "specifically requested since it was evident that some of the higher priority detainees had received some kind of resistance training, as evidenced by the Al Qaeda training manual." Before leaving the island, the two met with General Miller and discussed a "high level" directive that "outlined specific guidance regarding current and proposed ICE operation in dealing with detainees." Rankin added a handwritten note at the end of his report: "Maybe a good idea to plan/coordinate a return trip to see how things are progressing," he suggested.[434]

But by the time Rankin and Ross left Guantánamo on January 4, 2003, just over a month after Rumsfeld had signed the interrogation techniques memo, a rebellion was gaining force that would bring the Qahtani interrogation—now in its sixth week—to an end and interrupt talk of any future training sessions.

* * *

On December 17, 2002, the twenty-seventh day of his "special interrogation," interrogators forced the shackled Qahtani to wear a bra, placed a thong on his head, and began calling him a homosexual and his mother and sister prostitutes and whores. That same day David Brant, who headed the Navy's Criminal Investigative Service, visited Alberto Mora, the Navy's General Counsel, in his Pentagon office. As Mora later reported,

In a late afternoon meeting, NCIS Director David Brant informed me that NCIS agents attached to JTF-160, the criminal investigation task force in Guantánamo, Cuba, had learned that some detainees confined in Guantánamo were being subjected to physical abuse and degrading treatment. This treatment—which the NCIS agents had not participated in or witnessed—was allegedly being inflicted by personnel attached to JTF-170, the intelligence task force, and was rumored to have been authorized, at least in part, at a "high level" in Washington, although NCIS had not seen the text of this authority.

The NCIS agents at Guantánamo and civilian and military personnel from other services were upset at this mistreatment and regarded such treatment as unlawful and in violation of American values. Director Brant emphasized that NCIS would not engage in abusive treatment even if ordered to and did not wish to be even indirectly associated with a facility that engaged in such practices.

Director Brant asked me if I wished to learn more. Disturbed, I responded that I felt I had to. We agreed to meet again the following day. That evening, I emailed [Rear Admiral] Michael Lohr, the Navy JAG, and invited him to attend the next morning's meeting with NCIS.[435]

In a 2006 profile in *The New Yorker*, Jane Mayer describes Alberto Mora as "a cautious, cerebral conservative who admired President Reagan and served in both the first and second Bush Administrations as a political appointee." Mora's parents had fled Communist regimes in Hungary and Cuba; one of his great uncles had been tortured and hanged, and another had been sent to a Nazi concentration camp. "People who went through things like this tend to have very strong views about the rule of law, totalitarianism, and America," Mora told Mayer.

In that interview, Mora spoke of his reaction to Brant's report, the first he had heard of Qahtani's interrogation, and of the dangerous game of trying to parse what exactly constitutes torture. "To my mind, there's no moral or practical distinction" between torture and other cruel, inhuman, and degrading treatment, Mora insisted.

If cruelty is no longer declared unlawful, but instead is applied as a matter of policy, it alters the fundamental relationship of man to government. It destroys the whole notion of individual rights. The Constitution recognizes that man has an inherent right, not bestowed by the state or laws, to personal dignity, including the right to be free of cruelty. It applies to all human beings, not just in America—even those designated as "unlawful enemy combatants." If you make this exception, the whole Constitution crumbles. It's a transformative issue.

"[M]y mother would have killed me if I hadn't spoken up," Mora explained his subsequent actions to Mayer. "No Hungarian after Communism, or Cuban after Castro, is not aware that human rights are incompatible with cruelty."[436]

On the morning of December 18, 2002, Brant returned to Mora's office with NCIS Chief Psychologist Michael Gelles. As part of the CITF team, Gelles had computer access to Guantánamo interrogation logs, and since he had filed his fruitless protest to the Special Interrogation Plan on November 22, he had been tracking the daily reports of Qahtani's interrogation and briefing Brant on what they both believed was the increasingly unlawful behavior of the military interrogators. In his July 7, 2004 "Statement for the Record: Office of General Counsel Involvement in Interrogation Issues," one of the most vivid and stirring documents in the historical record of the Bush administration torture program, Alberto Mora presented Navy Vice Admiral Albert Church this narrative of that meeting and its aftermath:

> *18 Dec 02*
>
> *I met with Director Brant and NCIS Chief Psychologist Dr. Michael Gelles. Dr. Gelles had advised JTF-160 in interrogation techniques and had spent time at the detention facility. Also present were OGC Deputy General Counsel William Molzahn, RADM Michael Lohr, and my Executive Assistant, CAPT Charlette Wise.*
>
> *Dr. Gelles described conditions in Guantánamo and stated that guards and interrogators with JTF-170, who were under pressure to produce results, had begun using abusive techniques with some of the detainees. These techniques included physical contact, degrading treatment (including dressing detainees in female underwear, among other techniques), the use of "stress" positions, and coercive psychological procedures. The military interrogators believed that such techniques were not only useful, but were necessary to obtain the desired information. NCIS agents were not involved in the application of these techniques or witnesses to them, but had learned of them through discussions with personnel who had been involved*

and through access to computer databases where interrogation logs were kept. Dr. Gelles showed me extracts of detainee interrogation logs evidencing some of this detainee mistreatment.

These techniques, Dr. Gelles explained, would violate the interrogation guidelines taught to military and law enforcement personnel and he believed they were generally violative of U.S. law if applied to U.S. persons. In addition, there was a great danger, he said, that any force utilized to extract information would continue to escalate. If a person being forced to stand for hours decided to lie down, it probably would take force to get him to stand up again and stay standing. In contrast to the civilian law enforcement at Guantánamo, who were trained in interrogation techniques and limits and had years of professional experience in such practices, the military interrogators were typically young and had little or no training or experience interrogations. Once the initial barrier against the use of improper force had been breached, a phenomenon known as "force drift" would almost certainly begin to come into play. This term describes the observed tendency among interrogators who rely on force. If some force is good, these people come to believe, then the application of more force must be better. Thus, the level of force applied against an uncooperative witness tends to escalate such that, if left unchecked, force levels, to include torture, could be reached. Dr. Gelles was concerned that this phenomenon might manifest itself at Guantánamo.

Director Brant reiterated his previous statements that he and the NCIS personnel at Guantánamo viewed any such abusive practices as repugnant. They would not engage in them even if ordered and NCIS would have to consider whether they could even remain co-located in Guantánamo if the practices were to continue. Moreover, this discontent was not limited to NCIS; law enforcement and military personnel from other services were also increasingly disturbed by the practice.

Director Brant also repeated that NCIS had been informed that the coercive interrogation techniques did not represent simply rogue

activity limited to undisciplined interrogators or even practices
sanctioned only by the local command, but had been reportedly
authorized at a "high level" in Washington. NCIS, however, had no
further information on this.

The general mood in the room was dismay. I was of the opinion
that the interrogation activities described would be unlawful and
unworthy of the military services, an opinion that the others shared.
I commended NCIS for their values and their decision to bring this
to my attention. I also committed that I would try to find out more
about the situation in Guantánamo, in particular whether any such
interrogation techniques had received higher-level authorization.

Mora called his counterpart at the Army, which had command
authority for Guantánamo. Army General Counsel Steven Morello told
Mora he had more information about what was going on there and invited
Mora to meet with him and Tom Taylor, his Deputy General Counsel, the
following day.

19 Dec 02

In the Army OGC offices, Mr. Morello and Mr. Taylor provided
me with a copy of a composite document (Att 2) capped by an Action
Memo from DoD General counsel William Haynes to the Secretary of
Defense entitled "counter-Resistance Techniques." The memo, which I
had not seen before, evidenced that on December 2, 2002, Secretary
Rumsfeld had approved the use of certain identified interrogation
techniques at Guantánamo, including (with some restrictions) the
use of stress positions, hooding, isolation, "deprivation of light and
auditory stimuli," and use of "detainee-individual phobias (such as
fear of dogs) to induce stress." This composite document (further
referred to as the "December 2nd Memo") showed that the request
for the authority to employ the techniques had originated with an
October 11, 2002, memorandum from MG Michael Dunlavey, the
Commander of JTF-170, to the Commander, SOUTHCOM, and
had proceeded up the chain of command through the Joint Staff until

reaching the Secretary. The Dunlavey memo was accompanied by a legal brief signed by LTC Diane Beaver, the SJF to JTF-170, generally finding that application of the interrogation techniques complied with law.

Mr. Morello and Mr. Taylor demonstrated great concern with the decision to authorize the interrogation techniques. Mr. Morello said that "they had tried to stop it," without success, and had been advised not to question the settled decision further.

Upon returning to my office, I reviewed the Secretary's December 2nd memo and the Beaver Legal Brief more closely. The brief held, in summary, that torture was prohibited but cruel, inhuman, or degrading treatment could be inflicted on the Guantánamo detainees with near impunity because, at least in that location, no law prohibited such action, no court would be vested with jurisdiction to entertain a complaint on such allegations, and various defenses (such as good motive or necessity) would shield any U.S. official accused of the unlawful behavior. I regarded the memo as a wholly inadequate analysis of the law and a poor treatment of this difficult and highly sensitive issue. As for the December 2nd Memo, I concluded that it was fatally grounded on these serious failures of legal analysis. As described in the memo and supporting documentation, the interrogation techniques approved by the Secretary should not have been authorized because some (but not all) of them, whether applied singly or in combination, could produce effects reaching the level of torture, a degree of mistreatment not otherwise proscribed by the memo because it did not articulate any bright-line standard for prohibited detainee treatment, a necessary element in such a document. Furthermore, even if the techniques as applied did not reach the level of torture, they almost certainly would constitute "cruel, inhuman, or degrading treatment," another class of unlawful treatment.

In my view, the alleged detainee abuse, coupled with the fact that the Secretary of Defense's memo had authorized at least aspects of it, could—and almost certainly would—have severe ramifications unless the policy was quickly reversed. Any such mistreatment would be unlawful and contrary to the President's directive to treat the detainees "humanely." In addition, the consequences of such practices were almost incalculably harmful to U.S. foreign, military, and legal policies. Because the American public would not tolerate such abuse, I felt the political fallout was likely to be severe.

Mora gave a copy of the December 2 memo to Navy JAGs and asked them to do a legal analysis of the techniques, briefed Secretary of the Navy Gordon England, and demanded a face-to-face meeting with Jim Haynes.

20 Dec 02

That afternoon I met with Mr. Hayes in his office. I informed him that NCIS had advised me that interrogation abuses were taking place in Guantánamo, that the NCIS agents considered any such abuses to be unlawful and contrary to American values, and that discontent over these practices were reportedly spreading among the personnel on the base. Producing the December 2ⁿᵈ Memo, I expressed surprise that the Secretary had been allowed to sign it. In my view, some of the authorized interrogation techniques could rise to the level of torture, although the intent surely had not been to do so. Mr. Haynes disagreed that the techniques authorized constituted torture. I urged him to think about the techniques more closely. What did "deprivation of light and auditory stimuli" mean? Could a detainee be locked in a completely dark cell? And for how long? A month? Longer? What precisely did the authority to exploit phobias permit? Could a detainee be held in a coffin? Could phobias be applied until madness set in? Not only could individual techniques applied singly constitute torture, I said, but also the application of combinations of them must surely be recognized as potentially capable of reaching the level of torture. Also, the memo's fundamental problem was that it was completely unbounded—it failed to establish a clear boundary for prohibited treatment. That boundary, I felt, had to be at that point where cruel and unusual punishment or treatment began. Turning to the Beaver Legal Brief, I characterized it as an incompetent product of legal analysis, and I urged him not to rely on it.

I also drew Mr. Haynes's attention to the Secretary's hand-written comment on the bottom of the memo, which suggested that detainees subjected to forced standing (which was limited to four hours) could be made to stand longer since he usually stood for longer periods during his work day. Although, having some sense of the Secretary's verbal style, I was confident the comment was intended to be jocular, defense attorneys for the detainees were sure to interpret it otherwise. Unless withdrawn rapidly, the memo was sure to be discovered and used at trial in the military commissions. The Secretary's signature on the memo ensured that he would be called as a witness. I told Mr. Haynes he could be sure that, at the end of what would be a long interrogation, the defense attorney would then refer the Secretary to the notation and ask whether it was not intended as a coded message, a written nod-and-a-wink to interrogators to the effect that they should not feel bound by the limits set in the memo, but consider themselves authorized to do what was necessary to obtain the necessary information. The memos, and the practices they authorized, threatened the entire military commission process.

Mr. Haynes listened attentively throughout. He promised to consider carefully what I had said.

I had entered the meeting believing that the December 2nd Memo was almost certainly not reflective of conscious policy but the product of oversight—a combination of too much work and too little time for careful legal analysis or measured consideration. I left confident that Mr. Haynes, upon reflecting on the abuse in Guantánamo and the flaws in the December 2nd Memo and underlying legal analysis, would seek to correct these mistakes by obtaining the quick suspension of the authority to apply the interrogation techniques.[437]

Mora left Washington the next day for a two-week family vacation. There would be no let-up in the interrogation, now in its second month: the day he left, in fact, interrogators moved to the next phase of the Special

Interrogation Plan, introducing the ersatz detainee in a nearby cell in X-Ray; just before midnight that evening he was pinned to the floor by MPs while a female interrogator straddled his chest, taunting him. After five more days of twenty-hour interrogations, exposure to frigid temperatures, and repeated "invasions of personal space by a female," Qahtani would entreat interrogators to let him write his will.

That same day, December 26, 2002, the *Washington Post* ran a front-page story by Dana Priest and Barton Gellman under the headline "U.S. Denies Abuse but Defends Interrogations: 'Stress and Duress' Tactics Used on Terrorism Suspects Held in Secret Overseas Facilities." The article revealed the existence of secret CIA interrogation facilities at Bagram Air Base in Afghanistan, on the island of Diego Garcia in the Indian Ocean, and elsewhere where "those who refused to cooperate…are sometimes kept standing or kneeling for hours, in black hoods or spray painted goggles." "At times they are held in awkward, painful positions and deprived of sleep with a 24-hour bombardment of lights—subject to what are known as "stress and duress," Priest and Gellman reported. Sources identified as witnesses to the interrogations described a process in which MPs and special forces troops "softened up" detainees with beatings and confined them in tiny rooms where they were "blindfolded and thrown into walls, bound in painful positions, subjected to loud noises and deprived of sleep"—a process supposedly aimed at "piercing a prisoner's resistance."

> In some cases, highly trained CIA officers question captives through interpreters. In others, the intelligence agency undertakes a "false flag" operation using fake décor and disguises meant to deceive a captive into thinking he is imprisoned in a country with a reputation for brutality, when, in reality, he is still in CIA hands. Sometimes, female officers conduct interrogations, a psychologically jarring experience for men reared in a conservative Muslim culture where women are never in control.[438]

Priest and Gellman quoted a number of unnamed administration "national security officials" who "defended the violence against captives as just and necessary"; one insisted "If you don't violate someone's human rights some of the time, you probably aren't doing your job."

The article revealed something else as well: in the fourteen months since the commencement of hostilities in Afghanistan, the U.S. had rendered nearly one hundred detainees to Jordan, Egypt, Morocco, and Syria— precisely the kinds of countries whose torture methods are enumerated in the Manchester document. "We don't kick the [expletive] out of them. We send them to other countries so they can kick the [expletive] out of them" said one official who was described as being "directly involved in rendering captives into foreign hands."

The CIA personnel running these operations had learned their methods in SERE technique trainings like the October "fiasco." Three days after the *Washington Post* article ran, SERE trainers Rankin and Ross arrived in Guantánamo to teach many of these techniques to twenty-four of General Miller's GTMO interrogators. As Mora's vacation wound down, it was business as usual: anticipating the final phase of the Qahtani interrogation plan, the agenda for the January 7, 2003 National Security Council meeting included a discussion of the possible rendition of Qahtani to Egypt or Jordan.[439]

Mora returned to the office on Friday, January 3. The following Monday, as he reported to Admiral Church,

6 Jan 03

NCIS director Brant informed me that the detainee mistreatment in Guantánamo was continuing and that he had not heard that the December 2nd Memo had been suspended or revoked. This came as an unpleasant surprise since I had been confident that the abusive activities would have been quickly ended once I brought them to the attention of higher levels within DoD. I began to wonder whether the adoption of the coercive interrogation techniques might not have been the product of simple oversight, as I had thought, but perhaps a policy consciously adopted—albeit through mistaken analysis—and enjoying at least some support within the Pentagon bureaucracy. To get them curbed I would have to develop a constituency within the Pentagon to do so.

Three days later, on January 9, 2002, Mora went back to Haynes:

> *I met with Mr. Haynes in his office again that afternoon. He was*
> *accompanied by an Air Force major whose name I cannot recall. I*
> *told him that I had been surprised to learn upon my return from*
> *vacation that the detainee abuses appeared to be continuing and that,*
> *from all appearances, the interrogation techniques authorized by the*
> *December 2ⁿᵈ Memo were still in place. I also provided him a draft*
> *copy of the Navy JAG legal memo.*
>
> *Mr. Haynes did not explain what had happened during the*
> *interval, but said that some U.S. officials believed the techniques*
> *were necessary to obtain information from the few Guantánamo*
> *detainees who, it was thought, were involved in the 9/11 attacks*
> *and had knowledge of other al Qaeda operations planned against*
> *the United States. I acknowledged the ethical issues were difficult. I*
> *was not sure what my position would be in the classic "ticking bomb"*
> *scenario where the terrorist being interrogated had knowledge of,*
> *say, an imminent nuclear weapon attack against a U.S. city. If I were*
> *the interrogator involved, I would probably apply the torture myself,*
> *although I would do so with full knowledge of potentially severe*
> *personal consequences. But I did not feel this was the factual situation*
> *we faced in Guantánamo, and even if I were willing to do this as an*
> *individual and assume the personal consequences, by the same token*
> *I did not consider it appropriate for us to advocate for or cause the*
> *laws and values of our nation to be changed to render the activity*
> *lawful. Also, the threats against the United States came from many*
> *directions and had many different potential consequences. Does the*
> *threat by one common criminal against the life of one citizen justify*
> *torture or lesser mistreatment? If not, how many lives must the threat*
> *jeopardize? Where does one set the threshold, if at all? In any event,*
> *this was not for us to decide in the Pentagon; these were issues for*
> *national debate.*

These questions, Mora pointed out, were hardly theoretical exercises.

He raised, and listed for the record, five real-world consequences that extended or almost certainly would extend from Rumsfeld's memo:

- *The December 26th Washington Post article recounting allegations of prisoner mistreatment at Guantánamo and elsewhere demonstrated that the discontent of those in the military opposed to the practice was leaking to the media, as was inevitable.*
- *Even if one wanted to authorize the U.S. military to conduct coercive interrogations, as was the case in Guantánamo, how could one do so without profoundly altering its core values and character? Societal education and military training inculcated in our soldiers American values adverse to mistreatment. Would we now have the military abandon these values altogether? Or would we create detachments of special guards and interrogators, who would be trained and kept separate from the other soldiers, to administer these practices?*
- *The belief held by some that Guantánamo's special jurisdictional situation would preclude a U.S. court finding jurisdiction to review events occurring there was questionable at best. The coercive interrogations in Guantánamo were not committed by rogue elements of the military acting without authority, a situation that may support a finding of lack of jurisdiction. In this situation, the authority and direction to engage in the practice issued from and was under review by the highest DoD authorities, including the Secretary of Defense. What precluded a federal district court from finding jurisdiction along the entire length of the chain of command?*
- *The British government had applied virtually the same interrogation techniques against Irish Republican Army detainees in the '70s. Following an exhaustive investigation in which the testimony of hundreds of witnesses was taken, the European Commission of Human rights found the interrogation techniques to constitute torture. In* Ireland v. United Kingdom, *a later lawsuit brought by the victims of the interrogation techniques, the European court of Human Rights in a split decision held that the techniques did not rise to the level of torture, but did amount to "cruel, inhuman, and degrading"*

treatment, a practice that was equally in violation of European law and international human rights standards. The court awarded damages. Ultimately, the then-Prime Minister, standing in the well of Parliament, admitted that the government had used the techniques, forswore their further use, and announced further investigations and remedial training. This case was directly applicable to our situation for two reasons. First, because of the similarity between U.S. and U.K. jurisprudence, the case helped establish that the interrogation techniques authorized in the December 2nd Memo constituted, at a minimum, cruel, inhuman, and degrading treatment. Further, depending on circumstances, the same treatment may constitute torture—treatment that may discomfit a prizefighter may be regarded as torture by a grandmother. Second, at present, British Prime Minister Tony Blair had lost significant electoral support and was under heavy political pressure because of his staunch support for the United States in the War on Terror and Operation Iraqi Freedom. What would be the impact on Blair's political standing upon the disclosure that his partner, the United States, was engaged in practices that were unlawful under British and European law? Could the British Government be precluded from continuing to cooperate with us on aspects of the War on Terror because doing so would abet illegal activity? Besides Blair, what impact would our actions have with respect to the willingness of other European leaders, all of whom are subject to the same law, to participate with us in the War on Terror?

- *A central element of American foreign policy for decades had been our support for human rights. By authorizing and practicing cruel, inhuman, and degrading treatment, we were now engaged in the same sort of practices that we routinely condemned. Had we jettisoned our human rights policies? If not, could we continue to espouse them given our inconsistent behavior?*

Mr. Haynes said little during our meeting. Frustrated by not having made much apparent headway, I told him that the interrogation policies could threaten Secretary Rumsfeld's tenure and could even damage the Presidency. "Protect your client," I urged Mr. Haynes.

After the meeting, I reported back to Mr. Durnan by email (Att 9) Two sentences summarized my view of the meeting. Speaking of Mr. Haynes, I wrote: "He listened—as he always does—closely and intently to my arguments and promised to get back to me, but didn't say when. I've got no inkling what impact, if any, I made.[440]

Over the next six days, Mora met with Joint Chiefs legal advisor Jane Dalton, the Army and Air Force General Counsels, the Deputy General Counsel of the Defense Department, Undersecretary of the Navy Susan Livingstone, and Vice Admiral Kevin Green to make his case and build, as he put it, a constituency in the Pentagon for ending the abuse and repealing the Rumsfeld interrogation authorities. He also prepared to make his case in writing. Finally, on January 15, 2003,

Uncertain whether there would be any change to the interrogation policy and dissatisfied at what I viewed as the slow pace of the discussions, I prepared a draft memorandum addressed to Mr. Haynes and CAPT Dalton (Att 12) providing my views on the JTF-170 October 11, 2002 request (contained as part of the December 2nd Memo) requesting authority to engage in the counter-resistance interrogation techniques. My memo: (a) stated that the majority of the proposed category II and all of the category III techniques were violative of domestic and international legal norms in that they constituted, at a minimum, cruel and unusual treatment and, at worst, torture; (b) rejected the legal analysis and recommendations of the Beaver Legal Brief; and (c) "strongly non-concurred" with the adoption of the violative interrogation techniques. The memo further cautioned that even "the misperception that the U.S. Government authorizes or condones detention or interrogation practices that do not comply with our domestic and international legal obligations... probably will cause significant harm to our national legal, political, military and diplomatic interests."

I delivered the memo in draft form to Mr. Haynes's office in the morning. In a telephone call, I told Mr. Haynes that I was increasingly uncomfortable as time passed because I had not put down in writing my views on the interrogation issues. I said I would be signing out the memo late that afternoon unless I heard definitively that use of the interrogation techniques had been or was being suspended. We agreed to meet later that day.

In the later meeting, which Mr. Dell'Orto attended, Mr. Haynes returned the draft to me. He asked whether I was not aware of how he felt about the issues or the impact of my actions. I responded that I did not and, with respect to his own views, I had no idea whether he agreed totally with my arguments, disagreed totally with them, or held an intermediate view. Mr. Haynes then said that Secretary Rumsfeld would be suspending the authority to apply the techniques that same day. I said I was delighted and would thus not be signing out my memo. Later in the day and after our meeting, Mr. Haynes called to confirm that Secretary Rumsfeld had suspended the techniques. I reported the news widely, including to the Under Secretary (Att 13) and VADM Green (Att 14).

On that day, the Special Interrogation of Mohammed al-Qahtani came to an end. As interrogation experts had predicted for months, the sustained use of techniques that the U.S. long condemned as torture had failed. After seven weeks, the interrogation was at a standstill, but there would be no final phase, no rendition.

Annotations on this section from TheTortureReport.org

On the Manchester Document, former Air Force criminal investigator and interrogator Matthew Alexander wrote,

The Manchester Document was never widely read by members of Al Qaeda. The resistance techniques described within are nothing less than an amateur's approach to evading interrogation. Lying, alleging mistreatment, collaborating on cover stories...these are the techniques used by teenagers who conspire to steal candy from a convenience store.

On the use of guard dogs to intimidate detainees, based on the belief, as an FBI agent put it, that Arabs fear dogs because they view them as unclean, Matthew Alexander observed,

We've seen this theme repeated throughout The Torture Report, where prejudice-based stereotypes influence the interrogation techniques.

On General Myers and Jim Haynes scuttling a legal review of interrogation techniques by Joint Chiefs Legal Counsel Captain Jane Dalton, Matthew Alexander wrote:

This is one of the most important moments in the entire decision-making process that resulted in the torture and abuse of detainees. The senior ranking military officer in the United States stops a legal review of the techniques by the services when they advise that EITs violate the law. This was a perfect opportunity for General Myers to stand up and say that these techniques violated everything we stand for in the military and he would have had the full support of all four services behind him. Instead, he decided to 'play game,' sacrificing our principles in exchange for what was politically convenient, but morally incomprehensible. If the military had investigated torture and abuse as a crime, as it should have, this act could have led to several charges being filed against Gen Myers including abuse of authority and conspiracy, to name just two.

FORCE DRIFT

Donald Rumsfeld's January 15, 2003 memorandum suspending the interrogation techniques to which Qahtani had been subjected read,

My December 2, 2002 approval of the use of all Category II techniques and one Category III technique during interrogations at Guantánamo is hereby rescinded. Should you determine that particular techniques in either of these categories are warranted in an individual case, you should forward that request to me. Such a request should include a thorough justification for the employment of those techniques and a detailed plan for the use of such techniques.[441]

The day after Rumsfeld signed this rescission memo, General Miller's JTF-GTMO interrogators issued a draft interrogation plan titled "Methods and Approaches to Employ, Special Interrogation Operation of ISN 760," in which they proposed submitting a 32-year-old Mauritanian detainee named Mohamedou Ould Slahi to an ordeal very similar to the one Qahtani had suffered. Slahi was to face twenty-hour interrogations, during which interrogators would douse him with water to keep him awake and "enforce control." Military dogs would be used "to agitate the detainee and provide shock value." He would wear signs saying "liar," "coward," and "dog" and be forced to perform dog tricks "to reduce the detainee's ego." He would be forcibly shaved, strip-searched, and made to wear a burka. He would be refused opportunities to pray, and interrogators would exploit "religious taboos" like "close physical contact" with female interrogators to raise his stress level. Moreover, because Slahi "believes music is forbidden," his interrogation booth—"a bare white room designed to reduce outside stimuli and present an austere environment"—would be flooded with loud music and lurid red lighting; at other times, a strobe light would be used to "disorient [Slahi] and add to [his] stress level," or he would be hooded "to isolate him and increase his stress level."[442]

Ten months before, on March 6, 2002, CNN ran a story headlined "Al Qaeda Online for Terrorism" that featured an interview with a man who correspondent Mike Boettcher introduced as a "hacker" "who operates an Internet monitoring service from this Spartan loft in Zurich Switzerland"; in Guido Rudolphi's hands, Boettcher told viewers, "a keyboard can be a digital crime lab." Rudolphi, Boettcher said, was a private citizen who had been conducting a kind of freelance investigation since the 9/11 attacks and had stumbled upon Slahi.

> *First, he tracked down a classified French secret service report on bin Laden, including a secret list of suspected bin Laden associates. One name in particular caught Rudolphi's eye, a Mauritanian named Mohambedou Ould Slahi. Rudolphi became curious because Slahi operated an Internet site through a Swiss web space provider....Rudolphi discovered Slahi had twice been brought in for questioning during the investigation of two al Qaeda plots: the failed plan to blow up Los Angeles International Airport during the millennium celebration, and the successful September 11 attacks. Each time, Slahi had been released."[443]*

According to Boettcher, "by cracking a code on Slahi's website," Rudolphi found a digital trail leading to Duisberg, Germany, where Slahi had contact with several 9/11 hijackers, and then to Canada, "where he attended the same mosque" as Millennium bomb plotter Ahman Ressam, was questioned by Canadian intelligence after Ressam's arrest, and days later "fled." The story continued,

> *BOETTCHER: Guido Rudolphi and his colleagues were able to find Slahi using the web. They tracked him to his native country of Mauritania, in West Africa, where Slahi operates an Internet café, another fact that raised Rudolphi's suspicion.*
> *RUDOLPHI: If I want to use the Internet on a really sensitive matter, and under no circumstances want to run the risk that anybody can trace me back, I go to the Internet café.*
> *BOETTCHER: Or public libraries, where some of the September 11th hijackers went to access the Internet*

> *(on camera): What did you do with this information when you saw*
> *it and thought it looked suspicious?*
>
> *RUDOLPHI: First, I got in contact with the Swiss police. They were*
> *interested, but since then, I never heard back.*
>
> *BOETTCHER: (voice-over) But other law enforcement and intelligence*
> *agencies did have Slahi on their radar. Last September, the*
> *Mauritanian government detained and questioned Slahi at*
> *the request of the FBI, then released him. The FBI will not*
> *comment on Slahi.*
>
> *As far as we know, Mohambedou Ould Slahi is still in*
> *Mauritania. Not only did we try to contact him via the*
> *Internet or via fax, we had personal CNN representatives*
> *on the ground go to his family and friends to try to deliver*
> *a message to him that we wanted to speak to him. And in all*
> *cases we got nowhere.*[444]

Had CNN reporters actually contacted Slahi's family in Mauritania, they would have learned that a little over three months before, on November 20, 2001, Mauritanian police had come calling for Slahi. It was five o'clock in the evening, and he had just returned from work; he was in the shower when police arrived. They asked him to accompany them to the police station. Slahi was indeed used to being questioned by law enforcement and had always submitted willingly, and this time, too, he followed the police in his own car, telling his mother when he left home not to worry, he would return soon. He was never arrested. He also never returned. He was questioned for a week by Mauritanian officials and FBI agents, and on the eighth day, November 28, 2001, the U.S. took custody of Slahi, put him on a CIA rendition flight, and delivered him to a prison in Jordan.[445]

The Jordanians worked to connect Slahi with Ahmed Ressam. "Your government captured me for the wrong reasons; they thought I was part of the millennium plot," Slahi told the Military Commission at his CSRT hearing in Guantánamo late in 2004. "In Jordan, they made me crazy to admit I had something to do with it. Because there was so much pressure and bad treatment, I admitted to this. Your intelligence later realized this was not true and a mistake." On July 19, 2002, after eight months in Jordan, a team of masked men retrieved Slahi. At his Administrative Review Board hearing two years later, Slahi recalled,

They took my clothes off and I said this is an American technique not an Arabic one because Arabs don't usually take all your clothes off. So they stripped me naked like my mom bore me, and they put new clothes on me. The guy moved his mask a little bit and I could see he was pale and that way I knew he was American. It was like I know my life is God's, I didn't want my family to see me in such a condition on T.V. because I know Americans are about T.V. media. I did not want them to take my picture. I was in chains, a very bad suit, I had lost so much weight in Jordan I was like a ghost and I did not want my family to see me in this situation, that was my worst fear in the world. Besides that I had to keep my water (could not go to the restroom) for eight hours straight. Because the Americans [had me put] in a diaper but psychologically I couldn't [urinate] in the diaper. I tried to convince myself it was okay but I couldn't.

The leased CIA rendition jet flew Slahi from Amman to Kabul, where he was helicoptered and trucked on to Bagram. He was delivered to Guantánamo a month later, on August 14, 2002.[446]

Throughout the fall, as the military was gaining control of Qahtani's interrogation, Criminal Investigation Task Force agents managed to keep Slahi out of the hands of JTF interrogators. He was questioned by CITF investigator Britt Mallow, by three German intelligence agents, and by an FBI team, one agent in particular who reportedly managed to gain his trust. But by January, despite the service-wide outcry against the Qahtani interrogation and the apparent success of Mora's rebellion, General Miller's interrogators were now planning more of the same with Slahi.

Indeed, Rumsfeld's rescission memo had little effect on the base. In a meeting with General Miller two days after the memo was issued, CITF Deputy Commander Mark Fallon and Naval Criminal Investigation Service Chief Psychologist Michael Gelles pressed investigators' concerns about abusive interrogations. Miller—who had lobbied to continue Qahtani's interrogation even after Rumsfeld's memo was suspended—told the two "you have got to put on the same jersey if you want to be on the team."[447] An FBI agent who arrived in Cuba the day Qahtani's interrogation ended later recalled discussing interrogation methods with a psychiatrist from Walter Reed hospital who was on the base to consult with JTF-GTMO; "rapport building [is] for tree huggers," the psychiatrist told her.[448]

* * *

Rumsfeld issued a second memo on January 15, 2003, this one to his chief counsel Jim Haynes, directing him to "Establish a working group within the Department of Defense to assess the legal, policy, and operational issues relating to the interrogations of detainees held by the U.S. Armed Forces in the war on terrorism." It instructed,

> The working group should consist of experts from your Office, the Office of the Under Secretary of Defense for Policy, the Military Departments, and the Joint Staff. The working group should address and make recommendations as warranted on the following issues:
> Legal considerations raised by interrogation of detainees held by U.S. Armed Forces.
> Policy considerations with respect to the choice of interrogation techniques, including:
> - contribution to intelligence collection
> - effect on treatment of captured U.S. military personnel
> - historical role of U.S. armed forces in conducting interrogations
> Recommendations for employment of particular interrogation techniques by DoD interrogators.
> You should report your assessment and recommendations to me within 15 days.[449]

Alberto Mora was assigned to this Working Group, as were the general counsels of the Army and Air Force, the Judge Advocates General of the three services, and the staff judge advocate of the Marines. The Joint Chiefs had two representatives, including Legal Counsel Jane Dalton, and Doug Feith, Undersecretary of Defense for Policy, had one. Haynes appointed Air Force General Counsel Mary Walker to chair the group.

Mora went to work immediately to develop information and legal analyses that the group could use to counter what he knew was coming: another John Yoo memorandum, one that Haynes informed the group would provide the "definitive guidance" for Defense Department interrogations. He assigned Navy attorneys to write a paper on the applicability of the 5th, 8th, and 14th Amendments of the Constitution, and on January 17, 2003, he met with Gelles and Fallon. As he recorded in his memorandum for the record,

In the meeting, I mentioned my concern that simple opposition to the use of the coercive interrogation techniques may not be sufficient to prevail in the impending bureaucratic reexamination of which procedures to authorize. We couldn't fight something with nothing; was there anything in the scientific or academic literature that would support the use of non-coercive interrogation techniques? Dr. Gelles replied that there was. Most behavioral experts working in the field, he said, viewed torture as illegal, but also as ineffective. The weight of expert opinion held that the most effective interrogation techniques to employ against individuals with the psychological profile of the al Qaeda or Taliban detainees were "relationship-based," that is, they relied on the mutual trust achieved in the course of developing a non-coercive relationship to break down the detainee's resistance to interrogation. Coercive interrogations, said Dr. Gelles, were counter-productive to the implementation of relationship-based strategies.

At my direction, Dr. Gelles began the preparation of two memos, the first to be a summary of the thesis intended to be injected as quickly as possible into the Working Group and inter-agency deliberations, and the second a comprehensive discussion of the subject.[450]

At the Working Group's first meeting on January 23, 2003, David Becker, formerly JTF GTMO's Interrogations Chief and now a civilian employee of the Defense Intelligence Agency, was asked to present the

specific techniques DIA wanted the group to consider. Becker drew up
a list of thirty-six techniques: the standard techniques in the Army Field
Manual; the Category II and all four of the Category III techniques from
General Dunlavey's October 11, 2002 request memo, including mock
executions and other threats to the detainee or his family, exposure to cold
and water dousing, simulating drowning, and mild, non-injurious physical
contact; and three new, "less common" techniques:[451]

[1] Use of Drugs: Drugs such as sodium pentothal and demerol may
be used with some effectiveness. Significant policy issues must be
resolved. [2] Use of Female Interrogators: One al-Qaida resistance
method is to pray during interrogations. Prayer is only allowed if the
detainee is 'clean.' Having a woman rub scented oil on the detainee's
arms and face makes the detainee perceive that he is unclean and he
cannot pray until he cleans himself, which he is unable to do until
he returns to his cell. The use of female interrogators to put oil on a
detainee does not exceed limits already established by DoD policy or
the Geneva Conventions. [3] Sleep Deprivation: This can be effective;
however, there are obvious policy considerations. Guidelines as to the
use of sleep deprivation would have to be established.[452]

The Working Group received input from two other sources. General
Miller submitted a memo titled "Effectiveness of the Use of Certain
Category II Counter-Resistance Strategies" that described the techniques
used in the Qahtani interrogation as "essential to mission success." "These
techniques are humane, whether employed singly or in combination over
a period of time and are within the spirit and intent of humane detention,"
Miller asserted. "After consultation with the Staff Judge Advocate I believe
they are not in violation of the 8th Amendment of the United States
Constitution prohibiting cruel and unusual punishment; or Title 18 of the
United States Code, Section 2340 et seq. (the Federal Torture Statute)"[453]

The group also received a list of requested techniques from Afghanistan.
When the Justice Department's Inspector General was investigating the FBI's
involvement in detainee abuse in Guantánamo, Afghanistan, and Iraq, one

of its investigators recorded in his debriefing notes that an FBI agent he was interviewing, after describing Qahtani's interrogation, stated that "Camp X-ray was locally where harsh techniques were used," but "if you think this is tough, you should see what's happening in Afghanistan." The memo the Deputy Staff Judge Advocate of Afghanistan's CJTF-180 submitted to the Working Group on January 24, 2003 made clear that Category II and III techniques were in common use there, in addition to five others he was recommending be added to the list: "deprivation of clothing" for the purposes of placing detainees in a "shameful, uncomfortable situation"; "food deprivation"; "sensory overload—loud music or temperature regulation"; "controlled fear through the use of muzzled, trained, military working dogs"; and "use of light and noise deprivation."[454]

The Working Group also returned to the source of abusive methods, requesting information about the techniques directly from the Joint Personnel Recovery Agency and SERE instructors. By now, though, JPRA had grown skittish about the proliferating use of SERE-based interrogations and stalled, referring the group to information it had already provided to Haynes and the DIA. SERE instructor Joseph Witsch wrote to Daniel Baumgartner, the JPRA's Chief of Staff, alarmed. "The physical and psychological pressures we apply in training violate national and international laws," Witsch wrote in an email at the end of January. "We are only allowed to do these things based on permission from DoD management and intense oversight by numerous organizations within DoD. I hope someone is explaining this to all these folks asking for our techniques and methodology." Like Mora, Witsch clearly foresaw dangers of "force drift." "What do you think is more likely to happen when one of these organizations gets exposed and because of the significant 'drift' and a lack of oversight they go beyond what we do at SERE schools?" he asked. "The first question will be 'Where did you get your guidance?' Then we get investigated and exposed." "This is getting out of control!!" he concluded.[455]

The Working Group had specifically been instructed to "address and make recommendations" on the "legal considerations raised by interrogation of detainees held by U.S. Armed Forces," and by January 25, 2003, Mora, Dalton, and the rest of the group had produced a "Survey of

Legal and Policy Considerations" to serve as the framework for evaluating the individual techniques. The Senate Armed Services Committee, which was allowed to review that document but not to keep a copy, found

> *The draft reviewed U.S. obligations under international law and concluded that "obligations under the Torture Convention...apply to the interrogation of Operation Enduring Freedom detainees..." The draft analysis also included a review of articles of the UCMJ and the U.S. legal standards that were potentially applicable to U.S. interrogators....*
>
> *The draft analysis also assessed the legality of the techniques that had been requested for approval by GTMO in October 2002 including some of those that the Secretary of Defense had approved for use at GTMO in December 2002. In its draft, the Working Group adopted the conclusion that Navy JAG Corps CDR Stephen Gallotta had reached in his January 9, 2003 memo, writing that:*
>
>> *Category III techniques that threaten death to the detainee or his family (#1) or which create the misapprehension of suffocation (#3) would likely be judged to constitute torture under the statute and customary international law. They reflect conduct specifically defined as torture in [18 U.S.C.] §2340 and recognized as torture in international law. Category III, technique #4, mild, non-injurious grabbing and poking, is an assault under the UCMJ. Absent lawful purposes [defined elsewhere as inherent and necessary to custodial conduct], these techniques may be* per se *unlawful.*
>>
>> *Category II techniques could also, depending in their implementation, i.e., frequency of use, degree of pain inflicted, or combinations of techniques, rise to a level where they could be determined to be torture. Thus, additional analysis with specific guidance for implementation is recommended.*[456]

But Working Group chair Mary Walker already had in hand a draft of Yoo's new memorandum, addressed to Haynes and with the subject line "Military Interrogations of Alien Unlawful Combatants Held Outside the United States." The eighty-one-page memo dismissed almost every level of domestic and international legal restraint on the treatment of detainees in military custody. The Fifth and Eighth Amendments do not apply to interrogations outside the U.S. The War Crimes Act is not in force because Al Qaeda and Taliban detainees are not protected by the Geneva Conventions. The torture statute, which codifies the Convention against Torture in U.S. law, does not apply on U.S. territory or permanent military bases outside the U.S. Even if any of these prohibitions did apply, they were trumped by the president's absolute power to conduct war as Commander in Chief. If, for example, customary international law bans cruel, inhuman, and degrading treatment, "the President may decide to override customary international law at his discretion." And if the president ordered torture, "such an order would amount to a suspension or termination of the Convention [Against Torture]. In so doing, the President's order and the resulting conduct would not be a violation of international law because the United States would no longer be bound by the treaty."[457]

"Although the lengthy memo covered many issues and did so with seeming sophistication," Mora recalled in his 2004 Statement for the Record, "I regarded it as profoundly in error in at least two central elements."

> First, the memo explicitly held that the application of cruel, inhuman, and degrading treatment to the Guantánamo detainees was authorized with few restrictions or conditions. This, I felt, was a clearly erroneous conclusion that was at variance with applicable law, both domestic and international, and trends in constitutional jurisprudence, particularly those dealing with the 8th Amendment protections against cruel and unusual punishment and 14th Amendment substantive due process protections that prohibited conduct "shocking to the conscience." And second, the memo espoused an extreme and virtually unlimited theory of the extent of the President's commander-in-chief authority.... In summary, the OLC memo proved a vastly more sophisticated version of the Beaver Legal Brief, but it was a much more dangerous document

*because the statutory requirement that OLC opinions are binding
provided much more weight to its virtually equivalent conclusions."*[458]

The Working Group was not silent about its objections. Yoo and memo
co-author Jennifer Koester, an OLC staff attorney two years out of law
school, attended Working Group meetings from the outset, and Koester—
whose name is redacted throughout the July 29, 2009 Justice Department's
Office of Professional Responsibility report summarizing its investigation
into the Bush administration's OLC memos but inadvertently appears in
a footnote—got an earful when she met with members of the group on
January 28, 2003 and summarized the Yoo memo's conclusions. "Several
members of the Working Group were highly critical of the advice provided
by Yoo and [Koester]," the OPR reported. After the meeting, according to
the OPR report,

> *She reported back to Yoo by email that some members of the Working
> Group expressed concern that:*
>   - *the commander-in-chief section sweeps too broadly*
>   - *the necessity defense sweeps too broadly and doesn't make clear
>   enough that it would not apply in all factual scenarios*
>   - *the c-in-c argument (as with other defenses) is a violation of our
>   international obligations.*
>
> *[Koester] added that she was "not worried about the first two concerns
> but with respect to the third, I pointed them to national right of self-
> defense but I sense serious skepticism." Yoo responded that she should
> keep "plugging away" and that they would address the concerns in the
> editing process.*
>   *Yoo told us that he had "a lot of arguments" with members of the
> Working Group who disagreed with OLC's analysis. According to Yoo,
> he generally responded by pointing out that the criticism involved
> matters of policy, not legal analysis.*[459]

In fact, there was no substantive editing process. Two days after the meeting with Koester, Walker emailed Mora objecting to his efforts to correct the memo's 8th Amendment analysis. Mora, who would call the Yoo memo "a travesty of applicable law" in later testimony before the Armed Services Committee, wrote back to Walker warning that "The OLC draft paper is fundamentally in error: it spots some of the legal trees, but misses the constitutional forest. Because it identifies no boundaries to action—more, it alleges there are none—it is virtually useless as guidance as now drafted and dangerous in that it might give some a false sense of comfort." The reply was categorical: "Ms. Walker's response dismissed my warning. 'I disagree and moreover I believe DoD GC [Haynes] disagrees.'"[460] "There was a point where we were told that we could not argue against the OLC opinion…that any other legal ideas that we had would not be accepted, particularly when we commented on the draft report," Joint Chiefs legal counsel Captain Jane Dalton told the Committee.[461]

By early February, Walker was circulating a draft of what would become the group's report and recommendations; titled "Working Group Report on Detainee Interrogations in the Global War on Terrorism: Assessment of Legal Historical, Policy, and Operational Considerations," the report incorporated Yoo's legal analysis and applied it, in a literal, vivid red light/ green light grid, to Becker's list of thirty-six techniques. Decisions on whether to "green light" a technique would be made in the framework of Yoo's vision of near-limitless presidential power and expediency; the process was "essentially a risk benefit analysis that generally takes into account the expected utility of the technique, the likelihood that any technique will be in violation of domestic or international law, and various policy considerations." The second consideration was clearly subordinate to the first and third: "the lawfulness of the application of any particular technique, or combination of techniques, may depend on the practical necessity for imposition of the more exceptional techniques," and "legal justification for action that could otherwise be unlawful…depends in large part on whether the specific circumstances would justify the imposition of more aggressive techniques."[462]

Early drafts of the report juxtaposed a column labeled "Utility" (all rated "high" save for silence and threatened transfer to a third country, which were "medium") with four columns representing bodies of relevant law: the Torture Convention's ban on torture; its prohibition on cruel, inhuman, and degrading treatment; U.S. domestic law; and Customary International Law. The last column, a "very angry" Jane Dalton told the Senate Armed Services Committee, provided a particularly graphic example of how the working group process was "geared toward a particular conclusion" that was preordained by the White House via the OLC memo:

> [T]here was a column originally...in the stoplight chart, that was labeled "Customary International Law." So one of the things we were supposed to assess was whether or not the techniques were consistent with customary international law. The stoplight chart had all 36 techniques green under customary international law because the OLC opinion and thus the Working Group report maintained that customary international law did not impose any constraints on the actions...That green light was absolutely wrong legally...it was embarrassing to have it in there, and one of my comments to the report was...You need to delete that column entirely because it's embarrassing to have it in there and it's not reflective of the law.[463]

But Dalton and Mora were bucking an administration that had come to specialize in gearing information to a particular conclusion, regardless of facts or internal dissent; worse, it was an administration deeply invested in torture as a means of corroborating its conclusions. The Working Group had been presented with the first draft of its "Final Report" on February 4, 2003. The next day, Secretary of State Colin Powell appeared before the United Nations Security Council to present the case for invading Iraq. In that speech, Powell told the world,

> Al Qaida continues to have a deep interest in acquiring weapons of mass destruction. As with the story of Zarqawi and his network, I can trace the story of a senior terrorist operative telling how Iraq provided training in these weapons to Al Qaida.

Fortunately, this operative is now detained, and he has told his story. I will relate it to you now as he, himself, described it.

This senior Al Qaida terrorist was responsible for one of Al Qaida's training camps in Afghanistan. His information comes first-hand from his personal involvement at senior levels of Al Qaida. He says bin Laden and his top deputy in Afghanistan, deceased Al Qaida leader Muhammad Atta, did not believe that Al Qaida labs in Afghanistan were capable enough to manufacture these chemical or biological agents. They needed to go somewhere else. They had to look outside of Afghanistan for help. Where did they go? Where did they look? They went to Iraq.

The support that (inaudible) describes included Iraq offering chemical or biological weapons training for two Al Qaida associates beginning in December 2000. He says that a militant known as Abu Abdula Al-Iraqi had been sent to Iraq several times between 1997 and 2000 for help in acquiring poisons and gases. Abdula Al-Iraqi characterized the relationship he forged with Iraqi officials as successful.[464]

The supposedly loquacious source for this story was Ali Abdul Aziz al-Fakhiri, a Libyan who went by the name Ibn al-Shaykh al-Libi. Captured crossing into Pakistan in December 2001 during the battle of Tora Bora, al-Libi was questioned at Bagram air base by an FBI team led by two New York-based agents, Jack Cloonan and Russell Fincher. Fincher, a conservative Christian, developed a particular rapport with the former head of the al-Khalden training camp by praying alongside him and discussing religion, and al-Libi shared information about former camp trainees Zacarias Moussaoui and Richard Reid and an Al Qaeda-approved plot to attack the U.S. embassy in Yemen—information that did not, however, include any suggestions of connections between Al Qaeda and Saddam Hussein.

After several days, "Albert"—the same CIA agent who would threaten Abd al-Rahim al-Nashiri with a handgun and drill a year later in Poland—interrupted one of Fincher's sessions and announced that on White House orders, the CIA was taking over al-Libi's interrogation; "You're going to Egypt," Albert told al-Libi, "and while you're there, I'm going to find your mother, and fuck her." Soon after, Albert returned with a team that bound and hooded al-Libi and strapped him to a stretcher for the flight to Cairo. "We believed that al-Libi was withholding critical threat information at the time so we transferred him to a third country for further debriefing," George Tenet explained antiseptically in his 2007 memoir.[465]

Al-Libi spent two years in Egypt's "Scorpion" maximum-security prison, where he was tortured into creating the tale Powell related to the United Nations. When he was finally returned to U.S. custody in February 2004, he immediately recanted the story; citing CIA operational cables describing his debriefing, the Senate Select Committee on Intelligence reported in 2006,

> *After his transfer to a foreign government [redacted], al-Libi claimed that during his initial debriefings "he lied to the [foreign government service] [redacted] about future operations to avoid torture." Al-Libi told the CIA that the foreign government service [redacted] explained to him that a "long list of methods could be used against him which were extreme" and that "he would confess because three thousand individuals had been in the chair before him and that each had confessed."*
>
> *According to al-Libi, the foreign government service [redacted] "stated that the next topic was al-Qa'ida's connections with Iraq....This was a subject about which he knew nothing and had difficulty even coming up with a story." Al-Libi indicated that his interrogators did not like his responses and then "placed him in a small box approximately 50cm x 50 cm." He claimed he was held in the box for approximately 17 hours. When he was let out of the box, al-Libi claims that he was given a last opportunity to "tell the truth." When al-Libi did not satisfy the interrogator, al-Libi claimed that "he was knocked over with an arm thrust across the chest and he fell on his back." Al-Libi told CIA debriefers that he was "was punched for 15 minutes."*
>
> *Al-Libi told debriefers that "after the beating," he was again asked*

about the connection with Iraq and this time he came up with a story that three al-Qa'ida members went to Iraq to learn about nuclear weapons. Al-Libi said that he used the names of real individuals associated with al-Qa'ida so that he could remember the details of his fabricated story and make it more believable to the foreign intelligence service. Al-Libi noted that "this pleased his [foreign] interrogators, who directed that al-Libi be taken back to a big room, vice the 50 square centimeter box and given food."

According to al-Libi, several days after the Iraq nuclear discussion, the foreign intelligence service debriefers [redacted] brought up the topic of anthrax and biological weapons. Al-Libi stated that he "knew nothing about a biological program and did not even understand the term biological." Al-Libi stated that "he could not come up with a story and was then beaten in a way that left no marks." According to al-Libi, he continued "to be unable to come up with a lie about biological weapons" because he did not understand the term "biological weapons."[466]

The CIA cables from which the Senate Intelligence Committee constructed this account are dated February 4, 2004. But the intelligence community had long known that what al-Libi was telling the Egyptians was likely the fruit of torture. A Defense Intelligence Agency summary from February 2002—somewhere between a month and two months after al-Libi's rendition—flagged Egyptian intelligence reports that al-Libi was claiming three Al Qaeda operatives had sought nuclear weapons training in Iraq, cautioning,

This is the first report from Ibn al-Shaykh in which he claims Iraq assisted al-Qaida's [Chemical, Biological, Radiological, and Nuclear] efforts. However, he lacks specific details on the Iraqis involved, the CBRN materials associated with the assistance, and the location where training occurred. It is possible he does not know any further details; it is more likely this individual is intentionally misleading the debriefers. Ibn al-Shaykh has been undergoing debriefs for several weeks and may describing [sic] scenarios to the debriefers that he knows will retain their interest.[467]

It was these scenarios, sharpened by subsequent rounds of abusive interrogations, that Powell presented, without qualification or reservation, in his February 2003 speech before the UN Security Council.

The following day, Alberto Mora met directly with John Yoo himself to challenge the architecture of the legal memo the Working Group knew would not only govern military interrogations at Guantánamo and in Afghanistan, but very likely—and soon—in Iraq as well. As Mora recalled,

The principal author of the OLC Memo, Mr. Yoo glibly defended the provisions of his memo, but it was a defense of provisions that I regarded as erroneous. Asked whether the President could order the application of torture, Mr. Yoo responded, "Yes." When I questioned this, he stated that his job was to state what the law was, and also stated that my contrary view represented an expression of legal policy that perhaps the administration may wish to discuss and adopt, but was not the law. I asked: "Where can I have that discussion?" His response: "I don't know. Maybe here in the Pentagon?"[468]

A few days later, and less than a month after Mora had met with Haynes and Deputy Defense Department General Counsel Daniel Dell'Orto and threatened to circulate his memo denouncing the Rumsfeld-approved techniques, he again met with Haynes and Dell'Orto to discuss the Working Group report.

I informed them that the draft report was not a quality product. It was the product of a flawed working group process and deeply flawed OLC Memo. I believe I urged him to keep the report in draft form and not finalize it. I do recall suggesting that he should take the report, thank the Working Group leadership for its efforts, and the stick the report in a drawer and "never let it see the light of day again."

* * *

At 6:59 p.m. on Friday, March 7, 2003, an FBI agent stationed in Guantánamo sent an email to headquarters that begins, "Since I've got nothing else to do, a couple of Friday night thoughts." "I've been trying to get a handle on Detainees of interest to the FBI," says the agent. "In looking at the many lists that have been prepared on the ongoing FBI Special Projects, I've come up with 33 ISNs. Here they are with * denoting [FBI Terrorist Financing Operations Section] interest, ** [indicating] FBI lists, and other agency interest in parenthesis." One of the 33 detainees on his list, and one of eight he indicated were ongoing FBI "special projects," is ISN 760, Mohamedou Ould Slahi.

The agent asked HQ to review his list and confirm that these were indeed the FBI's priority cases, and then moved on to a second, and obviously more pressing, area of concern.

2. Given the DHS/DIA "incursion" which I believe will develop steam, I strongly believe we have to come up with a strategy that will make sense to the [Commanding General] and which does not sound like turf protection. From my perspective, there are several aspects of the strategy.

a. No real evidence that other techniques work (somebody has to do a real analysis of the 63 material and make that case but be careful. I've heard a lot of folks downplay purported DHS successes such as getting the detainee to salute but we also use very fuzzy behavioral standards such as he's talking to us/doesn't keep his head down etc).

b. Sufficiently articulated **real** *potential for a detainee to be a[n Article III] Court witness where any technique used will be at issue. While clearly this will also be at issue in the Commission cases, there is no indication that the exclusionary provisions will be as strict. (DoJ's take on the proposed Interrogation procedures and this issue will be critical.)*

c. No real exigencies which require extraordinary techniques.

*I'm sure these are not new issues, but I would like to get folks take on this. I don't like to lose and I do **not** feel completely comfortable with the arguments I've heard, especially if the new procedures get the DoJ nod. I think our strategy/argument must be sharper, and should probably include some level of collaboration with DHS/DIA. Which raises additional issues. If the new procedures are approved, DoJ and FBI OGC must also opine re: an agent's connection to a process which includes such techniques even if approved. We can't put our agents anywhere close to a problem area EVEN if DoJ says DoJ can employ. e.g. I can envision a collaborative process where Art III testimony may be relevant and where we develop a strategy where the FBI takes first crack for _____ weeks, DIA/DHS involved as analysts/monitors, Progress assessed as time goes on with DHS waiting in the wings for entry with their approved techniques if no FBI success. Does that still put FBI [Special Agents] at risk because they are knowingly part of a process which uses techniques not condoned in U.S. courts? In any event, couple thoughts. Would appreciate yours.*[469]

Rumsfeld's suspension of authorization for the Category II and Category III techniques meant that as of January 16, 2003 JTF GTMO interrogators were confined to the traditional Field Manual methods, but in the wake of the Qahtani interrogation military interrogators were regularly improvising variations on Qahtani's ritual humiliations. Around the time the FBI agent wrote this email, two of his colleagues were interviewing a detainee named Yussef Mohammed Mubarak al-Shihri. They later told the Justice Department's Inspector General that they had managed to build rapport with al-Shihri over the course of three interviews, but then, during the fourth interview,

Al-Shihri told them that "the mean ladies" came and got him from his cell in the middle of the night and interrogated him for hours. Al-Shihri said that during this interrogation he was also forced to listen to a recorded loop of the "meow mix" jingle for hours, was sprayed with perfume, and had a woman's dress draped on him. The agent told us he confronted a young female military intelligence contract interrogator whose name was unknown. She admitted to "poaching" his detainee and subjecting him to the treatment that he had alleged. The agent told us that after this incident al-Shihri became uncooperative and that the techniques employed on Al-Shihri were counterproductive.[470]

Perfume was evidently the idea of Miller's Chief Interrogator. While he was overseeing the Qahtani interrogation in December, Becker directed one of his female interrogators assigned to another detainee to purchase rose oil at the base PX and rub it on the detainee during questioning; the detainee "responded by attempting to bite the interrogator and lost his balance, fell out of his chair, and chipped his tooth," Lieutenant General Randall Schmidt and Brigadier General John Furlow reported in their 2005 "Investigation into FBI Allegations of Detainee Abuse at Guantánamo Bay, Cuba Detention Facility."[471] "The interrogator was not disciplined for rubbing perfume on a detainee since this was an authorized technique" that report concluded, citing the then-authorized Category III "mild, non-injurious physical touching." But the practice did not end when Rumsfeld rescinded approval for such techniques. A sergeant who served as a military interrogator at Guantánamo at the time told Furlow under oath that one of his female colleagues "used either perfume or Vaseline during interrogations" routinely. "She would put the lotion/perfume in her hand and then rub the detainee's hand and arms," he recalled. "She used Victoria Secret perfume so the detainees would smell like a woman."[472]

Explaining the concept of "force drift," Alberto Mora had warned, "if some force is good, [interrogators] come to believe, then the application of more force must be better"; so, too, if some religion-based gender coercion is good, more must be better. This dynamic appears to have been in play in March 2003, when a female interrogator rubbed not Victoria's Secret perfume but red ink on a detainee's arm. "She touched the detainee on the shoulder, showed him the red ink on her hand, and said, "by the way, I am menstruating," the Schmidt-Furlow report recorded. "The detainee threw himself on the floor and started banging his head."[473]

But rather than reining in his interrogators, General Miller was concentrating on winning renewed approval for the techniques that had been used to torture Qahtani. In advance of a February meeting with Deputy Defense Secretary Paul Wolfowitz—and with a draft interrogation plan for Slahi on the table—Miller had Diane Beaver write a memo to Haynes' staff insisting "We must have interrogation technique approval immediately and will speak to Mr. Wolfowitz about this. The hallmark is isolation and up to 20 hour interrogation" "We need commitment from senior leadership to let us do this mission," Beaver wrote. Wolfowitz told Miller the techniques would be approved within a week.

Almost a month later, Rumsfeld still had not acted. He had before him a draft of the Working Group's report that recommended approval of the thirty-six techniques Becker had proposed in January—twenty-six for general use, including hooding, dietary manipulation, sleep adjustment, and threat of transfer; and ten "exceptional" techniques for use with some limitations. These ten were: isolation, prolonged interrogations, forced grooming, prolonged standing, sleep deprivation, physical training, face slap/stomach slap, removal of clothing, increased anxiety by use of aversions, and waterboarding. Of these, waterboarding—which had earned red lights under domestic and international law—would require approval by "no lower than the Secretary of Defense." The draft listed three other techniques it said the Working Group lacked sufficient information to evaluate: stress positions, deprivation of light and auditory stimuli, and water immersion/wetting down.[474]

Also available to Rumsfeld were memos from the Judge Advocates General of the Army and Navy, the Deputy Air Force JAG, and the Staff Judge Advocate to the Commandant of the Marine Corps, all warning that that the Yoo memo failed to address the Uniform Code of Military Justice; that many of the techniques could place interrogators and their superiors at risk of criminal prosecution at home and abroad; that they were ineffective; that they could poison future attempts to prosecute detainees; and that they would leave U.S. servicewomen and men vulnerable to reciprocal treatment if captured.[475]

At a meeting with Rumsfeld and SOUTHCOM Commander General

James Hill on March 12, 2003, Joint Chiefs Chairman General Richard Myers echoed these warnings. An email a staffer sent to Diane Beaver afterwards reported that Myers suggested some of the techniques "could be illegal depending on how far they were used." Alarmed, Beaver wrote to Haynes office, "This email is not good news. It appears something went wrong." Hill followed up with a memo to General Myers insisting "both Geoff Miller and I believe that we need as many appropriate tools as possible," and insisted the previously-approved Category II and III techniques, including stress positions, deprivation of light and auditory stimuli, use of detainee phobias such as dogs, and "mild non-injurious physical touching" were "critical to maximizing our ability to accomplish the mission, now and in the future."[476]

A week later, Rumsfeld met with Wolfowitz, Haynes, Myers, Dalton, and Undersecretaries of Defense Stephen Cambone, Douglas Feith, and Marshall Billingslea. After the meeting, Rumsfeld announced he would authorize twenty-four of the proposed techniques, nineteen from the Army Field Manual plus dietary manipulation, environmental manipulation, sleep adjustment, and one of the techniques the Working Group had recommended for restricted use only, isolation. Myers subsequently submitted a memo formally requesting an approval memo along these lines; Billingslea countered with a memo of his own urging Rumsfeld to go further, approving the rest of these techniques in the Working Group's final report for use on a case-by-case basis with the Secretary's approval. That report, which had been selectively disseminated the previous day, retained the Yoo memo's legal architecture and endorsed thirty-five techniques, eliminating only waterboarding and the three techniques prior drafts suggested the Working Group lacked sufficient information to evaluate. Shockingly, at the direction of Daniel Dell'Orto, Haynes's deputy general counsel, the final report was withheld from the Working Group itself. "I should note that neither I, the Navy's [General Counsel] nor—to my knowledge—anyone else in the [Department of the Navy] ever received a completed version of the WG report," Mora wrote in his Statement for the Record. "It was never circulated for clearance. Over time, I would come to assume the report had never been finalized."

On April 16, 2003, Rumsfeld issued a memo to General Hill with the subject line "Counter-Resistance Techniques in the War on Terrorism" authorizing the twenty-four techniques. Four of these—incentive/removal of incentive, Pride and Ego Down, Mutt and Jeff, and isolation—required a determination of "military necessity" and advance notification to Rumsfeld personally, and came with caveats. Under Pride and Ego Down, for instance, the memo noted,

> *Caution: Article 17 of Geneva III provides, "Prisoners of war who refuse to answer may not be threatened, insulted, or exposed to any unpleasantness or disadvantageous treatment of any kind." Other nations that believe that detainees are entitled to POW protections may consider these techniques inconsistent with the provisions for Geneva. Although the provisions of Geneva are not applicable to the interrogation of unlawful enemy combatants, consideration must be given to these views prior to application of the techniques.*[477]

Likewise, for isolation,

> *Caution: The use of isolation as an interrogation technique requires detailed implementation instructions, including specific guidelines regarding the length of isolation, medical and psychological review, and approval for extensions of the length of isolation by the appropriate level in the chain of command. This technique is not known to have been generally used for interrogation purposes for longer than 30 days. Those nations that believe detainees are subject to POW protections may view the use of this technique as inconsistent with the requirements of Geneva III, Article 13 which provides that POWs must be protected against acts of intimidation; Article 14 which provides that POWs are entitled to respect for their person; Article 34 which prohibits coercion and Article 126 which ensures access and basic standards of treatment. Although the provisions of Geneva are not applicable to the interrogation of unlawful combatants, consideration should be given to these views prior to application of the technique.*

At the same time, Rumsfeld made clear that the list of twenty-four techniques was not definitive, and that other techniques would remain available to Miller's interrogators:

> *If, in your view, you require additional interrogation techniques for a particular detainee, you should provide me, via the Chairman of the Joint Chiefs of Staff, a written request describing the proposed technique, recommended safeguards, and the rationale for applying it with the identified detainee.*

* * *

The transcript of Mohamedou Ould Slahi's November 22, 2005 hearing before the Administrative Review Board at Guantánamo contains this passage:

> *Detainee: Then the FBI at GTMO Bay during the time era of General Miller, they released a list of the highest priority detainees here at GTMO Bay. It was a list of 15 people and I was, guess which number, number ONE. Then they sent a special FBI team and the leader was [redacted] and I worked with him especially for my case. He said 'you fucked up' and I was insulted because in Arabic that is a very bad word. That's like saying I have been raped or a homosexual or something. I asked why did he say that and he said because you are in a very bad situation. I did not believe him because the problem is interrogators lie and if a group of people lie, it is hard to tell who is telling the truth. But he was telling the truth on many aspects. I thought he was a truthful guy. I thought he was a decent guy. Since they are interrogators I guess it was a part of their job to lie. I thought he was just making fun of me when he said I was number ONE in the camp, but he was not lying he was telling the truth as future events would prove. He stayed with me until May 22, 2003.*
> *Presiding Officer: He stayed with you meaning he came back and interrogated you off and on?*

*Detainee: No, he stayed on this island and interrogated me on a
daily basis until May 22, 2003.*

Presiding Officer: Okay. Now I understand you.

*Detainee: His command, his boss told him I was involved in the
millennium plot and I told him I had nothing to do with the
millennium plot. They gave me a list of allegations with a lot
of suspicious answers. He wanted me to give him something
and I wouldn't give him anything because I didn't really do it,
I didn't kill anybody, I did not hijack anyone, but I did see this
dude [Ramzi Binalshibh]. I didn't know his name but I didn't
tell him that I just said I have never seen him. He said how did
you know? Then I took a polygraph and [Binalshibh] refused
to take a polygraph for many reasons. It turns out he is very
contradictory and he lies. They said that to me themselves.
They said my credibility is high because I took the polygraph.
This guy was also subjected to torture because I do my own
investigations too.*

Presiding officer: [Ramzi] was?

*Detainee: Yes, I asked the Yemenis, man, [Ramzi] said I sent him to
Afghanistan. I knew him I seen him but I didn't send him, why
did he say so. They said man you believe everything that they
tell you (this was a Yemeni guy who was captured with Ramzi).
He said, "The interrogators lie" and I said "no, they don't lie"
I have seen him but I did not send him to Afghanistan. They
said you forgot about something, that [Ramzi] was tortured.
We would hear his cries every night, we would hear his moans
every night.*

"Ramzi" is Ramzi Binalshibh, who had roomed with American
Airlines Flight 11 hijacker-pilot Mohamed Atta in Germany and had been
the subject of an international manhunt after 9/11 for his alleged role in
coordinating the "Hamburg cell." On the first anniversary of the attacks,
and just over a month after Slahi arrived in Guantánamo, via Bagram,
from his eight and a half-month interrogation in Jordan, Binalshibh was

captured with several other Al Qaeda suspects in a shootout in a suburb of Karachi. Five days after that raid, the *Los Angeles Times* reported that the United States was seeking to extradite him from Pakistan to the U.S. for a criminal trial, pledging to seek the death penalty. In fact, he was already in the hands of CIA agents, who had him shackled to the ceiling and were bombarding him with blaring music in a facility in Afghanistan, likely the "Dark Prison"; the following day the *Times* learned the U.S. authorities had "whisked" the men elsewhere "for interrogation at a secret location." That location was Morocco. Binalshibh was interrogated at the same facility near Rabat where Binyam Mohamed was then being tortured, remaining there through the fall and winter. Then, in March, 2003, days after Khalid Sheikh Mohammed was apprehended, Binalshibh was bundled and shipped to the CIA black site in Poland where Dr. James Mitchell was orchestrating Mohammed's enhanced interrogation, with its 183 episodes of simulated drowning.[478]

"Anyway," Slahi told the Administrative Review Board, "that is none of my business." He went on:

> *FBI said that I was playing games with them. Then on 22 May, 2003, [redacted], he said this was our last session, he told me that I was not going to enjoy the time to come. I am advising you to just tell the truth. I told him I don't care and he said goodbye, good friend. A couple of days later the new interrogators led by a female name [redacted], they called her [redacted], a very beautiful lady and decent lady, came to me as a task force it was Simmons from the FBI and another weird guy, I think he was CIA or something but he was very young. They said we will give you an opportunity to tell the truth or we will leave you in jail forever. I said, "Whatever you want to do, do it." "Why did you put me in jail what did I do?" We have proof and you just got to tell us. I said, "I haven't done anything, I told you everything. I am tired." [Redacted] and an army guy, [redacted], that's his real name, I found out his real name. Someone accidentally called his name and I*

remember he was the First Sgt. I didn't hate him but he was a
very hateful guy. Anyway she assigned him to me [redacted].
A couple of days later, [redacted], I don't know if that was her
real name but I heard them call her that. It was [redacted] who
was in charge. They assigned another guy named [redacted] or
[redacted], he was a special guy and we would never see his
face.

Presiding Officer: *When you said covered, I am not sure what you*
mean?

Detainee: *You know like in Saudi Arabia, how the women are*
covered.

Presiding Officer: *With a veil type thing, were there openings for his*
eyes?

Detainee: *He did have openings for his eyes. He also had gloves, OJ*
Simpson gloves on his hands. He was assigned to this special
mission. They started to talk to me and said, "look we are not
FBI and we need you to admit to the crime we have here.
That you were involved with the 11 September attack and
that you were involved in the millennium plot." I said "no I
*wasn't." They said okay, forget about it. Around June 18*th *2003,*
I was taken from Mike Block and put in India Block for total
isolation. They took all of my stuff from me. I complained to
[redacted] because I thought she was a decent lady. I could not
bear sleeping on the metal because of my back and you never
know how much pain I could take. I could end up dead or
something. She said, 'no, you are not going to die.' They tried
to give me painkillers and I refused them out of protest. How
could you give me a painkiller? Just give me something to sleep
on and I will be all right. They took me to the doctor here, a
Navy doctor, and he was a good guy. I told him that I am in a
very bad situation and he said okay I am going to recommend
that they give you some items, because you have a very serious
condition of Sciatic Nerve. But I cannot promise you because

those people decide not me. I would like for you to check my medical records.

At this point in the hearing, according to a bold-faced aside in the transcript, something remarkable happened:

During this portion of the ARB, the recording equipment began to malfunction. This malfunction has caused the remainder of tape 3 of 4 tapes from clicks 3487 to 4479 to become distorted. The Detainee discussed how he was tortured while here at GTMO by several individuals. The recording machine was swapped out with a new one and we finished out the session. The following is the board's recollection of the 1000 click malfunction:

The Detainee was explaining his medical treatment and noticed a Board Member passing a note to the Presiding Officer. The Detainee inquired as to why the Board Member was passing a note. The Presiding Officer told the Detainee the Board Member had a question regarding the Detainee's medical treatment. The Board Member asked the Detainee to summarize his medical treatment and the treatment he received at the hands of his interrogators. The Detainee stated the medical treatment he received was "good," however he decided to continue to go into great detail regarding the abuse he received from the hands of his interrogators.

The Detainee began discussing the alleged abuse he received from a female interrogator known to him as [redacted]. The Detainee attempted to explain to the Board [redacted's] actions but he became distraught and visibly upset. He explained that he was sexually harassed and although he does like women he did not like what [redacted] had done to him. The Presiding Officer noticed the Detainee was upset and told him he was not required to tell the story. The Detainee was very appreciative and elected not to elaborate on the alleged abuse from [redacted]. The Detainee gave detailed information regarding the alleged

abuse from [redacted] and [redacted]. The Detainee stated that [redacted] and [redacted] entered a room with their faces covered and began beating him. They beat him so badly that [redacted] became upset. [Redacted] did not like the treatment the Detainee was receiving and started to sympathize with him. According to the Detainee, [redacted] was crying and telling [redacted] and [redacted] to stop beating him. The Detainee wanted to show the Board his scars and location of injuries, but the board declined the viewing. The Board agrees that this is a fair recap of the distorted portion of the tape.[479]

The Justice Department's 2008 investigation of the FBI's role in abusive interrogations confirmed Slahi's account that FBI agents turned him over to Guantánamo's military interrogators in March, 2003. A military Memo for the Record dated March 23, 2003 blamed the FBI for the move. "FBI Special Agents have built strong rapport with [Slahi], but have generally not used that rapport to gain intelligence," the memo recorded. "While rapport is normally used as a means by which to gain intelligence, it seems as though FBI agents have not been willing to offend detainee or push him on matters on which he is uncomfortable because of the desire to maintain rapport."[480] The DoJ report also corroborated Slahi's account of being interviewed in June, after the turnover, by an interrogator who identified herself to him as FBI Agent "Samantha Martin"—but who was in fact an Army Sergeant on the DIA's GTMO "Special Projects Team." "Dressing casually and telling detainees they were FBI agents" turned out to be a popular ruse during 2003, and not only for military interrogators. The FBI's supervising agent in Guantánamo that summer reported it was also "common practice for CIA agents to say they were FBI so as not to reveal their presence" in the facility.[481]

Having military and CIA interrogators pose as FBI agents—a practice obviously intended to exploit the agency's reputation for non-abusive interrogation—threatened months of efforts by the agency to keep its personnel clear of the military's "fun and games." When one of its agents discovered later that year that Slahi had been interrogated in June by a counterfeit agent and that this interrogator continued to play this role throughout the Special Interrogation that was to follow, the agent flagged this episode in particular in relaying accounts of military abuses up the chain of command. "These tactics produced no intelligence of a threat neutralization nature to date and CITF believes that techniques have destroyed any chance of prosecuting this detainee," the message reported, and went on to warn, "If this detainee is ever released or his story made public in any way, DoD interrogators will not be held accountable because these torture techniques were done [by] the 'FBI' interrogators. The FBI will [be] left holding the bag before the public."[482]

Slahi's Special Interrogation, in fact, would feature a series of increasingly brutal deceptions. The interrogation plan was revised in the weeks following Rumsfeld's second approval memo, and on July 1 General Miller signed a request for "Special Projects Status" for Slahi and a ninety-day interrogation to include "techniques not specified in the Secretary of Defense guidance document." In Miller's plan, the interrogation was to begin by reenacting a favorite savagery of the Argentine military junta: after three to five days of questioning in Camp Delta, a team of MPs in full riot gear would force him from his cell, escort him past menacing dogs, and bundle him onto a helicopter, where he would be flown out over the ocean and threatened with death or rendition to another middle eastern dungeon. He would then be returned to the island and delivered to the recently-completed Camp Echo solitary confinement facilities just outside Camp Delta, where he would be subjected to "drastic changes in his environment," "shackled to the floor and left in the room for up to four hours while sound is playing continually," and interrogated for sixteen hours followed by four hours of sleep for several days.[483]

Miller's interrogators did not wait for Rumsfeld's approval to launch Slahi's Special Interrogation. The Senate Armed Services Committee reviewed military memos from July 2003 and reported,

The memoranda indicated that, on several occasions from July 8 through July 17, Slahi was interrogated by a masked interrogator called "Mr. X." On July 8, 2003, Slahi was interrogated by Mr. X

and "exposed to variable lighting patterns and rock music, to the tune of Drowning Pool's 'Let the Bodies Hit [the] Floor.'" On July 10, 2003, Slahi was placed in an interrogation room handcuffed and standing while the air conditioning was turned off until the room became "quite warm." The next day, Slahi was brought into the interrogation booth and again remained standing and handcuffed while the air conditioning was again turned off. After allowing Slahi to sit, the interrogator later "took [Slahi's] chair and left him standing for several hours." According to the memo, Slahi was "visibly uncomfortable and showed signs of fatigue. This was 4th day of long duration interrogations.

On July 17, 2003, the masked interrogator told Slahi about a dream he had had where he saw "four detainees that were chained together at the feet. They dug a hole that was six feet long, six feet deep, and four feet wide. Then he observed the detainees throw a plain, unpainted, pine casket with the number 760 [Slahi's internment serial number (ISN)] painted on it in orange on the ground.[484]

"The masked interrogator told the detainee that his dream meant that he was never going to leave GTMO unless he started to talk, that he would indeed die here from old age and be buried on "Christian... sovereign American soil," the military's own investigators found in 2005. "Mr. X" followed this two days later by telling Slahi "that his family was 'incarcerated.'" Over the next two weeks, as Miller's request was forwarded, with recommendations for approval, from Hill to Billingslea to Wolfowitz, interrogators denied Slahi sleep for extended stretches by bombarding him with strobe lights and music and by placing him in the "freezer," where guards doused him with ice and cold water to keep him awake.[485] Then, on August 1st or 2nd, a "messenger" visited Slahi. According to an August 2, 2003 memorandum for the record,

That message was simple: Interrogator's colleagues are sick of hearing the same lies over and over and are seriously considering washing their hands of him. Once they do so, he will disappear and never

be heard from again. Interrogator assured detainee again to use his imagination to this of the worst possible scenario he could end up in. He told Detainee that beatings and physical pain are not the worst thing in the world. After all, after being beaten for a while, humans tend to disconnect the mind from the body and make it through. However, there are worse things than physical pain. Interrogator assured Detainee that, eventually, he will talk, because everyone does. But until then, he will very soon disappear down a very dark hole. His very existence will become erased. His electronic files will be deleted from the computer, his files will be packed up and filed away, and his existence will be forgotten by all. No one will know what happened to him and, eventually, no one will care.[486]

On August 2, 2003, Slahi received another visitor, this time Miller's ICE chief posing as "Captain Collins," a Naval Captain dispatched directly from the White House. As the Schmidt-Furlow report recorded,

["Captain Collins"] indicated he was from the White House in an effort to convince the subject of the second special interrogation that he needed to cooperate with his interrogators. The Special Team Chief presented a letter to the subject of the second special interrogation, which indicated that because of the subject of the second special interrogation's lack of cooperation, U.S. authorities in conjunction with authorities from the country of origin of the subject of the second Special Interrogation Plan would interrogate the mother of the subject of the second Special Interrogation Plan. The letter further indicated that if his mother was uncooperative she would be detained and transferred to U.S. custody at GTMO for long term detention.[487]

That letter, the Senate Armed Services Committee found, stressed that Slahi's mother would become the only female to be detained in "this previously all-male prison environment."[488]

On August 7, 2003, Slahi asked to see "Captain Collins" again. Military interrogators recorded in a memo for the record the following day that they "understood that detainee had made an important decision and that the interrogator was anxious to hear what Detainee had to say." Slahi, the memo reported, "was not willing to continue to protect others to the detriment of himself and his family."[489] Evidently not satisfied, Rumsfeld approved the Special Interrogation Plan for Slahi five days later, on August 13, 2003, with one change: instead of a helicopter, Slahi would be ferried off the island on a boat. Becker himself later told the FBI's on-site supervisor that "Miller had decided that [the helicopter] was too difficult logistically to pull off, and that too many people on the base would have to know about it to get this done."[490]

By August 21, 2003, a construction crew was preparing a Camp Echo cell for Slahi, sealing it on the inside to "prevent light from shining" in and draping a tarp over the exterior to "prevent him from making visual contact with guards."[491] Then, on August 24, 2003, Slahi was fitted with blackout goggles, shackled, and taken aboard a boat that sailed out into Guantánamo Bay, where, as the 2005 Church report described it, "he was permitted to hear pre-planned deceptive conversations among other passengers."[492] The *Wall Street Journal* reported in 2007 that the boat trip "apparently led Mr. Slahi to think he was being killed and, in fear, he urinated in his pants."[493]

Slahi recounted the experience when recording resumed in his November 22, 2005 Administrative Review Board hearing:

> *Presiding Officer: . . . . Okay, could you take us from [before the 24ᵗʰ] because I got the August 2003 stuff between there, so if you could go to August 24ᵗʰ because you said that was a big day. Take us from there to this secret place so that we can move on a little bit.*
>
> *Detainee: Okay, exactly, I was taken by those two guys and the trip took about an hour, it was in a boat. Then they took me to a place and I was moaning and I recognized a voice and he was talking to two Arab guys, one claiming to be Egyptian and one claiming to be Jordanian. He was telling them how grateful he is that they are helping him. They told him in Arabic that they were there to torture me and they could not take me to*

Jordan or Egypt or something like that. Then they were telling him look into this. Then they gave me to the Arabic team and they took me to a place for about an hour and they took me to a place I don't know. They were hitting me all over (Detainee demonstrated the blows). They put ice in my shirt until it would melt. Then I arrived at that place and they gave me back to (redacted) when I arrived at the place and I was there and they brought in a doctor, who was not a regular doctor he was part of the team. He was cursing me and telling me very bad things. He gave me a lot of medication to make me sleep and I had special guards with masks so I couldn't see anybody. For like two or three weeks I was unconscious and after that I decided it is not worth it. Because they said to me either I am going to talk or they will continue to do this. I said I am going to tell them everything they wanted. I told them while I was in Canada, I was planning for a terrorist attack but I couldn't get it straight with Ressam because he was not talking back then and he was cooperating completely with the FBI, and of course he said he didn't know me because he didn't know me. But I told them I was on my own trying to do things and they said write it down and I wrote it and I signed it. I brought a lot of people, innocent people with me because I got to make a story that makes sense. They thought my story was wrong so they put me on a polygraph and I passed it. Then they wanted everything, they wanted me to tell them that I would tell them. I just wanted to get some peace. If nobody understands then they don't understand because I am the one who suffered with no food, the guards beat me, it was a very bad place.[494]

Slahi's "special interrogation" continued through September and October despite the fact, as Miller reported repeatedly in his weekly wrap-ups during that period, that he "continues to be cooperative." He was also beginning to exhibit some disturbing symptoms. On October 17, 2003, a JTF GTMO interrogator emailed Lieutenant Colonel Diane Zierhoffer, one of the BSCT psychologists, to report, "Slahi told me he is 'hearing voices' now.... He is worried as he knows this is not normal.... Is this something that happens to people who have little external stimulus such as daylight, human interaction, etc???? Seems a little creepy." Zierhoffer wrote back, "sensory deprivation can cause hallucinations, usually visual rather than auditory, but you never know.... In the dark you create things out of what little you have."[495]

* * *

On June 26, 2003, as JTF-GTMO interrogators were finalizing Slahi's "Special Interrogation Plan" for Rumsfeld's approval, President Bush issued the statement that CIA Inspector General John Helgerson would quote from in his Special Report the following year:

Today, on the United Nations International Day in Support of Victims of Torture, the United States declares its strong solidarity with torture victims across the world. Torture anywhere is an affront to human dignity everywhere. We are committed to building a world where human rights are respected and protected by the rule of law.

Freedom from torture is an inalienable human right. The Convention Against Torture and Other Cruel, Inhuman or Degrading Treatment, ratified by the United States and more than 130 other countries since 1984, forbids governments from deliberately inflicting severe physical or mental pain or suffering on those within their custody or control. Yet torture continues to be practiced around the world by rogue regimes whose cruel methods match their determination to crush the human spirit. Beating, burning, rape, and electric shock are some of the grisly tools such regimes use to terrorize their own citizens. These despicable crimes cannot be tolerated by a world committed to justice.

Notorious human rights abusers, including, among others, Burma, Cuba, North Korea, Iran, and Zimbabwe, have long sought to shield their abuses from the eyes of the world by staging elaborate deceptions and denying access to international human rights monitors. With Iraq's liberation, the world is only now learning the enormity of the dictator's three decades of victimization of the Iraqi people. Across the country, evidence of Baathist atrocities is mounting, including scores of mass graves containing the remains of thousands of men, women, and children and torture chambers hidden inside palaces and ministries. The most compelling evidence of all lies in the stories told by torture survivors, who are recounting a vast array of sadistic acts perpetrated against the innocent. Their testimony reminds us of their great courage in outlasting one of history's most brutal regimes, and it reminds us that similar cruelties are taking place behind the closed doors of other prison states.

The United States is committed to the world-wide elimination of torture and we are leading this fight by example. I call on all governments to join with the United States and the community of law-abiding nations in prohibiting, investigating, and prosecuting all acts of torture and in undertaking to prevent other cruel and unusual punishment. I call on all nations to speak out against torture in all its forms and to make ending torture an essential part of their diplomacy. I further urge governments to join America and others in supporting torture victims' treatment centers, contributing to the UN Fund for the Victims of Torture, and supporting the efforts of non-governmental organizations to end torture and assist its victims.[496]

The statement came amid an increasingly pointed exchange of letters between the Pentagon and Senator Patrick Leahy about American adherence to CAT. In April, as reports continued to circulate that detainees in U.S. custody were being subjected to "stress and duress" techniques that included shackling in stress positions, food and sleep deprivation, and beatings, Jim Haynes had written Ken Roth, Executive Director of Human Rights Watch, to say that "United States policy condemns and prohibits torture." "When questioning enemy combatants, U.S. personnel are required to follow this policy and applicable laws prohibiting torture," Haynes declared. Moreover, "If the war on terrorists of global reach requires transfer of enemy combatants to other countries for continued detention on our behalf, U.S. government instructions are to seek and obtain appropriate assurances that such combatants are not tortured."[497]

Leahy, as the ranking Democrat on the Senate Judiciary Committee, wanted to know more about how the administration viewed the applicable laws. In June, he made the first of several formal requests for copies of the secret OLC memos, and posed six specific questions to National Security Advisor Condoleezza Rice:

> First, Mr. Haynes' letter states that when questioning enemy combatants, U.S. personnel are required to follow "applicable laws prohibiting torture." What are those laws? Given that the United States has ratified the Convention Against Torture and Other Forms of Cruel, Inhuman or Degrading Treatment or Punishment (CAT), is this Convention one of those laws, and does it bind U.S. personnel both inside and outside the United States?
>
> Second, does the Administration accept that the United States has a specific obligation under CAT not to engage in cruel, inhuman and degrading treatment?
>
> Third, when the United States ratified the CAT, it entered a reservation regarding its prohibition on cruel, inhuman and degrading treatment, stating that it interprets this terms to mean "the cruel, unusual and inhumane treatment or punishment prohibited by the 5th, 8th, and/or 14th amendments to the Constitution." Are all U.S. interrogations of enemy combatants conducted in a manner consistent with this reservation?
>
> Fourth, in its annual country Reports on Human Rights Practices, the State Department has repeatedly condemned many of the same "stress and duress" interrogation techniques that U.S. personnel are alleged to have used in Afghanistan. Can you confirm that the United States is not employing the specific methods of interrogation that the State Department has condemned in countries such as Egypt, Iran, Eritrea, Libya, Jordan and Burma?
>
> Fifth, the Defense Department acknowledged in March that it was investigating the deaths from blunt force injury of two detainees

who were held at Bagram air base in Afghanistan. What is the status of that investigation and when do you expect it to be completed? Has the Defense Department or the CIA investigated any other allegations of torture or mistreatment of detainees, and if so, with what result? What steps would be taken if any U.S. personnel were found to have engaged in unlawful conduct?

Finally, Mr. Haynes' letter offers a welcome clarification that when detainees are transferred to other countries, "U.S. government instructions are to seek and obtain appropriate assurances that such enemy combatants are not tortured." How does the Administration follow up to determine if these pledges of humane treatment are honored in practice, particularly when the governments in question are known to practice torture?[498]

Leahy signed the letter with a handwritten note: "Condi – I want to make sure we are on the right moral plane if an American is held abroad. Pat."

Rice kicked Leahy's letter back to Haynes to answer, and on June 25, 2003, the day before the President's Torture Day statement, Haynes wrote Leahy that "we can assure you that it is the policy of the United States to comply with all of its legal obligations in its treatment of detainees, and in particular with legal obligations prohibiting torture." Those obligations, Haynes conceded disingenuously, included "undertak[ing] to prevent other acts of cruel, inhuman, or degrading treatment or punishment," as defined by the "cruel and unusual" standard incorporating 5th, 8th, and 14th Amendment protections. Haynes also insisted that the U.S. was in full compliance with CAT's prohibitions on renditions to torture, reiterating that the U.S. secured assurances in advance of renditions and "would take steps to investigate credible allegations of torture and take appropriate action if there were reason to believe that those assurances were not being honored."[499]

On September 9, 2003—days after Slahi had been subjected to the Rumsfeld-approved mock rendition and threatened execution—Leahy wrote back to Haynes welcoming his "clear statement" of U.S. compliance with CAT and its obligations regarding "cruel, unusual, and degrading treatment."

"This statement of policy rules out the use of many of the "stress and duress" interrogation techniques that have been alleged in press reports over the last several months," Leahy observed pointedly. "At the same time," he noted, "the ultimate credibility of this policy will depend on its implementation by U.S. personnel around the world." "In that spirit," he continued,

> I would appreciate it if you could clarify how the administration's policy to comply with the CAT is communicated to those personnel directly involved in detention and interrogation? As you note in your letter, the U.S. obligation under Article 16 of CAT is to "undertake... to prevent" cruel, inhuman or degrading treatment or punishment. What is the administration doing to prevent violations? Have any recent directives, regulations or general orders been issued to implement the policy your June 25 letter describes? If so, I would appreciate receiving a copy.
>
> I understand that interrogations conducted by the U.S. military are governed at least in part by Field Manual 34-52, which prohibits "the use of force, mental torture, threats, insults, or exposure to unpleasant and inhumane treatment of any kind." This field manual rightly stresses that "the use of force is a poor technique, as it yields unreliable results, may damage subsequent collection efforts, and can induce the source to say whatever he things the interrogator wants to hear." Are there further guidelines that in any way add to, define, or limit the prohibitions contained in this field manual? What mechanisms exist for ensuring compliance with these guidelines?
>
> Most important, I hope you can assure me that interrogators working for other agencies, including the CIA, operate from the same guidelines as the Department of Defense. If CIA or other interrogation guidelines in use by any person working for or on behalf of the U.S. government differ, could you clarify how, and why?

As for renditions, wrote Leahy,

I remain concerned...that mere assurances from countries that are known to practice torture systematically are not sufficient. While you state that the United States would follow up on any credible information that such detainees have been mistreated, how would such information emerge if no outsiders have access to these detainees? Has the administration considered seeking assurances that an organization such as the International Committee of the Red Cross have access to detainees after they have been turned over? If not, I urge you to do so.[500]

* * *

Two weeks, later, a Boeing 737 with no tail markings retrieved alleged 9/11 financier Mustafa al-Hawsawi from the Salt Pit prison and took off from Kabul for Szymany, Poland. After collecting Khalid Sheikh Mohammed, Abu Zubaydah, Abd al-Rahim al-Nashiri, and Ramzi Binalshibh and delivering Mohammed to a new black site in Bucharest, Romania, the CIA-leased aircraft made a stop in Morocco, taking off from Rabat at 8:10 p.m. on September 23, 2003 and arriving in Guantánamo before dawn the following morning. As Slahi was telling his interrogators in Camp Echo what they wanted to hear, Binalshibh, al-Nashiri, Zubaydah, and al-Hawsawi were installed in a new, secret facility outside Camp Delta dubbed "Strawberry Fields."[501]

Days later—and almost a year to the day after CIA attorney Jonathan Fredman visited Guantánamo and counseled Becker, Diane Beaver, and others to move selected detainees "away from the attention of" the ICRC—a Red Cross delegation carried out an official inspection of detention facilities on the base. By then, Fredman's advice had been incorporated into Camp Delta Standard Operating Procedures:

17-4. Levels of Visitation

All detainees will have a level of ICRC contact designated for them. These different levels are as follows:

a. *No Access. No contact of any kind with the ICRC. This includes the delivery of ICRC mail.*

b. *Restricted: ICRC is allowed to ask the detainee about health and welfare only. No prolonged questions.*

c. *Unrestricted: ICRC is allowed full access to talk to the detainee.*

d. *Visual: Access is restricted to visual inspection of the detainee's physical condition. No form of communication is permitted. No delivery of ICRC mail.*[502]

In flagrant violation of international law, which guarantees the Red Cross access to all POWs and civilians interned as a result of armed conflict, the presence of Guantánamo's four newest arrivals was not even disclosed to ICRC delegates during their October 2003 visit. Abu Zubaydah, Binalshibh, al-Nashiri, and al-Hawsawi remained as secret detainees on the island for seven months, and then, on March 27, 2004, were abruptly transferred back to CIA black sites—just as the Supreme Court was preparing to hear *Rasul v. Bush*, the case in which the court affirmed that Guantánamo detainees are entitled to file habeas corpus petitions.

The ICRC was, however, informed that four other detainees were "off limits" to the delegation "due to military necessity": Slahi, Abdullah Tabarak, Abdurahman Khadr, and Moazzam Begg. At a contentious one hour meeting with Miller at the end of the visit on October 9, 2003, ICRC Team Leader Vincent Cassard told the General,

[T]he ICRC does not feel bound by the previous SOP that was created between JTF and a previous ICRC team. MG Miller asked Mr. Cassard to point out the part(s) of the SOP they disagreed with. [ICRC team member Christophe] Girod responded by stating that the ICRC has their own SOP that they follow worldwide, which grants them unrestricted access to all areas and to all detainees. The ICRC acknowledged the JTF SOP, they will live with it but do not like it.[503]

During the meeting, Cassard warned Miller about the impact interrogations were having on the mental health of detainees, challenging in particular the "attempt to control the detainees through use of isolation" and "psychological pressure and…coercion." Miller insisted that detainees were being treated humanely; he insisted that 85 percent of Camp Delta detainees "get privileges above and beyond basic [Geneva Conventions] requirements, adding sarcastically, "Does the ICRC object to these additional privileges?" Cassard pressed ahead:

> *Mr. Cassard stated that the ICRC has a serious concern with the treatment of the Koran in the camps, particularly in August. Specifically, an incident of mishandling of the Koran. The ICRC heard from detainees that the MPs are mishandling the Koran. MG Miller responded by informing the ICRC that he conducted a complete investigation into that incident and he found that it was an accidental incident. MG Miller explained that cell searches were being conducted and an MP, while lifting up a mattress during a cell search, accidentally bumped the surgical mask that was holding the Koran. The Koran fell to the floor of the cell as a result of this accident. MG Miller continued by stating that the detainees were trying to use this incident to create disturbances throughout the camp. This was during a time when new MPs had just arrived at GTMO. Over 1200 new MPs arrived to GTMO during this time period. MG Miller emphasized that this was an accident and that JTF has the utmost respect for religion and the Koran. Mr. Cassard stated that he was pleased that such a thorough investigation was conducted. However, the ICRC takes the allegation very seriously and 20 detainees have informed the ICRC that as punishment for the disturbances they have been shaved. MG Miller stated that detainees were shaved only for hygienic purposes by a qualified barber. The approval to shave a detainee comes from the JDOG commander and is never done as a punishment.[504]*

Miller also denied that interrogators were using medical files to gain information to develop interrogation plans—a breach of confidentiality between a physician and a patient, Cassard insisted. When the general claimed that "interrogators do not have access to detainee medical files, only medical personnel may use the medical files of detainees" and told the ICRC to "confirm their facts," Cassard "raised a concern that MG Miller was not taking the discussion seriously." Finally, Miller lied outright to the delegation about the nature of Slahi's incarceration in Camp Echo and the reasons he was off limits to the ICRC:

> *Mr. Cassard stated that the ICRC was shocked to see that Camp Echo had expanded. The ICRC believes that Camp Echo is extremely harsh and has very strict interrogations. MG Miller explained that Camp Echo was built to hold detainees that are awaiting the commissions process. Camp Echo is an appropriate facility that allows detainees to have private conversations with their attorneys. Also that there are currently very few detainees in Camp Echo and they are there for serious assaults against MPs.*

The Red Cross knew nothing, of course, of Miller's "special projects" or Rumsfeld's approval memos or the outlandish legal contortions of Diane Beaver and John Yoo. Neither did another visitor who arrived in Guantánamo a few weeks after the ICRC team's departure.

Lieutenant Colonel Stuart Couch, a former Marine pilot turned Navy prosecutor, had retired from active service in 1999 for private legal practice, but returned to the military following the 9/11 attacks—in which his close friend Michael Horrocks was killed when the plane he was piloting was hijacked and crashed into the World Trade Center's south tower—to serve as a prosecutor for the Guantánamo Military Commissions. "I did that to get a crack at the guys who attacked the United States," he explained to *Wall Street Journal* reporter Jess Bravin in 2007. He had reported to the Commission's Crystal City, Virginia offices in August 2003 and was happy to find among those he was assigned to prosecute Mohamedou Ould Slahi, an alleged 9/11 recruiter. "You got one of the most important cases of all," his colleagues congratulated him.

When Lieutenant Colonel Couch landed in Guantánamo for the first time two months later, he was given a tour of the offices and future courtroom of the military commissions, and then reported to Camp Delta's interrogation rooms, where he was to observe his first interrogation. "I was going to sit in and watch the interrogation of one of the [other] cases that I was working on," he told an interviewer in 2007.[505]

> *I was going to watch him through a two-way mirror, just to kind of get an idea of what his demeanor was like. And it was while I was waiting for that—for the detainee to be brought over from his cell that I heard this really loud—you know, best way to describe it, "head-banger" you know, hardcore rock and roll being played— Metallica-type rock music, just down the hall. And so I came out of the booth were I was, and I looked down the hall. And I heard this, you know, head-banger music blaring out. And I could see what appeared to be like strobe light coming out of the doorway. And so I walked down the hallway and the door was open. And I turned around and I looked inside. And I saw a detainee sitting on the floor. He was in the orange jumpsuit. He was shackled. His hands were shackled, his feet were shackled, and from what I could see, his hands were next to the floor. So I'm assuming it was shackled to the floor. And the room was blacked out with the exception of the strobe light. And he was just—he was rocking back and forth. And I could see that he was praying; his lips were moving. And about that time these two civilian guys, you know, immediately got in the doorway and asked me, "Who are you? What do you want?" And I said I'm Lieutenant Colonel Couch, and you gotta—what's going on here? Turn that stuff down." And I was just so shocked by what I was seeing that, you know, I was having a hard time sort of registering. And they stepped out of the door and pulled the door behind them. And then they just said, you know, "Just move along," or words to that effect. And so I went back to the booth and there was a—there was an Air Force attorney that was accompanying me, giving me the tour. And I just said. "Did you see that?" And he goes, "Well, yeah." And I said, "You know, I got a problem with that." And he goes, "Well, that's approved."[506]*

Couch's experience was hardly unusual. Emails from FBI agents who worked in Guantánamo in 2002 and 2003 recount several such incidents: "I was situated in the observation booth in between two interview rooms, observing an interview," one begins.

> *The booth was quite crowded because there were several individuals present who were observing an "interview" in the room on the other side of the booth. In that room, the detainee was seated in a chair and was secured in the same method as I'd seen for all of the other detainees, shackled at his feet so that he could not leave the room. However, there wasn't much talking going on, because the lights had been turned off and a strobe light was flickering on and off, and loud rock music was being played. I estimate this went on for 30 to 60 minutes. I was told by quite a few FBI personnel that tactics such as this were quite common there at the time.*[507]

Another reports a similar scene, with a strange variation:

> *Following a detainee interview exact date unknown, while leaving the interview building at Camp Delta at approximately 8:30 p.m. or later, I heard and observed in the hallway loud music and flashes of light. I walked from the hallway into the open door of a monitoring room to see what was going on. From the monitoring room, I looked inside the adjacent interview room. At that time I saw another detainee sitting on the floor of the interview room with an Israeli flag draped around him, loud music being played and a strobe light flashing. I left the monitoring room immediately after seeing this activity. I did not see any other persons inside the interview room with the Israeli flag draped detainee, but suspect that this was a practice used by the DoD DHS since the only other persons inside the hallway near this particular interview room were dressed in green military fatigues, similar to the ones worn by DoD DHS and the DoD MP Uniformed Reservists.*[508]

"Is yelling, loud music, and strobe lights environmental manipulation?"

asks an undated military memo entitled "Historic Look at Inappropriate Techniques Used at GTMO." That document, which is still secret but which was described by the Senate Armed Services Committee in its 2008 report, reviewed interrogation practices under General Miller in Guantánamo and found it was "clear" that interrogators were routinely using "several if not all of the techniques that require SECDEF notification."[509] A third FBI account from the time vividly illustrates what Miller's interrogators believed could be done within the parameters of Rumsfeld's vaguely-defined temperature and environmental manipulation:

On a couple of occasions, I entered interview rooms to find a detainee chained hand and foot in a fetal position to the floor with no chair and no water. Most times they had urinated or defecated on themselves and had been left there for 18–24 hours or more. On one occasion, the air conditioning had been turned down so far and the temperature was so cold in the room, that the barefooted detainee was shaking with cold. When I asked the MP's what was going on, I was told that interrogations from the day prior had ordered this treatment, and the detainee was not to be moved. On another occasion, the A/C had been turned off, making the temperature in the unventilated room probably well over 100 degrees. The detainee was almost unconscious on the floor, with a pile of hair next to him. He had apparently been literally pulling his own hair out throughout the night. On another occasion, not only was the temperature unbearably hot but extremely loud rap music was being played in the room, and had been since the day before with the detainee chained hand and foot in the fetal position on the tile floor.[510]

By the summer of 2003 it was clear just how flexible an instrument even the revised list of approved techniques was meant to be. In Rumsfeld's April 16, 2003 memo, "sleep adjustment" is defined as "adjusting the sleeping times of the detainee (e.g., reversing sleep cycles from night to day.) This technique is NOT sleep deprivation." But when does "adjustment" become "deprivation"? On June 2, 2003, SOUTHCOM's General Hill issued clarifying instructions: interrogators were barred from keeping detainees awake for more than sixteen hours or allowing a detainee to rest briefly and then repeatedly awakening him, not to exceed four days in succession."[511] But an FBI agent who arrived in Guantánamo just after these guidelines were issued found himself in a command staff meeting with General Miller and GTMO department heads at which a new strategy, dubbed "Operation Sandman," was unveiled. An August 3, 2003 email from Maj. James Rogers, then Operations Officer for GTMO's Intelligence Control Element, described the "Sandman" scheme this way: interrogating a detainee for fifteen hours, letting him rest for five hours in his cell, and then having him transferred to a new cell every half hour for the rest of the twenty-four-hour cycle—at which point, he reported, "the fun begins again." By the fall, "non-cooperative" detainees camp-wide were being assigned to the "frequent flyer program," the duration of which was determined not by Hill's guidelines but by the "cooperativeness of the detainee."[512]

Indeed, by the time Lieutenant Colonel Couch arrived in Guantánamo, it was clear inside the "The Battle Lab" that the rebellion that led to the rescission of Rumsfeld's December 2002 memo had failed: FBI agents were avoiding certain interview trailers completely because the military's interrogations were so harsh and obtrusive, and in October 2003, the Criminal Investigative Task Force once again ordered CITF agents to stand clear of abusive interrogations. "[P]hysical torture, corporal punishment, and mental torture are not acceptable interrogation tactics and are not allowed under any circumstances," the memo read.

When CITF personnel are conducting a joint interrogation with another U.S. government organization, and a member of that other organization employs tactics that are, or appear to the investigator to be, inhumane or cruel and unusual, the CITF personnel will immediately disengage from the interrogation, report the incident to their CITF chain of command, and document the incident in a memorandum for record.[513]

Couch, who as a Marine pilot had been through SERE training, told a *Spiegel* reporter in 2008 he understood immediately what he was seeing in the interrogation room. "I was looking at the treatment of a prisoner-of-war in enemy detention. It resembled the abuse I had been trained to resist if captured"—abuse rogue nations use in violation of the Geneva Conventions, his SERE instructors had explained. He returned to the military commissions office in Virginia, but the incident "started keeping me up at night," he would later say. "I couldn't stop thinking about it." He wondered if he, too, should just stand clear. Barred from recounting his experience to family and friends, he sought the advice of a senior judge advocate of the Marine Corps, someone he knew was in a position "to know some of the aspects of the Guantánamo operation."[514]

"I described for him what I'd seen and how I felt about it," Couch said in the 2007 interview. "And he says, "Nope, you're not imagining things. You're not crazy. This is a real issue. This is a problem. And you need to work this—you need to work this problem.""[515]

* * *

Days before Lieutenant Colonel Couch's first visit to Guantánamo, President Bush nominated Jim Haynes for a federal judgeship on the U.S. Fourth Circuit Court of Appeals. Haynes hoped to follow Jay Bybee, who had seen his service as head of the Office of Legal Counsel rewarded with a seat on the 9th Circuit Court of Appeals earlier in the year. Yoo had moved on, too, accepting visiting scholar positions at the American Enterprise Institute and University of Chicago.

In October, Jack Goldsmith—who had served under Jim Haynes in the Defense Department but who had been excluded from the Working Group process—took over as head of the OLC. By the time the Senate Judiciary Committee began gearing up for the first hearings on Haynes' nomination six weeks later, Goldsmith had concluded that the March 2003 Yoo memo that had guided the Working Group and the August 1, 2002 "Standards of Conduct" Bybee memo were "legally flawed, tendentious in substance and tone, and overbroad." "My main concern," Goldsmith wrote in his 2007 memoir *The Terror Presidency*, "was that someone might rely on their green light to justify interrogations much more aggressive than ones specifically approved and then maintain, not without justification, that they were acting on the basis of OLC's view of the law."[516]

The week after Christmas, Goldsmith called Haynes to tell him the military could no longer rely on the March 14, 2003 legal opinion. Yet even the news that military interrogators were now operating without the cover of Yoo's memo seemed to have little impact on GTMO operations. On January 2, 2004, the Pentagon approved two more Special Interrogation plans, the contents of which remain classified.[517] But two weeks later, Army Specialist Joseph Darby, an MP in the 372nd MP Company deployed in Abu Ghraib prison in Iraq, left a CD full of photographs and an anonymous note for a CITF investigator stationed in the prison. Most of the photos had been taken between October 18 and October 31, 2003—just two months after General Miller led a Pentagon survey team to review detention and interrogation operations in Iraq and urged his counterparts to "GTMO-ize" their facilities. "You haven't broken [the detainees] psychologically," Miller complained to Major General Keith Dayton, Commander of the Iraq Survey Group, during his visit. Within days, plans had begun circulating to incorporate military working dogs, stress positions, "sleep management," twenty-four-hour interrogations, isolation, loud music, light control, and nudity in U.S. detention centers in Iraq.[518]

In the three months before Army Specialist Darby's photos were broadcast on 60 Minutes II, Lieutenant Colonel Couch was piecing together a picture of what had happened to Mohamedou Ould Slahi that previous summer and fall in Guantánamo.

As Slahi's designated prosecutor, Couch had been monitoring intelligence summaries of Slahi's interviews, and in the fall, he'd noticed that the Mauritanian suddenly "was being very prolific with what he was saying."

There were a lot of reports coming out. And just the volume—I got to the point where I just couldn't keep up with everything he was saying. I've got in mind what I had seen on that first trip. And I've also been told that Slahi is under "special project." All of that's kind of coming together. And I'm thinking, okay, why is he being this prolific? What's going on?[519]

During this time, Slahi provided what Couch would call "a Who's Who of al Qaeda in Germany and all of Europe"; he also reportedly corroborated Ramzi Binalshibh's allegations, extracted in the CIA's black sites, that Slahi had directed him and three of the Germany-based hijackers to Al Qaeda camps in Afghanistan to train for attacks on the United States. Couch knew those allegations: they were among the elements in Slahi's file that "got my attention," as he put it, and made him so enthusiastic to prosecute a person who might possibly have connections with the terrorist attack that killed his friend. But the file said nothing about the circumstances under which Binalshibh had offered this information. Later, when Slahi seemed to turn talkative, there was likewise no information about the conditions of his interrogation in Guantánamo. Slahi's confession came in sanitized ten-page summaries, the text all uppercase. "Why is he being this prolific?" Couch kept asking. "Is it physical coercion? Are they promising him things?" But even his top-secret clearance wasn't sufficient to see information about the circumstances of Slahi's interrogation. Anything beyond the interview summaries was off-limits and classified.

Couch had gathered that Slahi, as a "special project," had faced some kind of "enhanced" interrogation techniques, and he had a hint, from his October 2003 visit, of what the source of those techniques might be. And he knew, from his own SERE training, what those techniques were meant to do. That training involved "a mock invasion, and then you were captured," he explained in that 2007 interview. "It was clear that the fingerprints of Vietnam and the treatment of our Aviators at the hands of the North Vietnamese was the genesis of all the guiding principles they were trying to teach. What they were trying to get at was complete and total control of the individual. They controlled where you were, what you were wearing, what you were eating, what you're drinking, when you sleep—total and complete control." That control, in SERE exercises, is exerted toward coercing participants to sign false confessions. "Did you confess?" the interviewer asked. "I'm not going to go there," Couch answered.

It wasn't hard for Couch to imagine how the SERE techniques could come to form the backbone of a post-9/11 interrogation program. "They were seeing servicemen and women, Marines, Army Air Force, Navy Seals, special operations-type folks in these environments, and some of them were breaking," he said. "And they felt okay about adopting these techniques because the mantra is, we've been utilizing these same techniques with our own people."

> *But what gets dropped out of that analysis is that when we go to SERE school, we're volunteers. We go there, we know that we're going to be trained, and that that form of discipline, that form of harsh treatment, is ultimately for our good. And we know that it's going to be over in a week. Not so an individual who doesn't know that they're going to be released from captivity after a week, who has not volunteered to be there.*
>
> *I do want to note here, I was not the only one in the office that had concerns about these interrogation techniques. There were two other senior prosecutors, a Navy commander and another Marine, a lieutenant colonel, and there were other prosecutors in the office that had a concern. And we were looking at, what was the nature of the treatment of these detainees, from the moment we picked them up off the battlefield until today? What is this going to look like in a courtroom? What is this going to look like when we're standing in front of the military commission members and trying to convince them that this evidence is good evidence?*[520]

Couch put those concerns in writing in a March 2004 "Operational Assessment" to Brigadier General Scott Black: "Prosecutors in our office are very concerned about the allegations of detainee abuse at GTMO and Afghanistan, and we have individually taken steps to address this issue," he reported. "The techniques employed by the intelligence community in obtaining information is a policy decision that obviously affects our prosecution efforts, yet we are powerless to influence such activities."[521] Meanwhile, Couch was working with an NCIS agent assigned to Slahi's case to piece together the "great, big jigsaw puzzle" of his ordeal. With no official information forthcoming, the agent worked "under the table," talking to interrogators, hunting for documents like interrogation logs, bringing back bigger and bigger pieces.

Then, in the spring, the agent turned up the letter the phony White House emissary had shown Slahi reporting that his mother was in custody and was going to be brought to Guantánamo. "It was a clear implication that she was going to be harmed or could be harmed," Couch remembered. "We've got your family. We took them into custody, and they started crying. You better start telling us what you know." "And for me," Couch said, "That was it."

Slahi, Couch saw, had been tortured—and because Article 15 of the Convention against Torture requires every country that has signed the convention to "ensure that any statement which is established to have been made as a result of torture shall not be invoked as evidence in any proceedings," nothing in the interview summaries could be used even in the context of the relaxed evidentiary standards of the military commissions. But for Couch, who describes himself as an evangelical Christian, what to do about Slahi's prosecution cut much deeper than a question of what evidence he was willing to present. "The very cornerstone of the Christian faith is the dignity of human beings," Couch has said. "We believe that because as it says in the Bible, we were created in God's image. We were created in his image, and we owe each other a certain level of dignity—a certain level of respect." Exercising that respect, Couch concedes, is difficult in the face of visceral emotions like vengeance or fear, but "there's another aspect to it, too, and that is what God expects us to be doing to our fellow human being? Somebody that's been detained, they're off the battlefield, we are responsible for their care and feeding and their welfare, is it appropriate to treat them in a cruel and inhumane and degrading manner to get the information?"

Couch said he "had this abiding sense that God's not going to honor this. And I'm not honoring God by prosecuting a man with this type of evidence." But he worried that he was copping out, and struggled with pride—pride in his work, his "willingness to do the hard things, go the extra mile." Then,

Right in the middle of this time, when I had received this information from the NCIS agent—the documents, the State Department letterhead—and it was at the end of this, hearing all of this information, reading all this information, months and months and months of wrangling with the issue, that I was in church this Sunday, and we had a baptism. We got to the part of the liturgy where the congregation repeats—I'm paraphrasing here, but the essence is that we respect the human dignity of every human being and seek peace and justice on earth. And when we spoke those words that morning, there were a lot of people in that church, but I could have been the only one there. I just felt this incredible, all right, there it is. You can't come in here on Sunday, and as a Christian, subscribe to this belief of dignity of every human being and say I will seek justice and peace on the earth, and continue to go with the prosecution using that kind of evidence. And at that point I knew what I had to do. I had to get off the fence.[522]

Couch resigned. In a meeting with Colonel Bob Swann, the chief prosecutor of the military commissions, he called the techniques to which Slahi had been subject "morally repugnant," and made clear that for that reason alone he refused to participate further in his prosecution. According to a *Wall Street Journal* account of that meeting, Swann reacted indignantly, asking Couch, "What makes you think you're so much better than us?" "That's not the issue at all, that's not the point!" Couch shouted back. In the ensuing argument, Swann argued that the president's military commissions weren't bound by the Torture Convention; Couch countered by pressing Swann to cite one legal precedent establishing that the President of the United States could ignore a treaty the U.S. had ratified. Following the meeting, Couch wrote a formal letter of resignation and specifically requested that Haynes be informed of his concerns. A military commission spokesman told the *Wall Street Journal*, "Mr. Haynes was not informed of the issued raised by Lt. Col Couch nor did he expect to be told about all internal operations within the Office of Military Commissions."[523]

In the 2007 interview, Couch talked of his outrage at discovering "that these types of things were being done by the United States."

And one of the reasons was, when we're going through SERE school— just being in the military—we always think of ourselves as the good guys. The United States has always stood for goodness and fair play, is a good way to look at it. And we've always been outraged, as a nation, when other countries were using coercive methods and methodology on their prisoners. When I was in high school, I read several accounts of the prisoners of war that were held by the North Vietnamese, and what they endured at their hands in the Hanoi Hilton. I always had the utmost respect for them, and frankly a lot of outrage against the North Vietnamese for their treatment. In those accounts there's a lot of discussion about the Geneva Conventions, and about how these men and women who were being held in the prisoner of war camps always had that hope that somehow, with the Geneva Conventions as a backdrop, that world would be able to see what was wrong with what was being done to them and they would get justice.

That Vietnamese experience had a profound impact on interpretations of the Code of Conduct. It was directly attributable to even having SERE school to begin with, because that kind of behavior was out there. And so, for me, that was part of the backdrop when I started seeing what was being done to Slahi. I was just outraged, because if we stoop and we compromise on our ideals as a nation, then these guys have accomplished much more than driving airplanes into the World Trade Center and the Pentagon.

"It is the classic slippery slope," Couch concluded.

I believe when, as a government, we adopt a policy that allows for the degradation and dehumanization of another human being, whoever they may be, whatever they may be charged with or alleged to have done, when we adopt this as an acceptable and authorized method of interrogation with that individual, we have now embarked on a slippery slope that we can easily slip down ourselves. I go back to my Christian belief. We are human beings who are just inherently sinful. We are sinful beings. If we embark on a policy that allows us, by sanction of government, basically, to mistreat another human being, it can quickly get out of control when it's carried out by sinful human beings.[524]

ENDGAME

Mohamedou Ould Slahi

On April 9, 2010, U.S. District Judge James Robertson released a declassified Memorandum Order explaining his decision in the habeas corpus petition of Mohamedou Ould Slahi. His ruling concluded,

> *The government's problem is that its proof that Salahi gave material support to terrorists is so attenuated, or so tainted by coercion and mistreatment, or so classified, that it cannot support a successful criminal prosecution. Nevertheless, the government wants to hold Salahi indefinitely, because of its concern that he might renew his oath to al-Qaida and become a terrorist upon his release. That concern may indeed be well-founded. Salahi fought with al-Qaida in Afghanistan (twenty years ago), associated with at least a half-dozen known al-Qaida members and terrorists, and somehow found and lived among or with al-Qaida cell members in Montreal. But a habeas court may not permit a man to be held indefinitely upon suspicion, or because of the government's prediction that he may do unlawful acts in the future—any more than a habeas court may rely upon its prediction that a man will not be dangerous in the future and order his release if he was lawfully detained in the first place. The question, upon which the government had the burden of proof, was whether, at the time of his capture, Salahi was a "part of" al-Qaida. On the record before me, I cannot find that he was.*
>
> *The petition for writ of habeas corpus is granted. Salahi must be released from custody. It is SO ORDERED.*[525]

Slahi had initiated the habeas process five years before with a note he wrote by hand, in English, on March 3, 2005. "Hello," the petition begins. "I, Mohamedou Ould Slahi, detained in GTMO under ISN #760, herewith apply for a writ of habeas corpus." "As to my detention," it continues,

> *I turned myself [in] on Sep. 2001 to my government in Mauritania,*

*when they asked me to. My government extradited me eventually to
the U.S. and since then I am being detained here in GTMO, Cuba.*

*I have done no crimes against the U.S., nor did the U.S. charge me
with crimes, thus I am filing for my immediate release.*

For further details about my case, I'll be happy for future hearings.

*Best regards,
Ould Slahi*[526]

In a release posted on the Department of Defense website the next day,
the Pentagon touted the success of its "Battle Lab." The five hundred enemy
combatants still being held in Guantánamo had generated more than four
thousand intelligence reports, the release said, "an unprecedented body of
information [that] has expanded our understanding of al-Qaida and other
terrorist organizations." Credit for this success, it suggested, belonged to
JTF-GTMO:

*The Joint Task Force, Guantánamo Bay, Cuba (JFT-GTMO) remains
the single best repository of al-Qaida information in the Department
of Defense. Many detainees have admitted close relationships or other
access to senior al-Qaida leadership. They provide valuable insights
into the structure of that organization and associated terrorist groups.
They have identified additional al-Qaida operatives and supporters,
and have expanded our understanding of the extent of their presence
in Europe, the United States, and throughout the CENTCOM area of
operations. Detainees have also provided information on individuals
connected to al-Qaida's pursuit of chemical, biological, and nuclear
weapons.*[527]

"GTMO is currently the only DoD strategic interrogation center and
will remain useful as long as the war on terrorism is underway and new
enemy combatants are captured and sent there," the release concludes.
"The lessons learned at GTMO have advanced both the operational art of
intelligence, and the development of strategic interrogations doctrine."

By the spring of 2005, the broad outlines of that interrogation doctrine were well known. In an open letter to the Senate Judiciary Committee in opposition to the nomination of Alberto Gonzales to replace John Ashcroft as Attorney General, twelve retired generals and admirals pointed to Gonzales's role in the Bush administration's decision to deny detainees Geneva Convention protections—a decision that, they said, went "hand in hand with the decision to relax the definition of torture and to alter interrogation doctrine accordingly." The former commanders and senior military lawyers specifically criticized the series of OLC memos "prepared at [Gonzales's] direction" that replaced longstanding doctrine, elaborated in the Army Field Manual, "prohibiting 'threats, insults, or exposure to inhumane treatment as a means of or aid to interrogation.'" "The Manual was the product of decades of experience," they argued, "experience that had shown, among other things, that such interrogation methods produce unreliable results and often impede further intelligence. Discounting the Manual's wisdom on this central point shows a disturbing disregard for the decades of hard-won knowledge of the professional American military."[528]

By the spring of 2005 it was also clear, from the protests and defections of military prosecutors like Stuart Couch, from the chronic turmoil surrounding the military commissions, and from the on-again off-again possibility that detainees would be able to press their cases in habeas proceedings, that the administration's unwise decisions and deviations from international and domestic prohibitions on torture had poisoned potential prosecutions. Worse, Slahi's Administrative Review Board hearing later that year, with its convenient recording equipment failure, offered an uneasy glimpse of what the administration might be in for if its "Special Projects" were in fact able to tell their stories in federal courts to habeas judges.

A month after that hearing, in December 2005, President Bush signed the Detainee Treatment Act, prohibiting inhumane treatment but stripping federal courts of jurisdiction to hear Guantánamo habeas petitions. The administration tried to argue that the DTA likewise barred the Supreme Court from hearing Salim Ahmed Hamdan's challenge to the military commissions. When the court disagreed, finding that the Guantánamo commissions were not a "regularly constituted court affording all the judicial guarantees which are recognized as indispensable by civilized peoples," the White House went back to the Republican-controlled Congress to win passage of the Military Commissions Act, which supposedly addressed the issues of fairness in military commission proceedings while emphatically denying all Guantánamo detainees access to habeas proceedings.[529]

At Slahi's annual Administrative Review Board hearings, the government continued to maintain that he was an Al Qaeda operative, that he had recruited jihadists including members of the 9/11 hijacking teams, and that he had provided technical support for Al Qaeda communications networks—but it made no move to try him before the reconstituted military commissions, where his treatment was certain to be an issue. On March 9, 2006, Slahi wrote to Sylvia Royce, one of his attorneys:

> I've received both the letters from you Sylvy and the others from Nancy that contains the new DTA. I read the whole thing and as you might have noticed I am not subject to a trial by the [Military Commission] for I've done none of the mentioned crimes in the new law.
>
> You ask me to write you everything I told my interrogators. Are you out of your mind! How can I render uninterrupted interrogation that has been lasting the last 7 years. That's like asking Charlie Sheen, how many women he dated.
>
> Yet I provided you with everything (almost) in my book, which the gov't denies you the access to. Furthermore I was going to go deeper in details, but I figured it was futile.
>
> To make a long story short you may divide my time in two big steps.
>
> 1. Pre-torture (I mean that I couldn't resist): I told them the truth about me having done nothing against your country. It lasted until May 22nd, 2003.
>
> 2. Post-torture era: where my brake broke loose. I yessed every accusation my interrogators made. I even wrote the infamous confession about me was planning to hit the CN Tower in Toronto based on SSG [name redacted] advise. I just wanted to get the

> *monkeys off my back. I don't care how long I stay in jail. My belief comforts me.*
>
> *One of you have got to come visit me, or I am going loco!*
>
> *Nonetheless, I doubt that the gov't would provide you the intels I provided them. I mean a lot of it is true, though not incriminating. And the incriminating part are lies. Still, I persist that none of my statements in GTMO Bay or any other dictatorship countries are binding. Only the honest statements I'd make in front of a Fed judge and a jury would be binding.*
>
> *Around the subject: I believe that your leader acts like a bad chess player (patzer). He keeps doing the wrong moves, and if he is cornered, he cheats. Why just thinking before moving! Or resigning the game. Not everybody's meant to play chess or being a president :)*[530]

The week that Slahi wrote that letter, the Republican Party lost control of both houses of Congress in the 2006 midterm elections. As the new Congress was convening in January, the administration announced it was withdrawing the nomination of Jim Haynes to the Federal Court of Appeals. Haynes continued on as the Defense Department's General Counsel, and in November 2007, he intervened to block Lieutenant Colonel Stuart Couch from appearing before the House Judiciary Committee.

That hearing had been convened following Attorney General-designate Michael Mukasey's refusal to state whether waterboarding was torture at his Senate confirmation hearing, and was meant to probe detainee treatment. Couch—whose experiences as Slahi's would-be military prosecutor were made public in the March 2007 *Wall Street Journal* profile "The Conscience of the Colonel," had secured permission from his superiors to testify about the way in which Slahi's torture had derailed any possibility of a trial before a military commission and the tenuousness of many other detainee cases built on statements elicited under duress. On the eve of the hearing, Couch received an email advising him that Haynes "has determined that as a sitting judge and a former prosecutor, it is improper for you to testify about matters still pending in the military court system, and you are not to appear before the Committee to testify tomorrow."[531]

The Supreme Court finally ruled definitively in June 2008 in *Boumediene v. Bush* that Guantánamo detainees have a right to pursue habeas corpus petitions in federal court, and the following year Slahi and his attorneys pressed his case before Judge James Robertson, one of seventeen Washington, DC-based judges assigned to hear more than two hundred post-*Boumediene* petitions. In his April 9, 2010 unclassified opinion, Robertson summarized the government's case against Slahi this way:

> *Salahi has been in custody, without being charged with any crime, since November [redacted] 2001. He was first taken into custody by [redacted] on suspicion that he had been involved in the failed "Millennium Plot" to bomb the Los Angeles International Airport. The United States [redacted] transported him to Guantánamo Bay in August 2002. He has been there ever since....*
>
> *The government's case, essentially, is that Salahi was so connected to al-Qaida for a decade beginning in 1990 that he must have been "part of" al-Qaida at the time of his capture. The allegations are that Salahi was a recruiter for al-Qaida – that indeed he recruited two of the men who became 9/11 hijackers and a third who became a 9/11 coordinator; that he actively supported his cousin, who is or was one of Osama Bin Laden's spiritual advisors; that he carried out orders to develop al-Qaida's telecommunications capacity; and that he had connections with an al-Qaida cell in Montreal.*
>
> *Salahi concedes that he traveled to Afghanistan in early 1990 to fight jihad against communists and that there he swore bayat to al-Qaida. He maintains, however, that his association with al-Qaida ended after 1992, and that, even though he remained in contact thereafter with people he knew to be al-Qaida members, he did nothing for al-Qaida after that time.*
>
> *The government's case relies heavily on statements made by Salahi himself, but the reliability of those statements—most of them now retracted by Salahi—is open to question.*[532]

As Robertson explained in his ruling, previous court decisions in Guantánamo habeas cases had established that Congress's 2001 Authorization for the Use of Military Force gave the President "substantial authority to apprehend and detain those who pose a real danger to our security"; the AUMF specifically named "persons [the President] determined planned, authorized, committed, or aided the terrorist attacks that occurred on September 11, 2001...in order to prevent any future acts of international terrorism against the United States by such...persons." Early in the proceedings, the government argued that Slahi must remain detained because he was part of Al Qaeda when he was taken into custody and he had aided in the 9/11 attacks themselves by recruiting members of the Hamburg cell to join the hijacking teams. By the time Robertson heard arguments in the case, the government had abandoned its "aided in 9/11" claim, "acknowledging," as Robertson notes in his ruling, "that Salahi probably did not even know about the 9/11 attacks." Instead, in an "eleventh-hour brief," the government substituted another claim, formulated in the wake of a holding by another habeas judge in a case involving an alleged cook for a Taliban brigade, that those who were not "part of" but who had given "purposeful and material support" to Al Qaeda or the Taliban in hostilities against U.S. coalition partners could also be denied release.

Robertson rejected this late claim outright, calling it a "non-starter": "purposeful and material support" for Al Qaeda is a prosecutable offense under the 2006 and 2009 Military Commissions Acts, and Robertson could see from the evidence the government presented in Slahi's habeas proceedings that it "clearly has no triable criminal case of 'purposeful and material support' against Salahi." What remained was the government's claim that Slahi was "part of al-Qaeda." Under the standard established in previous Guantánamo habeas proceedings, the government has the burden of proving the lawfulness of holding a detainee without charge or trial under the AUMF by a preponderance of the evidence. In Slahi's case, the government argued, essentially, "once al-Qaeda, always al-Qaeda"; the fact that Slahi had sworn a loyalty oath to the organization nineteen years before the 2009 habeas hearing—at a time when the United States was supporting mujahideen forces in Afghanistan including Al Qaida—

meant that the burden shifted to Slahi to prove that he was no longer a member.

Slahi freely admitted he had sworn *bayat* in 1990, after training at the al-Farouq training camp in Afghanistan, and that he returned to Afghanistan in 1992 to fight in an Al Qaeda mortar battery against the pro-Soviet Afghan government in the town of Gardez. In video testimony from Guantánamo, Slahi told the court that was where his connection with al-Qaeda ended. "He testified that he was 'part of' al-Qaeda only to join the struggle against the communists, and that, after his final trip to Afghanistan in 1992, he severed ties with al-Qaeda and provided no further support to the organization," Judge Robertson recorded in his opinion.

The government countered that far from severing his ties with Al Qaeda in 1992, Slahi "actively recruited for al-Qaeda from 1991 to at least 1999" Its evidence consisted largely of statements Slahi made to interrogators. As Robertson explained,

> *The most damaging allegation against Salahi is that, in October 1999, he encouraged Ramzi bin al-Shibh, Marwan al-Shehhi, and Ziad Jarrah to join al-Qaida. Bin al-Shibh has been identified as the primary contact for the organizers of the 9/11 hijackers, and al-Shehhi and Jarrah became two of the hijackers. Under coercive interrogation, Salahi confessed to facilitating travel for "several of the 9/11 hijackers to Chechnya," justifying his assistance as "just" jihad. Salahi's testimony now is that he did nothing more than give bin al-Shibh and his friends lodging for one night.*[533]

This "confession," Robertson's citation reveals, was contained in an August 2, 2003 intelligence report from Guantánamo. August 2, 2003 is the day that Miller's interrogation chief, posing as a Naval Captain dispatched directly from the White House, visited Slahi during his "special interrogation" and presented him the letter threatening to transfer his mother to Guantánamo.

"There is ample evidence in this record that Salahi was subjected to extensive and severe mistreatment at Guantánamo from mid-June 2003 to September 2003," Robertson wrote. "Salahi made most, if not all, of the statements that the government seeks to use against him during the mistreatment or during the 2 years following it." Moreover, statements the government submitted from other detainees to bolster its case may also have been coerced. "The government proffered corroboration for Salahi's 2003 statements about recruitment consists of statements by [redacted] Karim Mehdi," he noted; however, "Salahi's attorney had submitted affidavits "that Mehdi's statements were coerced by mistreatment (sleep deprivation); that Mehdi was fed information by his interrogators; and that Mehdi has admitted to lying."[534]

Applying what he called "appropriate judicial skepticism to the jumble of evidence," Robertson concluded that "the government has credibly shown, and Salahi has not rebutted the showing, that [redacted] Salahi provided lodging for three men for one night at his home in Germany, that one of them was Ramzi bin al-Shibh, and that there was discussion of jihad and Afghanistan." However, "the government has not credibly shown Salahi to have been a 'recruiter.' What its evidence shows is that Salahi remained in contact with people he knew to be al-Qaeda members at least until November 1999, and that he was willing to make a referral to a known al-Qaeda member in 1997." Such contacts, Robertson decided, may show that Salahi was an Al Qaeda sympathizer, perhaps a "fellow traveler," but that did not prove he was part of Al Qaeda at the time he was detained.

> It is undisputed that Salahi swore bayat and was a member of al-Qaida in 1990, but the government had to show that he was still (or again) within its command structure when we was captured on November [redacted] 2001. Salahi's admission that he once was part of al-Qaida but that he severed his ties after 1992 raises burden-of-proof questions: May the burden lawfully be shifted to Salahi to prove his dis-association? If so, at what point does the burden shift?

Robertson observed that the DC Court of Appeals, in reviewing other habeas decisions, had ruled "there is nothing unconstitutional about shifting the burden to a detainee to rebut a credible government showing 'with more persuasive evidence.'"

> *If that is the rule, one might reasonably ask, how can Guantánamo detainees – locked up for years on a remote island, cut off from the world, without resources, with only such access to intelligence sources and witnesses as the government deigns to give them – how can such people possibly carry the burden of rebuttal, even against weak government cases? The answer, unfortunately for detainee petitioners, is that they are indeed at a considerable disadvantage, and that successful rebuttals of credible government cases will be rare events. The Court of Appeals has acknowledged this imbalance and approved it: "[P]lacing a lower burden on the government defending a wartime detention—where national security interests are at their zenith and the rights of the alien petitioner at their nadir – is... permissible."*
>
> *A habeas court must consider the government's factual showing of probable cause and look to the petitioner for rebuttal when that showing is both credible and significant. It is only fair to the petitioner, however—and, considering the government's built-in advantage, not unfair to the government—to view the government's showing with something like skepticism, drawing only such inferences as are compelled by the quality of the evidence.[535]*

In the end, Robertson rejected the government's contention that it was up to Slahi to offer evidence proving he had quit Al Qaeda. "The al-Qaeda that Salahi joined in 1991 was very different from the al-Qaeda that turned against the United States in the latter part of the 1990s," he held. Slahi had joined Al Qaeda to fight the rump Soviet regime in Afghanistan, and he had left Afghanistan at around the time Osama bin Laden, reacting to the buildup of U.S. troops in Saudi Arabia during and after the first Gulf

War, declared war on the United States. Instead, the government needed to demonstrate that Slahi was an active member of Al Qaeda closer to the time of his capture, when Al Qaeda was clearly targeting the U.S.; it had not done so, and he must be released.

Robertson's decision came as the Obama administration and Congress were negotiating how to fulfill Obama's post-inaugural pledge to close Guantánamo, and even before Robertson's opinion was declassified, Republicans were denouncing both the decision and the administration. Insisting that this ruling "clearly puts the American people in danger and should not be allowed to stand," Representative Lamar Smith wrote Attorney General Eric Holder demanding an appeal; the ranking member of the Senate Intelligence Committee, Kit Bond of Missouri, told reporters "while Holder's Justice Department should appeal the outrageous decision, I'm not holding my breath. Holder seems more intent on closing Guantánamo Bay than keeping terrorists locked up where they belong."[536]

The Obama administration appealed. Robertson had erred in two respects, it argued: in failing to shift the burden of proof onto Slahi to show he had left Al Qaeda, and in failing to find that the government's case established that Slahi remained part of Al Qaeda after 1992. Robertson had failed to reach that conclusion, moreover, partly because he had insisted on examining each piece of evidence individually and had given little weight to any inculpatory statements Slahi had made that were not corroborated by other evidence; at the very least the appeals court should remand the case back to Robertson and require him to consider statements Slahi had made after he was tortured.

The appeal was argued before a three-judge panel of the DC Circuit Court of Appeals on September 17, 2010. At that hearing, one of the judges grilled Slahi's attorneys on Judge Robertson's approach in evaluating the government's case:

> JUDGE SENTELLE: Was the Court properly assessing the evidence
>   when it treated the Government's evidence as being, viewing
>   the Government's evidence with something like skepticism?

MS. DUNCAN: *Yes, Your Honor. The District Court was doing what all of the District Courts have done in these Guantánamo Bay cases, and that is refusing to give the Government a presumption of reliability.*

JUDGE SENTELLE: *Now, he didn't say he was refusing to give them presumption of liability, he went beyond that, didn't he?*

MS. DUNCAN: *No, Your Honor, I don't believe-*

JUDGE SENTELLE: *No.*

MS. DUNCAN: *—he did. He—*

JUDGE SENTELLE: *What did he mean by that phrase then that he was viewing it with something like skepticism?*

MS. DUNCAN: *That he was—*

JUDGE SENTELLE: *It sounds as if he is downgrading the evidence before he ever hears it, like—*

MS. DUNCAN: *He was—*

JUDGE SENTELLE: *—the Government has some other burden to overcome besides a preponderance.*

MS. DUNCAN: *He was refusing to consider the Government's evidence without skepticism. And when you look at the, in his opinion at the place where he mentions I'm applying my judicial skepticism to this evidence, he's weighing the credibility of different types of evidence from different places and giving them the weight that he thinks it deserves. So, in his application of that comment—*

JUDGE SENTELLE: *That's not what he said, though. He said that he was viewing it with something like skepticism, and he said it twice, I think, didn't he?*

MS. DUNCAN: *Correct, Your Honor, he did say it twice. He said it at the very beginning, and I think there he's talking about not accepting the Government's evidence without skepticism, which—*

JUDGE SENTELLE: *That's two different things, to say not accepting it without skepticism, saying I'm applying skepticism to it.*

Judge Sentelle went on:

> *JUDGE SENTELLE: Have any of the other District Courts used that phrasing that I'm approaching the Government's evidence with skepticism?*
>
> *MS. DUNCAN: Your Honor, I don't recall if any other judge has worded—*
>
> *JUDGE SENTELLE: Have we ever approved that formulation?*
>
> *MS. DUNCAN: Not the word skepticism, but in Bensayah this Court did look at the Government's evidence with some skepticism and asking whether some, you know, outside evidence corroborated evidence at issue in the case, which is not accepting the Government's exhibit at face value, but rather approaching it, making your own credibility determinations of whether that evidence under the totality is reliable.*
>
> *JUDGE SENTELLE: But he has to make credibility determinations on all evidence in all cases.*
>
> *MS. DUNCAN: Correct, Your Honor.*
>
> *JUDGE SENTELLE: But he normally would not say all right, I'm going to look at your evidence, but I'm treating it with skepticism. He's doing something, or seems to be saying that he's doing something different here than he does in a run of the mill case.*
>
> *MS. DUNCAN: Well, I would agree with you to some extent, but it's not imposing a higher burden on the Government, rather it's recognizing the unique nature of this evidence, that the Government relied exclusively on interrogation reports in its case, and particularly interrogation reports of Mr. Salahi after admitting that Mr. Salahi was subjected to—*
>
> *JUDGE SENTELLE: Let us—I'm not sure where we crossed the line into classified.*
>
> *MS. DUNCAN: Your Honor, I promise you that I—*
>
> *JUDGE SENTELLE: Okay, good.*
>
> *MS. DUNCAN: —know that line and I'll—*
>
> *JUDGE SENTELLE: Be careful.*

MS. DUNCAN: —*honor it.*

JUDGE SENTELLE: *Good.*

MS. DUNCAN: *I promise.*

JUDGE SENTELLE: *Okay.*

MS. DUNCAN: *That the circumstances under which Mr. Salahi made the statements on which the Government relied were, I mean, the Government has admitted in public reports in a public pleadings that we would call it torture they would call it coercive circumstances, but nonetheless that those circumstances as Judge Robertson found rendered all of Mr. Salahi's statements to interrogators suspect. Given those circumstances, given the nature of the evidence in this case where we don't always know who the declarant is, we don't know what the circumstances, under what circumstances statements were made, evidence was gathered, judicial skepticism is really just a means of assessing the reliability of evidence under this unique circumstance of the Guantánamo cases. And when you read his opinion as a whole it's clear that he's not holding the Government to a higher standard, he's properly applying the preponderance of the evidence standard, but figuring out a way where you have conflicting accounts where things aren't corroborated to give the particular pieces of evidence and the Government's ultimate showing the weight it deserves.*[537]

In the end, the appeals court remanded the case to the District Court for another review of the record, not because Judge Robertson's skepticism was erroneous but because the Appeals Court had issued three other rulings in Guantánamo habeas cases since Robertson's decision that redefined the level of activity required to be considered a "part of" Al Qaeda. Under the prevailing standard, Robertson had looked for evidence that established that Slahi had been operating within Al Qaeda's command structure when he was detained—that is, that he had been carrying out Al Qaeda instructions and orders. Subsequent appellate rulings had held that it wasn't necessary for the government to show that a detainee had been within the organization's command structure to establish that he was "part of" Al Qaeda.

In its opinion, the court was careful to delineate "the precise nature of the government's case against Slahi." "The government has not criminally indicted Salahi for providing material support to terrorists or the 'foreign terrorist organization' al-Qaida," the court emphasized, quoting Judge Robertson's conclusion that "the government's problem is that its proof that Salahi gave material support to terrorists is so attenuated, or so tainted by coercion and mistreatment, or so classified, that it cannot support a successful criminal prosecution." "Nor," added the court, "does the government seek to detain Salahi under the AUMF on the grounds that he aided the September 11 attacks or 'purposefully and materially support[ed]' forces associated with al-Qaeda 'in hostilities against U.S. Coalition partners.'"[538] Rather, the government was asking the court to find that Slahi could still be considered part of Al Qaeda even though he was not taking orders from or actively plotting with the organization.

Judge Robertson has retired, and the case has now been reassigned to Judge Emmett Sullivan, who is currently presiding over a renewed round of fact discovery. Sometime later this year he will once again evaluate the government's claim that Slahi, who joined Al Qaeda in 1991 to fight communists in Afghanistan, remains part of Al Qaeda and poses an ongoing threat to the United States. Meanwhile, the man whose torture and mock execution Defense Secretary Donald Rumsfeld personally ordered remains in what the *Washington Post* has called "a gilded cage" in Guantánamo.

As Peter Finn reported in March, 2010, Slahi, who is now 40, and 53-year-old Tariq al-Sawah, a former explosives expert who renounced his past after his capture, "have become two of the most significant informants ever to be held in Guantánamo." "Today, they are housed in a little fenced-in compound at the military prison, where they live a life of relative privilege—gardening, writing, painting—separated from other detainees in a cocoon designed to reward and protect." "Their old jihadi comrades want them dead, revenge for the apostasy, now well known, of working with the

United States," Finn wrote. "The U.S. government has rewarded them for their cooperation but has refused to countenance their release."[539]

The treatment is an acknowledgement of what Slahi has long insisted: that he voluntarily provided useful information and intelligence from the time he was in U.S. custody, that he had been "honest, cooperative, and forthcoming," as he told the Guantánamo Administrative Review Board in 2005.[540] The gratuitous cruelty of his torture, meanwhile, had only served to extract what the habeas court concurred were useless, coerced confessions. That voluntary cooperation, Slahi had told the Combatant Status Review Board a year earlier, both left him vulnerable and merited special consideration from the U.S. "You do not want to return to your home country?" the Tribunal President asked Slahi when the subject of a possible future release arose at that hearing.

> [Slahi]: No, because I'm threatened because of the amount of information I've provided to the United States, I would be hunted down and killed. I want to be provided security.
>
> Tribunal President: We'll make a note of that; is there a particular country you are interested in going to? Not to say that we make that decision, someone else would make that decision, the Personal Representative is correct, but we'll put it on record.
>
> [Slahi]: United States.
>
> Tribunal President: You want to go to the United States?
>
> [Slahi]: I do.
>
> Tribunal President: OK, that is now made a part of this record, and the State Department will take note of this request."[541]

Slahi returned to the subject of a possible post-Guantánamo life at his Administrative Review Board hearing in 2005—this time stating that he had since been told there was no chance he would be resettled in the United States and asking to be released to Canada, where he had residency previously, instead. "If you were released to Canada, what would you do?" a board member asked. Slahi answered,

I have been kept out of the world for more than four years and I really don't know what is going on outside. I wish I could have a family a peaceful life without anybody trying to pin anything on me and some kind of money to make me comfortable, to make me serve God, have a house and take care of my big family. That is what I have been doing and most likely what I will do if the opportunity arises. Nonetheless, I need some assistance because to integrate myself back into society. Look at it for example, if I go now to look for a job somewhere I will have to write or they are going to ask me, who is your previous employer and I'm am going to write JTF-GTMO. I was a terror suspect and the guy will tell me are you crazy! Get out of my sight before I call the police. It is understandable, why should anybody take a chance like that. I wouldn't take a chance like that, so I definitely understand. I think just to let any Detainee out without giving some rehab or some help getting his way back into society, what they call reintegration, is bad.[542]

Mohammed al-Qahtani

On February 4, 2009, Mohammed al-Qahtani's attorneys filed a motion to hold the United States government in contempt for persistently refusing to turn over evidence essential to arguing his habeas corpus case. They wrote,

Petitioner al Qahtani has been incarcerated at Guantánamo since February 2002. Throughout his imprisonment, he has consistently maintained that he was repeatedly tortured and threatened with torture by U.S. military and civilian interrogators. And since Petitioner al Qahtani filed his habeas petition in October 2006, he has repeatedly asserted that any alleged "admissions" he made to U.S. personnel were extracted through this torture and threats of torture. Until recently, the Government had adamantly denied that any U.S. personnel engaged in acts of torture during Petitioner al Qahtani's interrogation. But on January 14, 2009, Military Commission Convening Authority Susan Crawford finally conceded that by subjecting Petitioner al Qahtani to systematic 20-hour interrogations, prolonged sleep deprivation, 160 days of severe isolation, forced nudity, sexual and religious humiliation, and other aggressive interrogation tactics, the Government had engaged in acts of torture so egregious that she was convinced Petitioner al Qahtani should not be subjected to prosecution before a military commission. In light of Ms. Crawford's admission, the Government can no longer deny that Petitioner al Qahtani was tortured at the hands of U.S. personnel. Yet the Government continues to rely upon his statements before this court as justification for his seven-year imprisonment.

At this juncture, Petitioner al Qahtani's habeas petition has been pending for almost three and a half years. The Government possesses readily available information that documents the torture he endured at the hands of interrogators at Guantánamo. Much of this information reached major media outlets nearly four years ago. Additional exculpatory records regarding Petitioner al Qahtani's torture have been searched, gathered, and provided to Executive and congressional investigatory bodies. These documents are undeniably exculpatory, since they are both "reasonably available" and "tend[] to materially undermine the information presented to support the Government's justification for detaining" him. Inexplicably, the Government still has not relinquished the underlying documents to Petitioner al Qahtani so that he may rebut the Government's evidence against him.[543]

The government's case against Qahtani largely consists of statements he made to interrogators beginning in April 2003, two and a half months after his fifty-day "Special Interrogation" and immediately following the capture and prolonged torture of Khalid Sheikh Mohammed in the CIA black site in Poland. According to the Justice Department's Inspector General, military interrogators reported that Qahtani became "fully cooperative" after failing a polygraph on March 31, 2003 and being "confronted with the fact that other al-Qaeda members were being apprehended and were providing valuable intelligence."[544] The Inspector General cited a JTF GTMO Memorandum for the Record dated April 7, 2003 stating that

Qahtani "is concerned with cutting the best deal possible for him, evading U.S. prosecution for his crimes, and avoiding incarceration in Saudi Arabia once he is returned home"; the next day, according to the Inspector General, another MFR recorded that "al Qahtani began to describe his knowledge of al Qaeda in great detail," and "from that point on he provided a significant amount of detailed information about al-Qaeda and its pre-September 11 operations."[545]

Fourteen of the seventeen "primary factors that favor continued detention" listed on Qahtani's October 5, 2006 "Unclassified Summary of Evidence" for the Administrative Review Board in Guantánamo were derived from information Qahtani provided interrogators during this "cooperative" period. These included, under the category of "Commitment,"

> 1. *The detainee stated he first traveled to Afghanistan from Saudi Arabia around the beginning of 2001 in order to participate in jihad, which he deemed a religious obligation. Once in Afghanistan, the detainee attended training at the al Farouq Training Camp.*
> 2. *The detainee stated he completed his training approximately three months after he entered Afghanistan, and he was then compelled to swear bayat to Usama bin Laden. The detainee stated he did this in person with Usama bin Laden, without any witnesses, while at Usama bin Laden's residence in Kandahar, Afghanistan.*
> 3. *The detainee stated that sometime in the summer of 2001, after he swore bayat to Usama bin Laden, the detainee was approached and asked to conduct a martyr mission from Usama bin Laden....*
> 5. *The detainee stated that at the time he agreed to conduct the mission there was no specific plan in place. However, the detainee knew that per his bayat and obligation, he would be called upon at a later time to conduct a martyr mission.*

And under the category of "Connections/Associations,"

> 3. *The detainee stated that on approximately 24 April 2001, after graduating from advanced training, he visited Usama bin Laden at*

his house to honor and praise him. The detainee told Usama bin Laden that he would continue to serve him as he would the prophet Mohammed. During this visit, Usama bin Laden instructed the detainee to contract a senior al Qaida official for instructions on how to serve his religion.

4. *The detainee stated that on approximately 22 June 2001, on his own initiative, he met with Usama bin Laden again at Usama bin Laden's house in Kandahar, Afghanistan, to greet him and to tell him that he was ready for his mission to the United States. Usama bin Laden called a senior al Qaida operative and advised him that the detainee had returned from the front line and was ready to complete his mission to America.*[546]

All of those statements, Qahtani told the Administrative Review Board at his hearing in 2007, were "information I only got from [interrogators] during interrogation sessions." "Interrogators provided me with this information and details and under pressure and coercion forced me to adopt the story that interrogators wanted to hear," he insisted. "The information I gave them was not valuable and did not help protect lives or property. I was unable to give any information about anything on the past or future. I just repeated the information given to me during interrogations."

"This is the first statement I am making of my own free will and without coercion or under threat of torture," Qahtani asserted in what remains the only publicly available personal account of his experiences. Recalling the litany of abusive methods to which he had been subjected from August 2002 through 2003, Qahtani told the Board, through a translator,

A human being needs four main things in life that were taken from me at Guantánamo. First, to honor religion and freedom to practice religion and respect it. Two, honoring his personal dignity by refraining from humiliating a human being through beatings or cursing him and bad treatment in general. Three, respect for his honor, which means not dishonoring him through sexual humiliation or abuse. Four, respect for human rights, by allowing a human being to sleep and be

comfortable where he is; to be in a warm shelter; to have security for
his life; to have sufficient food and beverage; to have means to relieve
himself and clean his body; to have humane medical treatment; and
to know that his family is safe from threats or harm. Again, all of
those rights were taken from me   It was only during this period
of physical and psychological torture and inhumane treatment that I
was forced to make false statements and fabricate a story.[547]

Qahtani's testimony before the Administrative Review Board was released to the public in September 2007. When his case came up again for review the following year, the Unclassified Summary of Evidence repeated the 2006 allegations, with some elaborations; now eighteen out of twenty-two factors favoring continued detention derived from Qahtani's statements to interrogators. The January 17, 2008 document added one item to the factors favoring release or transfer as well: "The detainee stated previous interviewers had coerced him into admitting that he had traveled to the United States to die," it recorded. "The detainee alleged that in return for this admission, these interviewers promised the detainee his freedom."[548]

A month later, the Bush administration announced it would try Qahtani before the military commissions for war crimes alongside Khalid Sheikh Mohammed, Walid Muhammad Salih Mubarek Bin 'Attash, Ramzi Binalshibh, Ali Abdul Azis Ali, and Mustafa Ahmed Adam al Hawsawi, all of whom had been transferred to Guantánamo in 2006 after prolonged detention in secret CIA prisons. All were to face the death penalty. The sworn charges were referred to Susan Crawford, the Convening Authority of the Military Commissions in April 2008. Qahtani, despairing, attempted suicide. His attorneys learned of the attempt during a visit in late April, when they saw the scars from three self-inflicted cuts, the worst of which "resulted in a deep wound, profuse bleeding, and hospitalization." Center for Constitutional Rights attorney Gitanjali Gutierrez recorded in her notes from that visit that Qahtani told her "I cannot accept this injustice. If I have to stay in this jail I want to put and end to this suffering."[549] On May 9, 2008, Crawford dismissed the charges against Qahtani, having concluded, as she would tell *Washington Post* reporter Bob Woodward shortly before

President Obama's inauguration the following January, that "we tortured Qahtani."

Despite this public admission, both the Bush and the Obama Justice Departments have repeatedly thwarted Qahtani's efforts to challenge the allegations against him in his habeas corpus proceedings. Following the Supreme Court's July 2008 *Boumediene* decision, which recognized that after years of extrajudicial detention the cost of legal delays "can no longer be borne by those who are in custody," the courts established specific guidelines to ensure the prompt resolution of habeas cases. One of those rules, devised by District Court Judge Thomas Hogan, gave the government two weeks to turn over all potentially exculpatory evidence to a habeas petitioner once it had filed a factual return in his case. In November 2008, as the deadline approached for the government to produce a long list of materials that Qahtani's attorneys had requested documenting his torture, the government sought a stay of all detainee cases assigned to Judge Hogan and an opportunity to relitigate the established groundrules.

Hogan reissued the guidelines, clarifying the government's obligation to give Guantánamo detainees access to potentially exculpatory evidence, and reset the deadline for December 30, 2008. When, a month after that deadline had passed, the now-Obama administration Justice Department finally responded that no exculpatory documents existed but at the same time allowed that "some arguably responsive documents" were still in the declassification process and might be produced some time in the future, Qahtani's attorney's filed a motion to compel the government to turn over documents relating to his interrogation.

This is not a case in which the Government must conduct a global search in order to identify those documents that are "exculpatory." Nor is this a case involving mere allegations of mistreatment, but one in which there is no dispute that the United States tortured Petitioner al Qahtani to procure incriminating evidence that it now relies upon to justify his continued detention. The Government can offer no justification for failing to comply with Section I.D.1 of the Amended [Case Management Order]. The Government's failure to comply with court-imposed deadlines has deprived Petitioner al Qahtani of information essential to rebut the Government's factual return, and has prevented this Court from adjudicating the substance of his challenge to his continued confinement. Accordingly, this Court should grant Petitioner al Qahtani's motion, order the Government to promptly comply with Section I.D.1 and hold the Government in contempt of Court.[550]

Among the materials Qahtani's attorneys had been seeking are videotapes of his interrogations. In June 2009, noting that Guantánamo habeas guidelines required courts to balance the value the government's materials would have for detainees against "the burden imposed on the government" of gathering and producing them to detainee's attorneys, Judge Rosemary M. Collyer ordered the government to assess the burden of producing any Qahtani videotapes. Judge Collyer summarized the government's response in a subsequent order:

In response to the Court's June 2, 2009 discovery order requiring the Government to report on the burden that would be imposed if the Court were to require the Government to produce all audio/video recordings of Petitioner from August 8, 2002 through January 15, 2003, [one and one-half line redaction]. Each tape is approximately [redacted] long. In order to clear these tapes for release, multiple agencies, including the Department of Defense ("DoD"), the FBI, and the Central Intelligence Agency would have to review the tapes frame-by-frame. Thus, to require the Government to produce all of these videotapes would be excessively burdensome.

However, the tapes created at the end of the period from August 13, 2002 to November 22, 2003 likely have some value to Petitioner. To justify Petitioner's detention, the Government relies on Petitioner's statements made from April 2003 through 2004. Petitioner challenges the veracity and reliability of the statements. He contends that his statements were so tainted by the cumulative effects of abusive treatment that took place previously that the statements cannot be credited or relied upon. Accordingly, Petitioner seeks information regarding his own mental and physical status both prior to and at the time he made the incriminating statements on which the Government relies. Thus, the audio/video recordings made later would be more likely to contain information relevant to Petitioner's challenge on voluntariness grounds than those made earlier. To provide relevant information to Petitioner and yet to ease the burden on the Government, the Court will order the Government to produce only these audio/video recordings of Petitioner created between November 15, 2002 and November 22, 2002.[551]

Qahtani's lawyers were requesting any and all videotapes recorded from the time Qahtani was placed in isolation in the Guantánamo brig on August 8, 2002 through the day his "special interrogation" was halted on January 15, 2003. The tapes Judge Collyer ordered the government to produce were those recorded the week before the Rumsfeld-ordered "special interrogation" began, after three and one-half months of isolation and the week-long Camp Delta interrogation that caused an FBI agent to recommend "leaving him alone, let[ting] him get healthy again."[552] The letter that T.J. Harrington, Deputy Assistant Director of the FBI's Counterterrorism Division, sent to the head of the Army's Criminal Investigation Command on July 14, 2004 gives a glimpse of what those videotapes may depict. "By late November," Harrington reported, "the detainee was evidencing behavior consistent with extreme psychological trauma (talking to non-existent people, reporting hearing voices, crouching in a corner of the cell covered with a sheet for hours on end)."[553]

Two years later, Qahtani's lawyers and the government continue to wrangle over what materials the government should be required to produce that would document his treatment at the hands of military interrogators in Guantánamo, and there are indications that the protracted habeas maneuverings themselves are exacting a toll on Qahtani. On September 10, 2010, the government submitted a "status report" to the court that suggested Qahtani had told military prosecutors in Guantánamo that he wanted to fire his attorneys and withdraw his habeas corpuspetition; in an attached affidavit, the Staff Judge Advocate of JTF GTMO reported that Qahtani had told the Assistant Staff Judge Advocate in late August that he wanted "to cancel his lawyer and cancel his case. ISN 063 said that in the future he would try to obtain new legal counsel, but for now he wanted to terminate everything."[554] In a subsequent status conference before Judge Collyer, Qahtani's attorneys disputed this, saying they met with al-Qahtani on September 13 and that "there is no chance" he intended to discharge he lawyers or dismiss his *habeas* action.[555]

Ibn al-Sheikh al-Libi

When President Bush announced the transfer of fourteen "high value detainees" from CIA black sites to Guantánamo in September 2006, conspicuously absent from the list was Ibn al-Sheikh al-Libi, the unnamed source of Colin Powell's assertion before the UN Security Council that Saddam Hussein had given two Al Qaeda operatives chemical and biological weapons training. As Human Rights Watch noted in a letter to the president in February 2007, al-Libi was one of thirty-eight men believed to have been held in CIA prisons who had effectively disappeared; the letter asked the president to "disclose the identities, fate, and current whereabouts of all prisoners held for any period of time at facilities operated or controlled by the CIA since 2001" and, for all those who had been transferred to the custody of other governments, to "disclose the date and location of the transfer."[556]

There were, by then, unconfirmed reports that al-Libi and four other Libyans the U.S. had been holding had been rendered to Tripoli. After years of ruptured relations and terrorism-related sanctions that began under Ronald Reagan in the 1980s, the Bush administration announced in May 2006 that it was restoring full diplomatic ties with Libya, specifically citing the Qaddifi regime's cooperation in the "War on Terror." "We are taking these actions in recognition of Libya's continued commitment to its renunciation of terrorism and the excellent cooperation Libya has provided to the United States and other members of the international community in response to common global threats faced by the civilized world since

September 11, 2001," Secretary of State Condoleezza Rice declared in a statement heralding "a new era in U.S.-Libya relations."[557] In October 2007, the *Washington Post*, citing a "Libyan security source," confirmed that al-Libi had been turned over to Tripoli not long before that announcement, and that he had told his Libyan jailers that, following his torture in Egypt and his debriefing in Afghanistan, where he recanted the alleged Al Qaeda–Iraq connection, he had been shuffled between CIA black sites in Jordan, Morocco, Afghanistan, and a "very cold" place his captors had told him was Alaska but which was likely the CIA black site in Poland.[558]

Neither the U.S. nor the Libyan government ever officially confirmed that al-Libi had been transferred to Qaddafi, but by early 2009 it was clear that he was among a group of former U.S. detainees being held in Tripoli's Abu Salim prison, and the Libyan government was facing growing pressure from human rights organizations and lawyers for other U.S. detainees to allow access to the group.

In the Spring of 2009, an attorney for Abu Zubaydah began working through intermediaries to request an opportunity to interview al-Libi, an associate of Abu Zubaydah at the Al Khaldan training camp in Afghanistan in the 1990s.[559] Then, on April 27, 2009, a Human Rights Watch delegation on a fact-finding mission to Libya was allowed into Abu Salim prison, where it was able to interview four former U.S. detainees, all of whom described being tortured in U.S. custody. One, Mohamed Ahmad Mohamed al-Shoroeiya, who was known as Hassan Rabi'i, described his treatment at the hands of Americans in what he believed was Bagram, Afghanistan: "The interpreters who directed the questions to us did it with beatings and insults," he told the delegation. "They used cold water, ice water. They put us in a tub with cold water. We were forced [to go] for months without clothes. They brought a doctor at the beginning. He put my leg in a plaster. One of the methods of interrogation was to take the plaster off and stand on my leg."[560]

The Human Rights Watch team also saw al-Libi, who they were told had been tried in secret by the Libyan State Security Court and sentenced to life in prison. It was the first time he had had contact with the outside world since he was captured in December 2001. Heba Morayef, a Human Rights Watch researcher, and another member of the delegation spoke with him briefly in the prison courtyard, telling him they wanted to interview him, too, about his experiences in U.S. custody. Al-Libi became angry. "Where were you when I was being tortured in an American prison?" was all he would say before walking away.[561]

Two weeks later, the Libyan newspaper *Oea*, a daily owned by Qaddafi's son Saif al-Islam Qaddafi, announced that al-Libi had committed suicide in his cell in Abu Salim prison. "Upon discovering the body, the police and a doctor were dispatched to the prison immediately to start the investigation," the report stated. The *Oea* story noted that al-Libi had been receiving regular visits from his family in recent months, and that friends were questioning the alleged circumstances of his death. Al-Libi's death was confirmed two days later by Human Rights Watch, which called on the U.S. and Libya to conduct a full and transparent investigation. Pressed for information about the reported suicide, a State Department spokesman told CNN, "I have to refer you to the government of Libya for any details regarding the matter."[562]

Notes

1 The United States signed but has not ratified the International Convention for the Protection of All Persons from Enforced Disappearance, and the Bush administration tried between 2003 and 2006 to renegotiate the scope of its prohibitions to shield CIA agents from prosecution under the treaty. See, e.g., R. Jeffrey Smith, "U.S. Tried to Soften Treaty on Detainees," *The Washington Post,* Sept. 9, 2009, http://www.washingtonpost.com/wp-dyn/content/article/2009/09/07/AR2009090702225.html. The article cites State Department documents secured by Amnesty International under the Freedom of Information Act. Regardless, enforced disappearance is barred under a variety of international human rights and humanitarian laws defining minimum due process rights.

2 For example, in 1994, the United Nations Commission on Human Rights, reviewing the case of a Libyan man who had been effectively "disappeared" by Libyan secret police and held in secret for three years, found that his prolonged incommunicado detention in an unknown location constituted torture and cruel and inhuman treatment (El-Megreisi v. Libyan Arab Jamahiriya, Communication No. 440/1990, UN Doc. CCPR/C/50/D/440/1990 (1994)). Likewise, the InterAmerican Court on Human Rights has ruled that "prolonged isolation and deprivation of communication are in themselves cruel and inhuman treatment, harmful to the psychological and moral integrity of the person and a violation of the right of any detainee to respect for his inherent dignity as a human being" (*Velásquez Rodríguez Fairen Garbi and Solis Corrales and Godinez Cruz Cases (Provisional Measures)*, Inter-American Court of Human Rights (IACrtHR), Jan. 19, 1988).

3 Fourth Declaration of Marilyn A. Dorn. Am. Civil Liberties Union v. Dep't of Def., N.1:04-CV-4151 (AKH) (S.D.N.Y. Mar. 30, 2005) ¶ XX. Cited in Am. Civil Liberties

Union v. Dep't of Def., 389 F. Supp. 2d 547, 557, 563, 565 (S.D.N.Y. 2005), http://www.aclu.org/torturefoia/legaldocuments/ccDorndecl.pdf.

4 President George W. Bush, Speech on Terrorism and High Value Detainees, Sept. 6, 2006, http://www.nytimes.com/2006/09/06/washington/06bush_transcript.html?pagewanted=all.

5 Eighth Declaration, of Marilyn A. Dorn, Hearing Transcript, Am. Civil Liberties Union v. Dep't of Def., No. 1:04-CV-4151 (AKH) (S.D.N.Y. May 12, 2003) ¶ XX; May 12, 2008, http://www.aclu.org/files/pdfs/natsec/20080512_transcript_directive.pdf.

6 CIA Office of the Inspector General (CIA OIG), "Counterterrorism Detention and Interrogation Activities, September 2001–October 2003," *CIA Office of the Inspector General Special Review*, May 7, 2004, 3, http://media.luxmedia.com/aclu/IG_Report.pdf. The report notes that the CIA had "intermittent involvement" with interrogations up through the Vietnam War, and had developed a Human Resource Exploitation (HRE) program to train interrogators in Latin American countries in the 1980s. That program was terminated in 1986 "because of allegations of human rights abuses in Latin America," and the agency had since avoided any role in interrogations. The CIA had no organizational background or experience in running detention facilities.

7 CIA OIG, 2.

8 The CIA is now withholding many of these communications, which include cables between the black sites and CIA headquarters and consultations between the CIA and the Justice Department's Office of Legal Counsel, partly on the grounds that the exchanges concern "the prospect of criminal, civil, or administrative litigation against the CIA and CIA personnel who participated in the program" and are thus privileged. "As subsequent events have shown" Ms. Hilton notes, "this anticipation was not unwarranted" (Decl. of Wendy M. Hilton, Am. Civil Liberties Union v. Dep't of Def., No. 1:04-CV-4151 (AKH) (S.D.N.Y. Aug. 31, 2009) ¶ XX).

9 CIA OIG, 94.

10 Bill Sammon, "Cheney Slams Obama's 'Politicized' Probe of CIA Interrogations," *Fox News*, August 30, 2009, http://www.foxnews.com/politics/2009/08/30/cheney-slams-obamas-politicized-probe-cia-interrogations.

11 CIA OIG, 100-01.

12 Ibid., 96.

13 Ibid., 105.

14 Michael V. Hayden, "A Conversation with Michael Hayden [Rush Transcript, Federal News Service]," *Council on Foreign Relations Publications,* Sept. 7, 2007. http://www.cfr.org/publication/14162/conversation_with_michael_hayden_rush_transcript_federal_news_service.html.

15 Matthew Cole and Brian Ross, "Deaths, Missing Detainees Still Blacked Out in New CIA Report," *ABC News,* 25 August 2009. http://media.abcnews.com/m/screen?id=8410340&pid=3029941.

16 Authorization for Use of Military Force in Response to the 9/11 Attacks, Pub. L. No. 107-40 (2006).

17 This original language could have been construed to authorize military action against Iraq, for example.

18 Congressional Research Service Report for Congress, "Authorization for Use of Military Force in Response to the 9/11 Attacks Pub. L. No. 107-40: "Legislative History"; and Tom Daschle, "Power We Didn't Grant," *The Washington Post,* December 23, 2005.

19 John Yoo, "The President's Constitutional Authority to Conduct Military Operations Against Terrorists and Nations Supporting Them," September 25, 2001, http://www.justice.gov/olc/warpowers925.htm; and "Authority for Use of Military Force to Combat Terrorist Activities Within the United States," October 23, 2001, http://www.justice.gov/olc/docs/memomilitaryforcecombatus10232001.pdf.

20 Edward R. Cummings, Email message. Department of State, 27 September 2001.

21 Article 2 of the Convention against Torture states:

1. Each State Party shall take effective legislative, administrative, judicial, or other measures to prevent acts of torture in any territory under its jurisdiction.

2. No exceptional circumstances whatsoever, whether a state of war or a threat of war, internal political instability or any other public emergency, may be invoked as a justification of torture.

3. An order from a superior officer or a public authority may not be invoked as a justification of torture.

22 Article 15 of the Convention against Torture states: Each State Party shall ensure that any statement which is established to have been made as a result of torture shall not be invoked as evidence in any proceedings, except against a person accused of torture as evidence that the statement was made.

23 Letter from the High Commissioner for Human Rights, October 11, 2001, http://dspace.wrlc.org/doc/get/2041/63353/00114display.pdf.

24 International Committee of The Red Cross, "ICRC Report on the Treatment of Fourteen 'High Value Detainees' in CIA Custody," February 2007, 28-31, http://www.nybooks.com/media/doc/2010/04/22/icrc-report.pdf. The ICRC was allowed to interview the 14 in Guantánamo in early October and early December 2006.

25 President George W. Bush, Speech on Terrorism and High Value Detainees, September 6, 2006. http://www.nytimes.com/2006/09/06/washington/06bush_transcript.html?pagewanted=all.

26 ICRC, 24.

27 Sworn Statement, Kandahar Detention Facility, February 13, 2002, http://www.aclu.org/files/projects/foiasearch/pdf/DOD043638.pdf.

28 United States Senate Armed Services Committee, "Inquiry into the Treatment of Detainees in U.S. Custody," November 20, 2008, 4. http://armed-services.senate.gov/Publications/Detainee%20Report%20Final_April%2022%202009.pdf. The report notes that, "Exploitation is a term the JPRA uses to describe the means by which captors use prisoners for their own tactical or strategic needs. Interrogation is only one part of the exploitation process."

29 Senate Armed Services Committee, xiii.

30 Ibid., 5.
31 John Yoo, Memorandum for William J. Haynes II General Counsel, Department of
    Defense, Re: Application of Treaties and Laws to al Qaeda and Taliban Detainees,
    January 9, 2002, http://www.gwu.edu/~nsarchiv/NSAEBB/NSAEBB127/02.01.09.pdf.
32 Senate Armed Services Committee, 1-2.
33 Alberto Gonzales, Memorandum for the President, Decision Re: Application
    of the Geneva Convention on Prisoners of War to the Conflict with al Qaeda
    and the Taliban, January 25, 2002, http://www.gwu.edu/~nsarchiv/NSAEBB/
    NSAEBB127/02.01.25.pdf.
34 Senate Armed Services Committee, 7.
35 Ibid., 9-11.
36 Ibid., 14.
37 Ibid., 21.
38 Photos are available at http://www.andyworthington.co.uk/wp-content/uploads/
    abughraib31.jpg and http://a.abcnews.com/images/Blotter/ht_Zubaydah1_071210_ssh.
    jpg.
39 Jane Mayer, *The Dark Side* (New York: Doubleday, 2008), 140-141. Mayer quotes a CIA
    source who disclosed that the CIA paid $10 million to Pakistan's intelligence services
    for Zubaydah's capture.
40 Michael Isikoff, "We Could Have Done This the Right Way," *Newsweek*, April 25, 2009,
    http://www.thedailybeast.com/newsweek/2009/04/24/we-could-have-done-this-the-
    right-way.html.
41 Ali Soufan, Testimony before the United States Senate Committee on the Judiciary,
    May 13, 2009, http://judiciary.senate.gov/hearings/testimony.cfm?id=e655f9e2809e5476
    862f735da14945e6&wit_id=e655f9e2809e5476862f735da14945e6-1-2.
42 Ibid.
43 According to several published accounts, Soufan repeatedly confronted Mitchell, at one
    point shouting, "We're the United States, and we don't do that kind of thing." Mitchell
    countered that his aggressive techniques were approved by the "highest levels" in
    Washington, and reportedly showed Soufan a document and said the approvals were
    coming from Alberto Gonzales. See, e.g., Michael Isikoff, "We Could Have Done This
    The Right Way," *Newsweek*, May 4, 2009; and Jane Mayer, *The Dark Side*.
44 Hon. Alvin K. Hellerstein, List of Cables, ACLU v. Department of Defense (04-cv-
    4151), http://www.aclu.org/torturefoia/legaldocuments/torturefoia_list_20090518.pdf.
45 Brian Ross, Interview with John Kiriakou, *ABC News*, December 10, 2007,
    http://abcnews.go.com/images/Blotter/brianross_kiriakou_transcript1_blotter071210.
    pdf.
46 Senate Armed Services Committee, 17.
47 John Yoo, *War By Other Means: an Insider's Account of the War on Terror* (New York:
    Atlantic Monthly Press, 2006).
48 Office of Legal Counsel, Memorandum for William J. Haynes II, Re: The President's
    power as Commander in Chief to transfer captured terrorists to the control and

custody of foreign nations, March 13, 2002, http://www.justice.gov/opa/documents/memorandumpresidentpower03132002.pdf.

49 See Jane Mayer, *The Dark Side*, 143, and Jan Crawford Greenburg, Howard L. Rosenberg, and Ariane de Vogue, "Sources: Top Bush Advisors Approved 'Enhanced Interrogation,'" *ABC News*, April 9, 2008, http://abcnews.go.com/print?id=4583256.

50 CIA OIG, 14.

51 Michael Isikoff, "We Could Have Done This the Right Way," *Newsweek*, April 25, 2009.

52 Office of Legal Counsel, Memorandum for Alberto R. Gonzales, Re: Standards of Conduct for Interrogation under 18 U.S.C. §§ 2340-2340A, August 1, 2002, 6, http://www.justice.gov/olc/docs/memo-gonzales-aug2002.pdf.

53 Ibid., 7.

54 Office of Legal Counsel, Memorandum for John Rizzo, Acting General Counsel of the Central Intelligence Agency, Re: Interrogation of an al Qaeda Operative, August 1, 2002, http://www.justice.gov/olc/docs/memo-bybee2002.pdf. An index of Bush-Era OLC Memoranda Relating to Interrogation, Detention, Rendition and/or Surveillance, released and still secret, is available at http://www.aclu.org/pdfs/safefree/olcmemos_2009_0305.pdf.

55 Memorandum for John Rizzo, 1-2.

56 Ibid., 7-8.

57 Ibid., 10.

58 Ibid.

59 Ibid., 13.

60 Ibid., 14.

61 Ibid., 15.

62 Ibid.

63 CIA OIG, 85.

64 Steven G. Bradbury, Memorandum to John A. Rizzo, Re: Application of United States Obligations Under Article 16 of the Convention Against Torture to Certain Techniques that May Be Used in the Interrogation of High Value al Qaeda Detainees, May 30, 2005 31, http://www.justice.gov/olc/docs/memo-bradbury2005.pdf.

65 CIA OIG, 36.

66 CIA OIG, 37.

67 Dana Priest, "CIA Avoids Scrutiny of Detainee Treatment," *The Washington Post*, March 3, 2005, http://www.washingtonpost.com/wp-dyn/content/article/2005/03/24/AR2005032402115.html; and Adam Goldman and Kathy Gannon, "Death Shed Light on CIA 'Salt Pit' Near Kabul," *MSNBC*, March 28, 2010, http://www.msnbc.msn.com/id/36071994/ns/us_news-security/#.TlFfo67qEvo.

68 Vaughn Index, "OIG Documents," November 20, 2009, documents 17, 55, 53, http://www.aclu.org/files/assets/20091120_Govt_Para_4_55_Hardcopy_Vaughn_Index.pdf.

69 Vaughn Index, documents 50, 11, 8, 46.

70 Armed Forces Regional Medical Examiner, "Final Report of Postmortem Examination," December 8, 2002, http://action.aclu.org/torturefoia/released/102405/3146.pdf.

71 Ibid. Within days, another detainee—this one a 22-year-old taxi driver who was incorrectly suspected of involvement in a rocket attack, was murdered by the same group of interrogators at the same facility.

72 CIA OIG, 35.

73 Al-Nashiri, Interrogation Summary, November 20, 2002, http://www.aclu.org/torturefoia/released/082409/cia_ig/oig196.pdf.

74 CIA OIG, 36, 44, and Giuseppa Sedia, "Further Evidence in CIA Torture Investigation," *Krakow Post*, September 13, 2010, http://www.krakowpost.com/article/2337.

75 CIA OIG, 44.

76 Ibid., 6.

77 Ibid., 31-32.

78 Ibid., 43. As in the January 2002 incident at Kandahar Detention Facility described in Chapter 2, this was not an isolated, improvised technique. The OIG Report notes: "A CIA officer [redacted] revealed that cigarette smoke was once used as an interrogation technique in October 2002. Reportedly, at the request of [redacted] an interrogator, the officer, who does not smoke, blew the smoke from a thin cigarette/cigar in the detainee's face for about five minutes. The detainee started talking so the smoke ceased. [Redacted] heard that a different officer had used smoke as an interrogation technique." And "[Redacted] admitted that he has personally used smoke inhalation techniques on detainees to make them ill to the point where they would start to 'purge.' After this, in a weakened state, these detainees would then provide [redacted] with information" (CIA OIG 72-73).

79 CIA OIG, 44.

80 In a footnote the OIG explains, "Racking is a mechanical procedure used with firearms to chamber a bullet or simulate a bullet being chambered."

81 CIA OIG, 42.

82 18 U.S.C. 2340(2).

83 CIA OIG, 14. See Chapter 2.

84 John Helgerson, Interview with *Der Spiegel*, August 31, 2009, http://www.spiegel.de/international/world/0,1518,646010,00.html.

85 CIA OIG, 1-2.

86 Ibid., 70-72.

87 Ibid., 42-43.

88 Ibid., 69.

89 Ibid., 2.

90 John Helgerson, Interview with *Der Spiegel*, August 31, 2009, http://www.spiegel.de/international/world/0,1518,646010,00.html.

91 Jane Harman, Letter to Scott Muller, February 10, 2003, http://www.house.gov/list/press/ca36_harman/Jan_3.shtml.

92 Vaughn Index, documents 32, 28.

93 Jane Harman, Letter to Scott Muller, February 10, 2003, http://www.house.gov/list/
press/ca36_harman/Jan_3.shtml.

94 International Committee of The Red Cross, ICRC Report on the Treatment of Fourteen
"High Value Detainees" in CIA Custody, February 2007, 34-35, www.nybooks.com/
icrc-report.pdf.

95 Ibid., 35.

96 Despite the death of the detainee at the Salt Pit, "water dousing" was emerging as a
preferred technique in the spring of 2002. The Inspector General reports, "According
to [redacted] and others who worked [redacted] 'water dousing' has been used
[redacted] since early 2003 when [redacted] officer introduced this technique to
the facility. Dousing involves laying a detainee down on a plastic sheet and pouring
water over him for 10 to 15 minutes.... A review [redacted] from April and May
2003 revealed that [redacted] sought permission from CTC [redacted] to employ
specific techniques for a number of detainees. Included in the list of requested
techniques was water dousing. Subsequent cables reported the use and duration
of the techniques by detainee per interrogation session. One certified interrogator,
noting that water dousing appeared to be a most effective technique, requested
CTC to confirm guidelines on water dousing. A return cable directed that the
detainee must be placed on a towel or sheet, may not be placed naked on the bare
cement floor, and the air temperature must exceed 65 degrees if the detainee will
not be dried immediately.... The DCI Guidelines do not mention water dousing as
a technique. The 4 September 2003 draft OMS Guidelines, however, identify 'water
dousing' as one of 12 standard measures that OMS listed, in ascending degree of
intensity, as the 11th standard measure. OMS did not further address 'water dousing'
in its guidelines" (CIA OIG, 76).

97 ICRC, 36.

98 ICRC, 36-37.

99 "...the individual is bound securely to an inclined bench.... The individual's feet
are generally elevated. A cloth is placed over the forehead and eyes. Water is then
applied to the cloth in a controlled manner. As this is done, the cloth is lowered
until it covers both the nose and mouth. Once the cloth is saturated and completely
covers the mouth and nose, the air low is slightly restricted for 20 to 40 seconds due
to the presence of the cloth. This causes an increase in carbon dioxide level in the
individual's blood. This increase in the carbon dioxide level stimulated increased
effort to breathe. This effort plus the cloth produces the perception of 'suffocation
and incipient panic,' i.e., the perception of drowning. The individual does not
breathe water into his lungs. During those 20 to 40 seconds, water is continuously
applied from a height of [12 to 24] inches. After this period, the cloth is lifted,
and the individual is allowed to breathe unimpeded for three or four full breaths.
The sensation of drowning is immediately relieved by the removal of the cloth.
The procedure may then be repeated. The water is usually applied from a canteen

cup or small watering can with a spout…[T]his procedure triggers an automatic
physiological sensation of drowning that the individual cannot control even though
he may be aware that he is in fact not drowning. [It] is likely that this procedure
would not last more than 20 minutes in any one application" (Memorandum for John
Rizzo, August 1, 2002, cited in CIA OIG, 21).

100 CIA OIG, 37.

101 Ibid.

102 Ibid., 21-22.

103 "Operational Issues Pertaining to the Use of Physical/Psychological Coercion in
Interrogation: an Overview," attached to July 26, 2002 memo from the Joint Recovery
Personnel Agency to the General Counsel's office of the Department of Defense,
available at http://www.washingtonpost.com/wp-srv/nation/pdf/JPRA-Memo_042409.
pdf.

104 CIA OIG, 83.

105 Ibid., 104.

106 Ibid., 89.

107 Ibid., 101.

108 Department of Justice, "Legal Principles Applicable to CIA Detention and Interrogation
of Captured Al-Qa'ida Personnel," April 28, 2003, www.aclu.org/torturefoia/
released/082409/olcremand/2004olc17.pdf and http://www.aclu.org/files/torturefoia/
released/082409/olcremand/2004olc151.pdf.

109 CIA OIG 93-94. See also President George W. Bush, Statement, "Torture, 'an Affront to
Human Dignity Everywhere,'" June 26, 2003, http://www.usembassy.it/file2003_06/alia/
A3062613.htm.

110 Mark Mazzetti and Scott Shane, "Interrogation Debate Sharply Divided Bush White
House," The New York Times, May 4, 2009, http://www.nytimes.com/2009/05/04/us/
politics/04detain.html, and Joby Warrick, "CIA Tactics Endorsed in Secret Memos," The
Washington Post, October 15, 2008, http://www.washingtonpost.com/wp-dyn/content/
article/2008/10/14/AR2008101403331.html.

111 CIA OIG, 24.

112 "HVT" is a High Value Target. See heavily redacted overview http://www.aclu.org/files/
torturefoia/released/082409/cia_ig/oig29.pdf. LS: FIX IT!

113 Vaughn Index, document 6.

114 Scott Shane and Mark Mazzetti, "Tapes by C.I.A. Lived and Died to Save Image," The
New York Times, December 30, 2007, http://query.nytimes.com/gst/fullpage.html?res=9
D06E6DC1639F933A05751C1A9619C8B63.

115 Mark Mazzetti and Scott Shane, "Bush Lawyers Discussed Fate of C.I.A. Tapes,"
The New York Times, December 17, 2007, http://www.nytimes.com/2007/12/19/
washington/19intel.html?_r=1&pagewanted=1.

116 Jane Mayer, The Dark Side, 292.

117 Jack L. Goldsmith III, Letter to John Helgerson, May 25, 2004, www.aclu.org/
torturefoia/released/082409/olcremand/2004olc26.pdf.

118 Jack L. Goldsmith III, Letter to Scott Muller, May 27, 2004, http://www.aclu.org/
     torturefoia/released/082409/olcremand/2004olc28.pdf.

119 George J. Tenet, Memorandum for the National Security Advisor, June 4, 2004,
     http://www.aclu.org/torturefoia/released/052708/052708_Other_3.pdf; and response:
     Condoleeza Rice, Memorandum for the Hon. George J. Tenent, June 4, 2004, http://
     www.aclu.org/files/assets/06112004_memotociadirector_0.pdf.

120 Dana Priest and R. Jeffrey Smith, "Memo Offered Justification for the Use of Torture,"
     The Washington Post, June 8, 2004, http://www.washingtonpost.com/wp-dyn/articles/
     A23373-2004Jun7.html.

121 Scott W. Muller, Memorandum for John Bellinger, July 2, 2004, http://www.aclu.org/
     files/projects/foiasearch/pdf/DOJOLC001079.pdf.

122 Joby Warrick, "CIA Tactics Endorsed In Secret Memos," *The Washington Post,* October
     15, 2008, http://www.washingtonpost.com/wp-dyn/content/article/2008/10/14/
     AR2008101403331.html.

123 Dana Priest, "CIA Holds Terror Suspects in Secret Prisons," *The Washington
     Post,* November 2, 2005, http://www.washingtonpost.com/wp-dyn/content/
     article/2005/11/01/AR2005110101644.html.

124 Douglas Jehl, "Report Warned C.I.A. on Tactics In Interrogation," *The New York Times,*
     November 9, 2005, http://www.nytimes.com/2005/11/09/politics/09detain.html.

125 Vaughn index, documents 3, 5, 2, and 4.

126 Mark Mazetti, "CIA Destroyed Two Videotapes Depicting Interrogations," *The
     New York Times,* December 7, 2007, http://www.nytimes.com/2007/12/07/
     washington/07intel.html.

127 Thomas H. Kean and Lee H. Hamilton, "Stonewalled by the C.I.A.," *The New York
     Times,* January 2, 2008, http://www.nytimes.com/2008/01/02/opinion/02kean.html.

128 Order Regulating Proceedings at 2, Am. Civil Liberties Union v. Dep't of Def.,
     No. 1:04-CV-4151 (AKH) (S.D.N.Y. Aug. 20, 2008), https://www.aclu.org/files/
     assets/20080820_ORDER_re_regulating_contempt_proceedings.pdf. The CIA tried to
     argue that because Helgerson's inquiry was a "Review" and not an "Investigation," and
     because he never physically had the tapes in his possession, they were not covered by
     the lawsuit. CIA's Mem. in Opp'n to Pls.' Mot. for Contempt and Sanctions at 2, 10-11,
     Am. Civil Liberties Union v. Dep't of Def., No. 1:04-CV-4151 (AKH) (S.D.N.Y. Jan. 10,
     2008), http://www.aclu.org/torturefoia/legaldocuments/Opposition011008.pdf.

129 Lev L. Dessin, Acting United States Attorney, Letter to Hon. Alvin K. Hellerstein,
     March 2, 2009, http://www.aclu.org/files/pdfs/safefree/lettertohellerstein_
     ciainterrogationtapes.pdf.

130 Transcript of Oral Argument at 16, Am. Civil Liberties Union v. Dep't of Def., No.
     1:04-CV-4151 (AKH) (S.D.N.Y. Sept. 30, 2009), t https://www.aclu.org/national-
     security/transcript-9302009-public-hearing-aclu-torture-foia-lawsuit.

131 *Id.* at 24.

132 *Id.* at 22-23, 26, 28.

133 CIA, "Background Paper on CIA's Combined Use of Interrogation Techniques,"

December 30, 2004, 1, www.aclu.org/torturefoia/released/082409/olcremand/2004olc97.
pdf.

134 Ibid., 9-10.

135 Ibid., 14-15.

136 Ibid., 17.

137 R. Jeffrey Smith, "Fired CIA Officer Believed CIA Lied to Congress," *The
Washington Post*, May 14, 2006, http://www.washingtonpost.com/wp-dyn/content/
article/2006/05/13/AR2006051301311.html.

138 Department of Justice, "Statement on the Investigation into the Destruction of
Videotapes by CIA Personnel," November 9, 2010, http://www.justice.gov/opa/pr/2010/
November/10-ag-1267.html.

139 CIA OIG, 41-42.

140 Adam Goldman, "Former FBI translator implicated in CIA interrogation abuse
at Polish jail," *Associated Press*, September 7, 2010, http://www.foxnews.com/
us/2010/09/07/ap-sources-fbi-translator-implicated-cia-interrogation-abuse-secret-
polish-jail-285427727/.

141 Department of Justice, "Statement of the Attorney General Regarding Investigation into
the Interrogation of Certain Detainees," Office of Public Affairs, June 30, 2011, http://
www.justice.gov/opa/pr/2011/June/11-ag-861.html.

142 In June, 2011, Army reservist Lynndie England was subpoenaed to testify before
a grand jury investigating al-Jamadi's death, which a Navy medical examiner
determined at the time to be homicide (see "Final Autopsy Report of Manadel
Al-Jamadi," January 9, 2004, http://www.npr.org/documents/2005/oct/jamadi/
autopsyreport.pdf). The grand jury is reportedly weighing the possible war crimes or
torture prosecution of a CIA agent identified as "Steve," who oversaw the interrogation
of CIA "ghost detainees" at Abu Ghraib and who was responsible for hooding and
shackling al-Jamadi in the fatal position. While England and ten other soldiers
working in the prison were court-martialed and convicted for offenses relating to the
other non-lethal abuse depicted in the Abu Ghraib photographs, Steve had merely
received a letter of reprimand from the CIA for failing to have a doctor examine
al-Jamadi when Navy Seals delivered him to the prison. One of Steve's superiors,
the CIA's deputy Baghdad station chief, was temporarily barred from field duty and
ordered to undergo retraining, but now reportedly runs the CIA Counterterrorism
Center's Pakistan-Afghanistan office.

143 Adam Goldman and Matt Apuzzo, "At CIA, Grave Mistakes, Then Promotions,"
Associated Press, February 9, 2011, http://abcnews.go.com/US/wireStory?id=12872725.

144 Maureen E. Mahoney and Everett C. Johnson, "Classified Response to the U.S.
Department of Justice Office of Professional Responsibility Classified Report
Dated July 29, 2009," October 9, 2009, http://judiciary.house.gov/hearings/pdf/
BybeeResponse090729.pdf.

145 Kathy Gannon and Adam Goldman, "Frustrated Family Wants CIA Detainee's
Remains," *Associated Press*, January 5, 2011, http://abcnews.go.com/International/

wireStory?id=12543525. The Bybee Classified Response as originally released is available at http://www.fas.org/irp/agency/doj/opr-bybeefinal.pdf.

146 Mohammed v. Obama, No. 1:05-CV-1347, 2009 WL 4884194, at *30 (D.D.C. Dec. 16, 2009), http://www.leagle.com/unsecure/page.htm?shortname=infdco20091217b92.

147 *Mohammed*, 2009 WL 4884194, at *5 and *4.

148 *Id.* at *15.

149 *Id.* at *15.

150 *Id.* at *15, citations omitted.

151 *Id.* at *16.

152 *Id.* at *24 and *25.

153 *Id.* at *26.

154 Peter Finn and Joby Warrick, "Detainee's Harsh Treatment Foiled No Plots," *The Washington Post,* March 29, 2009, http://www.washingtonpost.com/wp-dyn/content/article/2009/03/28/AR2009032802066_pf.html.

155 Noor al-Deen was reportedly eventually transferred from Morocco to Syria, but his current whereabouts are unknown.

156 George W. Bush, "Remarks by the President at Connecticut Republican Committee Luncheon," April 9, 2002, http://georgewbush-whitehouse.archives.gov/news/releases/2002/04/20020409-8.html.

157 "Declaration of Clive Stafford-Smith in Support of Plaintiffs'-Appellants' Opposition to United States' Motion to Dismiss," Exhibit A, Mohamed v. Jeppesen Dataplan, Inc., No. 08-15693 (9th Cir.), 1, http://www.aclu.org/national-security/declaration-clive-stafford-smith-support-plaintiffs-appellants-opposition-united-s.

158 *Id.,* 1-2.

159 See Part One, "The Experiment."

160 Ali Soufan, Testimony before the United States Senate Committee on the Judiciary, May 13, 2009, http://judiciary.senate.gov/hearings/testimony.cfm?id=e655f9e2809e5476862f735da14945e6&wit_id=e655f9e2809e5476862f735da14945e6-1-2.

161 There are conflicting accounts of what these details were, exactly. In 2004, *The New York Times* reported that Abu Zubaydah "did not name Mr. Padilla but described him physically and referred to him as a Latin American man who went by a Muslim name, an official with the Department of Homeland Security said. Intelligence agents began searching commercial and law enforcement databases under that Muslim name. At about the same time, Mr. Padilla was briefly detained in Pakistan on a passport violation. This helped a customs intelligence agent link the name give by Abu Zubaydah to 'an Arab alias not mentioned by the detainee,' the official said. That 'alias' led the agent to Mr. Padilla's Florida driver's license, the official said. The photo was shown to 'a detainee,' presumably Abu Zubaydah, who confirmed that Mr. Padilla was the 'Latin American' he had been describing. The Pakistanis also viewed the photo and made a confirmation" (Deborah Sontag, "Terror Suspect's Paths From Streets to Brig," *The New York Times*, April 25, 2004, http://www.nytimes.com/2004/04/25/national/25PADI.html?pagewanted=1). In *The Dark Side*, Jane Mayer reported, "Abu Zubaydah disclosed

Padilla's role accidentally, apparently. While making small talk, he described an Al Qaeda associate he said had just visited the U.S. embassy in Pakistan. That scrap was enough for authorities to find and arrest Padilla" (Jane Mayer, *The Dark Side*, 156).

162 "Al-Qaeda Claims 'Dirty Bomb' Know-How," BBC News, April 23, 2002, http://news. bbc.co.uk/2/hi/americas/1945765.stm.

163 David Rose, "How MI5 Colluded in my Torture: Binyam Mohamed Claims British Agents Fed Moroccan Torturers their Questions," *The Daily Mail*, March 8, 2009, http://www.dailymail.co.uk/news/article-1160238/How-MI5-colluded-torture-Binyam-Mohamed-claims-British-agents-fed-Moroccan-torturers-questions--WORLD-EXCLUSIVE.html.

164 Barbara Ehrenreich, "My Unwitting Role In Acts of Torture," *The Guardian*, February 21, 2009, http://www.guardian.co.uk/commentisfree/libertycentral/2009/feb/21/barbara-ehrenreich-guantanamo; and Barbara Ehrenreich, "How to Make Your Own H-Bomb," qtd in Zachary Heaton, "How (Not) to Build a Thermonuclear Bomb, *Port 80* (blog), March 13, 2005, http://port80.blogsome.com/2005/03/13/how-not-to-build-a-thermonuclear-bomb.

165 David Rose, "How MI5 Colluded in my Torture: Binyam Mohamed Claims British Agents Fed Moroccan Torturers their Questions," *The Daily Mail*, March 8, 2009.

166 Government's Response to Padilla's Objections to the Magistrate Judge's Report and Recommendation Denying Motion to Suppress Physical Evidence and Issues Writs Ad Testificandum, at 7-9, United States v. Padilla, No. 04-60001-CR (S.D. Fla. Nov. 16, 2006), http://www.pegc.us/archive/US_v_Padilla/gov_resp_20061116.pdf.

167 R (Mohamed) v. Sec'y of State for Foreign & Commonwealth Affairs, [2008] EWHC 2048 at *12, http://www.bailii.org/ew/cases/EWHC/Admin/2008/2048.html.

168 *Id.* at *9x

169 Declaration of Clive Stafford-Smith, 2-3.

170 *R (Mohamed)*, [2008] EWHC 2048, at ¶ 20.

171 *Id.* at ¶ 19.

172 *Id.* at ¶ 21.

173 John Ashcroft, Text of Announcement of Arrest of Suspected Terrorist Abdullah Al Muhajir, *Fox News*, June 10, 2002, http://www.foxnews.com/story/0,2933,54941,00.html.

174 Paul Wolfowitz, Justice Department Press Conference (transcript), June 10, 2002, http://www.defense.gov/transcripts/transcript.aspx?transcriptid=3498.

175 "Did Ashcroft Overstate Terror Arrest?" *ABC News*, June 13, 2002, http://abcnews.go.com/US/story?id=91559&page=1.

176 "'Dirty Bomb' Suspect had an Accomplice," *Fox News*, June 11, 2002, http://www.foxnews.com/story/0,2933,54908,00.html.

177 George W. Bush, "Remarks by the President on Homeland Security in Meeting with Congressional Leaders," Department of Homeland Security, June 11, 2002, http://www.dhs.gov/xnews/speeches/speech_0043.shtm.

178 Gov't's Resp. to Padilla's Objections, 5-6, *United States v. Padilla*.

179 *R (Mohamed)*, [2008] EWHC 2048, ¶¶ 29i-iv, 29v.

180 First Amended Complaint at ¶¶ 62-64, Mohamed v. Jeppesen Dataplan, Inc., No. 5:07-
     CV-2798 (N.D. Ca. Aug. 1 2007), http://www.aclu.org/files/pdfs/safefree/mohamed_v_
     jeppesen_1stamendedcomplaint.pdf.

181 First Amended Complaint at ¶ 61, *Mohamed v. Jeppesen.*

182 Declaration of Clive Stafford-Smith, 3.

183 *Id.*

184 Committee on Legal Affairs and Human Rights, "*Alleged secret detentions and unlawful
     inter-state transfers involving Council of Europe member states*," Parliamentary Assembly
     of the Council of Europe, July 6, 2006, ¶ 202, http://assembly.coe.int/Main.asp?Link=/
     CommitteeDocs/2006/20060606_Ejdoc162006PartII-FINAL.htm.

185 Binyam Mohamed, "One of them made cuts in my penis. I was in agony," (op-ed
     adapted from his attorney's notes of their May 2005 interview in Guantánamo), *The
     Guardian*, August 2, 2005, http://www.guardian.co.uk/uk/2005/aug/02/terrorism.
     humanrights.

186 Declaration of Clive Stafford-Smith, 7-8. Documents reviewed by the British High
     Court corroborate that UK agents gave questions and a photobook to US agents to
     pass through to his Moroccan interrogators. They also show one of the agents who
     interviewed Mohamed in Pakistan traveled to Morocco three times in late 2002 and
     early 2003. Despite this, the SyS maintains it did not know Mohamed was in Morocco
     (*R (Mohamed)*, [2008] EWHC 2048, ¶¶ 30-35).

187 Declaration of Clive Stafford-Smith, 9.

188 *Id.*, 11-12.

189 *Mohammed*, 2009 WL 4884194, at *20-21.

190 Re: Detainee issues, 15 April Report," April 17, 2002, http://www.aclu.org/pdfs/natsec/
     dod_emails_20081006.pdf ("No sitting or lying on your rack between reveille and taps
     unless you are on medical bedrest; likewise, you may not lie on the floor"; "All meals
     will be eaten in your cell; you must partake of all meals"; "You may not drill or march
     in military formation for any purpose except as authorized and directed by the facility
     commander"; etc.)

191 See, e.g., "Complaint," Jose Padilla v. John Yoo, http://jurist.law.pitt.edu/pdf/
     YooComplaint.pdf. The technical director of the Charleston Brig, Sanfred Seymour,
     confirmed many of these details in court testimony: Carol J. Williams, "New Light
     on Padilla's Treatment," *Los Angeles Times*, February 28, 2007, http://articles.latimes.
     com/2007/feb/28/nation/na-padilla28.

192 Emails, June 21 and June 28, 2002, http://www.aclu.org/pdfs/natsec/dod_
     emails_20081006.pdf.

193 Jack Goldsmith, *The Terror Presidency: Law and Judgment Inside the Bush
     Administration* (New York: Norton, 2007), 101-102.

194 Michael H. Mobbs, Special Advisor to the Under Secretary of Defense Policy,
     Declaration, August 27, 2002, 4, http://news.findlaw.com/hdocs/docs/padilla/
     padillabush82702mobbs.pdf.

195   Lowell Jacoby, "Declaration of Vice Admiral Lowell Jacoby," January 9, 2003, 3, http://
      www.pegc.us/archive/Padilla_vs_Rumsfeld/Jacoby_declaration_20030109.pdf.

196   Jacoby, 4-5

197   *Id.,* 7.

198   *Id.,* 8.

199   First Amended Complaint at ¶ 22, *Mohamed v. Jeppesen,*

200   Declaration of Clive Stafford-Smith, 15-16.

201   Bishir al-Rawi, Interview with ACLU, August 30, 2009, http://www.aclu.org/national-
      security/transcript-aclu-interview-bisher-al-rawi.

202   Mohamed elaborated on this later in his account: "For 20 days, 24 hours a day, they
      played some album by Slim Shady and Dr. Dre. I don't know the name of the album,
      and I've tried to block it out. But it has some song about 'America I love you' on it.
      There is talking on it by a girl, and it's about her. They used this music to torture us. It
      was blasting loud all around. There were speakers in every cell. Then they used horror
      sounds, like they were from the movies. 24 hours a day, for maybe two weeks. There
      was hardly any way to sleep. It was like a perpetual nightmare. After that, they came
      with other sounds, irritating things—thunder, planes taking off, cackling laughter, the
      screams of women and kids, that kind of thing. It was meant to drive you nuts. There's
      a prisoner in Guantánamo who was there who had totally lost his head" (Declaration
      of Clive Stafford-Smith, 17).

203   Declaration of Clive Stafford-Smith, 16-17.

204   *Id.,* 18.

205   Phil Hirschkorn, "Judge allows lawyers to visit 'enemy combatant,'" *CNN,* March 11,
      2003, http://www.cnn.com/2003/LAW/03/11/padilla.decision/index.html.

206   Donna R. Newman, "The Jose Padilla Story," *New York Law School Law Review,*
      2003/2004, http://www.nyls.edu/user_files/1/3/4/17/49/v48n1-2p39-67.pdf.

207   Paul Wolfowitz, Letter to James Comey, "Summary of Jose Padilla's Activities
      with Al Qaeda," May 28, 2004, 5-6, http://news.findlaw.com/cnn/docs/padilla/
      dod2doj52805sum.pdf. In one of the quirks of this document, the source of the
      statements is identified by a descriptor such as "al Qaeda detainee #2" but then almost
      immediately identified by name, in this case KSM.

208   *Id.,* 5-6.

209   *Id.,* 7.

210   James Comey, News Conference on Jose Padilla (transcript), *CNN,* June 1, 2004, http://
      edition.cnn.com/2004/LAW/06/01/comey.padilla.transcript/.

211   Declaration of Clive Stafford-Smith, 19.

212   *Mohammed,* 2009 WL 4884194, at *22.

213   Memorandum from the White House to Secretary of Defense Donald Rumsfeld, Re:
      Transfer of Jose Padilla to the Control of the Attorney General, November 20, 2005,
      http://www.aclu.org/national-security/memo-white-house-secretary-defense-donald-
      rumsfeld-regarding-transfer-jose-padilla.

214 Hamdi v. Rumsfeld, 542 U.S. 507, http://www.law.cornell.edu/supct/html/03-6696.
ZO.html.

215 Judge Luttig Opinion, Padilla v. Hanft, No. 05-6396 (4th Cir. Sept. 9, 2005), http://
news.findlaw.com/hdocs/docs/padilla/padhnft90905opn4th.pdf.

216 Alberto Gonzales, "Prepared Remarks of Attorney General Alberto R. Gonzales at the
Press Conference Regarding the Indictment of Jose Padilla," November 22, 2005, http://
www.justice.gov/archive/ag/speeches/2005/ag_speech_051122.html.

217 Superceding Indictment at 5, United States v. Padilla, No. 04-60001 (S.D. Fla. Nov. 17,
2005), http://abcnews.go.com/images/US/Padilla-Indictment-11-17-05.pdf. Adham
Amin Hassoun and Mohamed Hesham Youssef had been indicted a year before on
similar charges. Hassoun, who was arrested the same month as Padilla, in June 2002,
was originally charged with illegal possession of a firearm, see, e.g., http://www.
investigativeproject.org/documents/case_docs/122.pdf.

218 *Associated Press*, "Judge agrees Padilla case 'light on facts,'" *MSNBC*, June 21, 2006,
http://www.msnbc.msn.com/id/13462968/.

219 "Judge drops Padilla terror charge," CNN, August 21, 2006, http://www.cnn.com/2006/
LAW/08/21/padilla.charge/index.html.

220 Deborah Sontag, "Video Is a Window Into a Terror Suspect's Isolation," *The New York
Times*, December 4, 2006, available at http://www.nytimes.com/2006/12/04/us/04detain.
html.

221 Image at http://graphics8.nytimes.com/images/2006/12/03/us/04detain.xlarge1.jpg.

222 "Video Shows Treatment of Terrorism Suspect Padilla" (transcript), *NPR*, December 4,
2006, http://www.npr.org/templates/transcript/transcript.php?storyId=6576398.

223 Declaration of Andrew G. Patel at ¶5, United States v. Padilla, No. 04-60001 (N.D. Fla.
Dec. 1, 2006), http://cryptome.org/padilla/padilla-695-5.pdf.

224 *Id.*, ¶ 27.

225 *Id.*, ¶¶ 30, 31.

226 Affidavit of Angela Hegarty at ¶17, United States v. Padilla, No. 04-60001 (N.D. Fla.
Dec. 1, 2006), http://cryptome.org/padilla/padilla-695-3.pdf.

227 *Id.*, ¶ 15.

228 *Id.*, ¶¶ 4-7.

229 *Id.*, ¶ 11.

230 Deborah Sontag, "Defense Calls Padilla Incompetent For Trail," *The New York Times*,
February 23, 2007, http://www.nytimes.com/2007/02/23/us/23padilla.html.

231 Phil Hirschkorn, "The Case of the Missing Padilla Tape," CBS News Blogs, February 24,
2007, http://www.cbsnews.com/blogs/2007/02/24/primarysource/entry2510443.shtml;
and Michael Isikoff and Mark Hosenball, "Terror Watch: The Missing Padilla Video,"
Newsweek, February 28, 2007, http://www.newsweek.com/id/140851.

232 Curt Anderson, "Tape of Padilla Interrogation is Missing," *Associated Press*, March 9,
2007, http://www.usatoday.com/news/washington/2007-03-09-padilla-tapes_N.htm.

233 Government's Response to Defendant Padilla's CIPA § 5 Notice of Intent to Use

Classified Material at 1-2, United States v. Hassoun, No. 004-60001 (N.D. Fla, Feb 20, 2007), http://www.pegc.us/archive/US_v_Padilla/gov_resp_2_20070220.pdf.

234 *Id.*, 4.

235 *Associated Press*, "Prosecutors Can't Find Tape of Padilla's Final Interrogation in Navy Brig," *Fox News*, March 9, 2007, http://www.foxnews.com/story/0,2933,258075,00.html?sPage=fnc/us/lawcenter.

236 Carol J. Williams, "Aspects of Padilla's Treatment Confirmed," *Los Angeles Times*, February 28, 2007, http://warisacrime.org/node/19085.

237 Peter Whoriskey, "Judge Rules Padilla is Competent to Stand Trial," *The Washington Post*, March 1, 2007, http://www.washingtonpost.com/wp-dyn/content/article/2007/02/28/AR2007022801377.html.

238 Michael Isikoff and Mark Hosenball, "Terror Watch: The Missing Padilla Video," *Newsweek*, February 27, 2007, http://www.thedailybeast.com/newsweek/2007/02/27/the-missing-padilla-video.html.

239 Order Denying Def. Padilla's Motion to Dismiss at 8-10, United States v. Padilla, et al., No. 04-60001 (S.D. Fla. Apr. 9, 2007), http://www.discourse.net/archives/docs/Padilla-motion-denied.pdf.

240 *Id.* at 11.

241 *Id.* at 11.

242 *Id.* at 10.

243 Abby Goodnough, "Prosecutors Turn to Padilla for Closing Arguments," *The New York Times*, August 14, 2007, http://www.nytimes.com/2007/08/14/us/14padilla.html.

244 See e.g., Kirk Semple, "Padilla Gets 17 Years in Conspiracy Case," *The New York Times*, January 23, 2008, http://www.nytimes.com/2008/01/23/us/23padilla.html, and Warren Richey, "In Padilla Case, No Life Sentence," *The Christian Science Monitor*, January 23, 2008, http://www.csmonitor.com/USA/Justice/2008/0123/p11s01-usju.html.

245 Complaint at ¶ 20, Padilla v. Yoo, No. 08-0035 (N.D. Cal. Jan. 4, 2008), http://jurist.law.pitt.edu/pdf/YooComplaint.pdf.

246 *Id.* at ¶¶ 1, 3.

247 A parallel lawsuit Padilla filed against former Secretary of State Donald Rumsfeld, former Defense Department General Counsel Jim Haynes, and five others responsible for his treatment at the Charleston Brig was dismissed by a federal judge in South Carolina in February, 2011; see Introduction.

248 Ginsburg Dissent, Padilla v. Hanft, 547 U.S. 1062, 1651 (2006), http://www.supremecourt.gov/opinions/05pdf/05-533ginsburg.pdf.

249 Kennedy Opinion, *Hanft*, 547 U.S. 1062, 1651 (2006), http://www.texascollaborative.org/SilverblattModule/Padilla-v-Hanft-Supreme-Court.pdf.

250 Luttig Opinion, *Hanft*, 547 U.S.at 4-5, http://pacer.ca4.uscourts.gov/opinion.pdf/056396R1.P.pdf.

251 *Id.*, at 2-3.

252 *Id.*, 8-9.

253 CSRT Summary of Evidence, *The New York Times*, http://projects.nytimes.com/ guantanamo/detainees/1458-binyam-mohamed.

254 Personal Representative Notes Re: Binyam Mohamed, *The New York Times*, 3, http:// projects.nytimes.com/guantanamo/detainees/1458-binyam-mohamed.

255 See "Guantánamo Detainee Processes, " available at http://www.defense.gov/news/ Sep2005/d20050908process.pdf.

256 Clive Stafford Smith, *Eight O'Clock Ferry to the Windward Side* (New York: Nation Books, 2007), 51.

257 Captain John Carr and Robert Preston, Emails to Colonel Fred Borch, qtd in "Testimony of Lt. Commander Charles Swift before the Senate Judiciary Committee," July 11, 2006, http://fas.org/irp/congress/2006_hr/071106swift.html.

258 Charles D. Swift, "Statement of Lieutenant Commander Charles D. Swift before the Senate Committee on the Judiciary," July 11, 2006, http://fas.org/irp/congress/2006_ hr/071106swift.html.

259 Charge Sheet, United States of America v. Binyam Ahmed Muhammad, November 13, 2011, http://www.defense.gov/news/Nov2005/d20051104muhammad.pdf.

260 Referral, *Muhammad,* December 12, 2005, http://www.globalsecurity.org/military/ library/news/2005/12/d20051215muhammad.pdf.

261 Reuters, "Prosecutor likens Guantánamo defendants to vampires," *ABC News*, March 1, 2006, http://www.abc.net.au/news/2006-03-01/prosecutor-likens-guantanamo-defendants-to-vampires/808456.

262 Smith, *Eight O'Clock Ferry to the Windward Side,* 96-97, 101.

263 Ibid., 106-107.

264 Ibid., 106-116.

265 Two Republican co-sponsors of the DTA, Senators Lindsey Graham and Jon Kyl, had filed an amicus curiae brief in the case asserting that Congress had intended to apply the law retroactively to detainees with pending cases. In a footnote that is one of the most contentious passages of the majority opinion, Justice Stevens suggested the Senators' claims bordered on dishonesty. "While statements attributed to the final bill's two other sponsors, Senators Graham and Kyl, arguably contradict Senator Levin's contention that the final version of the Act preserved jurisdiction over pending habeas cases, those statements appear to have been inserted into the Congressional Record after the Senate debate," Stevens wrote. Stevens opinion, Hamdan v. Rumsfeld, 548 U.S. 557 (2006), www.law.cornell.edu/supct/html/05-184.ZS.html.

266 Stevens opinion, *Rumsfeld,* 548 U.S. 557 (2006).

267 *Id.*

268 *Id.*

269 "Notice of Military Commissions Act," October 18, 2006, http://www.pegc.us/archive/ DC_Gitmo_Cases_JHG/gov_MCA_notice_20061018.pdf.

270 The charges against Hamdan and Khadr were refiled almost immediately, and Hamdan was eventually convicted and sentenced on August 7, 2008 to 66 months in prison with

credit for 61 months time served. Khadr, a Canadian-born youth who was 15 at the time he allegedly threw a grenade that killed an American soldier in Afghanistan, pled guilty in October 2010 under a plea agreement that resulted in a 40-year sentence but also reportedly includes early repatriation to Canada.

271 Leigh Day & Co., Letter to Rt. Hon. David Miliband MP, March 28, 2008, http://graphics8.nytimes.com/packages/pdf/world/080328-LeighDay.pdf.

272 Ibid.

273 Ibid.

274 Charge Sheet, United States v. Binyam Ahmed Mohamed, 2008, www.defense.gov/news/Mohamed%20-%20sworn0603.pdf.

275 Clive Stafford Smith and Lt. Col. Yvonne Bradley, Letter to Susan J. Crawford and convening authority responses, May 30, 2008, cited in June 18, 2008 letter, http://www.scotusblog.com/wp-content/uploads/2008/06/mohamed-letter-6-18-08.pdf.

276 Clive Stafford Smith and Lt. Col. Yvonne Bradley, Letter to Susan J. Crawford, June 18, 2008.

277 Richard Stein, "The Foreign Office did try to conceal information from us," *The Guardian*, March 18, 2009, http://www.guardian.co.uk/world/2009/mar/18/binyam-mohamed-david-miliband; and *R (Mohamed)*, [2008] EWHC 2048 at ¶ 147x(4), http://www.bailii.org/ew/cases/EWHC/Admin/2008/2048.html. The UK court said of the US reaction, "The unreasoned dismissal by the United States Government of BM's allegations as 'not credible' as recorded in the letter of 22 July 2008 is, in our view, untenable, as it was made after consideration of almost all the material provided to us."

278 *R (Mohamed)*, [2008] EWHC 2048 at ¶ 87.

279 *Id.*at ¶ 147x.

280 *Id.* at ¶ 147xi-xii.

281 Declaration of Lieutenant Colonel Darrel J. Vandeveld, United States v. Mohammed Jawad, September 22, 2008, at ¶¶ 4, 7, and 10, http://humanrights.ucdavis.edu/projects/the-guantanamo-testimonials-project/testimonies/testimonies-of-prosecution-lawyers/vandeveld_declaration.pdf.

282 Declaration of Darrel J. Vandeveld, January 12, 2009, at ¶¶ 18-20, http://www.aclu.org/files/pdfs/safefree/vandeveld_declaration.pdf.

283 Vandeveld (2009) at ¶ 32.

284 *R (Mohamed)* [2008] EWHC 2519 at ¶ 17(vi), http://www.judiciary.gov.uk/docs/judgments_guidance/mohamed_judgment3_221008.pdf.

285 Carol J. Williams, "Charges dropped in terror cases," *Los Angeles Times,* October 22, 2008. See also *R (Mohamed)*, [2008] EWHC 2519 at ¶1 47xi-xii.

286 "Judge questions 'dirty plot' allegations by U.S.," *Los Angeles Times*, October 31, 2008, http://articles.latimes.com/2008/oct/31/nation/na-briefs31.

287 Documents available at http://www.scribd.com/doc/8615476/Habashi-v-Gates-Doc-1032.

288 Order, Habashi v. Bush, No. 05-CV-0765(EGS) (D.D.C. Dec. 8, 2008), http://www.aclu.org/national-security/al-habashi-v-bush-order.

289 R *(Mohamed)* [2008] EWHC 2519 at ¶ 40, http://www.bailii.org/ew/cases/EWHC/
     Admin/2008/2519.html.

290 *Id.* at ¶ 54-55.

291 *Id.* at ¶ 27.

292 R (Mohamed) v. Sec'y of State for Foreign & Commonwealth Affairs, [2009] EWHC
     571 at ¶ 5, http://www.reprieve.org.uk/static/downloads/2009_03_23_Binyam_
     Mohamed_v_Foreign_Office_Judgment_annex.pdf.

293 *Id.* at ¶ 6, 10.

294 *Id.*at ¶ 15-17.

295 "UK visit to Guantánamo detainee," BBC, February 11, 2009, http://news.bbc.
     co.uk/2/hi/uk_news/7884216.stm; and Clive Stafford Smith, Letter to President
     Obama, February 10, 2009, http://image.guardian.co.uk/sys-files/Guardian/
     documents/2009/02/11/CSSlettertoObama.pdf.

296 Yvonne Bradley, "Bring Binyam Home," *The Guardian,* February 11, 2009,
     http://www.guardian.co.uk/commentisfree/2009/feb/11/binyam-mohamed-
     guantanamo-torture.

297 Binyam Mohamed, Full Statement, *The Guardian,* February 23, 2009, http://www.
     guardian.co.uk/world/2009/feb/23/binyam-mohamed-statement-guantanamo.

298 R *(Mohamed)* [2009] EWHC 2549 at ¶ 10, http://news.bbc.co.uk/2/shared/bsp/hi/
     pdfs/16_10_09_mohamed_judgement.pdf.

299 *Id.* at ¶ 13-14.

300 *Id.* at ¶ 66iv.

301 R (Mohamed) v. Sec'y of State for Foreign & Commonwealth Affairs, [2010] EWCA
     Civ 65, http://www.reprieve.org.uk/static/downloads/2010_02_10_Binyam_Mohamed_
     Court_of_Appeals_Judgment.pdf, and Foreign Office, Statement on Binyam Mohamed
     Case, February 10, 2010, http://www.fas.org/irp/news/2010/02/binyam.html.

302 First Amended Complaint at ¶ 8, Mohamed et al. v. Jeppesen Dataplan, Inc., No. 5:07-
     CV-2798 (N.D. Ca. Aug. 1 2007), http://www.aclu.org/files/pdfs/safefree/mohamed_v_
     jeppesen_1stamendedcomplaint.pdf.

303 Opinion, *Mohamed v. Jeppesen*, No. 08-15693 (9th Cir. Apr. 28, 2009) at 8-9, http://
     www.aclu.org/files/pdfs/safefree/mohamedvjeppesen_districtcourtopinion.pdf.

304 *Mohamed v. Jeppesen*, 579 F.3d 943 (9th Cir. 2009), http://www.ca9.uscourts.gov/
     datastore/opinions/2010/09/08/08-15693.pdf.

305 Appendix, http://www.ca9.uscourts.gov/datastore/opinions/2010/09/07/08-15693-
     appendix.pdf.

306 *Mohamed v. Jeppesen*, 579 F.3d 943 (9th Cir. 2009).

307 *Id.*

308 "Binyam Mohamed: police to investigate claims British agents colluded in torture,"
     The Telegraph, July 10, 2009, http://www.telegraph.co.uk/news/newstopics/politics/
     lawandorder/5796601/Binyam-Mohamed-police-to-investigate-claims-British-agents-
     colluded-in-torture.html.

309 Andrew Johnson, "Goldsmith calls for investigation into UK's role in torture," *The*

Independent, February 14, 2010, http://www.independent.co.uk/news/uk/home-news/
goldsmith-calls-for-investigation-into-uks-role-in-torture-1899128.html.

310 Abu Zubaydah, "Verbatim Transcript of Combatant Status Review Tribunal Hearing
for ISN 10016," Closing Unclassified Section, 22-30, http://www.aclu.org/pdfs/safefree/
csrt_abuzubaydah.pdf.

311 "Respondent's Memorandum of Points and Authorities in Opposition to Petitioner's
Motion for Discovery and Petitioner's Motion for Sanctions," *Husayn v. Gates,*
08-cv-1360 (D.D.C. Oct. 27, 2009), http://big.assets.huffingtonpost.com/1295-
00oppositiontodiscovery.pdf.

312 Bob Woodward, "Detainee Tortured, Says U.S. Official," *The Washington Post,* January
14, 2009, http://www.washingtonpost.com/wp-dyn/content/article/2009/01/13/
AR2009011303372.html.

313 United States v. William J. Kreutzer, http://www.armfor.uscourts.gov/newcaaf/
opinions/2005Term/04-5006.pdf.

314 Morris D. Davis, "AWOL Military Justice," *Los Angeles Times,* December 10, 2007,
http://humanrights.ucdavis.edu/projects/the-guantanamo-testimonials-project/
testimonies/testimonies-of-prosecution-lawyers/awol-military-justice.

315 Charge Sheet, United States v. Khalid Sheikh Mohammed, et al., April 15, 2008, http://
www.defense.gov/news/Mohamed%20al%20Kahtani%20Dismissed%20Charges%20
9%20May%202008%20R.pdf. (Facsimile of April 15 Charge Sheet with Susan
Crawford's May 20 amendments.)

316 Woodward asked Crawford whether the other five had also been tortured. "I
assume torture," she answered, citing CIA Director Michael V. Hayden's public
acknowledgements that Khalid Sheik Mohammed had been waterboarded. However,
as Woodward reported, "Crawford said she let the charges go forward [against the
five] because the FBI satisfied her that they gathered information without using harsh
techniques. She noted that Mohammed has acknowledged his Sept. 11 role in court,
whereas Qahtani has recanted his self-incriminating statements to the FBI."

317 Bob Woodward, "Guantánamo Detainee Was Tortured, Says Official Overseeing
Military Trials," *The Washington Post,* January 14, 2009, http://www.washingtonpost.
com/wp-dyn/content/article/2009/01/13/AR2009011303372.html.

318 This and all the log quotations that follow in this section are from the Qahtani
Interrogation Log: "Interrogation Log Detainee 063," November 23, 2002, http://www.
ccrjustice.org/files/Al%20Qahtani%20Interrogation%20Log.pdf

319 T.J. Harrington, Letter to Major General Donald J. Ryder, July 14, 2004, http://www.
pegc.us/archive/In_re_Gitmo/pet_mot_disc_20050110_ex_C.pdf.

320 *AMA Code of Medical Ethics,* "Opinion 2.067 – Torture," December 1999, http://www.
ama-assn.org/ama/pub/physician-resources/medical-ethics/code-medical-ethics/
opinion2067.shtml.

321 In his October 12, 2006 statement before the Administrative Review Board in
Guantánamo, Qahtani described the interrogation methods recorded in the
Interrogation Log and told the Board, "As a result of the intense physical and

psychological stress from these methods, I went from approximately 160 pounds to 100 pounds and was sent to the hospital twice when I was close to death during interrogation" ("Summary of Administrative Review Board Proceedings for ISN 063," 7, http://projects.nytimes.com/guantanamo/detainees/63-mohammed-al-qahtani). Official weight records of Mohammed al-Qahtani available at http://humanrights.ucdavis.edu/ resources/library/documents-and-reports/gtmo_heightsweights.pdf/view.

322 An alternate, heavily redacted Qahtani interrogation log released as an attachment to the Schmidt-Furlow report describes this scene in greater detail: "The doctor spoke with the detainee. He was given an 800mg Motrin for chest pains. The detainee was attempting to gain the sympathy of the doctor. The detainee complained of having a hard time breathing but after the doctor examined the detainee he determined that the detainee could and was breathing just fine. The detainee also told the doctor that he was tired and needed to get some sleep. The doctor informed the detainee that he was getting ample sleep" ("Extracts from Shift logs 13 Dec 02 – 14 Jan 03," enclosure #64 to the Schmidt-Furlow report, http://action.aclu.org/torturefoia/released/061906/ Schmidt_FurlowEnclosures.pdf).

323 Enclosure #65 to the Schmidt-Furlow Report, *Investigation into FBI Allegations of Detainee Abuse at Guantánamo Bay, Cuba Detention Facility*, http://action.aclu.org/ torturefoia/released/061906/Schmidt_FurlowEnclosures.pdf.

324 The Manchester Document, "Seventeenth Lesson, Interrogation and Investigation," *The Smoking Gun*, http://www.thesmokinggun.com/file/seventeenth-lesson?page=0.

325 Ibid., 2.

326 Ibid., 8-9.

327 Ibid., 11-12.

328 Donna Miles, "Al Qaeda Manual Drives Detainee Behavior at Guantánamo Bay," American Forces Press Services, June 29, 2005, http://www.defense.gov/news/ newsarticle.aspx?id=16270.

329 United States Senate Armed Services Committee, *Inquiry into the Treatment of Detainees in U.S. Custody*, November 20, 2008, 6-7, http://armed-services.senate.gov/ Publications/Detainee%20Report%20Final_April%2022%202009.pdf.

330 Department of Justice Office of the Inspector General, *A Review of the FBI's Involvement in and Observations of Detainee Interrogations in Guantánamo Bay, Afghanistan, and Iraq*, May 2008, 27, www.justice.gov/oig/special/s0805/final.pdf.

331 Secretary Donald Rumsfeld and Gen. Meyers, Department of Defense News Briefing, January 11, 2002, http://www.defense.gov/transcripts/transcript.aspx?transcriptid=2031.

332 Ibid.

333 Senate Armed Services Committee, 1-2.

334 President George W. Bush, Memorandum, Re: Humane Treatment of Taliban and al Qaeda Detainees, http://www.pegc.us/archive/White_House/bush_memo_20020207_ ed.pdf.

335 DoJ IG Witness Interviews, February 25, 2009, 787, http://www.aclu.org/files/pdfs/ natsec/dojfbi20100514/55_interview1_5pp.pdf.

336 Measurements and Weights of Individuals Detained by the Department of Defense at Guantánamo Bay, Cuba, March 16, 2007, http://humanrights.ucdavis.edu/resources/library/documents-and-reports/gtmo_heightsweights.pdf/view.

337 DoJ IG Witness Interviews, February 24, 2009, 85, http://www.aclu.org/files/pdfs/natsec/dojfbi20100514/08_interview1_or_interviewnotes_20050304_5pp.pdf.

338 DoJ IG Witness Interviews, February 24, 2009, 400, http://www.aclu.org/files/pdfs/natsec/dojfbi20100514/24_interview1_or_interviewnotes_20051116_6pp.pdf.

339 DoJ IG, 183.

340 Central Intelligence Agency Directorate of Operations, Technical Services Division, "Communist Control Techniques: An Analysis of the Methods Used by Communist State Police in the Arrest, Interrogation, and Indoctrination of Persons Regarded as 'Enemies of the State,'" April 2, 1956, 25-26, http://dspace.wrlc.org/doc/bitstream/2041/70937/00064_560402display.pdf.

341 Alert D. Biderman, "Communist Attempts to Elicit False Confessions From Air Force Prisoners of War," Bulletin of the New York Academy of Medicine, September 1957, 620-621, http://www.ncbi.nlm.nih.gov/pmc/articles/PMC1806204/.

342 Senate Armed Services Committee, 7-8.

343 Ibid., 9.

344 Ibid., 9.

345 Ibid., 11.

346 MG Michael E. Dunlavey, "Summarized Witness Statement of MG (Retired) Mike Dunlavey," March 29, 2005, 9-17, http://www.aclu.org/pdfs/safefree/dod_release_07022009.pdf.

347 Ibid.

348 Rick Baccus, "The Torture Question," Frontline, PBS, August 27, 2005, http://www.pbs.org/wgbh/pages/frontline/torture/interviews/baccus.html.

349 Memorandum Opinion, Abdah et al. v. Obama, 2010 WL 3270761 (D.D.C.), https://ecf.dcd.uscourts.gov/cgi-bin/show_public_doc?2004cv1254-873.

350 Tim Golden and Don Van Natta, Jr., "U.S. Said to Overstate Value of Guantánamo Detainees," The New York Times, June 21, 2004, http://www.nytimes.com/2004/06/21/politics/21GITM.html.

351 Army Spc. Shanita Simmons, "Manchester Manual the Code of Conduct for terrorism," JTF Guantánamo Public Affairs, August 14, 2007, http://www.jtfgtmo.southcom.mil/storyarchive/2007/August/081407-2-manmanual.html.

352 DoD News Briefing, January 11, 2002.

353 Senate Armed Services Committee, 41.

354 Ibid.

355 Ibid., 39.

356 DoJ IG, 181, 204.

357 DoJ IG, 78.

358 DoJ IG Witness Interviews, July 30, 2010 release to ACLU, 1000, http://www.aclu.org/pdfs/natsec/DOJOIGFOIA_CasemapInterviewSummaries_07302010release.pdf.

359 See Part One, "The Experiment."

360 DoJ IG Witness Interviews, 1000.

361 DoJ IG Witness Interviews, 300, February 24, 2009, http://www.aclu.org/files/pdfs/
natsec/dojfbi20100514/21_interview2_8pp.pdf.

362 DoJ IG Witness Interviews, 300.

363 DoJ IG, 81. Explaining Qahtani's exaggerated sense of how long his experience in the
brig lasted, Soufan told the IG, "One of the side-effects of isolating a detainee is that
they lose their anchor to time or a sense of time."

364 DoJ IG Witness Interviews, 300. In its 1956 study "Communist Control Techniques,"
CIA researches documented the effects of isolation regimens on prisoners. After
four to six weeks in isolation, prisoners weep, mutter, pray aloud in their cells, and
follow the orders of guards "with the docility of a trained animal." Ultimately, "Some
prisoners may become delirious and have visual hallucinations. God may appear to
such a prisoner and tell him to cooperate with his interrogator. He may see his wife
standing beside him…If he is given an opportunity to talk, he may say anything
which seems to be appropriate, or to be desired by his listener; for in his confused
and befuddled state he may be unable to tell what is 'actually true' from what 'might
be' or 'should be' true. He may be highly suggestible and may 'confabulate' the details
of any story suggested to him…. [Some prisoners,] especially those with pre-existing
personality disturbances, may become frankly psychotic. However, frank psychotic
manifestations, other than those of the 'prison psychosis' described above, are not
usual, primarily because those having charge of the prisoners usually break the routine
of total isolation when they see that disorganization of the prisoner's personality is
imminent."

365 DoJ IG, 82, and OIG Witness Interviews, 300.

366 Senate Armed Services Committee, 24-29.

367 Bob Drogin, "No Leaders of Al Qaeda Found at Guantánamo," Los Angeles Times,
August 18, 2002, http://articles.latimes.com/2002/aug/18/nation/na-gitmo18.

368 Tim Golden and Don Van Natta, Jr., "The Reach of War: U.S. Said to Overstate Value
of Guantánamo Detainees," The New York Times, June 21, 2004, http://www.nytimes.
com/2004/06/21/world/the-reach-of-war-us-said-to-overstate-value-of-Guantánamo-
detainees.html?pagewanted=all&src=pm.

369 Declaration of Colonel Lawrence B. Wilkerson (Ret.), Adel Hassan Hamad v. George
Bush et al., March 24, 2010, http://humanrights.ucdavis.edu/projects/the-guantanamo-
testimonials-project/testimonies/testimonies-of-foreign-affairs-officials/declaration-by-
lawrence-b-wilkerson-in-the-case-of-adel-hamad.

370 Julian Borger, "'Soft' Guantánamo chief ousted," The Guardian, October 16, 2002,
http://www.guardian.co.uk/world/2002/oct/16/usa.afghanistan.

371 Senate Armed Services Committee, 43.

372 Col. Brittain P. Mallow, Memorandum for Record, XX September 2002, http://www.
aclu.org/files/projects/foiasearch/pdf/DOD045174.pdf.

373 Percival later told the Senate Armed Services Committee that at the July 2002 CIA

training, Witsch "acted as the 'beater' while he was the 'beatee.'" Senate Armed Services Committee, 22.

374 Senate Armed Services Committee, 47.

375 Ibid., 48.

376 DoJ IG, 82.

377 Senate Armed Services Committee, 58.

378 Jack Goldsmith, *The Terror Presidency: Law and Judgment Inside the Bush Administration* (New York: W.W. Norton & Company, 2007).

379 Office of the Staff Judge Advocate, "Trip Report, DoD General Counsel Visit to GTMO," September 27, 2002, http://dspace.wrlc.org/doc/bitstream/2041/70968/00411_020927_001display.pdf.

380 Senate Armed Service, 49.

381 DoJ IG Witness Interviews, 495, http://www.aclu.org/files/pdfs/natsec/dojfbi20100514/32_interview1_or_interviewnotes_20050621_9pp.pdf.

382 DoJ IG Witness Interviews, 495.

383 FBI email, October 1, 2002, http://www.aclu.org/pdfs/natsec/DOJOIG07036.pdf.

384 MG Michael E. Dunlavey, Memorandum for Commander, Joint Task Force 160, October 2, 2002, http://dspace.wrlc.org/doc/bitstream/2041/63492/00253display.pdf.

385 Senate Armed Services Committee, 50.

386 Ibid., 52.

387 Barry Rhodes, Peter Zolper, and Mark Fallon, "Counter Resistance Strategy Meeting Minutes," October 2, 2002, http://www.torturingdemocracy.org/documents/20021002.pdf.

388 Ibid.

389 Mark Fallon, Email to Sam McCahon, October 28, 2002, http://www.torturingdemocracy.org/documents/20021002.pdf.

390 Senate Armed Services Committee, 57.

391 DoJ IG, 83-84. Qahtani, when he was interviewed by the OIG, described how a dog was used "as a tool to intimidate him" during the interrogation. He said that the dog was not ordered to attack him, but rather was walked around the interrogation room and allowed to get very close to him, barking and growling the whole time. Qahtani said the dog tried to bite him but was restrained by its handler.

392 FBI email, October 8, 2002, http://www.aclu.org/pdfs/natsec/DOJOIG06961.pdf.

393 Senate Armed Services Committee, 61.

394 MG Michael E. Dunlavey, Memorandum, Counter-Resistance Strategies, October 11, 2002, http://www.defenselink.mil/news/Jun2004/d20040622doc3.pdf.

395 Lt. Col. Diane Beaver, Memorandum, Legal Brief on Proposed Counter-Resistance Strategies, October 11, 2002, http://www.defenselink.mil/news/Jun2004/d20040622doc3.pdf.

396 Ibid., 5-6.

397 Ibid., 5.

398 Senate Armed Services Committee, 96.

399 Gen. James T. Hill, Memorandum for Chair, Joint Chiefs of Staff, October 25, 2002,http://www.torturingdemocracy.org/documents/20021025.pdf.

400 Lt. Col. Mark Gingras, Interview with Army Inspector General, qtd. in Senate Armed Services Committee, 67.

401 Senate Armed Services Committee, 67-69.

402 Ibid., 72.

403 Ibid., 71.

404 DoJ IG, 191-192 and DoJ IG Witness Interviews, 442, http://www.aclu.org/files/pdfs/natsec/dojfbi20100514/26_interview1_or_interviewnotes_20051003_10pp.pdf.

405 DoJ IG, 106.

406 Ibid., 110.

407 Ibid., 86.

408 ibid., 86.

409 Ibid., 113-115.

410 Ibid., 115.

411 Julian Borger, "'Soft' Guantánamo chief ousted," *The Guardian*, October 16, 2002, http://www.guardian.co.uk/world/2002/oct/16/usa.afghanistan/print.

412 Senate Armed Services Committee, 76.

413 Ibid., 75-78, and DoJ IG report, 87-88.

414 Senate Armed Services Committee, 76.

415 Ibid., 78.

416 Senate Armed Services Committee, 78-79, and DoJ IG report, 88-89.

417 DoJ IG, 88. While the FBI adamantly opposed the rendition plan, its position was clouded by the fact that since September some FBI personnel had been suggesting that Qahtani be sent from Guantánamo to a CIA black site for interrogation. In the course of his 2008 investigation, the Justice Department's Inspector General uncovered a draft of a letter that was to be sent by Attorney General John Ashcroft to the National Security Council proposing the move so that al-Qahtani could be "debriefed by highly knowledgeable personnel, and dissemination regarding the results of these debriefings would be released to the appropriate U.S. intelligence entities expeditiously." The proposal evidently was developed around the time the military took over Qahtani's interrogation, and seems to have been part of a strategy the FBI devised with Chertoff, Ashcroft, and Thompson to remove Qahtani's interrogation from the military's control. The letter was never finalized or sent. DoJ IG, 93-101.

418 DoJ IG, 89.

419 Ibid., 90-91.

420 FBI, Email, "Interrogation Plan #63," date redacted, www.aclu.org/pdfs/natsec/DoJOIG007034.pdf.

421 DoJ IG, 91, and FBI email to Marion Bowman et al., "To document BAU assistance and challenges encountered during TDY assignment in Guantánamo Bay," May 30, 2003, http://action.aclu.org/torturefoia/released/022306/1261.pdf.

422 Senate Armed Services Committee, 83.

423 Ibid.

424 Ibid., 87.

425 FBI, Email to Major General Geoffrey Miller, November 21, 2002, www.aclu.org/pdfs/natsec/admin_of_torture_p139.pdf.

426 Senate Armed Services Committee, 81.

427 "Measurements of Heights and Weights of Individuals Detained by the Department of Defense at Guantánamo Bay," Center for the Study of Human Rights in the Americas, UC Davis, March 16, 2007, http://humanrights.ucdavis.edu/resources/library/documents-and-reports/gtmo_heightsweights.pdf/view.

428 Senate Armed Services Committee, 88.

429 Ibid., 87.

430 Ibid., 85.

431 William J. Haynes II, Memorandum for Secretary of Defense, Counter-Resistance Techniques, November 27, 2002, www.gwu.edu/~nsarchiv/NSAEBB/NSAEBB127/02.12.02.pdf.

432 Senate Armed Services Committee, 98.

433 Ibid., 91-94.

434 John P. Rankin, "After Action Report Joint Task Force Guantánamo Bay (JTF-GITMO) Training Evolution," January 15, 2003, http://www.torturingdemocracy.org/documents/20030115-4.pdf.

435 Alberto Mora, Statement for the Record, "Office of General Counsel Involvement in Interrogation Issues," July 7, 2004, http://www.newyorker.com/images/pdf/2006/02/27/moramemo.pdf.

436 Jane Mayer, "The Memo," The New Yorker, February 27, 2006, http://www.newyorker.com/archive/2006/02/27/060227fa_fact.

437 Mora, "Statement for the Record."

438 Dana Priest and Barton Gellman, "U.S. Decries Abuse but Defends Interrogations," The Washington Post, December 26, 2002, http://www.washingtonpost.com/wp-dyn/content/article/2006/06/09/AR2006060901356.html.

439 DoJ IG, 94. An attachment to the agenda included a note claiming that Qahtani's ongoing interrogation was now producing intelligence and so rendition "may not be appropriate."

440 Mora, "Statement for the Record."

441 Memorandum for Commander USSOUTHCOM, Re: Counter-Resistance Techniques, January 15, 2003, http://www.aclu.org/files/projects/foiasearch/pdf/DOJOLC000020.pdf.

442 Senate Armed Services Committee, 135-136.

443 Mike Boettcher, "Al Qaeda Online for Terrorism" (transcript), CNN report, March 6, 2002, http://edition.cnn.com/TRANSCRIPTS/0203/06/lt.15.html.

444 Ibid.

445 "From Germany to Guantánamo: The Career of Prisoner No. 760," Der Spiegel, September 10, 2008, http://www.spiegel.de/international/world/0,1518,583193,00.html.

446 "Summary of Administrative Review Board Proceedings for ISN 760 (Mohamedou

Ould Slahi)" (transcript), http://online.wsj.com/public/resources/documents/couch-slahiARB-03312007.pdf; and "Combatant Status Review Board" (transcript), November 27, 2004, http://projects.nytimes.com/guantanamo/detainees/760-mohamedou-ould-slahi.

447 United States Senate Armed Services Committee, 107-108.

448 DoJ IG Witness Interviews, 468, http://www.aclu.org/files/pdfs/natsec/dojfbi20100514/27_interview1_7pp.pdf.

449 Memorandum for the General Counsel of the Department of Defense, Re: Detainee Interrogations, January 15, 2003, http://www.dod.gov/pubs/foi/operation_and_plans/Detainee/additional_detainee_documents/07-F-2406%20doc%207.pdf.

450 Mora, "Statement for the Record."

451 Becker's memo asserted that the four Category III techniques were being used, with OLC approval, by the CIA. This was not entirely true: the August 2, 2002 Yoo memo specifically left off mock executions and did not extend approval for exposure to cold. Nevertheless, two months before, CIA agents had killed the detainee in its Salt Pit facility in Afghanistan by dousing him with water and leaving him exposed to the elements (see Part One, "Black Sites, Lies, and Videotapes").

452 Senate Armed Services Committee, 113. Becker told the Senate Armed Services Committee in 2007 he had included the use of drugs as an option and his description of their efficacy based "on a rumor that [the CIA] had used drugs in their interrogation program."

453 JTF GITMO, Memorandum, Effectiveness of the Use of Certain Category II Counter-Resistance Strategies, http://americantorture.com/documents/gitmo/04.pdf; see also Senate Armed Services Committee, 113-115.

454 Senate Armed Services Committee, 114-115, and FBI, Interview Notes, "CTORS/MLDU FBIHQ-AFGHANISTAN," July 23, 2009, http://www.aclu.org/files/pdfs/natsec/dojoig_5_007132_876179_2.pdf.

455 Senate Armed Services Committee, 116-117.

456 Senate Armed Services Committee, 118-119.

457 Office of Legal Counsel, Memorandum for William J. Haynes II, Re: Military Interrogation of Alien Unlawful Combatants Held Outside the United States, March 14, 2003, 73, 58, at http://www.justice.gov/olc/docs/memo-combatantsoutsideunitedstates.pdf.

458 Mora, "Statement for the Record."

459 Office of Professional Responsibility, "Investigation in the Office of Legal Counsel's Memoranda Concerning Issues Relating to the Central Intelligence Agency's Use of 'Enhanced Interrogation Techniques' on Suspected Terrorists," July 29, 2009, 78, http://cdm266901.cdmhost.com/cdm4/item_viewer.php?CISOROOT=/p266901coll4&CISOPTR=2317&CISOBOX=1&REC=3.

460 Mora, "Statement for the Record."

461 Senate Armed Services Committee, 120.

462 "Working Group Report on Detainee Interrogations in the Global War on Terrorism:

Assessment of Legal, Historical, Policy, and Operational Considerations," April 4, 2003, 65-66, http://www.gwu.edu/~nsarchiv/NSAEBB/NSAEBB127/03.04.04.pdf.

463 Senate Armed Services Committee, 122.

464 Colin Powell, Speech to the United Nations on Iraq, February 5, 2003, http://www.washingtonpost.com/wp-srv/nation/transcripts/powelltext_020503.html.

465 Michael Isikoff and David Corn, *Hubris: The Inside Story of Spin, Scandal, and the Selling of the Iraq War* (New York: Crown Books, 2006), 120-121; Jane Mayer, *The Dark Side*, 104-108, 134-138; George Tenet, *At the Center of the Storm* (New York: Harper Collins, 2007), 353; and Adam Goldman, "Ex-CIA officer linked to detainee abuse," *Associated Press*, September 8, 2010, http://www.philly.com/inquirer/world_us/20100908_Ex-CIA_officer_linked_to_detainee_abuse.html.

466 Senate Select Committee on Intelligence, "Postwar Findings About Iraq's WMD Programs and Links to Terrorism and How They Compare With Prewar Assessments," September 8, 2006, 80-81, http://intelligence.senate.gov/phaseiiaccuracy.pdf.

467 Defense Intelligence Agency DITSUM #044-02, February 2002, cited in John D. Rockefeller IV and Carl Levin, Letter to Vice Admiral Lowell E. Jacoby, October 18, 2005, http://www.fas.org/irp/news/2005/11/DIAletter.102605.pdf.

468 Mora, "Statement for the Record."

469 FBI, Email to Pasquale J D'Amuro et al., March 14, 2002, 12-13, www.aclu.org/files/pdfs/natsec/dojoig_2_006979_876175.pdf.

470 Department of Justice Office of the Inspector General, "A Review of the FBI's Involvement in and Observations of Detainee Interrogations in Guantánamo Bay, Afghanistan, and Iraq," May 2008, 195, www.justice.gov/oig/special/s0805/final.pdf.

471 Schmidt-Furlow, "Army Regulation 15-6: Final Report Investigation into FBI Allegations of Detainee Abuse at Guantánamo Bay, Cuba Detention Facility," 7, http://www.defense.gov/news/Jul2005/d20050714report.pdf.

472 Schmidt-Furlow, Attachments to Report, 858, http://action.aclu.org/torturefoia/released/061906/Schmidt_FurlowEnclosures.pdf.

473 Schmidt-Furlow, 8.

474 Senate Armed Services Committee, 128-129.

475 Ibid., 126-128.

476 Ibid., 129.

477 Memorandum for the Commander, US Southern Command, Counter-Resistance Techniques in the War on Terrorism, April 16, 2003, http://www.aclu.org/files/projects/foiasearch/pdf/DOJOLC000023.pdf.

478 John Daniszewski and Shamim Ur-Rehman, "Terror Suspect Likely to Face Charges in U.S.," *Los Angeles Times*, September 16, 2002, http://articles.latimes.com/2002/sep/16/world/fg-pakistan16; John Daniszewski, "Al Qaeda Suspect in U.S. Hands," *Los Angeles Times*, September 17, 2002, http://articles.latimes.com/2002/sep/17/world/fg-ramzi17; and Adam Goldman and Matt Apuzzo, "CIA Tapes of Terrorist Interrogation Found Under Desk," *Associated Press*, August 17, 2010, http://www.huffingtonpost.com/2010/08/17/cia-tapes-of-terrorist-in_n_684366.html.

479 "Summary of Administrative Review Board Proceedings for ISN 760," November
    22, 2005, 24-27, http://online.wsj.com/public/resources/documents/couch-
    slahiARB-03312007.pdf.
480 DoJ IG, 298.
481 Ibid., 200.
482 Ibid., 126.
483 DoJ IG, 126-127 and Senate Armed Services Committee, 136-138.
484 Senate Armed Services Committee, 139.
485 DoJ IG, 124.
486 Schmidt-Furlow, 25.
487 Ibid., 24.
488 Senate Armed Services Committee, 140.
489 Schmidt-Furlow, 25.
490 DoJ IG, 127, and DoJ IG Witness Interviews, 1007, http://www.aclu.org/national-
    security/doj-ig-witness-interviews.
491 Senate Armed Services Committee, 140.
492 DoJ IG, 123.
493 Jess Bravin, "The Conscience of the Colonel," *The Wall Street Journal,* March 31, 2007,
    http://pierretristam.com/Bobst/07/wf040107.htm.
494 Administrative Review Board, 27. The Schmidt-Furlow report recorded that Slahi
    "reported 'rib contusions' from an altercation with MPs when moved between camps"
    and that notes from a doctor's examination recorded an "'edema of the lower lip'" and
    a "small laceration' on his head," but that the notes gave "no indications of swelling or
    contusions to support a conclusion that the subject of the second special interrogation
    was hit "very hard all over."
495 Senate Armed Services Committee, 140-141.
496 President George W. Bush, Statement, "Torture 'an Affront to Human Dignity
    Everywhere,'" June 26, 2003, http://www.usembassy.it/viewer/article.asp?article=/
    file2003_06/alia/A3062613.htm.
497 William J. Haynes II, Letter to Kenneth Roth, April 2, 2003, Appendix, www.abcny.org/
    pdf/HUMANRIGHTS.pdf.
498 Sen. Patrick Leahy, Letter to Condoleezza Rice, June 2, 2004, Appendix, www.abcny.
    org/pdf/HUMANRIGHTS.pdf.
499 William J. Haynes II, Letter to Sen. Patrick Leahy, June 25, 2003, Appendix, www.
    abcny.org/pdf/HUMANRIGHTS.pdf.
500 Sen. Patrick Leahy, Letter to William J. Haynes II, September 9, 2003, Appendix, www.
    abcny.org/pdf/HUMANRIGHTS.pdf.
501 Adam Goldman and Matt Apuzzo, "CIA Flight Carried Secret from Gitmo,"
    Associated Press, August 6, 2010, http://www.boston.com/news/nation/washington/
    articles/2010/08/07/ap_exclusive_cia_flight_carried_secret_from_gitmo/.
502 Maj. Gen. Geoffrey D. Miller, JTF-GITMO, Camp Delta Standard Operation Procedure,
    March 28, 2003, 17.1, http://www.comw.org/warreport/fulltext/gitmo-sop.pdf.

503 Memorandum for Record, ICRC Meeting with MG Miller, October 9, 2003, http://
www.washingtonpost.com/wp-srv/nation/documents/GitmoMemo10-09-03.pdf.

504 Memorandum for Record, ICRC Meeting.

505 Jess Braver, "The Conscience of the Colonel."

506 Lt. Col. Stuart Couch, Interview, October 9, 2007, http://www.gwu.edu/~nsarchiv/
torturingdemocracy/interviews/stuart couch.html.

507 FBI, Email "Re: GITMO," August 2, 2004, http://www.aclu.org/torturefoia/released/
FBI_4744_4745.pdf.

508 FBI, Email "Re: GITMO," August 16, 2004, http://www.aclu.org/torturefoia/released/
FBI.121504.4737_4738.pdf.

509 Senate Armed Services Committee, 134. That document noted that "[d]espite these
revelations by interrogators, the supervisory chain of command reports that these
techniques are not used."

510 FBI, Email "FW: GITMO," August 2, 2004, http://www.aclu.org/torturefoia/released/
FBI.121504.5053.pdf.

511 Schmidt-Furlow, 10.

512 DoJ IG, 184, and Senate Armed Services Committee, 148.

513 Senate Armed Services Committee, 143.

514 "From Germany to Guantánamo: The Career of Prisoner No. 760," *Der Speigel*,
September 9, 2008; and Jess Bravin, "The Conscience of the Colonel," *The Wall
Street Journal*, March 31, 2007, http://pierretristam.com/Bobst/07/wf040107.htm.

515 Lt. Col. Stuart Couch, Interview, October 9, 2007, http://www.gwu.edu/~nsarchiv/
torturingdemocracy/interviews/stuart_couch.html.

516 Jack Goldsmith, *The Terror Presidency: Law and Judgment Inside the Bush
Administration* (New York: W.W. Norton, 2007), 153.

517 Senate Armed Services Committee, 146.

518 Ibid., 190-200.

519 Lt. Col Stuart Couch, Interview.

520 Ibid.

521 Senate Armed Services Committee, 141.

522 Lt. Col. Stuart Couch, Interview.

523 Jess Bravin, "The Conscience of the Colonel."

524 Lt. Col. Stuart Couch, Interview.

525 Memorandum Order, Mohammedou Ould Salahi v. Barack H. Obama, No. 1:05-cv-
00569-JR, Memorandum Order at 1-3 (D.D.C. Apr. 4, 2010) (internal citations
omitted), available at http://www.aclu.org/files/assets/2010-4-9-Slahi-Order.pdf.

526 Mohammedou Olud Salahi, handwritten Habeas Corpus petition, March 15, 2005,
http://media.miamiherald.com/smedia/2010/03/22/16/slahi.source.prod_affiliate.56.
pdf.

527 US Department of Defense, "JTF-GTMO Information on Detainees," March 4, 2005,
http://www.defense.gov/news/mar2005/d20050304info.pdf.

528 Brig. Gen. David M. Brahms et al., "An Open Letter to the Senate Judiciary

Committee," January 3, 2005, http://www.globalsecurity.org/military/library/
report/2005/senate-judiciary-committee-letter_03jan2005.htm.

529 Hamdan v. Rumsfeld, 548 U.S. 557 (2006), http://www.law.cornell.edu/supct/html/05-184.ZS.html.

530 Mohammedou Ould Salahi, Letter to Attorney Sylvia Royce, March 9, 2006, http://online.wsj.com/public/resources/documents/couch-slahiletter-03312007.pdf. As he indicates in this letter, Slahi has reportedly written a memoir of his experiences; his manuscript remains classified.

531 Jess Bravin, "Pentagon Forbids Marine to Testify," *The Wall Street Journal*, November 8, 2007, http://www.military-quotes.com/forum/pentagon-forbids-marine-testify-t47678.html.

532 Memorandum Order, *Salahi v. Obama*.

533 *Id.* at 15-16 (internal citations omitted).

534 The statements were made during interrogations following Mehdi's arrest in France in 2003. Mehdi, a Moroccan immigrant who was living in Germany at the time of the 9/11 attacks, was prosecuted in France in 2006 in connection with an alleged plot to carry out a bombing on Reunion Island in the Indian Ocean.

535 Memorandum Order, *Salahi* at 9 (internal citations omitted).

536 Susan Crabtree, "GOP denounces terror suspect release," *The Hill*, March 24, 2010, http://thehill.com/homenews/house/88853-gops-denounce-release-of-terror-suspect.

537 Transcript of Oral Argument at 29-31, 33-35, *Salahi v. Obama*, 625 F.3d 745 (D.C. Cir. 2010), http://www.aclu.org/national-security/transcript-oral-argument-29-31-33-35-salahi-v-obama-625-f3d-745-dc-cir-2010.

538 *Salahi v. Obama*, 625 F.3d at 749-750.

539 Peter Finn, "For two detainees who told what they knew, Guantánamo becomes a gilded cage," *The Washington Post*, March 24, 2010, http://www.washingtonpost.com/wp-dyn/content/article/2010/03/24/AR2010032403135.html.

540 In his 2010 article, Peter Finn quoted military officials who believe this privileged treatment is not a sufficient reward for Salahi's cooperation, and that he should be given political asylum and placed in a witness protection program in the United States. "If we don't do this right, it will be much harder to get other people to cooperate with us," one retired senior military intelligence officer told Finn. "And if I was still in the business, I'd want it known we protected them. It's good advertising."

541 Mohammedou Olud Salahi, Summarized Sworn Detainee Statement, Combatant Status Review Board, 10, http://media.miamiherald.com/smedia/2010/03/22/16/slahi.source.prod_affiliate.56.pdf.

542 Ibid, 29.

543 Expedited Motion to Compel the Government's Compliance with Section I.D.1 of the Amended Case Management Order, Mohammed Al-Qahtani et al. v. Barack H. Obama, et al. No. 05-cv-1971 (D.D.C. Sept. 17, 2010), http://ccrjustice.org/files/2009-02-04%20Al%20Qahtani%20-%20Mot%20to%20Compell%20and%20Hold%20in%20Contempt.pdf.

544 The IG report indicates that Qahtani had been asking to be given a polygraph exam for four months.

545 Department of Justice Office of the Inspector General, "A Review of the FBI's Involvement in and Observations of Detainee Interrogations in Guantánamo Bay, Afghanistan, and Iraq," May 2008, 117-120, www.justice.gov/oig/special/s0805/final.pdf.

546 Administrative Review Board, Memorandum for Maad Al Qahtani, Re: Unclassified Summary of Evidence, October 5, 2006, http://projects.nytimes.com/guantanamo/detainees/63-mohammed-al-qahtani/documents/3.

547 Ibid., 8.

548 Administrative Review Board, Memorandum, Re: Unclassified Summary of Evidence for Administrative Review Board, January 17, 2008, http://projects.nytimes.com/guantanamo/detainees/63-mohammed-al-qahtani/documents/1/pages/91.

549 Center for Constitutional Rights Justice, "Newly Declassified Notes Reveal Guantánamo Detainee Mohammed al Qahtani Suicidal After Military Commission Capital Charges," Press Release, May 20, 2008, http://ccrjustice.org/newsroom/press-releases/newly-declassified-notes-reveal-guantanamo-detainee-mohammed-al-qahtani-suic.

550 Expedited Motion, Al-Qahtani v. Obama.

551 Memorandum Opinion and Order, Al-Qahtani v. Obama, http://ccrjustice.org/files/MAQ%20Order%20to%20Disclose%20Videotapes.pdf.

552 Senate Armed Services Committee, 61.

553 T.J. Harrington, Letter to Major General Donald J. Ryder, July 14, 2004, http://www.pegc.us/archive/In_re_Gitmo/pet_mot_disc_20050110_ex_C.pdf.

554 Don A. Martin, "Declaration of Captain Don A. Martin," September 16, 2010, http://www.aclu.org/national-security/declaration-captain-don-martin-september-16-2010.

555 Transcript of Status Conference, Al-Qahtani v. Obama, No. 05-cv-1971 (D.D.C. Sept. 17, 2010), http://www.aclu.org/national-security/transcript-status-conference-al-qahtani-v-obama-no-05-cv-1971-ddc-september-17-201.

556 Joanne Mariner, "Letter to Bush Requesting Information on Missing Detainees," Human Rights Watch, February 26, 2007, http://www.hrw.org/en/news/2007/02/26/letter-bush-requesting-information-missing-detainees.

557 "U.S. to renew diplomatic relations with Libya," NBC News and news services, May 15, 2006, http://www.msnbc.msn.com/id/12799651/ns/world_news-mideast/n_africa/.

558 Craig Whitlock, "From CIA Jails, Inmates Fade Into Obscurity," The Washington Post, October 27, 2007, http://www.washingtonpost.com/wp-dyn/content/article/2007/10/26/AR2007102602326.html.

559 Michael Isikoff, "Death in Libya," Newsweek, May 12, 2009, http://www.newsweek.com/2009/05/11/death-in-libya.html.

560 Human Rights Watch, "Libya/US: Investigate Death of Former CIA Prisoner," May 11, 2009, http://www.hrw.org/en/news/2009/05/11/libyaus-investigate-death-former-cia-prisoner.

561 Peter Finn, "Detainee Who Gave False Iraq Data Dies in Prison in Libya," The Washington Post, May 12, 2009, http://www.washingtonpost.com/wp-dyn/content/

article/2009/05/11/AR2009051103412.html; and Human Rights Watch, "Libya/US: Investigate Death of Former CIA Prisoner."

562 Matt Smith, "Al Qaeda figure who provided link to Iraq reportedly dead in Libya," *CNN*, May 12, 2009, http://edition.cnn.com/2009/WORLD/africa/05/12/libya.al.qaeda.prisoner/index.html; and Peter Finn, "Detainee Who Gave False Iraq Data Dies in Prison in Libya."

SAMPLE DOCUMENTS

except as noted (b)(6)2

SWORN STATEMENT
For use of this form, see AR 190-45; the proponent agency is ODCSOPS

LOCATION	DATE	TIME	FILE NUMBER
KANDAHAR DETENTION FACILITY	13 FEB 02	1100	

LAST NAME, FIRST NAME, MIDDLE NAME	SOCIAL SECURITY NUMBER	GRADE/STATUS
██████████	██████████	E4 SPC

ORGANIZATION OR ADDRESS
A CO 202 JIF KANDAHAR AF

████████████████████████████ , WANT TO MAKE THE FOLLOWING STATEMENT UNDER OATH:

I am writing this in response to events that I witnessed while performing my duties as an interrogator with the TF 202 JIF.

SPC ████ & I were conducting an interrogation of MP ████ (b)(6)4 on 3 Jan 2002. Special forces personnel had been visiting the booth area previously & helping out by giving information that they had from their raids. ████ & I took a break to regroup & check our notes. I was the translator. While we were out of the booth several special forces members entered the booth. At the time I did not think anything of it, & thought they were just observing him based on previous experiences with their people. This was a different group of people I hadn't seen before. ████ & I finished the break & went back to continue the interrogation. When we entered the booth, we found the special forces members all crouched around the prisoner. They were blowing cigarette smoke in his face. The prisoner was extremely upset. It took a long time to calm him down & find out what had happened. The prisoner was visibly shaken & crying. ████ immediately told them to get out & not to come back anywhere near anyone that we were talking to. I could tell that something was wrong. The prisoner was extremely upset. He said that they had hit him, told him that he was going to die, blew smoke in his face, & had shocked him with some kind of ~~torture~~ device. He used the term "electricity". ████ & I immediately notified our NCOIC of what had happened. The chain of command took actions to ensure that nothing of the sort could happen again. A new policy was established requiring that any of the special forces members who wanted to assist with any part of the interrogation process had to first check in with the interrogation control element (ICE). The individuals who committed the acts were told that they were no longer welcome in the facility. I was very upset that such a thing

EXHIBIT	INITIALS OF PERSON MAKING STATEMENT	PAGE 1 OF 2 PAGES

STATEMENT (Continued)   STATEMENT OF ████████████████ TAKEN AT KANDAHAR DATED 13 FEB 02 CONTINUED

could happen. I take my job & responsibilities as an interrogator & as a human being very seriously. I understand the importance of the Geneva Convention & what it represents. If I don't honor it, what right do I have to expect any other military to do so?

112115-74.00

Sworn statement of a military interpreter, Kandahar Detention Facility, February 13, 2002, available at http://www.aclu.org/files/projects/foiasearch/pdf/DOD043638.pdf.

Ramifications of Determination that GPW Does Not Apply

The consequences of a decision to adhere to what I understood to be your earlier determination that the GPW does not apply to the Taliban include the following:

Positive:

* Preserves flexibility:
  o As you have said, the war against terrorism is a new kind of war. It is not the traditional clash between nations adhering to the laws of war that formed the backdrop for GPW. The nature of the new war places a high premium on other factors, such as the ability to quickly obtain information from captured terrorists and their sponsors in order to avoid further atrocities against American civilians, and the need to try terrorists for war crimes such as wantonly killing civilians. In my judgment, this new paradigm renders obsolete Geneva's strict limitations on questioning of enemy prisoners and renders quaint some of its provisions requiring that captured enemy be afforded such things as commissary privileges, scrip (i.e., advances of monthly pay), athletic uniforms, and scientific instruments.
    Although some of these provisions do not apply to detainees who are not POWs, a determination that GPW does not apply to al Qaeda and the Taliban eliminates any argument regarding the need for case-by-case determinations of POW status. It also holds open options for the future conflicts in which it may be more difficult to determine whether an enemy force as a whole meets the standard for POW status.
  o By concluding that GPW does not apply to al Qaeda and the Taliban, we avoid foreclosing options for the future, particularly against nonstate actors.
* Substantially reduces the threat of domestic criminal prosecution under the War Crimes Act (18 U.S.C. 2441).
  o That statute, enacted in 1996, prohibits the commission of a "war crime" by or against a U.S. person, including U.S. officials. "War crime" for these purposes is defined to include any grave breach of GPW or any violation of common Article 3 thereof (such as "outrages against personal dignity"). Some of these provisions apply (if the GPW applies) regardless of whether the individual being detained qualifies as a POW. Punishments for violations of Section 2441 include the death penalty. A determination that the GPW is not applicable to the Taliban would mean that Section 2441 would not apply to actions taken with respect to the Taliban.
  o Adhering to your determination that GPW does not apply would guard effectively against misconstruction or misapplication of Section 2441 for several reasons.
    o First, some of the language of the GPW is undefined (it prohibits, for example, "outrages upon personal dignity" and "inhuman treatment"), and it is difficult to predict with confidence what actions might be deemed to constitute violations of the relevant provisions of GPW.
    o Second, it is difficult to predict the needs and circumstances that could arise in the course of the war on terrorism.
    o Third, it is difficult to predict the motives of prosecutors and independent counsels who may in the future decide to pursue unwarranted charges based on Section 2441. Your determination would create a reasonable basis in law that Section 2441 does not apply, which would provide a solid defense to any future prosecution.

Negative:

On the other hand, the following arguments would support reconsideration and reversal of your decision that the GPW does not apply to either al Qaeda or the Taliban:

Alberto R. Gonzales's January 25, 2002 Memorandum for the President, "Decision re: Application of the Geneva Convention on Prisoners of War to the Conflict with Al Qaeda and the Taliban," available at http://www.torturingdemocracy.org/documents/20020125.pdf

cloth or cover over the outside of the box to cut out the light and restrict my air supply. It was difficult to breathe. When I was let out of the box I saw that one of the walls of the room had been covered with plywood sheeting. From now on it was against this wall that I was then smashed with the towel around my neck. I think that the plywood was put there to provide some absorption of the impact of my body. The interrogators realized that smashing me against the hard wall would probably quickly result in physical injury

During these torture sessions many guards were present, plus two interrogators who did the actual beating, still asking questions, while the main interrogator left to return after the beating was over. After the beating I was then placed in the small box. They placed a cloth or cover over the box to cut out all light and restrict my air supply. As it was not high enough even to sit upright, I had to crouch down. It was very difficult because of my wounds. The stress on my legs held in this position meant my wounds both in the leg and stomach became very painful. I think this occurred about 3 months after my last operation. It was always cold in the room, but when the cover was placed over the box it made it hot and sweaty inside. The wound on my leg began to open and started to bleed. I don't know how long I remained in the small box, I think I may have slept or maybe fainted.

I was then dragged from the small box, unable to walk properly and put on what looked like a hospital bed, and strapped down very tightly with belts. A black cloth was then placed over my face and the interrogators used a mineral water bottle to pour water on the cloth so that I could not breathe. After a few minutes the cloth was removed and the bed was rotated into an upright position. The pressure of the straps on my wounds was very painful. I vomited. The bed was then again lowered to a horizontal position and the same torture carried out again with the black cloth over my face and water poured on from a bottle. On this occasion my head was in a more backward, downwards position and the water was poured on for a longer time. I struggled against the straps, trying to breathe, but it was hopeless. I thought I was going to die. I lost control of my urine. Since then I still lose control of my urine when under stress.

I was then placed again in the tall box. While I was inside the box loud music was played again and somebody kept banging repeatedly on the box from the outside. I tried to sit down on the floor, but because of the small space the bucket with urine tipped over and spilt over me. I remained in the box for several hours, maybe overnight. I was then taken out and again a towel was wrapped around my neck and I was smashed into the wall with the plywood covering and repeatedly slapped in the face by the same two interrogators as before.

I was then made to sit on the floor with a black hood over my head until the next session of torture began. The room was always kept very cold.

This went on for approximately one week. During this time the whole procedure was repeated five times. On each occasion, apart from one, I was suffocated once or twice and was put in the vertical position on the bed in between. On one occasion the suffocation was repeated three times. I vomited each time I was put in the vertical position between the suffocation.

30

Abu Zubaydah's statement to the International Committee of the Red Cross, from the ICRC's February 2007 "Report on the Treatment of Fourteen 'High Value Detainees' in CIA Custody," available at http://www.nybooks.com/media/doc/2010/04/22/icrc-report.pdf.

TOP SECRET

individual do not result in severe pain. The facial slap and walling contain precautions to ensure that no pain even approaching this level results. The slap is delivered with fingers slightly spread, which you have explained to us is designed to be less painful than a closed-hand slap. The slap is also delivered to the fleshy part of the face, further reducing any risk of physical damage or serious pain. The facial slap does not produce pain that is difficult to endure. Likewise, walling involves quickly pulling the person forward and then thrusting him against a flexible false wall. You have informed us that the sound of hitting the wall will actually be far worse than any possible injury to the individual. The use of the rolled towel around the neck also reduces any risk of injury. While it may hurt to be pushed against the wall, any pain experienced is not of the intensity associated with serious physical injury.

As we understand it, when the waterboard is used, the subject's body responds as if the subject were drowning—even though the subject may be well aware that he is in fact not drowning. You have informed us that this procedure does not inflict actual physical harm. Thus, although the subject may experience the fear or panic associated with the feeling of drowning, the waterboard does not inflict physical pain. As we explained in the Section 2340A Memorandum, "pain and suffering" as used in Section 2340 is best understood as a single concept, not distinct concepts of "pain" as distinguished from "suffering." See Section 2340A Memorandum at 6 n.3. The waterboard, which inflicts no pain or actual harm whatsoever, does not, in our view inflict "severe pain or suffering." Even if one were to parse the statute more finely to attempt to treat "suffering" as a distinct concept, the waterboard could not be said to inflict severe suffering. The waterboard is simply a controlled acute episode, lacking the connotation of a protracted period of time generally given to suffering.

Finally, as we discussed above, you have informed us that in determining which procedures to use and how you will use them, you have selected techniques that will not harm Zubaydah's wound. You have also indicated that numerous steps will be taken to ensure that none of these procedures in any way interferes with the proper healing of Zubaydah's wound. You have also indicated that, should it appear at any time that Zubaydah is experiencing severe pain or suffering, the medical personnel on hand will stop the use of any technique.

Even when all of these methods are considered combined in an overall course of conduct, they still would not inflict severe physical pain or suffering. As discussed above, a number of these acts result in no physical pain, others produce only physical discomfort. You have indicated that these acts will not be used with substantial repetition, so that there is no possibility that severe physical pain could arise from such repetition. Accordingly, we conclude that these acts neither separately nor as part of a course of conduct would inflict severe physical pain or suffering within the meaning of the statute.

We next consider whether the use of these techniques would inflict severe *mental* pain or suffering within the meaning of Section 2340. Section 2340 defines severe mental pain or suffering as "the prolonged mental harm caused by or resulting from" one of several predicate

TOP SECRET

John Yoo and Jay Bybee's August 1, 2002 memorandum for the CIA, "Interrogation of al Qaeda Operative," available at http://media.luxmedia.com/aclu/olc_08012002_bybee.pdf.

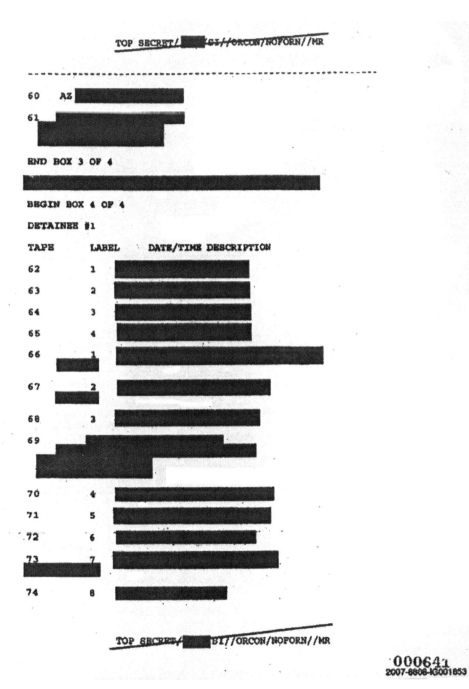

Inventory of 92 videotapes of the interrogation of Abu Zubaydah in the CIA black site in Thailand, available at http://www.aclu.org/files/assets/cia_release20100415_ p10-18.pdf.

CLASSIFICATION: SECRET
codeword:
caveats: ▮▮▮▮▮▮▮▮▮ EYES ONLY

▮▮▮▮▮▮▮▮▮▮▮▮▮▮▮▮▮▮▮▮▮▮▮▮▮▮▮▮▮▮▮▮

S.E.G.R.E.T 090627Z NOV 05 ▮▮▮▮
▮▮▮▮▮▮▮▮▮▮▮▮▮▮

TO: PRIORITY DIRECTOR.

FOR: ▮▮▮▮▮▮▮▮▮▮▮▮
▮▮▮▮▮▮▮▮▮▮▮▮▮▮▮▮▮▮

SUBJECT: EYES ONLY FOR ▮▮▮▮▮ - DESTRUCTION OF ▮▮▮▮▮ VIDEO TAPES

REF: ▮▮▮▮▮▮▮▮▮▮▮▮▮

TEXT:

▮▮▮▮▮▮▮▮▮▮▮▮▮▮▮▮▮▮▮▮▮▮▮▮▮▮▮▮▮▮

1. ACTION REQUIRED: FYI

2. PER REF A, ALL 92 ▮▮▮▮▮▮ VIDEO TAPES WERE DESTROYED ON 09 NOVEMBER. DESTRUCTION ACTIVITY WAS INITIATED AT 0910HRS AND COMPLETED AT 1230HRS.

3. FILE: ▮▮▮▮▮
▮▮▮▮▮▮▮▮▮▮▮▮▮▮▮▮▮▮▮▮▮

CABLETYPE: ▮▮▮▮▮▮▮▮

END OF MESSAGE   SECRET

2007-8808-IG000235
00062b

November 9, 2005 CIA cable confirming destruction of Abu Zubaydah interrogation tapes, available at http://www.aclu.org/files/assets/cia_release20100415_p10-18.pdf.

e.

The interrogators will likely use walling once interrogators determine the HVD is intent on maintaining his resistance posture.

f. The sequence may continue for multiple iterations as the interrogators continue to measure the HVD's resistance posture.

g. To increase the pressure on the HVD,

water douse the HVD for several minutes.

h. The interrogators, assisted by security officers, will place the HVD back into the vertical shackling position to resume sleep deprivation. Dietary manipulation also continues, and the HVD remains nude. White noise (not to exceed 79db) is used in the interrogation room. The interrogation session terminates at this point.

i. As noted above, the duration of this session may last from 30 minutes to several hours based on the interrogators' assessment of the HVD's resistance posture. In this example of the second session, the following techniques were used: sleep deprivation, nudity, dietary manipulation, walling, water dousing, attention grasp, insult slap, and abdominal slap. The three Conditioning Techniques were used to keep the HVD at a baseline, dependent state and to weaken his resolve and will to resist. In combination with these three techniques, other Corrective and Coercive Techniques were used throughout the interrogation session based on interrogation objectives and the interrogators' assessment of the HVD's resistance posture.

13

December 30, 2004 CIA "Background Paper on CIA's Combined Use of Interrogation Techniques," available at http://www.aclu.org/torturefoia/released/082409/olcremand/2004olc97.pdf.

28 December 2002 and 1 January 2003, the debriefer used an unloaded semi-automatic handgun as a prop to frighten Al-Nashiri into disclosing information.[44] After discussing this plan with ████ ████ the debriefer entered the cell where Al-Nashiri sat shackled and racked the handgun once or twice close to Al-Nashiri's head.[45] On what was probably the same day, the debriefer used a power drill to frighten Al-Nashiri. With ████████ consent, the debriefer entered the detainee's cell and revved the drill while the detainee stood naked and hooded. The debriefer did not touch Al-Nashiri with the power drill.

93. (S//NF) The ████ and debriefer did not request authorization or report the use of these unauthorized techniques to Headquarters. However, in January 2003, newly arrived TDY officers ████████████who had learned of these incidents reported them to Headquarters. OIG investigated and referred its findings to the Criminal Division of DoJ. On 11 September 2003, DoJ declined to prosecute and turned these matters over to CIA for disposition. These incidents are the subject of a separate OIG Report of Investigation.[46]

Threats

94. (TS ████████ During another incident ██████████ the same Headquarters debriefer, according to a ████████████who was present, threatened Al-Nashiri by saying that if he did not talk, "We could get your mother in here," and, "We can bring your family in here." The ████████ debriefer reportedly wanted Al-Nashiri to infer, for psychological reasons, that the debriefer might be ████ ████████intelligence officer based on his Arabic dialect, and that Al-Nashiri was in ████████custody because it was widely believed in Middle East circles that ████████interrogation technique involves

---

[44] (S//NF) This individual was not a trained interrogator and was not authorized to use EITs.
[45] (U//FOUO) Racking is a mechanical procedure used with firearms to chamber a bullet or simulate a bullet being chambered.
[46] (S//NF) Unauthorized Interrogation Techniques ████████ 29 October 2003.

42

CIA Inspector General John L. Helgerson's May 2004 classified report, "Counterterrorism Detention and Interrogation Activities, September 2001-October 2003," available at http://media/luxmedia.com/aclu/IG_Report.pdf.

SECRET

all that went before." Clewis, 386 U.S. at 710.

First, Binyam Mohamed's lengthy and brutal experience in detention weighs heavily with the Court. For example, this is not a case where a person was repeatedly questioned by a police officer, in his own country, by his own fellow-citizens, at a police station, over several days without sleep and with only minimal amounts of food and water. See Ashcraft v. State of Tenn., 322 U.S. 143, 153-54 (1944); Reck v. Pate, 367 U.S. 433, 440-41 (1961) (murder suspect held incommunicado for eight days, questioned extensively for four, and interrogated while sick). While neither the Ashcraft nor Reck scenarios are to be approved, they can hardly compare with the facts alleged here.

The difference, of course, is that Binyam Mohamed's trauma lasted for two long years. During that time, he was physically and psychologically tortured. His genitals were mutilated. He was deprived of sleep and food. He was summarily transported from one foreign prison to another. Captors held him in stress positions for days at a time. He was forced to listen to piercingly loud music and the screams of other prisoners while locked in a pitch-black cell. All the while, he was forced to inculpate himself and others in various plots to imperil Americans. The Government does not dispute this evidence.

SECRET
-64-

Judge Gladys Kessler's November 19, 2009 opinion in the habeas corpus petition of Guantánamo detainee Farhi Saeed bin Mohammed, available at http://www.leagle.com/xmlResult.aspx?xmldoc=in%20fdco%2020091217b92.xml&docbase=cslwar3-2007-curr.

(iv)   It was reported that a new series of interviews was conducted by the United States authorities prior to 17 May 2002 as part of a new strategy designed by an expert interviewer

(v)   It was reported that at some stage during that further interview process by the United States authorities, BM had been intentionally subjected to continuous sleep deprivation.   The effects of the sleep deprivation were carefully observed.

(vi)   It was reported that combined with the sleep deprivation, threats and inducements were made to him. His fears of being removed from United States custody and "disappearing" were played upon.

(vii) It was reported that the stress brought about by these deliberate tactics was increased by him being shackled during his interviews;

(viii) It was clear not only from the reports of the content of the interviews but also from the report that he was being kept under self-harm observation, that the interviews were having a marked effect upon him and causing him significant mental stress and suffering.

(ix)   We regret to have to conclude that the reports provided to the SyS made clear to anyone reading them that BM was being subjected to the treatment that we have described and the effect upon him of that intentional treatment.

(x)   The treatment reported, if had been administered on behalf of the United Kingdom, would clearly have been in breach of the undertakings given by the United Kingdom in 1972. Although it is not necessary for us to categorise the treatment reported, it could readily be contended to be at the very least cruel, inhuman and degrading treatment of BM by the United States authorities.

British Court of Appeals' seven redacted paragraphs summarizing 42 CIA documents describing the treatment of Binyam Mohamed, publicly released February 10, 2010, available at http://www.fco.gov.uk/en/news/latest-news/?view=News&id=21735373.

BSCT continued:

- Psychological stressors are extremely effective (ie, sleep deprivation, withholding food, isolation, loss of time)

COL Cummings   We can't do sleep deprivation
LTC Beaver   Yes, we can - with approval.

- Disrupting the normal camp operations is vital. We need to create an environment of "controlled chaos"

LTC Beaver   ·We may need to curb the harsher operations while ICRC is around. It is better not to expose them to any controversial techniques. We must have the support of the DOD.

Becker.   We have had many reports from Bagram about sleep deprivation being used.

LTC Beaver   True, but officially it is not happening. It is not being reported officially. The ICRC is a serious concern. They will be in and out, scrutinizing our operations, unless they are displeased and decide to protest and leave. This would draw a lot of negative attention.

COL Cummings   The new PSYOP plan has been passed up the chain
LTC Beaver   It's at J3 at SOUTHCOM.

Fredman   The DOJ has provided much guidance on this issue. The CIA is not held to the same rules as the military. In the past when the ICRC has made a big deal about certain detainees, the DOD has "moved" them away from the attention of ICRC. Upon questioning from the ICRC about their whereabouts, the DOD's response has repeatedly been that the detainee merited no status under the Geneva Convention. The CIA has employed aggressive techniques on less than a handful of suspects since 9/11.
Under the Torture Convention, torture has been prohibited by international law, but the language of the statutes is written vaguely. Severe mental and physical pain is prohibited. The mental part is explained as poorly as the physical. Severe physical pain described as anything causing permanent damage to major organs or body parts. Mental torture described as anything leading to permanent, profound damage to the senses or personality. It is basically subject to perception. If the detainee dies you're doing it wrong. So far, the techniques we have addressed have not proven to produce these types of results, which in a way challenges what the BSCT paper says about not being able to prove whether these techniques will lead to permanent damage. Everything on the BSCT white paper is legal from a civilian standpoint.[Any questions of severe weather or temperature conditions should be deferred to medical staff.] Any of the techniques that lie on the harshest end of the spectrum must be performed by a highly trained individual. Medical personnel should be present to treat any possible accidents. The CIA operates without military intervention. When the CIA has wanted to use more aggressive techniques in the past, the FBI has pulled their personnel from theatre. In those rare instances, aggressive techniques have proven very helpful.

LTC Beaver   We will need documentation to protect us

Minutes of the October 2, 2002 "Counter Resistance Strategy Meeting" with Guantánamo Staff and CIA Attorney Jonathan Fredman, available at http://www. torturingdemocracy.org/documents/20021002.pdf.

0700: Detainee walked, refused water, and allowed to begin four hour rest period.

1100: Detainee awakened and offered coffee – refused.

1115: Detainee taken to bathroom and walked 10 minutes. Offered water – refused. Interrogators began telling detainee how ungrateful and grumpy he was. In order to escalate the detainee's emotions, a mask was made from an MRE box with a smiley face on it and placed on the detainee's head for a few moments. A latex glove was inflated and labeled the "sissy slap" glove. This glove was touched to the detainee's face periodically after explaining the terminology to him. The mask was placed back on the detainee's head. While wearing the mask, the team began dance instruction with the detainee. The detainee became agitated and began shouting. The mask was removed and detainee was allowed to sit. Detainee shouted and addressed lead as "the oldest Christian here" and wanted to know why lead allowed the detainee to be treated this way.

1300: Detainee taken to bathroom and walked 10 minutes.

1320: Detainee offered food and water – refused. Detainee was unresponsive for remainder of session. Afghanistan / Taliban themes run for remainder of session.

1430: Detainee taken to bathroom and walked 10 minutes.

1500: Detainee offered water – refused.

1510: Corpsman changed bandages on ankles, checked vitals – O.K.

1530: Detainee taken to bathroom and walked 10 minutes.

1600: Corpsman checks vitals and starts IV. Detainee given three bags of IV.

1745: Detainee taken to bathroom and walked 10 minutes.

1800: Detainee was unresponsive.

1833: Detainee was allowed to sleep.

1925: The detainee was awakened by interrogation team. He was offered food and water but he refused.

1945: The interrogation team and detainee watched the video "Operation Enduring Freedom".

2120: Detainee was sent to the latrine. Offered water but he refused.

2200: Detainee exercised for good health and circulation. Medical representative took detainee's vital signs and removed the IV housing unit from the detainee's arm. The detainee's pulse rate was low (38) and his blood pressure was high (144/90). Detainee complained of having a boil on his left leg, just below his knee. The medical representative looked at the his leg and phoned the doctor. The doctor instructed the corpsman to recheck the detainee's vitals in one hour.

2300: Detainee refused water and food. He was taken to the latrine and exercised in order to assist in improving the detainee's vital signs.

2345: The medical representative rechecked the detainee's vital signs. The detainee's blood pressure had improved but it was still high (138/80) and his pulse rate had improved but it remained low (42). The corpsman called the doctor to provide an update and the doctor said operations could continue since there had been no significant change. It was noted that historically the detainee's pulse sometimes drops into the 40's in the evenings.

14 DECEMBER 2002

Interrogation Log of Mohammed al-Qahtani, November 23, 2002 to January 11, 2003, available at http://www.time.com/time/2006/log/log.pdf.

UNCLASSIFIED

GENERAL COUNSEL OF THE DEPARTMENT OF DEFENSE
1600 DEFENSE PENTAGON
WASHINGTON, D. C. 20301-1600

GENERAL COUNSEL

2002 DEC -2 AM 11: 03

OFFICE OF THE
SECRETARY OF DEFENSE

ACTION MEMO

November 27, 2002 (1:00 PM)

DEPSEC _____

FOR: SECRETARY OF DEFENSE

FROM: William J. Haynes II, General Counsel

SUBJECT: Counter-Resistance Techniques

- The Commander of USSOUTHCOM has forwarded a request by the Commander of Joint Task Force 170 (now JTF GTMO) for approval of counter-resistance techniques to aid in the interrogation of detainees at Guantanamo Bay (Tab A).

- The request contains three categories of counter-resistance techniques, with the first category the least aggressive and the third category the most aggressive (Tab B).

- I have discussed this with the Deputy, Doug Feith and General Myers. I believe that all join in my recommendation that, as a matter of policy, you authorize the Commander of USSOUTHCOM to employ, in his discretion, only Categories I and II and the fourth technique listed in Category III ("Use of mild, non-injurious physical contact such as grabbing, poking in the chest with the finger, and light pushing").

- While all Category III techniques may be legally available, we believe that, as a matter of policy, a blanket approval of Category III techniques is not warranted at this time. Our Armed Forces are trained to a standard of interrogation that reflects a tradition of restraint.

RECOMMENDATION: That SECDEF approve the USSOUTHCOM Commander's use of those counter-resistance techniques listed in Categories I and II and the fourth technique listed in Category III during the interrogation of detainees at Guantanamo Bay.

SECDEF DECISION

Approved _____ Disapproved _____ Other _____

Attachments
As stated

cc: CJCS, USD(P)

However, I stand for 8-10 hours a day. Why is standing limited to 4 hours?

D.R DEC 0 2 2002

UNCLASSIFIED

X04030-02

Secretary of Defense Donald Rumsfeld's December 2, 2002 approval of "Counter-Resistance Techniques," available at http://www.gwu.edu/~nsarchiv/NSAEBB/NSAEBB127/02.12.02.pdf.

I provided RADM Lohr with a copy of the December 2nd Memo
and requested that Navy JAG prepare a legal analysis of the
issues. I also decided to brief Secretary of the Navy Gordon
England and take my objections to DOD GC Haynes as quickly as
possible.

Later that day, RADM Lohr wrote via email that he had
brought the allegations of abuse to the attention of the Vice
Chief of Naval Operations, ADM William Fallon. (Att 4)

20 Dec 02

At 1015, in a very short meeting, I briefed Navy
Secretary Gordon England on the NCIS report of detainee abuse,
on the December 2nd Memo authorizing the interrogation
techniques, and on my legal views and policy concerns. I told
him I was planning to see DOD GC Haynes that afternoon to
convey my concerns and objections. Secretary England
authorized me to go forward, advising me to use my judgment.[*]

That afternoon I met with Mr. Haynes in his office. I
informed him that NCIS had advised me that interrogation
abuses were taking place in Guantanamo, that the NCIS agents
considered any such abuses to be unlawful and contrary to
American values, and that discontent over these practices were
reportedly spreading among the personnel on the base.
Producing the December 2nd Memo, I expressed surprise that the
Secretary had been allowed to sign it. In my view, some of
the authorized interrogation techniques could rise to the
level of torture, although the intent surely had not been to
do so. Mr. Haynes disagreed that the techniques authorized
constituted torture. I urged him to think about the
techniques more closely. What did "deprivation of light and
auditory stimuli" mean? Could a detainee be locked in a
completely dark cell? And for how long? A month? Longer?
What precisely did the authority to exploit phobias permit?
Could a detainee be held in a coffin? Could phobias be
applied until madness set in? Not only could individual
techniques applied singly constitute torture, I said, but also
the application of combinations of them must surely be
recognized as potentially capable of reaching the level of
torture. Also, the memo's fundamental problem was that it was

---

[*] At this time, Secretary England's nomination to serve as Deputy
Secretary of the Department of Homeland Security had been announced, and
he was transitioning out of the DON. He would ultimately transfer out of
the Department on January 23, 2003. This would be my only conversation
with him on the issue until months later, well after his return as Navy
Secretary.

Navy General Counsel Alberto Mora's July 7, 2004 "Statement for the Record:
Office of General Counsel's Involvement in Interrogation Issues," available at http://
www.aclu.org/pdfs/safefree/mora_memo_july_2004.pdf.

b6 Per FBI
b7C

b6 Per FBI
b7C

b6 Per FBI
b7C

	Memorandum from the Director re: Conducting Federal Bureau of Investigation Investigations Overseas. Office of the Inspector General requested he locate the document. [redacted] stated that this document was not the file he would have expected and that he had his secretary find it. After reviewing the memorandum, he said that he did not recall receiving it or reading it, but that it was something he would have normally received. Substantively, [redacted] said that the material covered is not new, that it just provides the same information he knows about how to work with Legats. According to [redacted] he thought the memorandum was not related to the issue of how to interview or interrogate detainees held at U.S. Naval Base Guantanamo Bay, Cuba. This memorandum addresses overseas investigations, U.S. Naval Base Guantanamo Bay, Cuba is a United States military base.	Interview 1
Fri 09/27/2002	email from [redacted] and [redacted] While at Delta in the morning, he received a call to return to the Command Post (CP) immediately. "FBIHQ [redacted] etc.) had issues regarding # 63, surprise, surprise." [redacted] explained there was a disagreement with Department of Defense as to how to handle # 63. The "fun and games" identified in the email refers to non-standard investigative techniques. [redacted] did not recall participating with this conversation with [redacted]	Notes 6/21/05, at 9, Interview 1
Mon 09/30/2002	email from [redacted] to [redacted] cc: [redacted] and [redacted] email describes "current Defense Humint Services plan" for # 63 including taking to Camp X-Ray for six (6) hour sessions with the detainee and giving a four hour break for before beginning again. [redacted] speak with [redacted] suggested that [redacted] asked to provide guidance because Defense Humint Services wanted federal Bureau of Investigation to be part of one of the interrogation teams. [redacted] said as long as there was no 'torture' involved that we were within our guidelines. He actually encouraged us to be a part of this as we would be able to provide FBIHQ with 'updates' of what was happening." When asked about this	Notes 6/21/05, at 10, Interview 1

Interview notes concerning Guantánamo interrogation of Mohammed al-Qahtani, gathered for the Justice Department's "Review of the FBI's Involvement in and Observations of Detainee Interrogations in Guantánamo Bay, Afghanistan, and Iraq," available at http://www.aclu.org/files/pdfs/natsec/dojfbi20100514/32_interview1_or_interviewnotes_20050621_9pp.pdf

| | Fwd: Impersonating ...l at GTMO | Page 1 |

b6 -1
b7C -1

b6 -1
b7C -1

From:
To: Bald, Gary, BATTLE, FRANKIE, CUMMINGS, ARTHUR, ...
Date: Fri, Dec 5, 2003 9:53 AM
Subject: Fwd: Impersonating FBI at GTMO

b6 -1
b7C -1

Frank

I am forwarding this EC up the CTD chain of command. MLDU requested this information be documented to protect the FBI. MLDU has had a long standing and documented position against use of some of DOD's interrogation practices, however, we were not aware of these latest techniques until recently.

b2 -3
b6 -4
b7C -4
b7E -1
b7F -1

Of concern, DOD interrogators impersonating Supervisory Special Agents of the FBI told a detainee that ____ These same interrogation teams then ____ The detainee was also told by this interrogation team ____

These tactics have produced no intelligence of a threat neutralization nature to date and CITF believes that techniques have destroyed any chance of prosecuting this detainee.

If this detainee is ever released or his story made public in any way, DOD interrogators will not be held accountable because these torture techniques were done the "FBI" interrogators. The FBI will left holding the bag before the public.

b6 -1
b7C -1

SSA
CTD/MLDU

CC: ____   b6 -1
                                            b7C -1

DETAINEES-3168

3977

December 5, 2003 FBI email reporting on Guantánamo interrogation of Mohamedou
Ould Slahi, available at http://www.aclu.org/torturefoia/released/FBI_3977.pdf

Presiding Officer: With a veil type thing, were their openings for his eyes

Detainee: He did have openings for his eyes. He also had gloves, O.J Simpson gloves on his hands. He was assigned to this special mission. They started to talk to me and said, "look we are not FBI and we need you to admit to the crime we have here. That you were involved with the 11 September attack and that you were involved in the millennium plot." I said "no I wasn't". They said okay, forget about it. Around June 18ᵗʰ 2003, I was taken from Mike Block and put in India Block for total isolation. They took all of my stuff from me. I complained to ▌▌▌▌▌ because I thought she was a deceit lady. I could not bear sleeping on the metal because of my back and you never know how much pain I could take. I could end up dead or something. She said 'no, you are not going to die." They tried to give me painkillers and I refused they out of protest. How could you give me painkiller? Just give me something to sleep on and I will be all right. They took me to the doctor here, a Navy doctor, and he was a good guy. I told him that I am in a very bad situation and he said okay I going to recommend that they give you some items, because you have a very serious condition of Sciatic Nerve. But I cannot promise you because those people decide not me. I would like for you to check my medical records.

During this portion of the ARB, the recording equipment began to malfunction. This malfunction has caused the remainder of tape 3 of 4 tapes from clicks 3407 to 4479 to become distorted. The Detainee discussed how he was tortured while here at GTMO by several individuals. The recording machine was swapped out with a new one and we finished out the session. The following is the board's recollection of that 1000 click malfunction:

The Detainee was explaining his medical treatment and noticed a Board Member passing a note to the Presiding Officer. The Detainee inquired as to why the Board Member was passing a note. The Presiding Officer told the Detainee the Board Member had a question regarding the Detainee's medical treatment. The Board Member asked the Detainee to summarize his medical treatment and the treatment he received at the hands of the interrogators. The Detainee stated the medical treatment he received was "good", however he decided to continue to go into greater detail regarding the alleged abuse he received from the hands of his interrogators.

The Detainee began by discussing the alleged abuse he received from a female interrogator known to him as ▌▌▌▌▌ The Detainee attempted to explain to the Board ▌▌▌▌▌ actions but he became distraught and visibly upset. He explained that he was sexually harassed and although he does like women he did not like what ▌▌▌▌▌ had done to him. The Presiding Officer noticed the Detainee was upset and told him he was not required to tell the story. The Detainee was very appreciative and elected not to elaborate on the alleged abuse from ▌▌▌▌▌ The Detainee gave detailed information regarding the alleged abuse from ▌▌▌▌▌ and ▌▌▌▌▌ The Detainee stated that ▌▌▌▌▌ and ▌▌▌▌▌ entered a room with their faces covered and began beating him. They beat him so badly that ▌▌▌▌▌ became upset. ▌▌▌▌▌

ISN 760
Enclosure (6)
Page 26 of 33

20959

Transcript of Mohamedou Ould Slahi's November 22, 2005 Administrative Review Board Proceedings, Guantánamo, available at http://online.wsj.com/public/resources/documents/couch-slahiARB-03312007.pdf.

31. Irrespective of the failed Commissions proceedings, I personally do not believe there is any lawful basis for continuing to detain Mr. Jawad. There is no reliable evidence of any voluntary involvement on Jawad's part with any terrorist groups. Even a statement that we believed linked him to HIG, and was thought to contain Mr. Jawad's fingerprint, was sent to the Army's crime lab for analysis, which concluded that the fingerprint was not Mr. Jawad's.

32. Ultimately, I decided that I could no longer ethically prosecute Mr. Jawad or, in good conscience, serve as a prosecutor at OMC-P. I have taken an oath to support and defend the Constitution of the United States, and I remain confident that I have done so, spending over four of the past seven years away from my family, my home, my civilian occupation -- all without any expectation of or desire for any reward greater than the knowledge that I have remained true to my word and have done my level best to rise to our Nation's defense in its time of need. I did not "quit" the Commissions or resign; instead, I personally petitioned the Army's Judge Advocate General to allow me to serve the remaining six months of my two year voluntary obligation in Afghanistan or Iraq. In the exercise of his wisdom and discretion, he permitted me to be released from active duty. However, had I been returned to Afghanistan or Iraq, and had I encountered Mohammed Jawad in either of those hostile lands, where two of my friends have been killed in action and another one of my very best friends in the world had been terribly wounded, I have no doubt at all – none – that Mr. Jawad would pose no threat whatsoever to me, his former prosecutor and now-repentant persecutor. Six years is long enough for a boy of sixteen to serve in virtual solitary confinement, in a distant land, for reasons he may never fully understand. I respectfully ask this Court to find that Mr. Jawad's continued detention is unsupported by any credible evidence, any provision of the Detainee Treatment Act of 2005, the MCA, international law or our own hallowed Constitution. Mr. Jawad should be released to resume his life in a civil society, for his sake, and for our own sense of justice and perhaps to restore a measure of our basic humanity.

Pursuant to 28 U.S.C. § 1746, I hereby declare and state under penalty of perjury that the foregoing is true and correct to the best of my knowledge, information and belief.

Darrel J. Vandeveld

Executed on: January 2009.

14

Lt. Col. Darrel Vandeveld's January 12, 2009 Declaration in support of the habeas corpus petition of Mohammed Jawad, available at http://www.aclu.org/national-security/declaration-lt-col-darrel-vandeveld-habeas-corpus-case-mohammed-jawad.

INDEX